THE EXODUS AFFAIR

Religion, Theology, and the Holocaust
Alan L. Berger, Series Editor

THE
EXODUS AFFAIR

Holocaust Survivors and the Struggle for Palestine

AVIVA HALAMISH

Translated by Ora Cummings

Syracuse University Press

Published in the United States by
Syracuse University Press, Syracuse, New York 13244-5160,
by arrangement with Vallentine Mitchell and Company Limited,
London, United Kingdom.

Originally published in Hebrew in 1990 by Am Oved Publishers,
Tel Aviv and Tel Aviv University as *Exodus—ha-Sippur ha-Amiti*
(Exodus – The Real Story).

Library of Congress Cataloging-in-Publication Data

Halamish, Aviva.
    [Eksodus—ha-sipur ha-amiti. English]
    The Exodus affair : Holocaust survivors and the struggle for
Palestine / Aviva Halamish : translated by Ora Cummings.—1st ed.
        p.   cm.
    Includes bibliographical references and index.
    ISBN 0-8156-0516-1 (alk. paper).
    1. Exodus 1947 (Ship)   2. Refugees, Jewish.   3. Holocaust
survivors.   4. Palestine—Emigration and immigration.   I. Title.
HV6405.J4.H2513   1998
304.8'5694'09044—DC21   98-9408

Typeset by Vitaset, Paddock Wood, Kent
Printed in Great Britain on acid-free paper by
Creative Print and Design (Wales), Ebbw Vale

In loving memory of my father,
Mordechai Halamish (Flint)

Contents

List of Illustrations

List of Abbreviations

The following abbreviations are used in the Notes and Works Cited:

Adm   Admiralty
BGA   Ben-Gurion Archives, Sde Boker
Cab   Cabinet
CO   Colonial Office
CP   Cunningham Papers, Middle East Center, St Antony's College, Oxford
CZA   Central Zionist Archives, Jerusalem
FO   Foreign Office
FRUS   Foreign Relations of the United States
HPIC   Ha'apalah Project Information Center, Tel Aviv University, Tel Aviv
HHA   Haganah Historical Archives, Tel Aviv
ISA   Israel State Archives, Jerusalem
JANY   American Joint Distribution Committee Archives, New York
JDCJA   American Joint Distribution Committee Archives, Jerusalem
JIA   Jabotinsky Institute Archives, Tel Aviv
LA   Labor Archives, Tel Aviv
LPA   Labor Party Archives, Beit Berl
MA   Moreshet Archives, Giv'at Haviva
OHC   Oral History Center, Institute for Contemporary Jewry, Hebrew University, Jerusalem
PRO   Public Record Office, London
SHA   Ha-Shomer ha-Tza'ir archives, Giv'at Haviva
YBZA   Yad Yitzhak Ben-Zvi Archives, Jerusalem

Key to Coded Names

Ami	David Ben Gurion
Amnon	Yossi Hamburger (later Har'el)
Amos	Germany
Arnon	Mossad Headquarters in Tel Aviv
Artzi	Palestine
Ben-Yehuda	Shaul Meirov (later Avigur)
Berg	Pino Ginzburg, Mossad's treasurer
Danny	Ze'ev Schind, also: the United States
Delphi	Haganah's Intelligence Service
Elisha	Grisha Sheinkman, Mossad activist
Ernest	Ephrayim Frank, Mossad activist
Galoni	Mordechai Roseman
Ha-kli	*Exodus 1947* (Lit: The vessel)
Hannan	Germany
Hillel	Israel Galili, Commander of the Haganah
Hofi	Mossad office in Haifa
Hofshi	Davidka Nameri, Mossad activist
Itay	Ehud Avriel, Mossad activist
Kalir	Ada Sereni
Leonard	Mossad branch in Italy
Matityahu	Israel Galilee, Commander of the Haganah
Neter	France
Rise	Cyprus
Rudy	Shemarya Zameret, Mossad activist, also: Southern France
Sidney	Marseilles
Tal	Akiva Levinsky, Mossad activist
Ur	Shaul Meirov (later Avigur)
Yiftach	Yigal Peikovitz (later Allon)
Yis'ar	Venia (Ze'ev) Pomerantz (later Hadari) also: Mossad branch in France
Yoram	Yugoslavia
Zehava	Golda Myerson (later Meir)
Zelig	Tel Aviv

Foreword

In her book, *The Exodus Affair*, historian Aviva Halamish clarifies and explains how the illegal immigrant ship *Exodus* became not only the flagship of her 64 sister ships which sailed "illegally" between the years 1945 and 1948 into the coast of Palestine, with thousands of illegal immigrants on board, but also became a legend which summarized the courage and steadfastness of Holocaust survivors against the destroyers of His Britannic Majesty's Navy.

This fascinating book, a wonderfully exciting blend of precise historical facts with personal and political drama, highlights the following points. First of all, the name *Exodus* conjures up a kind of motto, which fluttered the hearts of millions of Jews and non-Jews alike. "Exodus" is the Latin name for the second of the five books of Moses; it is a name which harbors within it the vast biblical ethos of the Jewish liberation from slavery to freedom. This ship, previously called *President Warfield*, was honored with a name which resounded like the blowing of a ram's horn. The other illegal immigrant ships, including the *Ulua*, which I had the privilege of commanding, were given less vibrant names.

A second factor which raised the profile of the ship to legendary status was the battle between *Exodus* and the British warships off the Palestine coast – a war of the weak against the power of the Empire – which received widespread international press coverage. More than in any of the other violent confrontations which accompanied much of the illegal immigrant operation, this time the blood of the dead and the cries of the injured were seen and heard the world over.

A third factor, which powerfully reinforced the two previous ones, was the development of the Exodus Affair into an international struggle. The unsuccessful British attempt at sending the illegal immigrants in deportation ships back to their port of departure in France and, following this débâcle, expelling them to detention camps in Germany – which just a few years before had been the country in which the hell of the Holocaust had been conceived and implemented – drew not only the outraged Jewish world into the whirlpool, but also the governments of Britain, France and the United States, as well as the United Nations and the world media.

Today there is a debate in Israel as to whether the illegal immigrants were no more than passive statistics, puppets manipulated by the Zionist leadership which ostensibly tried to "exploit" their misery and forced them, through the emissaries of the Haganah from Palestine, to undergo the harsh voyages on board those illegal immigrant ships in order to win points in a struggle for the foundation of a Jewish state; or whether the immigrants themselves, survivors of the death camps and former partisan fighters, were the very force which activated the Jewish odyssey on its way to the Land of Israel and it was they who, through utmost determination, found their way to the people of the Haganah to help lead them.

Not for a moment does Aviva Halamish understate the tensions between the members of the Haganah and the illegal immigrants, friction which was the result of different mentalities, different languages and different life experiences. But, in the final analysis, she states unequivocally that in those difficult and trying days, they all came together in a true partnership. Together they stood against their common enemy, together they fought and struggled, and together they participated in bringing about the birth of the State of Israel.

ARIE LOVA ELIAV
Commander in the Illegal Immigration Operation
and a prominent figure in the Israeli peace camp
January 1998

Preface

It was sheer chance that led me on board *Exodus*, many years after the wrecked ship had sunk to the bottom of the sea, but her name was known world wide. I had been asked, to my great surprise, to write a monograph on the Exodus Affair, as part of a research project on the illegal immigration of Jews into Palestine (*Ha'apalah*). "But surely," I said, "everything that needs to be known about that legendary ship, which was one of the symbols of the struggle for a Jewish state, has already been told. What else is there to tell about the affair?" It was not long before I found out how wrong I was.

Indeed, I found that most of what had been written on *Exodus* before was either lacking or inaccurate. Early writings had been based on the personal accounts of people who had taken part in the operation, and these are by nature problematic, because of the limitations of human memory and the partial observation of those who participated in certain aspects of the events only. Moreover, most of these accounts were recorded when *Exodus* had already become a symbol and even a myth, and there was a tendency to combine facts, on the one hand, with commentary, analysis, evaluation, polemic and even wishful thinking, on the other. Another weakness lay in the use of archival sources. For the first thirty years following the affair, the writers were aided, if at all, by documents available from the Jewish side only. But even books written after British documents became available to the researchers contained ingrained errors, which require amendment and revision in order to present things in as accurate a way as possible. And, as in any other affair which took place many years before and which has had layer upon layer of stories told about it, so too in the case of *Exodus* it was necessary to examine what had been written, to ratify the various versions and details and to review the existing historiography against the "new" primary sources – those which were revealed only years afterwards.

I was soon bewitched by the Exodus Affair. I found myself carried away by an extraordinary human and political drama, one which sheds light on the entire period between the end of the Second World War and the founding of the State of Israel. Being a particular incident which also has a general significance, it satisfied my dilemma as a historian, between the legitimacy of describing a single, unique phenomenon and the search for a wider generalization.

Moreover, the words of the Italian philosopher Benedetto Croce, that "all history is contemporary history" took on a significant actuality for me, when, at the end of 1987 the *Intifada* (revolt) of the Palestinian Arabs broke out against the Israeli occupation. The events which I was to witness forty years after the Exodus Affair drove home to me the difficulties faced by the British during the years 1945–1948, when, as rulers of Palestine, they had to stand opposite the un-armed struggle of Holocaust survivors making their way to what, for them, was their homeland. The pictures which filled the TV screen at this time served to increase my respect for the correct behavior of the soldiers of the British Navy and Army toward the illegal immigrants. At the same time, I learned to value even more the illegal immigration as a unique method chosen by the Jewish national liberation movement – Zionism – in its struggle for independence. Not personal or blind terror, nor acts of violence involving physical attacks on the enemy and casualties on the part of the strugglers, but a calculated blend of political and diplomatic activity and a struggle which took advantage of the weakness of the strong and the power of the weak.

And in addition to this, the Exodus Affair also bears a universal message which traverses the boundaries of time and place: that of the human spirit, of the willingness of people to struggle and of their ability to overcome hardship, especially when faced with an objective in which they believe and are convinced of their ability to contribute to its achievement.

Acknowledgements

I would like to thank all those who helped me during the research, writing, translating and publishing of this book, first in Hebrew and then in English. Anita Shapira at Tel Aviv University was the one who suggested the idea of researching the Exodus Affair and who, with good advice, accompanied the writing of the Hebrew version. Israel Oppenheim at Ben-Gurion University of the Negev, himself an *Exodus* immigrant, read the entire manuscript, and his encouragement throughout was no less important than his valuable comments. Thanks to Yaacov Shavit and Zohar Shavit at Tel Aviv University, devoted scholars and faithful friends, for their help and advice in getting the English version published. Yosef Gorni and Ron Zweig of the Institute for Research in the History of Zionism at Tel Aviv University were also helpful in this.

It is a pleasure to thank the directors and staff of the archives who assisted me in locating the relevant material: Haganah Historical Archives in Tel Aviv, Central Zionist Archives in Jerusalem, Israel State Archives in Jerusalem, Moreshet Archives and the ha-Shomer ha-Tza'ir Archives in Giv'at Haviva, the JDC Archives in Jerusalem, the Ben-Gurion Heritage Archives in Sde Boker, the Labor Archives in Tel Aviv, the Jabotinsky Institute Archives in Tel Aviv, the Oral History Center of the Institute for Contemporary Jewry at the Hebrew University of Jerusalem and Yad Yitzhak Ben-Zvi Archives in Jerusalem, as well as the Jewish National and University Library at the Hebrew University of Jerusalem. Special thanks to the staff of the Ha'apalah Project Information Center, situated at the Tel Aviv University campus and headed by Hava Mustigman, for whom no time or trouble was too much in helping me locate the material I needed. For assistance in obtaining the photographs used in the book I thank the Haganah Historical Archives, the Ha'apalah Project Information Center, the photograph Archives of Beth Hatefutsoth in Tel Aviv, Reuven Koppler of the Central Zionist Archives and Yoram Weinberg of the Open University of Israel.

It is a pleasant duty to thank the institutions and foundations which helped finance the book's English translation. First and foremost, the Ha'apalah Research Association Founded in Memory of Shaul Avigur, which also funded the research and publication of the book in Hebrew, especially board member Zachary Kikayon; Yad Avi Ha-Yishuv of the Rothschild Foundation; the Yoran-Schnitzer Foundation at the School of Jewish Studies at Tel Aviv University; the President of Israel's Amos Foundation for the encouragement of scholars and writers. My thanks also to the Open University of Israel for its generous assistance throughout the research, writing and translation of the book.

My translator, Ora Cummings, deserves thanks and praise for finding the golden road between maintaining the original spirit of the book as it was written in Hebrew and its current version, in fluent, readable English – no easy task. Thanks to the staff of Am Oved Publishers in Tel Aviv and the editor Eli Shaltiel for their part in the Hebrew version of the book. Also to Robert Mandel, Director of Syracuse University Press and his staff and the editor Rachel Joseph and the staff at Vallentine Mitchell Publications.

Two good friends deserve special mention: Bat-Chen Furst at the Open University, who helped me to overcome the mysteries of the computer and its ever-changing programs, and Judith Tydor Baumel at the University of Haifa, a friend in every sense of the word, whose willingness to help is boundless and for whom no words of the kind used at the beginning of books to express thanks have the power to convey the level of gratitude I feel for her.

Last but not least, I thank my close friends and family, especially my mother, Hanna Halamish, who stood by me throughout the project and helped me overcome the hardships caused by time. And above all I thank my children Ilan and Maya Goldstein. Their consideration, understanding and the way in which they took part with me in the long journey were a source of strength without which the book would never have seen the light of day.

My father, Mordechai Halamish, followed the early stages of the work with intellectual interest, tempered by parental concern. Sadly, he did not live to see the completed product, and I dedicate this book to his dear memory, as an expression of love and esteem.

Introduction

Ten o'clock on the evening of Thursday 17 July 1947 and the Jews in Palestine were waiting with bated breath by their radio sets for a broadcast from the ship *Exodus 1947*. They had learned from the Haganah's hastily posted billboard notices that same afternoon that the ship, bearing some 4,500 men, women and children, was "making its way toward the shores of the homeland" and that at ten o'clock in the evening "our brothers, the Ma'apilim, will broadcast their message to the Jews of Eretz Israel".

At exactly ten o'clock, the broadcaster came on the air to unfold the story of the ship and the suffering of her passengers – the horrors they had experienced during the Holocaust, and their anguish up to that very moment when they were but a few kilometers off the shores of the Promised Land. No sooner had he finished speaking, than the air was filled with the sound of joyful Hebrew singing, followed by the hymn of the Jewish partisans, sung in the high clear voices of the ship's youth choir. "Ha-Tikvah", the national anthem of hope, brought the emotionally charged broadcast to an end.

A few hours later, the *Exodus* was attacked by ships of the British Navy, which blocked her entry into Palestine. Dozens of British soldiers charged the ship to be met by stubborn resistance of the passengers on board. For more than two hours a fierce face-to-face battle took place on the decks of the ship and in her nether regions. Three of the *Exodus* people were killed and dozens, including British soldiers, were injured. Accompanied by about half a dozen British warships, the damaged ship then floated of her own accord into the port of Haifa. Here the illegal immigrants were transferred to three deportation ships. The following day, Saturday, they set sail westwards.

Where exactly were they heading for?

Since August 1946, the British had been deporting all illegal immigrants caught trying to get into Palestine, to detention camps in Cyprus.

This time they changed their normal practice, trying a new tactic in their futile efforts to put a stop to Jewish illegal immigration into Palestine. They decided to return the illegal immigrants to the port from which they had set off.

Thus, once SS *Exodus 1947* was safely moored at Haifa's "shadow dock" (for illegal immigrant ships), her task completed, the story of what would go down in posterity as the "Exodus Affair" began to unfold. It would reach its climax with the expulsion of the illegal immigrants to Germany, after having refused to disembark in France.

Ha'apalah, the organized illegal immigration of Jews into Palestine in violation of British Mandatory regulations, was initiated in 1934, and gained momentum in the second half of the 1930s, as the plight of the Jews in Europe deteriorated and the British restricted immigration into Palestine. On the eve of the Second World War, the Ha'apalah, also known as *Aliyah Bet*, was adopted by the Zionist leadership as the primary means in the struggle against British policy in Palestine. After the outbreak of the war, organized illegal immigration of Jews to Palestine was gradually diminished and eventually came to a virtual halt. However, the infra-structure of shipping connections and experienced personnel was not totally lost, including *ha-Mossad le-Aliyah Bet*, the Haganah branch responsible for the illegal immigration operation, thus facilitating the renewal of its activity shortly after the war.

Following the Second World War, the Ha'apalah was aimed first and foremost to serve as a lever for founding a Jewish state in Palestine. The architects of Zionist policy assigned it a key role in creating a link in the minds of world public opinion and decision makers between a solution for the problem of the Jewish DPs (displaced persons) and the establishment of a Jewish state in Palestine. The idea was to keep the plight of the Jewish DPs, languishing in Europe so many months after the end of the war, alive in the newspaper headlines, and to drive home the fact that they were yearning to come and settle in Palestine, notwith-standing any and all the hardships they would have to face in doing so. Illegal immigration had the potential to embarrass the British for callously preventing the entry of Jewish survivors of the Holocaust into their homeland, and thus making full use of the moral force of the Zionist cause.

Exodus is without doubt the most famous of all the 64 ships used by the Mossad during the years 1945–1948. She is considered to be the flag ship of the illegal immigration fleet and a symbol of the entire operation. Moreover, although the Exodus Affair was a unique event, it is nevertheless a microcosm not only of the illegal immigration operation in the years 1945–1948, but also of the history of the Holocaust survivors and of the Yishuv in those years.

About ten years after the Exodus Affair, the book *Exodus* by Leon Uris and the subsequent movie, made the name of the ship a household word and joined it in the minds of millions of people all over the world with the story of the founding of the State of Israel. Although the book and film are only loosely connected to the real-life Exodus Affair, they aroused and sustained public interest in the fate of the original ship and her passengers.

This book presents as comprehensive a picture as possible of all the aspects and stages of the 1947 Exodus Affair. It follows the chain of events, describes the actions and motives of all the participants, attempts to explain the reasons behind these actions and to identify their goals, and to evaluate the ways in which these were achieved and at what price.

On a political level, the book deals with the policies and activities of the British, French, Americans and the Zionists, as well as the United Nations Organization and its Special Committee on Palestine. It deals also with the role the Yishuv played in illegal immigration in general and the Exodus Affair in particular. On a human level, the book brings a tale of genuine, unassuming heroism, the heartrending story of thousands of men, women and children, survivors of the Holocaust in Europe, who happened by chance upon a lengthy and trying test and came through it with quiet courage and dignity. Where did they draw their immense spiritual power from? And from a social point of view, the book attempts to define the interaction between the American volunteers, the Ma'apilim and the escorts from Palestine, as well as the relationships within each of these groups.

Even as it was unfolding, the Exodus Affair was showing signs of becoming a legend, a myth. The steadfast, dignified stance of the illegal immigrants against the intransigent impotence of the giant British Empire imparted a kind of David and Goliath character to the struggle. The fact that the decision by the British Government (on 20 September 1947) to withdraw its army from Palestine and the UN decision of 29 November 1947 on the partition of Palestine and the establishment of a Jewish state in part of it, all came hot on the heels of the Exodus Affair, created a kind of circumstantial connection between the events, in Zionist consciousness and contemporary historiography, which labeled it as a victory for the Zionist cause. And ever since, the Exodus Affair has been part of the myth surrounding the founding of the State of Israel.

Now, about half a century after the Exodus Affair, when the lava has long since ceased to flow but has not yet cooled completely and solidified, the time has come not only to tell things as they happened (with the help of as many and as varied sources as possible), and to offer some new interpretations, but also to ponder over the myth: how did it evolve, and which needs of the Yishuv and the young State of Israel was it supposed to answer?

The Hebrew name of *Exodus 1947* was *Yetzi'at Eiropa Tashaz* (Exodus from Europe [in the Hebrew year] 5707). To paraphrase a section from the Passover Haggadah that millions of Jews all over the world repeat every year at the Feast of Passover, this book fulfills the command: "And the more is told about the 'Exodus from Europe', the better." And I believe that the story of *Exodus 1947* will continue to be told and retold in the future as the last word has not yet been said on the matter.

1 · Crisis

Like the exodus of their Biblical forefathers from Egypt, the departure of European Jews out of Germany to board the ship *Exodus 1947* was a hurried affair. The order to swiftly transfer a large number of displaced persons (DPs) to France was issued by the Mossad le-Aliyah Bet (Mossad) toward the end of June 1947. In less than two weeks, some 5,000 people left the DP camps in Germany (Yahil 1981, 143–44; Habbas 1954, 23). Most of them set sail on 11 July 1947 aboard a ship, whose name at that time was still *President Warfield*.

In the spring of 1947, the Jewish DPs in the American occupied zone in Germany were in a state of near crisis. Two years after the end of the war there were some 150,000 Jews still living in the zone, after having experienced seven years of hell and whose future was foggy at best. At the end of the Second World War, at a time when displaced persons from other nations were making their way eastward back to their countries of origin, the Jews were moving southward to the Mediterranean coast in the hope of eventually reaching Palestine. It was soon evident, however, that the way to Palestine was neither short nor swift and by an ironic twist of history, many Jews were forced to "seek refuge for the night" on their way to the Promised Land, in Germany of all places. This temporary overnight stop stretched from months into years, and as time passed, wave upon wave of Holocaust survivors gathered on German soil.

By spring of 1947, more than half of all the Jewish DPs in Europe were living in the American occupied zone in Germany.[1] There were several reasons for the fact that this region served as a lodestone for these people. In August 1945, the Americans began setting up special camps to house the displaced Jews. The British, on the other hand, did not recognize the Jews as having a separate national identity, and placed them together with other nationalities, claiming that "it is undesirable to accept the Nazi theory that the Jews are a separate race. Jews, in common with all other religious sects, should be treated according to their nationality, rather than as a race or religious sect."[2] Furthermore, the refugees who kept flowing into the British zone were not recognized as "displaced persons", and were dispersed among groups of Germans and received the same meager food rations as the Germans (Bauer 1970, 268). The American authorities on the other hand, showed more tolerance and compassion toward the waves of Jewish DPs who came in from the East and tended to make their stay as bearable as possible. They issued a statement that Jewish refugees from Poland arriving in the American occupied zone would not be turned back against their will,[3] and even set up special camps to house the new arrivals (Slutzky 1972a, 1019, 1040–41). The better conditions in the American zone drew to it not only Jews from the East, but also those who had settled in regions occupied by others, especially the British.

There were, in theory, four main ways to solve the problem of the displaced Jews. The first solution would have been to settle them in Germany; the second, to return them, as was done with millions of other such people, to the countries in which they had lived before the war; the third one was for them to emigrate to Western European countries or countries overseas; and emigration to Palestine was the fourth solution.

The DPs themselves saw their stay in Germany only as a temporary respite. They considered Europe on the whole, and especially Germany, to be defiled territory, which they wanted to leave as soon as they possibly could. There was nothing they wished for less than to settle in Germany. Moreover, as if their terrible memories so fresh after their awesome ordeals were not sufficient, the antisemitic attacks they were now exposed to after the war further fueled their desire to leave Germany as fast as they could. As their stay in the camps lengthened and the chances of their ever leaving Germany seemed ever dimmer, some of the DPs moved away and settled in nearby towns and villages. Most of these did not see this move as a permanent solution, rather as a refuge from the life of inactivity and atrophy offered by the camps and as a way of "making money" for the sake of their future rehabilitation.[4]

As far as they were concerned, repatriation to the countries in which they had lived prior to the outbreak of the Second World War was not a practical solution either. On the contrary: haunted by the events of the war and by the incessant antisemitism which followed, and suffering from the harsh economic conditions of postwar Eastern Europe, the Jews started moving westward. Only a few of them returned to Poland from the Western occupied zones, and many Jews – including those who had already made their way back to Poland only to discover that this was no longer their home – left Poland and other Eastern European countries to join their brothers in Germany.

And what about the West? The United States was not in any hurry to legislate amendments in her immigration laws, and agreed at first only to give preferential treatment to DPs, but not necessarily Jewish ones, within the framework of existing immigration quotas. Thus by the summer of 1948 no more than 45,000 DPs had been allowed entry to the United States, and about one-third of these were Jews (Wischnitzer 1948, 262–63, 267, 349; Divine 1957, 112–13: Bauer 1970, 205). From the end of the war and until the time the *Exodus* set sail for Palestine, only some 25,000 Jewish DPs had emigrated to the West – USA, England, Canada, Australia, France, Belgium, Scandinavia and Latin America (Wischnitzer 1948, 273; Bernstein 1947).

And then there was Palestine, both as a preferred choice in her own right and as the single ray of hope in a given situation. The Jewish DPs' wish to emigrate to Palestine first became known with the publication of the Harrison Report in the summer of 1945. Earl G. Harrison, Dean of the Law School at the University of Pennsylvania, had been sent by President Truman to review the general situation of the displaced persons' camps in Germany and Austria, and that of the Jewish inmates in particular. He was asked, furthermore, to determine what would be the preferred alternative destination for those of the DPs who were not able to return to their countries of origin. In his report to the President, Harrison stated that for most of the Jews in the DP camps "Palestine is definitely and pre-eminently the first choice. Many now have relatives there, while others, having experienced intolerance and persecution in their homelands [for] years, feel that only in Palestine will they be welcomed and ... given an opportunity to live and work." Some chose Palestine because they had always been devoted Zionists and there were others who realized that the "possibility of settling in the US or the Western Hemisphere was slight". However, Harrison felt that the number of the latter was not large. He suggested to the President to allow "reasonable numbers" of Jewish DPs into the US, without deviating from existing immigration laws, remarking that these potential immigrants would be relatively few, since most of the Jewish DPs preferred to make their way to Palestine (Wischnitzer 1948, 260–62; Hurewitz 1950, 229–30).

The issue was reviewed a few months later by several other bodies, in preparation for a visit by the Anglo-American Committee of Inquiry Regarding the Problems of European Jewry and Palestine. The findings showed that the majority of the DPs (between 60 percent and 96.8 percent) wished to emigrate to Palestine.[5] The Committee itself reached

similar conclusions after its visit to Poland, Czechoslovakia, Austria and
Germany at the beginning of 1946. The Committee's members discovered that the Jewish DPs had completely and irrevocably severed
their ties with the countries in which they had lived prior to the war, and
recommended that permission be granted for the immediate entry into
Palestine of 100,000 Jews, victims of the Nazi and Fascist atrocities.

However, the British Government chose to keep the gates of Palestine
securely closed and left only a tiny opening through which a mere 1,500
certificate-bearing immigrants could enter each month. These certificates were allocated according to a predetermined set of priorities, whose
main aim was that of reducing the number of Jewish DPs in the British
held zone in Germany and easing the burden on the British authorities
in that region. With this in mind, the British exercised a strict policy to
prevent the entry of any more DPs into the area under their control and
refused to acknowledge the DP status of any who succeeded in smuggling
themselves in. At the same time, they were relatively generous with
immigration permits to Palestine to inhabitants of their zone – to the tune
of some 350 a month. Thus, by August 1947, they were able to reduce
the number of Jewish DPs under their control to a mere 12,000. Of these,
some 4,000 emigrated to Palestine before the founding of the State of
Israel.[6]

Requests by the American Government and the Jewish Agency to
the British Government to increase the quota of immigration permits
to Jewish inhabitants of the American occupied zone – whose number
was ten times greater than that of the area under British control – were
refused.[7] During its entire term of activity since the end of the war, the
Palestine Office of the Jewish Agency in Munich, which was responsible
for immigration to Palestine from the American occupied zone, was
granted only a single quota of certificates in 1946 (461 in number) which
were given to orphans (The Jewish Agency 1949, 40).

The British devoted a significant portion of the certificate quota to
their struggle against illegal immigration to Palestine, an issue which had
been placed high on their list of priorities. In the period between January
and August 1946, any illegal immigrant caught by the British was automatically imprisoned at a detention camp near Atlit, some ten miles south
of Haifa, only to be released shortly afterward. The monthly quota of immigrants was then reduced accordingly, which meant, in effect, that illegal
immigration took place at the expense of officially issued certificates. All
in all, some 10,444 certificates were deducted in this way from the official
quota, during the first 18 months prior to the *Exodus* departure.[8]

Several big illegal immigration ships were sailing toward Palestine during the spring of 1946 and there was intelligence regarding an imminent wave of illegal immigration during the summer months, which would exceed all the quotas. In the middle of August that year, the British began deporting all the illegal immigrants they caught to Cyprus, and holding them there in detention camps specially constructed for that purpose. Fearing that, at this rate, the camps would soon be overcrowded, the British then found themselves having to allocate one-half of their monthly quota of immigration certificates to transferring the illegal immigrants from Cyprus to Palestine (Sha'ari 1981, 244; Bogner 1991, 63–69).

After 750 immigration certificates had been allotted to the Cyprus detainees and another 300–400 distributed to Jews in the British occupied zone in Germany, around 300 to 400 certificates still remained in the monthly quota. These were allocated by the British Mandatory Authorities to people whose relations in Palestine had requested immigration permits on their behalf. Here too, the authorities preferred to supply certificates to those Jewish DPs living in the area under British control in Germany. Thus, between 1945 and 1948 a total of less than 1,000 immigration permits to Palestine were issued to Jewish DPs living in the American held zone in Germany – as compared with 6,000 such permits issued between March 1947 and May 1948 alone, to people in the British-held zone (The Jewish Agency, 1949).

This British policy, therefore, dealt a double blow to the Jews in the American-held zone. Not only did they cause overcrowding by obliging the DPs to move from the British zone into the area under American control, but the British also almost entirely denied them the opportunity to immigrate legally into Palestine. Thus, in effect, the only channel left open for the Jews in the American controlled area to reach Palestine was through illegal immigration. But here too, there was a considerable dragging of heels. From the end of the war until spring of 1947, only about 10,000 people from the American zone were able to use the illegal immigration option for reaching Palestine,[9] and the last few months before the mass exodus toward the *Exodus* saw a dwindling of even this meager flow (Slutzky 1972a, 1902–903; Sha'ari 1981, 74–79).

The long standstill in illegal immigration from Germany took place when living conditions and morale were deteriorating rapidly in the Jewish DP camps in the American-held zone. The severe winter of 1946/47 was especially harsh on the inhabitants of the DP camps. Everyone, the DPs, the emissaries from Palestine, the Americans as well as members of international relief organizations active in the camps, were concerned about the negative consequences of keeping the DPs in the camps for a further winter.[10] Members of the United Nations Special Committee on Palestine (UNSCOP), who visited the camps in the summer of 1947, were convinced that, unless significant changes would take place, a further winter under present conditions would result in considerable restlessness and possible outbreaks of violence (UNSCOP 1947b, 27). The American occupation authorities were deeply concerned at growing evidence of negative and even criminal activity within the DP community, especially with regard to the flourishing black market. There were signs of insufficient cooperation on the part of the DPs and some of them had even developed hostile attitudes toward the camps' military personnel. A further source of concern for the authorities was the suspicion that the Jewish DPs may be susceptible to communist propaganda (Eilat 1982, 161–63; Bain 1979, 162).

With the passing of time, the American military personnel (at the lower echelons) underwent a deterioration of attitude toward the Jewish DPs. In 1947, the American soldiers serving in Germany were young men who had only recently arrived in Europe. These were no longer the same soldiers who had taken part in liberating the concentration camps, who, horrified by the sights they had seen, identified sympathetically with the victims of Nazi atrocities. These new soldiers, who knew little about what the DPs had been through, found their behavior repulsive (Lippman testimony; Bernstein 1947). As a rule, the lower the rank of the American soldier, the more negative his attitude was to the Jewish DPs in his care. Although HQ personnel and the higher ranks were exposed to the moderating influence of Army Rabbis and advisors on Jewish affairs – as well as being, presumably, more in tune with political considerations back home – it was still the lower ranks who came in daily contact with the DPs.

As relations between soldiers and military authorities and the Jewish DPs gradually cooled, spring 1947 saw a further change for the worse, which came in the form of "orders from above". Ever since the end of the war, the Americans had been facing a dilemma. On the one hand, they wanted to placate the Germans by helping them rebuild their economy; on the other hand, they were overwhelmingly aware of the necessity to help and rehabilitate the millions of displaced persons, victims of the Nazi oppression of the previous decade. At first, the latter issue was of primary importance, but, as the events of the Second World War faded into the past and the shadow of the Cold War loomed ever greater, feelings and attitudes inevitably changed. In April 1947, an order was issued to the American forces in Europe not to admit any more DPs into the already overcrowded camps. This order did not specify that the borders should be closed to the DPs, nor that their entry to the camps should be blocked forcibly, so that, in practical terms, the meaning of the order was that future arrivals in the camps would no longer be recognized as DPs and would not be eligible for the aid given to people of this status (Proudfoot n.d., 342; Bauer 1970, 304).

Unlike previous occasions in which orders were issued to limit the flow of Jewish DPs into the American zone in Germany, only to be revoked shortly thereafter (Bauer 1970, 198–99), this time the financial assets to maintain the DPs were indeed frozen. Since more DPs continued to arrive, there evolved a new situation whereby support per person in the camps was significantly reduced, with existing budgets now having to be stretched to cope with ever-growing numbers of DPs. At the same time, changes were taking place among the international relief organizations responsible for taking care of the DPs. The United Nations Relief and Rehabilitation Agency (UNRRA) was replaced by the International Refugee Organization (IRO), who had less manpower and lower budgets. As a result of these changes, there was a considerable drop in the quality and quantity of food handed out in the camps, and overcrowding increased.[11]

Morale was low among the Jewish DPs in spring 1947, a kind of anticlimax to the hopes and expectations of the previous year. President Truman's call to the British to allow 100,000 Jewish DPs to enter Palestine, the visit of the Anglo-American Committee in the camps, its conclusions (which also included a recommendation to permit the immediate immigration of 100,000 DPs into Palestine), and the intensive political activity which followed publication of these conclusions, all kindled hopes among the displaced persons that their problems were about to be solved. Toward the end of 1946, it seemed that a more comprehensive political solution was about to be found, which would not limit itself to the immigration of 100,000 DPs to Palestine, but would eventually bring about the formation of a Jewish state. The camps were charged with activity in the wake of the elections to the 22nd Zionist Congress to be held in December 1946, accompanied by high hopes for a political breakthrough. Disappointment was therefore great when this was not forthcoming. The hopes and expectations of 1946 were replaced in the first few months of 1947 by feelings of disillusion and dejection.

In the spring of 1947, some two years after the end of the war, with millions of DPs of other nationalities already back in their homelands, the future of the Jewish DPs (whose numbers rose from 60,000 at the end of the war to some quarter of a million) seemed less than promising. The inhabitants of the camps in Germany were showing distinct signs of demoralization. Chaim Barlas, Director of the Jewish Agency Immigration Department, who visited Europe during the spring and summer of 1947, found changed attitudes toward immigration to Palestine. He felt that there was now a mood of resignation, of acquiescence, that might well threaten the desire to immigrate to Palestine. The camps' inhabitants began quarreling over whether it might not be better all round if they were to emigrate to countries other than Palestine (1947b). Many of them were sick and tired of this situation of uncertainty and constant inactivity. More and more people were leaving the camps for the nearby towns, many of them to become involved in black market activity, while the queues grew longer outside the offices of the organizations dealing with emigration to countries in the West.

However, the Jewish DPs did not completely rule out immigration to Palestine by registering for immigration to other countries (Habbas 1954, 28). On the contrary, they were willing to become part of what was known as Aliyah Bet, and even fought for a place on it. The American Jewish Joint Distribution Committee (JDC) and the Hebrew Sheltering and Immigration Aid Society (HIAS), the Jewish organizations who registered DPs for emigration out of Germany, made a point of not supplying the Jewish Agency with information, for fear that the latter would then punish the DPs by refusing them the right to immigrate to Palestine (Levin 1947a; Barlas 1947a). People were signing up for immigration to other countries because they were exhausted and disillusioned by their empty and atrophic lives in the camps, and because they had lost hope of ever being able to make it to Palestine. They did so out of a desire to get out of Germany, to embark on a new life, to rehabilitate themselves as soon as possible and wherever possible, and not because there was any real reason for them to believe that there was any better chance now to obtain a visa to any Western country.[12]

In October 1946, as part of the mid-term election campaign, President Truman announced his intention to ask Congress to permit numbers of displaced persons to enter the United States in excess of the regular quota (Divine 1957, 113). However, the President was not referring in this to Jewish DPs – for them he had a different plan altogether. This plan, which was announced at the very same time, was to become known as the "Day of Atonement Statement" and referred to the immediate admission into Palestine of 100,000 Jews (Hurewitz 1950, 264–65). Only six months later, very shortly before the sailing of the *Exodus*, Representative William Stratton of Illinois introduced a bill in which he proposed that 400,000 non-quota European DPs be allowed to immigrate to the United States over a period of four years. The legal process for this bill took until the middle of 1948, and the law, which was very different from the original draft proposal, was passed only one month after the founding of the State of Israel.[13]

On the eve of the sailing of the *Exodus*, rumors were rife in the DP camps of an imminent visit by a Canadian committee, which was coming to pick out some 2,500 skilled tailors. These would be granted entry permits to Canada, where they would be given jobs in the country's clothing industry. The source of the rumors was a decision taken by the Canadian Government at the beginning of June 1947, to admit 2,000 tailors and their families from among the displaced persons in Europe. The decision was taken at the request of industrialists and Union officials in the clothing industry (who were mostly Jewish), and had the specific aim of allowing the immigration to Canada of Jewish DPs, in the framework of the Canadian Government's bulk labor program for the admission of DPs. This program in its wording as well as its *modus operandi*, openly discriminated against Jewish DPs, and the Canadian representatives, as did those of other countries, habitually overlooked the Jewish DPs when choosing potential candidates for immigration. In April 1947, the International Labor Organization came to the conclusion that Jewish DPs had only a slight chance of being able to emigrate out of Germany in the foreseeable future, both because of the many restrictions placed on immigration (which were usually based on considerations of race and nationality) and because most of the countries willing to accept immigrants, were interested only in healthy, able-bodied people who would be useful and productive additions to their economies (Wischnitzer 1948, 273). The Jewish DPs did not meet with these demands – both from a professional and from a health point of view – since what these countries wanted were mainly laborers for their heavy industries, mines and agriculture. The "tailor's quota" was actually the first time a specific demand had been made for Jews. However, the Canadian committee arrived in Germany only at the beginning of August 1947, so that among the many other rumors flying around during the early months of the year, news of its arrival did not really constitute any special reason for excitement (Levin 1947a; Habbas 1954, 28; Troper 1985, 16–25).

In the spring of 1947, on the eve of the mass departure from the camps toward the ship *Exodus*, there was no real reason for the Jewish DPs to believe that any significant changes were afoot with regard to their chance of leaving Germany in the foreseeable future – notwithstanding the frequent rumors that they might be able to emigrate to this country or that.

The Zionist leaders were seriously disturbed by the long queues for emigration to the United States, by the rumors of "tailors for Canada", by news of possible changes in American immigration policies, and by the attempts being made by non-Zionist Jewish organizations to solve the problems of the displaced persons.[14] To the humane concern of these Zionist leaders about the fate of their brethren rotting away for so long in the DP camps, was now added the fear – on the political level – lest the connection would be weakened, which they had been working so hard to reinforce, between the solution to the plight of the Jewish DPs and the foundation of a Jewish state in Palestine.

For some time, Zionists and non-Zionists alike had been pessimistic with regard to the situation of the Jewish DPs in Germany. In the summer of 1946, a JDC observer reported that "people are getting more and more discouraged daily ... the feeling of frustration is reaching the stage where it is demoralizing" (Bauer 1970, 262). At the same time, Haim Hoffman (later Yahil), head of the Palestine delegation in Germany, sent a report to his colleagues in Jerusalem in which he described the mood prevalent among the DPs as defeatist and informed of the registration for emigration to the United States. "If they are not able to immigrate [to Palestine] soon," he wrote, deeply concerned, "the situation can only get worse" (Yahil 1946). In other words, the trend to emigrate (to the West) would increase.

And, as we have seen, matters did not improve with regard to immigration to Palestine and did indeed deteriorate. The number of people applying for emigration to the West grew and the JDC, HIAS and other Jewish organizations did their best to assist the Jewish DPs to make their way to America and other Western countries. During the summer and autumn of 1946, Rabbi Philip Bernstein, the official Jewish Advisor to the Commander of American Forces in Europe, whose concern was triggered both by a sincere desire to help his brethren and by the wish to lighten the load of his own army, raised several ideas for the partial solution of the problem. These ideas included: resettling 10,000 DPs in Czechoslovakia, transferring 25,000 DPs to Italy, and a similar number of children to Norway. He even tried to persuade Pope Pious XII to work toward improving conditions for the Jews in Poland. Bernstein believed that efforts should be made to rehabilitate the Jews inside Europe as well, and not only to send them to Palestine, and he said as much to President Truman in October 1946 (Bauer 1970, 251–55, 276–77). Nor did he hide this opinion from the Zionist leadership. In December 1946, he warned the Zionist Congress of the disintegrating morale in the camps (Zionist Organization Executive, n.d., 208–211), and at the beginning of 1947, at a meeting with Zionist leaders in London, he said that he was "very worried that these people will not hold out, and that the consequences will be terrible. Something has to be done to reduce the tension, to find immediate relief, by transferring people to other countries."[15]

As the stay in the DP camps drew out, they became, whether intentionally or by circumstances, a human reservoir and a political lever in the struggle for the founding of a sovereign Jewish State in Palestine. Suggestions, such as those put forward by Rabbi Bernstein, together with the low morale, and the increasing numbers of people registering for emigration to the West, constituted a severe threat to Zionist policies. Concern was increased among the Zionist leaders and their emissaries upon the appointment of UNSCOP. As one of the top emissaries from Palestine in Germany put it, the threat posed by the JDC and HIAS, with their registration for other countries, "lay not in the fact that there won't be enough candidates for immigration to Palestine, but that this registration for emigration to other countries might weaken our position in front of the international organizations, such as the United Nations. They might come to the conclusion that the Jews are indiscriminate as to where they want to emigrate" (Levin 1947a).

By the spring of 1947, many months had passed since the end of the war, and many changes had taken place in the number and character of the Jewish DPs in Germany. When Harrison made his tour in the summer of 1945, the camps in the American zone were inhabited by no more than 50,000 Jewish DPs, most of them survivors of the concentration camps in that area. The visit of the Anglo-American committee took place prior to the arrival of the large numbers of repatriates from the Soviet Union and before the wave of Jewish refugees following the pogrom at the Polish town of Kielce in July 1946. During the months of July–October 1946 alone, some 70,000 Jews who had left Poland entered the American zone. Over the two years following the war, whole "generations" of DPs had settled in the camps, differing from each other in their countries of origin, family status (i.e. married couples, singles, with or without children) and experience during the war years. Those who had managed to survive the Nazi-occupied regions were mostly on their own – "one from this town, another from that family" – whereas among the repatriates from the Soviet Union there was a fairly large number of entire families including women, children and old people. By spring 1947, the number of families with children had been vastly increased, due to high marriage and birth rates among the Holocaust survivors during those years. There was an exceptionally large number of children, including orphans and others who had been sent by their parents to the children's institutions run by the Zionist youth movements, believing that this might precipitate their chances of reaching Palestine.

The reliability of the various surveys, and the level of the DPs' determination to immigrate to Palestine, are still a subject for research and dispute. We ourselves are concerned with the thoughts and feelings of the people involved at the time – by which we mean the eve of the sailing of the ship *Exodus*. When UNSCOP began its inquiry, the possibility was raised of conducting a referendum among the inhabitants of the camps, to determine the countries to which they would most like to emigrate – similar to that held in advance of the Anglo-American committee's visit eighteen months previously. The Palestine emissaries at the camps had serious doubts as to whether this would be worthwhile. In an official report Barlas summed up his lengthy tour of Europe with impressions similar to those of Hoffman a year before: "People are becoming resigned to the situation – which constitutes a serious threat to the prospect of Aliyah, if this situation continues and no change takes place in the near future" (Barlas, 1947a). At an unofficial gathering at his home, he was adamant that "if no possibilities are created for immigration to Palestine very soon, it is quite possible that no one will remain who wants to go there" (Barlas, 1947b). It was at exactly that time that Rabbi Bernstein believed that, as long as the gates of other countries were closed to them, at least 90 percent of all the Jewish DPs would emigrate to Palestine. And even if they had a choice and the United States would change her immigration laws, 75 percent of them would still prefer Palestine and only 25 percent would go to the United States (1947).

The question is, how was it that non-Zionist persons and organizations had a much stronger tendency to believe that the DPs preferred to immigrate to Palestine no matter what, than did Zionist emissaries and politicians? Could the answer to this lie in the fact that the Zionists had more at stake in the potential immigration of the DPs to Palestine, so that they tended to be more outspoken about their fears regarding the DPs' reduced determination to do so? Is it possible, on the other hand, that they were aware also that preparations and indoctrination had been made among the DPs in advance of the various committees' visits, and that, despite the fact that most of the DPs would clearly choose Palestine, the size of this majority was still somewhat artificial?

On her return to Palestine in July 1947, following an eighteen month tour of duty at DP camps in Germany, an emissary revealed that the assessment in the Yishuv of the prevailing mood among the DPs in Germany was not a realistic one. In her summary to the Supervisor of emissaries at the Jewish Agency, she wrote that it would be misleading to believe that all the Jews in the camps in Germany were eager to come only to Palestine. "If they were all issued with certificates, then without a doubt most would come [here]. However, in the event that no certificates are available, every effort must be invested constantly, on education and indoctrination, in order to encourage the people to use any means possible to make their way to Palestine" (Kinnarti 1947).

Her letter hints at an aversion to illegal immigration, certainly a widely held sentiment at the time. People were aware of the difficulties and dangers in this option, which anyway could not guarantee a safe arrival in Palestine. It was a well-known fact that since August 1946 most of the illegal immigrants had been caught and taken to detention camps on Cyprus. However, for those Jews stuck in the American zone in Germany, illegal immigration was almost the only option – not only to reach Palestine, but to get out of Germany at all. Moreover, the youth movements and kibbutzim were always willing to supply volunteers to help in this kind of immigration, but could it serve as the main avenue for the masses?

In spring 1947, two years after the end of the war, emigration to Palestine was no more than a "dribs and drabs" affair and there seemed no solution in sight, either Zionist or non-Zionist. Signs were appearing even among the members of Zionist youth movements – those DPs who constituted the strongest element within the camps' population – of "far-reaching deviations from the pioneer ethic, serious social complications, a cynical attitude, and on top of everything else, desertion".[16] The ground was now fertile for some impressive action to be taken which would bring renewed hope to the DPs, and it is not surprising that emotions were aroused when news came of the headlines in the American press, announcing that the Jews were preparing for a "Mass Exodus" of all the 150,000 Jewish DPs from the camps toward the European coastline.[17] Hoffman was sure that the origin of this rumor was in the propaganda being spread by the American Revisionist group, headed by Peter Bergson (Yahil 1947; 1981, 142). At the end of April 1947, a question was raised in the British Parliament regarding a recently uncovered plan for the illegal immigration of some 125,000 Jews from the American occupied zone in Germany to Palestine. The British Foreign Secretary replied that this information is probably connected with Rabbi Bernstein's declaration at a press conference, according to which some 125,000 European Jews were now "marching on Palestine".[18]

Less than three months had gone by since this confusing and unbased information, and new rumors were flying around the camps regarding an unprecedented mass departure toward a giant illegal immigrant ship.

This time the stories were not unfounded. People were indeed making their way to a ship which would later be known by the very symbolic name of *Exodus 1947*. However, it was only a strange trick of fate which brought all these people from the DP camps in Germany to the decks of the *Exodus*. The original plans for this ship, which at the time was still known officially as the *President Warfield*, were very different.

2 · "The Yanks Are Coming"

The ship *President Warfield* was sold in September 1946 to a maritime scrap company, who paid $8,028 for her. Shortly afterwards, the wreck was bought for $40,000 by the Chinese–American Industrial Company. Within less than ten days, she changed hands yet again, this time for $50,000 and to the Weston Trading Company, which was no less than a cover for the purchasing activity of the Mossad in the United States. By November, the *President* had joined the illegal immigration fleet, and within a short time she underwent intensive renovations (Habbas 1954, 9–15; Holly 1969, 133–70; Derogy 1972, 13– 33). It must have seemed somewhat strange for a ship that only three months before had been sold for scrap, to be now undergoing renovations involving an investment far exceeding her original purchase price.

People who lived in and around Baltimore followed the activity surrounding the elderly vessel with great interest. They could still remember the ship in her prime, when she had sailed the Baltimore–Norfolk line, bearing a passenger cargo of holidaymakers and honeymooners. Their affection for the ship was tinged with pride because, having been found suitable for military service, she had served during the Second World War under both British and American flags. The British were interested in the flat-bottomed ship, whose design made her particularly useful for crossing the English Channel. However, before she could be handed over by the Americans on a lend-lease program, she had been prepared for her new task. From once having been a coastal and river boat, she had now been transformed into a ship fully able to tackle the ocean – the capacity of her fuel and water tanks had been increased and a wooden structure had been built on deck, which would serve as shelter for passengers. It is something of an irony that those same renovations made on the ship by order of the British during the Second World War were what had made her so desirable a candidate for the Aliyah Bet fleet after the war.

In August 1942, the ship flew the flag of the British merchant navy. She spent most of her time on the British shores static, sunk deep in a mud bank, where she was used as British Royal Navy barracks – in preparation for the Normandy landings. In May 1944, the British flag was removed from her mast and she was handed over to the American Navy. In July that same year, she landed for the first time – although not the last – on the shores of France, where she again dropped anchor and was used as control office for ships bringing in supplies to the allied bridgehead in Normandy. It was only toward the end of her stay in Europe that her talents as a riverboat were put into effect at last, and she was used to ferry soldiers, around 800 each trip, from the port of Le-Havre to their camp on the banks of the Seine (Holly 1969, 31–64).

Emotional editorials in the Maryland and Virginia press welcomed her on her return to the United States in July 1945. But sentiment and nostalgia are not sufficient to overcome the ravages of time, and when it became apparent that it was not economically viable to renovate the old ship, her fate was cast – to scrap she would go. Was it no wonder then, that the inhabitants of the region were curious, to say the least, when, in November 1946, a year after being banished, the *President Warfield* returned, to be prepared for a new lease on life?

The *President Warfield* was not the first ship to be purchased by the Mossad in the United States. She had been preceded by four, and four more were to follow. The last two, *Kibbutz Galuyot* (Ingathering of the Exiles) and *Atzma'ut* (Independence) – which were known as the "Pans" because of their original names, *Pan York* and *Pan Crescent* – were the largest of all the illegal immigrant ships, and between them these two ships carried some 15,000 passengers. Altogether, some 70,000 illegal immigrants set sail in the Mossad's ships after the war. About 30,000 of them made their way to Palestine on the nine ships purchased in America and manned by crews of American Jews. The *Ben Hecht*, which had been acquired in America by the Revisionist American League for a Free Palestine, bore some 600 immigrants.

At the same time as it was buying up ships in the United States, the Mossad was also busy recruiting Jewish volunteers to serve as crew members on them (Halamish 1995). The British, who were struggling unsuccessfully against the waves of illegal immigration, were wary of this new development and suspected that the objective of having American crews on illegal immigration ships was to "embroil us with the US over any untoward incidents or prosecutions which may result".[1] The real reasons for recruiting Jewish volunteers in the United States were quite different. These men were destined to replace the foreign, professional crews. For reasons of economy, the Mossad preferred to employ Jewish volunteers rather than having to pay non-Jews for doing the work (Schind 1947; Aran 1947). Although the natural candidates for this were young Jewish men who had had seafaring experience with the US Navy or Merchant Marines, the easiest to recruit and most readily available were members of the pioneer Zionist youth movements. However, the number of professionals increased as compared with that of the youth movement members, as methods for recruitment improved.

Members of the American crew started arriving at the *President Warfield* in December 1946. They were a representative cross-section of all of the some 250 American Jewish volunteers in the illegal immigration project. Some were members of the pioneer youth movements, planning this way to make their own Aliyah to Palestine (Holly 1969, 128–69; Derogy 1972, 13–29; Habbas 1954, 9–16; Sela 1987, 165–66). The eight members of the ha-Shomer ha-Tza'ir youth movement impressed and won the respect of the captain, Yitzhak Aharonowitz (later Aran), who was known to everyone as Ike. He described the pioneer youth movement members as the "moral backbone and the most disciplined part of the entire crew". Aharonowitz defined the second category of American volunteers as "ordinary Jewish youngsters, mostly non-Zionist to begin with, but who were drawn to us out of idealism". The third category consisted of professional merchant marines, excited by the idea of Aliyah Bet, who had already been trying to find their way to the Mossad ships. Many of these youngsters however, had been in contact with the Revisionist Bergson group, who, despite all the fuss and publicity, actually succeeded in sending out only one ship (Aran 1947; Sela 1987, 165; Habbas 1954, 9–15). The *President Warfield* was ultimately manned by several highly experienced professionals, including her Second Officer, William (Bill) Bernstein, of San Francisco. Bernstein was a graduate of the Merchant Marine Academy at Kings Point, with much experience in the Merchant Marines. He was 24 years old when he was killed in the battle with the British near the Palestine coast early on the morning of 18 July 1947.

It was more guilt than any Jewish or Zionist education which motivated the American volunteers – a feeling they shared with many American Jews, who had not had any direct experience of the Holocaust. As the American journalist I. F. Stone wrote after sailing in the spring and summer of 1946 aboard the illegal immigration ships *Haganah* and *Josiah Wedgewood*: "[The volunteers] were simply American sailors who happened to be Jews, boys with little if any past contact with Jewish life. They spoke neither Yiddish nor Hebrew. They were not very articulate, but for them the trip was more than a heroic adventure. They all felt deeply about the treatment of the Jews in Europe and this was their way of doing something about it" (1946, 149).

After Bill Bernstein's death, his brother was nonplussed as to his motives for joining the project: "He was not connected with any Jewish organizations. It was the experience with the refugees in Europe that decided him."[2] Indeed, it was direct contact with the refugees in Europe during their military service that most influenced the desire of young American Jews to help the survivors of the Holocaust. Even members of the youth movements, for whom Aliyah Bet was a good way of "making Aliyah", believed that their eagerness to volunteer for the mission was influenced by their meeting with Holocaust survivors (Stone 1946, 149; Sela 1987, 156–57).

Nevertheless, the volunteers were not motivated by humanitarian or patriotic considerations alone, but also by a zest for adventure and a quest for meaning to their lives. By volunteering for this mission, some of them may have been hoping to stop time, to postpone having to grow up and face the demands of an adult world, or maybe it was also an act of youthful rebellion. Bernstein wrote to his mother: "You ask me to settle down, go to school. That's all very fine, Mom, but one doesn't find happiness by continually telling himself he's happy. Don't you think I would like a nice wife and kids and a good job? Of course I would, but I can't do that now. I say this knowing that your thoughts and heart are with me wherever I am and whatever I'm doing."[3]

All but two of the American crew members of the *President Warfield* were Jewish. One of the first to climb aboard was the 28-year-old Methodist minister, John Stanley Grauel, who had been active in the Christian Committee for Palestine. The Committee continued to pay Grauel his salary for the period he was away on the ship, the idea being that the journey would serve as an important source of information and inspiration in furthering his work in the United States for the Zionist cause. In the period prior to the sailing, he proved himself to be a devoted and hardworking man, willingly fulfilling every task he was given, and making light work of even the most menial of them. He had considerable influence over the young American men. Grauel was very eager to reach Palestine and, it seems, he had told the Mossad organizers that as soon as he reached Cyprus, he would disclose his true identity to the British authorities. As it turned out, however, he would do this not in Cyprus, but in Haifa, where he disembarked after the battle with the British Navy and testified before UNSCOP. He returned to America in September 1947 where he joined the struggle for the Zionist cause.[4]

On Sunday 16 February 1947, a shipboard ceremony organized by the Mossad was held in the presence of about one hundred people, at which an oath of allegiance to the Haganah Organization was taken by the team. It was an opportunity to thank all the Zionist activists and supporters of Aliyah Bet in the region for their financial and spiritual help. The Mossad was especially keen on cultivating the goodwill of people such as Rudolph Sonnenborn, one the of leading fundraisers in America for Aliyah Bet, and the writer I. F. Stone, author of the book *Underground to Palestine*. Ya'akov Dostrowsky (later Dori), head of the Haganah delegation to North America was also there, as was Ze'ev ("Danny") Schind, Mossad Head in that continent. Schind delivered a short speech in which he quoted the words of Berl Katznelson, one of the leaders of the Labor Movement in Palestine, at the 21st Zionist Congress in 1939. On the very eve of the Second World War, Katznelson had argued with Abba Hillel Silver, a prominent leader of American Zionists, who, at the time, opposed illegal immigration to Palestine:

> If I were a Jewish leader in America, I would behave differently. First of all, I would make sure that each and every Jew, whether Zionist or not, would take an active part in helping those asking for assylum. If the Jews of America are prevented from undertaking the task of saving the refugees from Hell, as they themselves were once taken in and saved, let them at least offer some fair help to those who dare and can save them. I would go even further: Young Jews, the cream of American youth, again regardless of whether they are Zionist or not, must be educated to accompany the Jewish wonderers and suffer with them their suffering, and live with them during those difficult hours in which they are struggling with fate, and when they succeed in achieving salvation – in order to feel deeply the common fate of the Jewish people. (Habbas 1954, 11)

On the deck of the *President Warfield*, in the presence of American Jews who had contributed money to finance illegal immigration, as well as some forty Zionist and non-Zionist crew members about to set sail for Europe and from there to take Jews to Palestine, Schind's quoting of Katznelson's words could be construed as something of a prophecy fulfilled.

The large crowd witnessed how the blue and white flag together with a copy of the Bible were handed over to Ike Aharonowitz. Ike was introduced as the ship's captain, although the post would be made official only two months later in Marseilles. Secrecy, therefore, was hardly the order of the day at the time and, as if to complete this rather festive picture, crew member Cy Weinstein held his wedding aboard ship, just a few days before it set sail from Baltimore.

On the *President Warfield* the problems which accompanied the

Mossad's activity in America were revealed in all their pungency. It was virtually impossible to stick to the principles of secrecy and confidentiality which characterized the Mossad's activity on the other continents, in a country in which many of whose five million Jewish population and more than a few non-Jews as well, were so fascinated by the illegal immigration operation. This fascination was indeed welcome, so long as monies collected in America were financing the purchase of ships in Europe. Once the purchasing started taking place in the United States itself, the Mossad found itself facing a new kind of problem – because the American benefactor has never liked being sold a "pig in a poke", and insisted on being kept informed of what is being done with his money. Moreover, in America the Mossad found itself trapped between the cloak of secrecy demanded of its activity, and competition with the Revisionists, who were having considerable success in fundraising and recruiting volunteers. It seemed to the Mossad people that Bergson's Revisionist group had managed to raise more money than them, and that "at any rate, they are better known than we are, and the American Jewish public have the idea that all the Aliyah Bet ships are theirs" (Aran 1947).

The Mossad were assisted in their activities in America by Jewish professionals, whose excellent work was largely voluntary. One man who played an important role in the purchasing of the *President Warfield* and its renovation was Captain William Ash, Vice President of the Masters, Mates and Pilots Union. However, alongside his help, which was no doubt invaluable to the project, he also succeeded in causing the kind of publicity which the Mossad could well have done without. The veil of secrecy, which by now was very transparent indeed, was lifted by William Schlegel, the captain of the *President Warfield*, who made a habit of "convening the press at every port we called at. He had a kind of thirst for publicity and was a megalomaniac to the extent that the sight of his photograph in the papers as one of the admirals of the Jewish Aliyah Bet, was capable of adding at least ten years to his life expectancy" (Aran 1947).

The media, always an important and very powerful element in America, soon came to realize that stories of Aliyah Bet were a marketable comodity as far as the American reader is concern. The Exodus Affair at its later stages did indeed benefit from the interest of the American press and public, although this interest very nearly put a spoke in the ship's wheel at the very beginning of her career in the illegal immigration operation fleet. The newly renovated ship first sailed for Europe on 25 February 1947, was caught in a storm at sea and returned to Philadelphia, battered and water-logged. By the time she set sail once again, this time successfully, at least 12 articles had been published about her in the Baltimore press, accompanied by detailed and quite accurate evaluations of her future plans (Holly 1969, 294–98). The most dangerous item published on the matter appeared in *The New York Times* on 7 March 1947 under the headline: "Palestine-Bound Mystery Ship" and set off alarms in the British Foreign Office.

On 29 March 1947, a fully repaired *President Warfield* finally set off for Europe, and the problem of the flag (which will be discussed in the next chapter) was also solved. The head of the Mossad in America saw fit to warn his colleagues in Europe of possible problems with the crew members: "You will undoubtedly have grave difficulties with them, but be advised that they have been on board since 20 December [1946], in a state of tense expectation, waiting for the sailing date. Although frustrated by the manifold delays, they have managed to overcome their disappointment. Certainly there are several immoral lads among them. But, on the whole, it's not a bad bunch, and if there are no further delays, they will fulfill their tasks with devotion" (Schind 1947).

Indeed, more difficulties arose once they arrived in Europe. The Mossad organizers in America had hoped that by recruiting Jews for illegal immigration operation rather than foreign (non Jewish) crews, it would be easier to stick to the rules of conspiracy, which by necessity surrounded Aliyah Bet. But sailors will be sailors, and as soon as the American lads reached dry European land, off they went in search of all the entertainments common to healthy seafaring men. They made a habit of picking fights with British soldiers they came across in the pubs and bars of the harbors, although more dangerous still was the verbal side of these confrontations. Their Palestinian counterparts would try to shut them up by whispering "Shush ..." whenever they felt things were getting out of hand – and were soon given the nickname, "Shu-Shu" by the Americans. Mossad documents refer to the Americans as "Sams", from the term "Uncle Sam".

The British had little trouble getting information on the ship and her crew. Within two weeks of the ship's dropping anchor at Porto Venere, Italy, the British knew the name of her captain, and the number and background of all her crew members – 31 Americans, three Mexicans, one Pole and one stateless person – which their Embassy in Rome was quick to report to London.[5]

Schind and Aharonowitz, who were by now familiar with the mentality of the American crew members, were almost paternally forgiving and understanding toward their wayward behavior. They felt that the lads behaved as they did because they were simply not suitably trained and had not received the guidance necessary for this kind of mission. The Mossad people in Europe and the Palmachniks who escorted the illegal immigrants were less tolerant. Ada Sereni, head of the Mossad's Italian branch, complained to her colleagues back in Palestine about the American crews, who "only succeeded in making the work, which was hard enough in itself, that much harder" (1947).

The Palestinian escorts had little faith in their American counterparts and did not share with them all the shipboard rights and obligations. Their attitude was a combination of several factors. The well-known haughtiness of Palestinian Jews toward Diaspora Jews; the language barrier; the difficulty of a closed group sharing mutual experiences and established behavioral codes to absorb outsiders; and the intense pressure to accomplish the task at hand.

The Americans became resigned to the suspicious and disrespectful attitudes of their fellow crew members. As one of them (Dov Mills) wrote later: "The relations between us and the Palestinian guys were not ... the best. We felt we were being rejected and left out of the leadership and the secret planning they were involved in. It was only later that we came to understand how wise they had been, because they didn't know us well enough [then] and they had no way of assessing us" (Habbas 1954, 77).

Fired by their volunteer spirit and completely sympathetic to the mission they were involved in, it was not enough for the Americans to just do the jobs they were taken on for; they insisted on helping the Palestinian escorts and the passengers on the way from Europe to the shores of Palestine. To their credit, the Palestinians did show respect and comradeship when introducing their American counterparts to the illegal immigrants, and made a point of presenting them as full partners in the mission. As the ship's commander said over the ship's Tannoy system at the start of the journey from France to Haifa: "The naval crew on this ship are all young Jewish men from America, who left behind everything and volunteered – not for any possible gain, but for the sole purpose of bringing Jews to Palestine" (Habbas 1954, 224).

The time they spent together on board ship *en route* to Palestine, together with the challenge of the forthcoming battle with the British, did succeed in bringing down barriers and promoting mutual confidence. "On the last night, before we reached the coast of Palestine," continued the American crew member, "they told us everything and included us in everything – and the atmosphere was much lighter, and from that night on we were given more responsibility, and we knew how to handle it" (Habbas 1954, 77). In the last part of the sentence he was referring to the contribution made by the Americans to the organizing and handling of life on board the deportation ships, on which the illegal immigrants were transported from Haifa to France and then to Germany.

In time, Bill Bernstein's evaluation of his fellow American crew members also improved. His initial assessment had at first been less than complimentary: "But the crew! We have everything aboard except sailors," he wrote to his brother at the time the ship was still undergoing repairs in America.[6] Still, after spending time with his fellow seamen and together struggling against the elements, his attitude had softened toward them: "The motley mess of philosophers, mathematicians and assorted intellectuals have begun to shape up into some sort of good working crew. More team work ... The ship is beginning to run like a ship and the sailors are beginning to act like seamen ... The crew is really catching on."[7]

Of all the Palestinians on board the *President Warfield*, Ike Aharonowitz had developed the closest relations with the Americans. A special bond had developed between them of affection and mutual respect. He was their captain, and they admired him because of his professionalism, his personality and the very fact that he was a Palestinian Jew. He in turn valued their professionalism and the fact that they had volunteered for the mission. They were also bound to each other by their experiences over the long months of close proximity on board ship and the kind of male pastimes they all shared at their various ports of call in Europe. Years later, he described the young Americans as "youngsters who were no less determined than the people of the Palmach, and far better trained professionally than we ourselves were in those days" (Aran 1963).

Aharonowitz's opinion of the Americans was more positive than that of the other Palestinians. The ship *Chaim Arlozoroff* (*Ulua*), which brought in 1,348 illegal immigrants in the winter of 1947, had a crew of 37 sailors, most of them Jewish volunteers from America. When the trip was over, the Palestinian escorts on the ship claimed that it would have been better if paid foreign sailors had been employed, than to have to put up with the Jewish volunteers, who were an undisciplined and unprofessional bunch – even if in the breast of each one of them beat a warm Jewish heart (Sha'ari 1981, 75). The Mossad leaders were particularly perturbed by the large numbers of the sailors. After the journey of the ship *Ha-Tikvah* – which sailed in May 1947 with 1,414 immigrants aboard and a crew of 26 Americans – Davidka Nameri, a central figure in the Mossad, pointed out that "it is not necessary to send out such a large number of sailors in such a small vessel" (Sha'ari 1981, 65–66).

The main problem involved in having so large a crew was the need to extricate its members when they reached Cyprus, a job which would have to be done either surreptitiously or at the expense of the certificates allotted by the British for bringing the immigrants into Palestine. It wasn't so bad if the crew members had intended to remain in Palestine, but many of them had then to be returned to the United States. The Mossad, therefore, tried to reduce the number of "Sams" sailing on the *President* and sent the following message to the ship when it was anchored in Italy: "There is a crew of 38 Sams on the President, as far as we are concerned this number is enormous. You should keep only those of them who intend to settle in Artzi [Palestine], and any others essential to the vessel. The remainder must be left behind and sent to Rudy [France]. Such a large number will only cause unnecessary expense and hardship."[8]

At the end of June, after the *President* had moved to France, an order was issued to "reduce as far as possible the number of foreign workers before they arrive here. Their presence causes us hardship and complications, as well as considerable expense."[9]

The American volunteers on the *President Warfield* claimed that they had been promised in America that they would be able to spend some time in Palestine, before being returned home. This worried the Mossad in Palestine and they repeated the order that only those crew members who complied with one of two criteria were to be allowed to remain on the ship: those who are essential to the mission and those who planned to remain in Palestine. The Mossad people in France were requested to explain to the Americans that "their way via Rise [Cyprus] involves great hardship and discomfort and it will take five months. Getting them out of here [Palestine] involves great expense and causes considerable problems."[10]

Nevertheless, the ship sailed with 36 Americans on board and the Mossad prepared to prevent their arrival in Cyprus. On her way to Palestine, the ship received this order: "If you are unable to disembark, and you are towed in to Haifa, you must find yourselves safe hiding places for a few dozen workers and let us know where these are. Once the immigrants have been taken off the ship, [the workers] must remain in hiding until our people come on board the following day to swab down the vessel. Make sure you have enough food, water and masks. You'll know it's safe to come out, when you hear our people singing in Hebrew."[11]

The crew prepared four hiding places: under the bridge; in a storeroom at the ship's prow, between the sandbags of the ballast; behind the large refrigerator at the stern; and on the second deck beneath the stairs leading to the third deck.[12] The entire crew, with the exception of one Palestinian who was to accompany the immigrants on their journey to Cyprus, were meant to get into these hiding places and to wait there for the cleaning staff to come and extricate them. The ship entered the port of Haifa during the afternoon of a hot summer Friday. The crew was to remain hidden on board until the following Sunday morning – more than forty hot and suffocating hours. Most of the Americans preferred to disembark with the immigrants, assuming that a way would be found to release them from Cyprus within a short time (Mills 1986; Einav 1988). This eventually turned out to be something of a blessing. Twenty five American crew members returned with the immigrants to France,[13] and some of them helped get things organized on board the deportation ships.

William Bernstein was killed in the battle with the British. John Grauel, the Methodist minister, presented himself to the British and disembarked the ship on 18 July 1947. One American was injured in the battle and taken to hospital. The First Officer, Bernard (Berny) Marks, was presented to the British as being the ship's captain, so as not to expose Aharonowitz, and was arrested together with two other volunteers. The latter four were flown back to the United States in the middle of September.[14] Five of the American volunteers were taken out of hiding and off the ship together with the Palestinian escorts.

On reaching Port de Bouc in France, some of the American crew members were ordered to disembark the deportation ships and join the "ships on the way" (Sela 1987, 166). Some of the volunteers disembarked on their own volition and evidently made their way back to America. The rest remained with the immigrants and went with them to Hamburg and the camps in Germany. Some returned ultimately to the United States, and others settled in Israel.

3 · Crescendo

"Palestine-Bound Mystery Ship, Battered by Sea, Is Back in Port" was the title of an item run by *The New York Times* on 7 March 1947. Using a dramatic style, veiled in cloak-and-dagger-like allusions to conspiracy, it recounted the way in which the ship *President Warfield* was supposed to cross the Atlantic Ocean with the ultimate aim of reaching the Middle East and charging the British blockade of Palestine. The item – which contained several gross inaccuracies – was relayed by the British Embassy in Washington to the Foreign Office in London,[1] where it ignited yet another fuse in the "war room" against illegal immigration into Palestine.

Only two weeks before, the ship *Chaim Arlozoroff* (*Ulua*) with 1,348 illegal immigrants on board, had managed to evade the ships of the British Navy and to land near Haifa, where she deliberately hit a sand bank, and her passengers started jumping into the water. They were caught immediately, and British soldiers took control of the ship. This was the third illegal immigration ship that month (February 1947) to get close to the shores of Palestine and it seemed the illegal immigration operation was in full swing again. Not a single ship had approached shore during the previous two months, December 1946 and January 1947, but the British had succeeded in capturing some 2,800 illegal immigrants during February alone. On the day *The New York Times* item reached London, the ship *Shabtai Lojinsky* (*Suzannah*) landed on a beach near Nitzanim, south of Tel Aviv, where many of her passengers were picked up by Haganah activists and taken to the nearby Jewish settlements, before the British security forces had a chance to arrive on the scene.

With the approach of spring, the British anticipated an even larger wave of illegal immigration. According to their reckoning, 14 ships with a capacity to take aboard some 15,000 illegal immigrants, were waiting to set sail within a short time for Palestine.[2] This fleet would be joined by the *President Warfield*, which was larger than all her predecessors.

Palestine's narrow strip of territorial waters, which at the time was

only three miles wide, made it hard to intercept the relatively large immigrant ships, so that the Navy demanded Cabinet approval to circumvent
the illegal immigration ships outside of the territorial waters. However,
international law did not approve of mid-sea handling of ships suspected
of carrying illegal immigrants, so that at the end of 1946 the Cabinet
ordered the Admiralty to cease examining this option.[3] The result was
that a discrepancy had now been created between theory and practice –
the British Cabinet was opposed to capturing illegal immigration ships on
the high seas,[4] but this was exactly what the Royal Navy was in fact doing.[5]

The situation was causing considerable concern to all those responsible for blocking illegal immigration to Palestine. They were still
considering the possibility of having to intercept larger and swifter ships,
when they started noticing the first signs of new tactics – the Jews were
now bringing in two or more ships at the same time. So many illegal
immigrants were now coming in over a relatively short period of time,
and this was causing the British problems in transferring them to Cyprus,
due to the limited number of crafts and their capacity. The proposal that
the illegal immigrants be held temporarily in Palestine, pending
deportation to Cyprus, was discarded as being too problematic for it to
be feasible. The Cyprus camps were filled almost to overflowing and
when this happened – where would the illegal immigrants be held?
Deporting them elsewhere, to Benghazi or East Africa, required additional
means of transportation and these were not available.[6]

The British Mandatory authorities were deeply concerned by the
significant increase in the volume of illegal immigration activity, and it
is no wonder that *The New York Times* article on the *President Warfield*
caused them great discomposure. Without even bothering to first check
the reliability of the information presented in the newspaper article, the
British Embassy in Washington took action, by contacting the Paraman-
ian Ambassador requesting that his government withdraw Panamanian
registry from the *President Warfield*, "should *The New York Times* story
prove to be substantially accurate".[7]

The British were quite right to be cautious. Panama had been
mentioned in *The New York Times* story by mistake. The ship had indeed
been under Panamanian registration when she had been purchased by
the Weston Trade Company on behalf of the Mossad. However, by the
time she made her first sailing east from Baltimore on 25 February 1947,
when she was caught in a storm and had to return, she was already flying
the flag of Honduras. Why did Panama deny the *President Warfield*
registry in November 1946? That was the time that the American League
for a Free Palestine was publishing notices in the American press

declaring that the ship, *Abril* (later the *Ben Hecht*) – which was flying a Panamanian flag – was about to charge the British blockade of Palestine. The British automatically began suspecting all ships flying the Panamanian flag, and the *President Warfield*, which had changed hands often in so short a time, immediately became a prime suspect.

By the end of 1946, when the Government of Panama acquiesced to the British request to cancel the ship's registration, the Mossad began a frenzied search for a substitute flag for the *President* (Holly 1969, 148–49). This turned out to be no easy task, since it was already public knowledge that the ship was about to join the illegal immigration fleet and the British were making great efforts to prevent her sailing. Only after several tricks and many stratagems were the Mossad successful in obtaining Honduran registration for the ship, and they were then justifiably worried that the British Government would put pressure on Honduras to cancel the registration (Schind 1947).

So that before she had even arrived in Europe, the British already had their eye on the *President Warfield* and were scrupulously following her every move in order to prevent her achieving her objective.[8] When, on 29 March 1947, the *President Warfield* sailed eastward from the United States, the British Government asked the Government of Portugal to refuse the ship permission to refuel in the Azores.[9] The British, unsuccessful with their efforts at getting the Honduran Government to annul the ship's registration, now achieved permission (first verbally, later in writing) to apprehend at mid-sea all ships flying the flag of Honduras, and which were suspected of being involved in illegal immigration to Palestine.[10]

At the same time, although unconnected with the *President Warfield*, the British were going full steam ahead in their deployment to block the growing wave of illegal immigration into Palestine. In mid-March 1947, the Cabinet Defense Committee authorized the Foreign Office to create a strategic plan for combating illegal immigration. One proposal involved the increased control of the European ports from which the Mossad was attempting to launch ships full of illegal immigrants bound for Palestine; another proposal was that these ships be returned to their ports of origin or to have them redirected to the countries registered in the passengers' documents as being their destination. In order to ensure the success of these plans, the Foreign Office was authorized to put diplomatic pressure on the countries involved in illegal immigration and to ask all United Nations member states for cooperation on this issue. The Colonial Office was authorized by the Committee to write up a plan, in consultation with the War and Transport Offices and the Admiralty, whereby illegal immigrants could be transferred to other regions such as, for example, East Africa, when no room could be found for them in Cyprus.[11]

On 20 March 1947, for the first time in three months, the issue of illegal immigration into Palestine was raised in the British Cabinet, although the *President Warfield* was still not mentioned by name. The Cabinet was concerned about the new tactic the Jews were using, which involved beaching ships carrying illegal immigrants if they succeeded in eluding the Naval patrols, as had the *Chaim Arlozoroff* and the *Shabtai Lojinsky*. The overcrowding of these ships increased the risk of a major disaster, which could result in heavy loss of life. The spirit and content of the Cabinet discussion – which concluded without reaching any decision – show us that the struggle against illegal immigration of Jews into Palestine was hardly at the top of the British Government's list of priorities. The First Sea Lord informed the Cabinet that four escort vessels had been transferred from the Pacific to the Mediterranean in order to reinforce the preventive measures against illegal immigration, but he made a point of ensuring his colleagues that this would not prejudice the mine sweeping program. When the discussion turned to the matter of the arrangements being made to provide accommodation in Cyprus for an additional 10,000 illegal immigrants, the Cabinet agreed that no building materials would be provided for this purpose which were not surplus to the United Kingdom requirements. It was therefore decided that the additional numbers of immigrants would be for the most part accommodated in tented camps.[12]

The reasoning behind the British Government's policies toward illegal immigration was complex and contradictory. One element to be taken into consideration was the Arab position. The British were also worried about the way in which the Yishuv would react to their strong-arm policies toward illegal immigrants and the effect these policies might have on the relationship between the Mandatory Government and the Yishuv leadership, and on the status of the dissident Revisionist groups (IZL and Lehi). Also to be taken into consideration was the effect this war on illegal immigration would have on American public opinion, the Administration and the Congress. Since summer 1946, the British had become increasingly mindful of Arab reactions, which dictated that strict policies and measures be taken to block illegal Jewish immigration. As the numbers of illegal immigrants increased and intelligence reports prophesied even more for spring and summer 1947, the British were showing growing political intransigence, which reached a peak with the Exodus Affair.

However, the need to block illegal immigration conflicted with

Britain's interest to put an end to terrorist activity in Palestine, which she was attempting to do by isolating the dissident Revisionist groups and preventing any form of conciliation between them and the organized Jewish community. On 20 March 1947, the Cabinet devoted a lengthy discussion to this issue. The British, well aware of the consensus in the Yishuv with regard to their immigration policies – the only issue on which all the various sectors of the Jewish community were united – realized that the Yishuv was much more conciliatory toward the terrorist organizations after particularly harsh action had been taken against illegal immigrants. Zionist leaders made it clear that as long as the British were expelling illegal immigrants from Palestine, it would be impossible to unite public opinion against Revisionist terror, and, in a conversation with the British High Commissioner at the beginning of February 1947, Golda Myerson (later Meir) claimed that if the Government wants to help the Yishuv authorities to fight terror, it must stop expelling illegal immigrants (Jewish Agency Executive, 9 Feb. 1947).

Thus, by spring of 1947, the British were looking into the possibility of redirecting the illegal immigration ships in mid-sea and sending them directly to Cyprus. In this way, they believed, they would prevent the heartrending sight of illegal immigrants being removed forcibly and transferred to the deportation ships in Haifa, and this would put an end to the process of conciliation between the organized Jewish community and the terrorists. But for this, they would have to intercept the ships in mid-sea and it was at this point – the same time as the *President Warfield* was under close scrutiny – that they reached a dead-end and came to the conclusion that the issue required renewed Cabinet discussion.[13]

On 1 May 1947, the Cabinet in London resumed its discussions of illegal immigration into Palestine. This time, the *President Warfield* played a central role in the debate.

> The Prime Minister recalled that on 15 December 1946, the Cabinet had considered a proposal that officers commanding His Majesty's ships should be authorized to arrest on the high seas certain specified categories of vessels suspected of carrying illegal immigrants to Palestine, but had rejected that proposal as the Lord Chancellor had advised that it could not be justified in international law. The Foreign Office and Colonial Office has subsequently put forward the alternative proposal that His Majesty's ships should be authorized to arrest on the high seas any illegal immigrant ships whose flag State had agreed to interception; and the Lord Chancellor had advised that this would not be open to the same legal objection. If this policy were approved, it might be applied to the *President Warfield*, a 5,000 ton ship now

at Genoa, which was known to be embarking illegal immigrants for Palestine and was capable of carrying 5,000 immigrants.

The Cabinet was informed that the Admiralty were opposed to this proposal on two grounds. First, the conclusion of bilateral agreements with individual States for rights of interception might prove an embarrassing precedent. It might lead other States to demand rights of interception and search of British vessels, which would be unacceptable to us.... Secondly, interception involved serious practical difficulties. Illegal immigrants usually sabotaged their ship's engines on interception, and had to be towed into harbour. This created no special difficulty when ships were intercepted off the Palestine coast and towed into a local port. If, however, they were intercepted on the high seas and diverted to Cyprus, the immigrants were likely to resist being taken into tow and effective control of the intercepted ship could only be secured by placing a large guard on board.

The issue of the *President Warfield* was again raised toward the end of the discussion. The Secretary of State for the Colonies said "that every possible step should be taken to prevent the arrival in Palestine waters of a ship carrying as many as 5,000 illegal immigrants. Their custody and transfer to Cyprus would present very great difficulties." The Cabinet then "invited the Foreign Secretary to consider this matter further, in consultation with the Minister of Defense, the Secretary of State for the Colonies, the First Lord of the Admiralty and the Minster of Transport."[14]

This was to be the last time the Cabinet would discuss the issue of illegal immigration until after the *Exodus* immigrants had been returned to France. Between 1 May and 31 July 1947, all discussions on the subject of illegal immigration took place in ministerial committees, cabinet committees or at lower levels, under the auspices of the Foreign Secretary, Ernest Bevin.

The day after the described Cabinet meeting, Bevin appointed the Cabinet Illegal Immigration Committee, consisting of a small group of government ministers, who were most connected with the issue – and himself as leader. It was Bevin's decision that this group of ministers would take sole responsibility for the matter and they would make only *ad hoc* consultations with the Cabinet or the Defense Committee.[15]

That same day, 2 May 1947, talks were held with the ministers named in the Cabinet decision and it transpired that despite the fact that the Colonial Office, as well as the Foreign Office, was in support of intercepting illegal immigration ships flying the flags of countries who agree to this; and although Honduras, whose flag flew on the *President Warfield*, was included in this category, the objections raised in the Cabinet meeting against this kind of action were too heavy for it to be feasible to adopt this method. It was concluded that firm action should be taken to stem illegal immigration at its source, referring not only to European countries, but to the United States as well.[16]

Believing that most of the funding for illegal immigration activity was raised in the United States, Britain had already opened an American front in her war against illegal immigration. Approaches had been made to the American Government complaining that American citizens were allowed to finance a "war" against a friendly nation and fund-raising organizations were tax exempt (Hurewitz 1950, 300, 359). In April 1947, the British Prime Minister, Clement Attlee, made a personal bid to President Truman, asking him to prevent the sale of American ships to Zionist agents, who use them for illegal immigration into Palestine (*Manchester Guardian*, 24 April 1947). Undoubtedly, this bid resulted from the enormous publicity which was already accompanying the *President Warfield*.

On 2 April 1947, as the *President Warfield* was making her way eastward from America to Europe, Britain asked that a special meeting of the United Nation's General Assembly be convened to discuss the issue of Palestine. On 21 April 1947, one week before the session, the British Ambassador to the UN sent a memo to the Secretary General of the organization, Trygve Lie, which he asked to distribute among all the member nations. The memo called on the UN members to do "all in their power to discourage illegal immigration of Jews into Palestine".[17] However, the British inexplicably withdrew the memo before it was distributed. The American State Department apparently had a hand in this, by advising them to postpone distribution until the end of the special session – so as to avoid having to raise the question of illegal immigration in the course of the discussions. The State Department was in favor of applying to the member nations only after the Special Committee for Palestine had been appointed, since the British could then rationalize their request by claiming that nothing must interfere with the Committee's work.[18]

In the meantime, Italy was Britain's main objective in her attempts to stem illegal immigration at its source. As soon as the *President Warfield* docked at Porto Venere on 25 April 1947, the British Foreign Secretary instructed his Ambassador in Rome to "take all possible steps to prevent embarkation of Jews and departure of ship either from Genoa or elsewhere".[19] Quick to follow orders, the Ambassador presented this particular ship to the Italians as a "test case".[20]

Italy, who was applying for membership in the United Nations at that time, was therefore being doubly cautious. The armistice agreement forbade her to act against the interests of UN member nations, therefore she was careful not to do anything which would harm Honduras, the country whose flag the ship was flying. The Italians were worried also that if they were to take measures against the *President Warfield*, they might find themselves facing a conflict with the United States Government as well as with powerful American interests. The Italian Government was willing to use all legal means against the strange ship anchored in her waters. She would happily exploit any possible excuse – irregular maritime documents, unprofessional crew, the limited scope of movement defined by the ship's license, safety issues – in order to postpone the ship from sailing. She was adamant, however, in refusing to take any steps which could not be legally upheld.[21]

Throughout May the British did their utmost to delay the *President Warfield* from sailing, and indeed the ship remained anchored in Italy until almost the middle of June. Preparations for her journey to Palestine went on nonstop.

At the same time, the British were making approaches in an attempt to return the illegal immigrants to the port countries from which they had set off for Palestine in the first place. Italy agreed to accept the returning immigrants, on the condition that they would then be transferred to Germany, although this was in fact tantamount to a negative response, since on the way from Italy to Germany, the immigrants would have to pass through the American-occupied zones in Austria and Germany.[22] At the beginning of June it was clear to the British that Italy was not going to permit returning immigrants into her territory.[23]

The United Nations Special Session on Palestine opened on 29 April 1947 and closed on 15 May 1947, during which time the General Assembly appointed a United Nations Special Committee on Palestine (UNSCOP), which was composed of representatives of 11 countries. The General Assembly also adopted a resolution calling upon "all Governments and peoples, and particularly upon the inhabitants of Palestine, to refrain [pending action on UNSCOP's report] from the threat or use of force or any other action which might create an atmosphere prejudicial to an early settlement of the Palestine question" (United Nations 1947, 6–7).

Britain attached great diplomatic importance to the General Assembly's decision, but was not entirely satisfied by it, since it made no explicit mention of illegal immigration into Palestine. Eight days after the special session, they were back with the Secretary General, to present him with the document asking all member nations to do their utmost to prevent illegal immigration of Jews into Palestine, while the Palestine question was still under consideration. Lie distributed the letter on 29 May 1947, and added his own personal hope that consideration be given to this letter in the light of the resolution on the Palestine question adopted by the General Assembly. He even asked the members to confirm receipt of the letter and to report to him on any action they were planning to take on the issue (Lie 1947; United Nations 1949, 303).

All this time, work was going on in the ship, with rows upon rows of wooden berths being built into the hold, to sleep the thousands of expected immigrants. But at which port would the passengers embark? It had been planned originally to take on illegal immigrants in Yugoslavia, once constructions had been completed in Italy.[24] However, in the middle of May, the Mossad people in France reported to the main office in Palestine: "We have very painful news regarding Yoram [Yugoslavia]. Yoram's men have suddenly and categorically changed their minds. Not only with regard to transferring people, but also in connection with preparing vessels. We still have to clarify the reason for this .... They have informed us that there is nothing further to discuss until *September*."[25]

The reason for Yugoslavia's sudden announcement was the appointment of its representative to serve as a member of UNSCOP. The Committee was required to present the report together with recommendations no later than 1 September 1947, and, in accordance with the United Nations General Assembly decision, Yugoslavia preferred not to involve herself in the illegal immigration issue in any way, so long as the Committee was active.

The Mossad at that time was busy preparing a program of unprecedented proportions – the transfer to Palestine of thousands of Jews from Romania. When it turned out that the *President Warfield* would not be able to set sail from Yugoslavia, the possibility was raised of sending her to Romania. The idea was discarded very shortly afterwards, however, since "the *President* stinks to high heaven and it started as far back as Danny [the United States]" and if she is sent to Romania, "this may very well ruin our entire grand plan".[26]

During the second half of May, the Mossad were toying with yet another idea: To bring the *President* to Bremen, an American enclave in the British held zone in northern Germany, where 4,000–5,000 people could be brought on board. The Bremen enclave was the only exit to the sea from the American zone in Germany, but the British-held zone had to be crossed in order to get there. The transportation of would-be illegal immigrants to Bremen involved no little hardship, even if the Americans were willing to lend a hand, or at least, to turn a blind eye, which is what they seemed at the beginning to be about to do. However, the program which to the Mossad people seemed no less than "fantastic" soon had to be discarded.[27] The American War Office was too reserved about it and intervention of the State Department put paid to the whole affair (Yahil testimony; Bauer 1970, 316).

Thus, of all the European countries in which the Mossad was operating at the time, the only two which might be considered a feasible launching point for the *President Warfield* were France and Italy.[28] There were not large concentrations of potential immigrants on French soil. The thousands of Jews who had entered France had done so of their own free will and in order to settle there. Unlike the occupied Austria and Germany, and, immediately after the War, Italy, no DP camps were set up in France, nor did that country have an international refugee welfare network. In order for the *President Warfield* to be able to set off from the south of France, the Mossad would have had to bring immigrants in from other countries, as soon as possible before the date of sailing and be responsible for housing and feeding them while they waited to set sail.

Yet, as far as the Mossad was concerned, France was a convenient place to carry out their activity. This was due mainly to the ties they had managed to form with various French people in high places and because, in those days, the French Government still had quite a friendly attitude toward Zionism (Derogy 1972, 49–85). In May 1947, David Ben-Gurion, who was then Chairman of the Jewish Agency Executive, was convinced that "if there is one truly pro-Zionist country in Europe, it's France, but she would never publicly admit to anything of the sort" (Jewish Agency Executive, 22 May 1947). That was the time when the first signs of Britain's pressure on France, regarding the illegal immigration issue, were beginning to be felt. This pressure did not actually threaten illegal immigration activity in France, but it did cause considerable delays, hindrance and hardships which did much to slow down the Mossad's work there.[29]

Thus in the spring of 1947, France was not the most suitable place for the *President Warfield* to set sail from. Which left only Italy. But here too, there was a considerable dragging of heels. The British, together with the Italian security forces, were guarding the country's northern border, so as to prevent the entry of Jews intent on emigrating to Palestine. By April 1947 the flow of Jewish immigrants into Italy had ceased almost altogether.[30] Not content with preventing the entry of new immigrants into Italy, the British also did their best to deny exit to those already there. At the insistence of the British, Italian security forces were stationed around the railway stations in the vicinity of the DP camps in Italy, thus effectively preventing a mass movement to the illegal immigration ships. And to make things even harder, the Italians placed a physical blockade around the *President*, to make sure that she would not be able to slip out of port surreptitiously. "The [Italian] authorities displayed a complete change of attitude, under pressure of our friends [the British]," reported Ada Sereni, then head of the Mossad in Italy. "We had to go back to subversive underground activity, with all the difficulties and hardship this entailed" (1947).

Italy's capitulation to British demands also made work on the ship that much harder.[31] By the beginning of June, the Mossad had come to the conclusion that France was, after all, the only country in which the *President* could be made ready for accepting the immigrants.

It is interesting to note that the decision not to sail the *President* out of Italy came as a result of "the difficult situation" there,[32] and the decision that the ship would leave from France was one of no-choice, a last resort, and not as a solution to the near-crisis situation in the DP camps in Germany. And it should be perfectly clear that had the ship been able to set sail from Italy, she would not have taken immigrants from Germany, but would have dipped into the reserves already waiting in Italy. Since the ship had been transferred from Italy to France in the middle of June, the Mossad found itself having to round up some 4,500 people from the American zone in Germany and to bring them, in next to no time, to France.

From the moment the *President Warfield* arrived in Italy at the end of April, the British had been busy urging the Italians to prevent the ship from sailing from her territories – with or without a cargo of passengers. And, as we have seen, the Italians were willing to cooperate with the British, within the scope of international law. They were aware, however, that they would not be able to delay the ship's departure indefinitely, and indeed, they were rather eager to get rid of this hot potato with which they had been inadvertently presented.[33] The British on the other hand, were keen for the ship to remain anchored in Italy, under their watchful eye. For a certain length of time, therefore, there was a consensus of interests (if from different motives) between the British and the Mossad. The latter wanted the ship to remain in Italy until she could be fully fitted out for her journey to Palestine, and hoped that she could eventually set sail with a cargo of immigrants after all. When they realized that this was not going to happen, the Mossad returned the ship to France, and there was nothing the Italians could do about it.

Thus, accompanied by an Italian warship, the ship set sail on 12 June 1947, and as she entered France's territorial waters opposite Toulon on the morning of 13 June, the Italians turned on their heels.[34] The *President*'s crew got the impression that the warship did not merely return to her home port once she had reached French territorial waters, but had "lost" the *President* as a result of a crafty trick played by the latter's crew. The *President* was traveling at a speed of 11 knots, when she suddenly increased her engine pressure. The ship braked all at once, and, when the surprised Italian warship had slipped by, the *President* made a quick 90 degree turn and beat a hasty retreat, without lights, in the direction of Toulon. They didn't see the Italian warship again (Habbas 1954, 16; Har'el testimony; Har'el 1985; Aran 1985).

One way or another, the *President Warfield* arrived at Port de Bouc on 14 June 1947. The British were still confused as to where the immigrants were supposed to be embarking the ship. While the ship was still anchored in Italy, the British asked the French to "keep an eye" on her and to do their best to prevent the embarkation of illegal immigrants.[35] Once she had returned to France, on the other hand, they were convinced that her passengers would actually go on board in Italy.[36]

It was probably for this reason that on the eve of setting sail from Europe, the *President Warfield* was not at the top of Britain's list of priorities in her diplomatic efforts to block illegal immigration into Palestine via France. In fact, Britain's seeming urgency and intensity of effort on the French front were due to other reasons. First of all was the fear that France's refusal to allow the re-entry of immigrants who had set sail from her shores might have an adverse effect on the Italian Government. This in turn would put a spoke in the wheel of the British efforts in this matter on the Italian front, where the problem seemed most acute. Second was the information which had accumulated on five or six illegal immigration ships anchored at French ports.[37]

By joining the fleet of suspect ships in the middle of June, the *President Warfield* was adding more fuel to the already burning embers. Nonetheless, during the second half of this month, the British were putting no more than moderate pressure on the French with regard to the *President Warfield* – probably because they were fairly certain that Italy was still the main objective for blocking the ship; and also because they were afraid that overpressuring the French with regard to this particular ship may very well ruin their chances of getting France to join the struggle against illegal immigration in general.[38] It should be borne in mind that the *President Warfield* was only one of the hurdles to be overcome in Britain's ongoing struggle against illegal Jewish immigration to Palestine.

Britain's talks with France included all aspects of illegal immigration, from the preliminary stage during which people were removed from Germany, right up to and including the time when illegal immigrants were caught trying to get into Palestine and were sent back to France. The French had demands of their own. First of all, they demanded that the certificates to Palestine be distributed equally among the Jews in the three occupied zones, and not as before, mainly to those in the zone under British control. A further demand was that the British accept back into their zone those Jews who had managed to filter their way out and across the border to France. More than anything, however, the French were disturbed at the growing shortage of manpower in their country and in return for British help in recruiting German manpower for work in France, they were willing to help the British block illegal immigration of Jews to Palestine.[39]

As for permitting the re-entry into France of immigrants who had been caught trying to filter their way into Palestine, the French distinguished between two categories of emigrants. France permitted 8,000 emigrants to stay in transit within her territory and when some of these had left, others could take their place, so that at any one time, up to 8,000 emigrants were legally in transit on French territory. The French were willing to take back those Jews who had entered French territory within the quota of transit emigrants, and were subsequently caught on their way to Palestine as illegal immigrants. This they would do, they said, not out of legal obligation, but as an act of friendship toward Britain. However, the French pointed out, most of the Jews caught trying to enter Palestine illegally had also entered France illegally – which the British could hardly disclaim. The French reckoned that these Jews should be returned to their countries of origin and not to France.

A further differentiation made by the French and of significance in the Exodus Affair was their refusal to furnish any details on people who had entered and left France on personal visas. They did, on the other hand, agree to supply details and even check their data on people who had entered on collective visas and passports, against lists which would be sent over from Jerusalem.

May 1947 saw some advance on the French front of Britain's struggle against illegal immigration to Palestine. The French were prepared to be more scrupulous in examining the visas of emigrants leaving via French ports; to make careful examinations of the ships' safety measures; to stop trains bearing illegal immigrants and to prevent their entry into the French zone in Germany and Austria. The French asked the British not to make these facts widely known.

By the beginning of June it seemed to Bevin that Britain's diplomatic attack on illegal immigration was proving fruitful. A few days after the Secretary General of the United Nations handed out Britain's letter regarding illegal immigration, President Truman appealed to "every citizen and resident of the United States ... to meticulously refrain, while the United Nations is considering the problem of Palestine, from engaging in or facilitating any activities which tend further to inflame the passions of the inhabitants of Palestine, to undermine law and order in Palestine, or to promote violence in that country" (*FRUS* 1947, 1101). The illegal immigration issue was not mentioned outright in Truman's declaration, but at a meeting of the Ministerial Committee on Illegal Immigration, Bevin expressed hope that this declaration – which as he said, denies terror and illegal immigration – will stop donations and support for this matter, especially by trade unions. Not all those participating shared the Foreign Secretary's optimism, although they agreed that further approach should be made to those governments who have dealing of any kind with illegal immigration into Palestine. They also authorized the Foreign Secretary to call on his counterparts on this issue.[40]

At the end of June, Bevin sent out personal letters to the Foreign Ministers of the United States, France, Italy, Greece, Holland, Belgium, Sweden, Denmark and Portugal. With slight amendments according to the country in question, mention was made of the UN decisions at the time of the formation of UNSCOP, President Truman's speech and the British Ambassador's letters which had been distributed by the Secretary General about a month before. Britain explained her need for help in blocking illegal immigration first and foremost by the necessity to maintain stability in Palestine and in the Middle East in general. Of all the nine letters sent out, only the one addressed to the French Foreign Minister made any reference to the *President Warfield*.[41]

More proposals for fighting illegal immigration were raised at a meeting of the Cabinet Committee at the beginning of June. Most of them were rejected for one reason or another. One proposal, which had been discussed on various occasions in the past, was to return illegal immigrants to the countries from which they had set off originally. It was agreed unanimously that putting such a proposal into operation would involve complicated diplomatic problems, but Bevin insisted that Britain should not be reluctant to take drastic action, if it might be effective in suppressing illegal immigration.[42]

During the month of June 1947, therefore, Britain followed a four-pronged path in her determined struggle against illegal immigration.

First, she was left with no choice but to return illegal immigrants to their countries of origin. Second, she took an ever firmer, impatient and threatening tone with the other countries involved – first of all Italy and then France. Third, Bevin's personal involvement was becoming more and more marked; and fourth, the weight of the threat had grown regarding the negative repercussions France's position on the issue would have on the Arabs. At the beginning of July, Bevin wrote to the French that their refusal to act against illegal Jewish immigration to Palestine was already resulting in negative repercussions among the Moslem population, and especially the Arabs living in the overseas French territories.[43]

After the *President Warfield* returned to France, in the middle of June, Bevin made it clear to his ambassador in Paris, that he attached "the very highest importance to stopping this ship which has the largest capacity of any at present engaged in the traffic". He asked the ambassador to bring to France's notice that Britain expected help in everything connected with this ship, as did the Italians, who were able to hold her for several weeks in their port.[44]

The French authorities did indeed seem to be cooperating with the British, although like the Italians, they too agreed to do so on the condition that they acted within the confines of international law. Thus, for example, they rejected the British demand that fuel be refused to illegal immigration ships, especially the *President Warfield*, claiming that this would be discriminatory. At that very time, the French merchant naval authorities detained the *President Warfield* at Port de Bouc, on the pretext that her safety arrangements were insufficient and her licensing was limited to coastal sailing.[45] Nevertheless, the staff of the British consulate in Marseilles were unable to shake off the feeling that it was a matter of days before the ship would be sailing out of Marseilles.[46] At the beginning of July the French denied a British request that should the *President Warfield* make a successful launching, she would be accompanied by a French warship until such a time as she would come into the vicinity of a British warship.[47]

It was no secret that the lower echelons among the French authorities were often more agreeable to British requests than were the Government Ministers responsible for them, who tended to be more sympathetic to the issue of illegal immigration to Palestine. The British also noticed that people in the French Foreign Office were more inclined to cooperate than were those in the Ministry of the Interior. Duff Cooper, the British ambassador in Paris, noticed the difference in attitude between the French Foreign Minister, George Bidault, who was inclined to capitulate to him on the issue of the ship, and his colleagues in the French Cabinet. Tensions such as these would continue to hound the Exodus Affair.

When Duff Cooper realized the strength of Bevin's determination on the *President Warfield* issue, he found it necessary to point out a few accuracies and to make some clarifications with regard to the broad aspect of the relationship between the two countries. He attracted Bevin's attention to things he had heard from a senior French government official, that there is no room for comparison between what Italy did on the issue and what Britain was expecting France to accomplish, since Britain still had, to a certain extent, the power to issue orders to the Italian government, whereas with regard to France ... this stands to reason.[48] Italy was no longer conquered territory at that time, but she was still largely dependent on Britain. Duff Cooper also called Bevin's attention to the fact that too much pressure on France with regard to this specific ship may well harm Britain's attempts to recruit France as an ally in the struggle against illegal immigration in general.[49]

On 23 June 1947, the British got wind of the fact that the ship had managed to obtain a license to sail to the Black Sea and they immediately began acting on several levels simultaneously to prevent her sailing. On a local level, they applied to the port authorities not to permit her sailing, on the pretext that she was breaching the conditions of her license, according to which the ship could set sail for the Black Sea only in good weather and without a cargo of passengers.[50] And on a higher level, Bevin instructed his ambassador in Paris to do his utmost to stop the ship from getting away.[51]

That same day, Bevin sent a letter to Bidault as well as to other colleagues in several countries, in an attempt to put a stop to illegal immigration. As far as Bevin was concerned, the *President Warfield* was the highlight of this "illicit traffic". According to his belief, the ship was capable of bearing some 2,000 (*sic*) people, whose arrival in Palestine may well threaten peace in the entire Middle East. The request which Bevin lay before his colleague illustrates clearly Britain's dual objectives at that time. In general, he was asking for Bidault to prevent the sailing of illegal groups from the south of France without official visas to a destination; and in particular that special attention be paid to Britain's request with regard to the *President Warfield*.[52] In the first week of July, Bevin instructed Duff Cooper to demand that the French refuse to service all the six suspect ships currently anchored at French ports. He justified himself by pointing out that, like England, France too was suffering from a serious shortage of petrol, food and shipyards, therefore the supply of 315 tons of petrol to the *President Warfield* constituted an unnecessary sacrifice on the part of the French people and an imposition on the country's fuel reserves.[53]

Despite efforts at persuading the French to cooperate on the *President Warfield*, the British were still convinced at the beginning of July, that in the final reckoning, the ship would take on her passengers in Italy! Therefore, preparations to repatriate the illegal immigrants, once they had been apprehended, were being made mainly in Italy. The Admiralty and the Ministry of Transport did not anticipate any special technical problems in bringing back immigrants from Palestine to Europe, although it was clear to everyone that it would not be possible for them to disembark on Italian soil without the consent of this government. For that reason they were forced to look into other options. If Italy should refuse to re-accept her immigrants, they should at least be permitted to pass through Italy on their way back to the British zone in Austria. This, too, was a way of returning the illegal immigrants to European soil.

The British were fully determined, therefore, to put into operation a new method in their war against illegal immigration – the return of illegal immigrants to the country from which they had set off on their way to Palestine. This policy became known as *refoulement*. At the beginning of July, as thousands of immigrants were already making their way from Germany to the South of France to set sail on the *President Warfield* to Palestine, the British were still making a concentrated effort to implement their refoulement policy in Italy![54]

Just to be on the safe side, the British held a warship of their own, not far from the port in which the *President* was anchored. At four o'clock, on the afternoon of 9 July, the *President Warfield* left Port de Bouc. At the same time, thousands of illegal immigrants were swarming out of a dozen camps in the region in the direction of the small port of Sete.

4 · A Ship for All Jews

As soon as it was clear to the Mossad that they would be unable to board immigrants on the *President* in Italy, they began making preparations for sailing from France. About ten days after the ship's return from Italy to Port de Bouc, they ordered the emissaries in Germany to get about five thousand immigrants organized and brought to France. These immigrants were categorized into two distinct types: The first was referred to as "pioneers" – kibbutz members and members of the pioneer youth movements, including children in shelters run by these organizations. The other category consisted of individuals, or, as they were known in those days, "ordinary Jews".

The Mossad, as usual, did not interfere in the process of choosing would-be immigrants (Yahil testimony; Frank testimony), a process which was conducted according to a party key.[1] People wanting to immigrate to Palestine had to be members of Zionist movements or parties (or to Agudat Israel). Where the "pioneers" were concerned, each movement was allocated a quota of immigrants, according to the number of members in its kibbutzim. The "ordinary Jews" were selected according to the relative strength of the political parties in the American occupied zone in Germany (Jewish Agency 1949, 11–12; Yahil testimony; Yahil 1980, 28).

The organizers of Aliyah Bet enacted a firm and irrevocable rule: the right to join the illegal immigration operation was reserved solely to inhabitants of the DP camps and to people taking part in training programs provided by the youth pioneer movements. This principle aimed at increasing the attraction for remaining within the organized framework of the camps, as opposed to the temptation to go out to the towns, and is based on the cornerstone of Zionist policy at the time, which tied the solution to the Jewish DPs in Europe with the founding of a Jewish state in Palestine. Thus the Zionist leadership was interested in having the DPs concentrated in the camps, and not scattered all over the countryside, both so as to ensure that Zionism does not lose a valuable reserve of immigrants to Palestine, and in order to use them as a means for pressuring the British into opening the gates to Palestine (Habbas 1954, iv; Braginsky 1965, 374–75). The Jews who did leave the camps and went to live in the towns and villages of Germany, were considered by those who remained in the camps – especially the "pioneers" – to be traitors and the scum of the earth, lowly outcasts (Roseman 1984; Leichter 1985). Incidentally, the British adhered to a similar principle in their zone in Germany, albeit for different reasons. In an attempt to ease the burden of maintaining the DPs, they gave out immigration certificates (to Palestine) to camp inhabitants only – it was not, after all, the responsibility of the occupying authorities to support people living in German towns and villages.

At first only "pioneers" were taken on board Mossad ships from Germany to Palestine. In Autumn 1946, however, individual immigrants were also being sent out, and constituted up to about one-third of each shipload of passengers. Between January and March 1947, the pioneers made up about 80 percent of the DPs who left the camps to join the immigrant ships, whereas only 60 percent of the *Exodus* passengers were "pioneers" – the remainder being "individuals" (Yahil testimony; Frank 1947). As a rule, babies under one year old were not included on Aliyah Bet ships, nor were people over 60, or obviously pregnant women. Nonetheless, a few exceptions succeeded in fooling the doctors and the immigration committees. The *Exodus* had a completely different composition of passengers. There was a higher proportion of "individuals" compared with other Mossad ships, and the "pioneers", too, included a relatively large number of pregnant women and families with small children.

Was this deliberate, or was it merely the result of circumstances? Several testimonies have it that rumors were rife in the camps that this was to be a large, comfortable and swift ship and not only would checking of potential passengers be lax, the organizers were actually interested in taking on "difficult human material", i.e. families with children, pregnant women and even handicapped people (Habbas 1954, 50; Greenstein 1964; Perlov n.d., 52–53). The British were aware of the fact that among the ship's passengers were "a notably high proportion of children, many of whom were unattached and whose parents were 'coming along later'. Many moderately pregnant Jewesses were to be seen, although it must be admitted that they were, on the whole, less fat than is customary."[2]

There were those who made *post factum* attempts to find significant reasons for this, as if orders had actually been issued from above that immigrants should be selected to "suitably represent a cross section of the DP population, so that this particular Mossad ship could make the most of any and all available symbolism. Under the command of 'Moses of Palestine', this exodus (from Europe) would set an example to the world – no less than had the first, Biblical, exodus from Egypt" (Derogy 1972, 73). However, the "mixed bag" composition of the illegal immigrants who would make up the passengers of the *Exodus*, was due more to circumstances in the DP camps, than to any carefully thought out program. In fact, the need to beat as hasty a retreat as possible from the camps, created a situation whereby the organizers no longer had control over who would be selected to go and who would be obliged to remain. Furthermore, the relatively small number of "pioneers" on *Exodus* stemmed also from the fact that by this time Germany had virtually been "emptied" of Zionist youth movement members and kibbutz movement trainees and it was inconceivable to leave thousands of DPs without the cream off the top of the milk (Frank 1947).

Among those making their way toward the *Exodus* were people who had previously signed on for emigration to countries other than Palestine. The American Methodist minister, Grauel, who accompanied the immigrants on their journey from France to Haifa, was impressed that most of the people on board had cited Palestine as their first choice for immigration, although many added that they would have wanted to go to the United States, were this possible (*PM*, 21 July 1947).

This dwelling on the immigrants' characteristics and motives exceeds somewhat from the obvious necessity to get to the root of the facts. It becomes more relevant in light of the people's experiences on the long and arduous journey to Palestine and back, via France, to Germany, only to return, ultimately, to Palestine. The material presented here will serve as background to the behavior of these people throughout the Exodus Affair and is of particular importance in light of the heroic aura attached to the immigrants during and after the affair.

For better or for worse, the *Exodus* passengers represented an accurate cross-section of the Jewish DP population in the American zone of Germany in spring 1947, not only from the point of view of the division between "pioneers" and "individuals", but also the various "generations" in the camps; the diversity of the countries of origin – Poland, Russia, Lithuania, Czechoslovakia, Hungary, Rumania; and the experience of the Jews during the war years. Some of them had lived under Nazi occupation – in ghettos, concentration and death camps, forced labor camps, in hiding places in towns and forests, or as partisans and underground fighters. Others had spent the war years in places out of the Nazi's reach, especially in Asiatic Russia. Many of them were lonely people, who had no kin left alive in the whole world, and there were others who came aboard ship with their families – in some cases, these were old established families, mainly of repatriates who had come back to their countries of origin, after having spent the war years in Russia, bringing with them children of various ages. And there were families which had been established after the war – men and women who had met and formed unions and were now coming on board with small babies. There were among the immigrants several Christian women, who had harbored Jewish children during the war, and could not bear the thought of parting from them before seeing them safely settled in their homeland, thereby fulfilling their vows to the children's parents.

At the end of June 1947, within a period of less than two weeks, some 5,000 Jewish men, women and children left the camps in the American zone of Germany. This mass exodus of people was felt keenly in all the DP camps and did much to improve the general atmosphere in them. It also rekindled in the remaining DPs their waning desire to immigrate to Palestine via Aliyah Bet. Once again queues began forming in front of the Jewish Agency offices, with people asking to be allowed to immigrate to Palestine by any means available (Yahil 1981, 144), and a renewed uplifting of the spirits was felt among the members of the pioneer youth movements.[3] The exodus itself, however, was fairly modest considering all the illusions and the raised hopes of a "mass exodus", but it was, nevertheless, the largest migration to date out of the camps, and coming after such a long dry period in which no one had left, it was no wonder so many people felt that salvation was at hand.

On 7 July, the French branch of the Mossad proudly sent a coded telegram to their colleagues in Palestine: "We have removed four thousand five hundred people out of Hannan. Of these, one thousand seven hundred in plants and the rest – as an enema."[4] Uncoded, this meant: We have taken 4,500 would-be immigrants out of Germany, of which 1,700 enter with an official visa and the remainder, illegally. The entire operation took place within a short space of time. The official visa had been received on 25 June.[5] Four days later the transfer of immigrants began from Germany to France and this was completed within eight days. The transfer was conducted in two stages, on Sunday 29 June and on Sunday 6 July. Sundays were chosen since on those days the military personnel, the police and the civilian personnel were less alert than usual and were concerned mainly with getting through their shift and making their way home. Bribes and other ruses were offered to smooth the way across international borders – American cigarettes were very popular in those days.

The collective French visa contained 850 fictitious names. The visa had arrived in duplicate, so that it was possible to use it twice, at two different crossing points. The exit of 1,700 people, whose "names" were included in the visa, was quite official and above board, and they arrived in France by train. They were looked after by the International Refugee Organization, which had recently taken over activity in the camps from UNRRA. Probably this situation, in which the camp authorities were somewhat in limbo – one international organization had left, while another was still in the process of taking over the care of the DPs – made the operation that much easier. The Jewish Refugee Aid Society – an organization set up by the Mossad in France as a welfare organization for Jewish refugees, and allegedly registered legally in the United States – provided the remaining immigrants with identity cards. The immigrants were driven in trucks by the Brichah organization. The American army helped both the legal and the illegal stages of the operation to succeed, mainly by turning a blind eye. There is very little doubt that the Americans knew more or less what was going on, but as long as there was some semblance of official cover to the transports, they were happy to continue in their work without delving too deeply or asking too many questions (Habbas 1954, 17–21, 24–32, 263–69; Braginsky 1965, 377; Slutzky 1972a, 377, 1154–55; Bauer 1970, 317).

Once they had arrived in France, the immigrants were taken by train to the Marseilles region. Of these, 4,200 were to find themselves eventually on the *Exodus*, some 600 boarded other ships at later dates and some 200 children were sent to "Youth Aliyah" institutions in France (Habbas 1954, 23; Yahil 1981, 143–44). The 4,200 DPs who arrived from Germany in order to board the *Exodus* were joined in France by a further 300 mainly young people from North Africa – Tunisia, Morocco and Algeria; and members of pioneer youth movements from France, Belgium, Holland, Italy and England.[6]

The immigrants were also joined in France by a group of 27 young men – most of them demobilized soldiers – and women from France and Algeria, who had no previous Zionist background. The Second World War and all its repercussions, general as well as specifically Jewish, and all they and their families had been through, made them realize that Palestine was the only place for them. They joined the "Jewish Scouts" and spent a year on a training farm in the south of France, where they were sworn in as members of Haganah and waited for their turn to join an immigrant ship which would take them to Palestine. By the time they arrived at the transit camp at the beginning of July 1947, they considered themselves to be recruited soldiers, ready and willing to fulfill any task required of them (Tubul 1985). As a group of healthy young people, unburdened by personal experiences of the Holocaust, and with no dependent relatives to worry about, they were of great help to the Palestinian emissaries and to the immigrants themselves while preparations were being made at the camp, during the journey to Palestine and later, on the deportation ship *Empire Rival*. In many ways, there were similarities between them and the American crew.

On her way from France to Palestine, the ship carried 1,561 men, 1,282 women, 1,017 youths and 655 children (total: 4,515).[7] The British deportation ships on their way from Haifa to France, carried 1,842 men, 1,632 women, and 955 children (total 4,429 immigrants).[8] The discrepancy in the total figures reflects the number of casualties and their families who had remained in Palestine. When the *Exodus* immigrants arrived in September 1947 at the two camps prepared for them by the British in north Germany, they included 56 babies under one year old (including those born on the *Exodus* and on the deportation ships); 114 children under the age of three; 107 aged between four and six years; 238 aged between seven and 11; 598 adolescents aged between 12 and 15; 538 aged between 16 and 18 and 2,541 aged over 18 (JDC 1947a).

All the political parties and movements were represented among the ship's passengers.[9] The level of commitment to party or movement was not uniform among the immigrants. Some of them were totally devoted to their movement and had strong ties to their fellow members, based on common experience, ideology and future plans; others had various ulterior motives for joining one or other of the groups. Again, selection of immigrants was carried out according to a party key, and it was clear to the camp inhabitants that their ability to immigrate to Palestine depended on their being members in one or other of the Zionist parties. The decision to join a particular party often had nothing to do with ideology, and could be based merely on the individual's opinion of his chances of being included in a transport to Palestine.

The first people to reach the training camps in the region of Marseilles at the end of June, were obliged to endure several days of waiting. Others were there for a short period of time only, which was spent in intensive training for the forthcoming voyage. First of all, it was necessary to organize the immigrants in groups of 30, as was customary in the illegal immigration ships. Thirty was the number chosen because of the size of the food pails used for handing out food on board ship and it was also a suitable number for transferring people and luggage in trucks from the camps to port. Those who had arrived in France within the framework of one or other of the movements knew already how to organize themselves and individuals were allocated to existing groups to make up their numbers to 30, or organized into their own groups. Some of this "matching up" paid no attention to the ideological identity of the people involved. The objective was simply to get all the people organized in groups of 30. In order to withstand the long journey ahead – both on *Exodus* and on the deportation ships – it was imperative for everyone to belong to a group. It would have been virtually impossible for people to manage on their own. Everything was distributed on a group basis – food, water, blankets, privileges, etc. Several homogenous groups were formed in order to ease things for people with special needs, the common denominators of these groups being age or health – e.g. small children, pregnant women and youngsters. Each group elected its own "group head" or "commander" and there were altogether around 150 such leaders (Habbas 1954, 35; Roseman 1984; Ganuz 1985, 131 and 139–40; Katzanelson 1985; Leichter 1985; Peker 1985; Perry 1985; Tubul 1985).

The few days and nights remaining before sailing were spent preparing the immigrants for their journey to Palestine. They practiced food and water drill and were taught how to behave in the event of a warning siren. Most difficult for all involved, immigrants and emissaries alike, was the task of packing personal belongings. Everyone was allowed to take on board one package, weighing no more than ten kilos and this had to be packed in such a way as to allow swift and easy mobility along the ship's narrow passage ways. The immigrants had to relinquish their most precious belongings, often the last material possessions left to them on earth, all of immeasurable sentimental value. For people who had already lost everything, yet succeeded in collecting a few meager items from here and there, the necessity to choose only the most important and discard the rest was too heartbreaking and some of them gave vent to their stress by picking fights and cursing the emissaries, whom they held responsible for this harsh edict. Once the immigrant had packed his meager belongings, he had to load them on his shoulders and make his way along a narrow gangway between two rows of benches. Anyone who upset a bench, had to go back and repack his baggage (Habbas 1954, 35–36; Ganuz 1985, 130–45; Har'el 1985; Leichter 1985; Perry 1985; Livyathan testimony; Einav 1988).

The documents necessary for their organized exit from France to Colombia (so it said on the certificates) were prepared during the immigrants' brief stay in the training camps. Marseilles street photographers were brought in to take passport photographs of 4,500 people. The Aliyah Dalet people, who were by now experts in preparing "authentic" papers, set to work to produce for each and every immigrant his own personal identity card with a genuine picture of the bearer, although the name on the card was, once again, fictitious – and different from that used in the earlier stage of the operation. The immigrants were again required to assume new names and to get used to them (Habbas 1954, 36; Ganuz 1985, 140–41). It was vital for each of them to be equipped with a personal passport stamped with a Colombian visa, in order to exit France in an apparently legal manner. When Britain demanded of the French to take back the immigrants after they had been apprehended off the shores of Palestine, the French shrugged them off with the seemingly correct claim that the ship's passengers had all boarded with *personal* passports and visas to Colombia.

The Palestinian emissaries had been somewhat concerned by the uncontrolled behavior of some of the immigrants during the train journey from the French border to the camps near Marseilles. The actual boarding of the ship, however, was orderly and organized, each group of 30 going on board with its own leader. The Haganah commander in Europe praised "our lads", the Haganah members from Palestine, responsible for the training camps in southern France, for this changed behavior.[10] These young men and women were indeed devoted and tireless, although their work was made easier because the immigrants worshipped the emissaries from Palestine and their every word was almost like the word of God. The sea crossing served only to increase this admiration. "We were led by Jewish lads, an outstanding example of humility and honesty," wrote one of the immigrants to his friends, describing the journey of the *Exodus* from France to Palestine. "We were not able to reach their standard and I doubt if we shall ever be able to do so. These are members of Haganah – and I have nothing but respect for them. You, of course, are familiar with our Jews, but I must admit, that under the supervision of such as those, they, too, behaved like human beings" (Habbas 1954, 165–66).

Obviously it was an exaggeration to believe that a handful of young people from Palestine, no matter how talented and devoted, were able to accomplish all the preparations single-handed and to be the cause of such an overwhelming change in the behavior of so large a group of people. The fact was that the immigrants connected to a youth movement had their own recognized leadership. The groups of children and youths arrived with their teams of leaders and instructors, whom they followed everywhere and obeyed implicitly. The change in behavior was the result mainly of changed circumstances. From being displaced persons with no hope, and their future foggy at best, they had become Ma'apilim facing a common objective, of the importance of which they were well aware, and it had great personal significance to each and every one of them. They had set forth upon a path which was to bring them, even if not directly, to a safe harbor and to the beginning of a new life.

Of all the *Exodus* passengers, the members of ha-Shomer ha-Tza'ir were outstanding in their leadership qualities and the way in which they organized themselves. On the eve of embarkation, Mordechai Roseman, the recognized leader of ha-Shomer ha-Tza'ir in Germany, appointed a six member team who, with him, constituted the movement's official management on board ship. He also composed an "order of the day" in Hebrew, illustrating the sense of mission common to members of pioneer youth movements, which was also shared by many of those immigrants defined as "ordinary Jews". The order read thus:

> Today we are about to board a ship, through which the Jewish nation is fighting for its existence.
>
> We shall march upright to victory, hand in hand with the rest of the Israeli people – leading them, at their side and in their defense, the way our comrades in the underground and the ghettos did before us, in the mission to save Jews and struggle for the honor of the Jewish people.
>
> Throughout the journey we shall exhibit the pioneering spirit and moral strength of our movement, we shall set an example to ourselves and to our fellow passengers.
>
> We shall fulfill faithfully all Orders of the Hour and take upon ourselves any directive, task and mission.
>
> We shall be prepared for our meeting with the motherland and even to cruelly push away from her.
>
> We shall meet head on the agents of the White Paper with dignity and with pride, in keeping with our movement's tradition.

The Order of the Day ends with the call: "be prepared and ready for the final and decisive order," and concludes with the movement's motto: "Be strong and of good courage."[11]

5 · *The Bird Flew the Coop*

With the sailing of the *Exodus*, illegal immigration activity was restored, after having been for several months at a standstill. The fact that the halt in illegal immigration had coincided with the appointment of UNSCOP set forth a series of rumors that there was a direct link between the two events. In June 1947, some European newspapers claimed that the Haganah spokesperson had announced a temporary halt in illegal immigration activity. One version had it that this halt was the result of difficulties caused by the British authorities, and another said that it was "in order not to interfere with the work of the investigation committee". "We were amazed," cabled the Mossad head Shaul Meirov (later Avigur), and his colleagues in France, to their counterparts in Palestine, and demanded to be told "if this announcement has really been released, and if it has, by whom?"[1] Similar information had been released by the *STA* news agency, according to which "The Resistance Movement" had claimed that "the British blockade on European ports had succeeded, and was seriously hindering illegal immigration activity." However, "The Hebrew Resistance Movement" would continue in its endeavors for illegal immigration.[2]

The reply from Palestine was that both versions had been distributed without official authorization. "The objective seems to be to spread confusion and discord." Whose objective? Was the use of the term "The Hebrew Resistance Movement" about a year after it had ceased to exist, supposed to show that the report had originated with the IZL? "Mossad and Haganah spokespersons are completely denying the reports of a halt in immigration activity," the Mossad in Palestine reassured their colleagues in France. "The Haganah also published 'ha-Homa' billboard notices denying this. But the fact that no ships are arriving makes further rumors possible. Let us know what the chances are."[3] Palmach commander Yig'al Peikovitz (later Allon), made it quite clear to his fellows that there was absolutely no truth in the rumors that there was a deliberate dearth of illegal immigration ships. And with the Palmach displeased at the moderate line taken by the political leadership since summer 1946, he found it right to stress that "this time, the delays are not being caused by the people responsible for illegal immigration and they have nothing to do with the political line" (Allon 1947, 841).

The fact that no ships sailed between 13 May and 11 July 1947 was due mainly to the Mossad's financial and manpower problems during the first months of that year.[4] The pressure put by Britain on Italy and France to prevent the sailing of illegal immigration ships from their ports, and the difficulty in congregating large numbers of immigrants at the ports of exit, made the matter more complicated still.

The news of a halt in illegal immigration arrived when the country was enjoying the atmosphere of ceasefire accompanying the UNSCOP's activity in Palestine. Both sides, the British Mandatory authorities and the Zionist leadership, were eager to keep things as quiet as possible while the committee was doing its work. On 12 June 1947, most of the Haganah prisoners were pardoned and released, in honor of the birthday of King George VI. On the 15th and 16th of the month, the committee members arrived in the country and on the 18th the Haganah successfully frustrated an IZL attack on the British in Tel Aviv's Hadar Building – one of the Haganah members was killed. This atmosphere succeeded in deceiving even the British administration in Palestine, which was convinced that the Jews had decided to halt illegal immigration during the committee's stay in the country.[5] This, then, may have been the source of the rumors – whether because of mistaken evaluation or, indeed, with the aim of "spreading confusion and discord".

In fact, the Zionist leadership had no intention of exercising any kind of truce on illegal immigration activity. Between the summer of 1945 and the end of 1947, illegal immigration had been the cornerstone of the struggle against British policies in Palestine. Practical and political considerations brought about changes in resistance and breakthrough plans and determined the character of the Yishuv's reactions, but they did not effect the scope of the operation and certainly had nothing to do with suspending it.

In other words, orders were not issued by the Zionist leadership and the Mossad to delay the sailing of illegal immigration ships from European ports during the activity of UNSCOP, which makes it necessary to determine if – as was written *post factum* – the Mossad people in Europe were ordered to speed up sailings, so that the ships' arrival in Palestine would coincide with UNSCOP's stay in the country. As early as August 1947, the Lehi paper *ha-Ma'as* claimed that "the arrival of [the

ship] *Yetzi'at Eiropa* was timed to serve as a political demonstration to
coincide with the UN committee's visit in Palestine." This claim appears
over and over again in books by British historians, sometimes firmly and
at times in more cautious terms (Kirk 1954, 243; Sykes 1965, 381; Bethell
1979, 324). Others too wrote it in their books (Cohen 1982, 252), including
Ada Sereni, Mossad head in Italy at the time, who wrote in her memoirs
that "the Yishuv leadership wanted the committee [UNSCOP] to be
present when a ship enters the country bearing illegal immigrants, so
that its members can witness the drama first hand: How the British overcome the ship and the desperate resistance on the part of the immigrants.
Meirov was allocated the job of seeing to it that one of the immigrant
ships arrive at Palestine, during the visit of the investigative committee"
(Sereni 1975, 140).

Documents written at the time present a different picture altogether.
In his letter dated 21 June 1947, the Palmach commander claimed that
"the absence of any immigrant ships, at the time of the UN investigation,
is no doubt a political blow ... and it is construed and misconstrued by
our own people and the entire world" (Allon 1947, 841). Sereni replied
to this letter on 20 July 1947: "I hear from Yiftach's letters, that he does
not understand how we were unable to bring a ship to Palestine at the
time of the committee. I would like to say this ... if we want to have a
ship arrive at a specific time, we have to have advance notice of the fact,
so that appropriate plans can be made. It is no use coming up with the
idea at the last moment." Yiftach's letter was written five days *after* the
committee's arrival in Palestine.

In all the correspondence between the Mossad and its people in
Europe, with regard to the June 1947 rumors, no mention was made
about speeding up the sailing of *The President*, so as to coincide with the
committee's stay. Despite the denial of reports that illegal immigration
activity was being suspended temporarily; and notwithstanding messages such as "the fact that there are no ships arriving, makes it easy to
spread rumors. Let us know what the chances are", no requests or
demands were made to speed up the sailing of *The President*.

The idea to bring in illegal immigrant ships to Palestine while
UNSCOP was visiting had apparently first been raised in that Palmach
commander's letter (dated 21 June 1947), in which he wrote: "The danger
of this failure can still be avoided [the political blow caused by the absence
of illegal immigrant ships at the time UNSCOP was in Palestine] if the
ships hurry up and make a point of arriving in large numbers." But when
this letter arrived in Europe, the *Exodus* had already set sail (Aran 1985;
Har'el 1985; Katzanelson 1985; Perry 1985).

In fact, the sailing date from France had been determined according to on the spot conditions and the people responsible for preparing the ship were unaware of any target date connected with UNSCOP activity (Aran 1985; Har'el 1985; Katzanelson 1985; Perry 1985). In order to mislead and to guard against leaks, the Mossad let it be known that the ship would leave on 20 July 1947 (Zameret 1964), although it was decided secretly to bring the date forward and to load the ship at the same time as the Tour de France was passing near to Sete – in the belief that the authorities would be so involved with that event as to pay little attention to what was going on at the port (Shadmi 1964).

The sailing of *Exodus* from France, like all other Mossad activity in that country, would have been impossible were it not for the sympathetic support of French people in various levels of authority. This was not a matter of French Government policy, which has already been discussed, but of people, who saw the issue as humanitarian, without giving too much thought to the harmful implications of their activity on French–British relations and on the position of France in the Arab world. The Mossad was assisted by people of reputation, especially Jews, who held various key positions in spheres connected with the matter at hand. The Mossad activists were helped also by ex-Resistance officers who, during the war had developed good connections and a certain *esprit de corps* with senior and junior officials in the relevant government offices. In the first few years following the end of the war, days which constituted a transition from being a resistance movement and all this entailed, to the formal framework of a sovereign state – great significance was attached to personal relationships which had been formed through shared experiences during the war.

The positive attitude of some of those French functionaries to the Mossad activity was based first and foremost on sympathy, and in some cases a feeling of guilt toward the Jews, victims of the Holocaust, whose only wish was to set sail for their homeland. As far as the French were concerned, the "bad guys" in this story were none other than the British, and the Jews were seen not only as the "good guys", but also as the underdog. Furthermore, the French had a long historic account to keep with the British, and the Middle East – a region from which the French had so recently been expelled, tail between their legs, by the British – played a vital and bitter role in this account (Kimche 1954, 186). French Foreign Office officials often ridiculed the idea that they would help the British get out of the swamp they got themselves into in the Middle East, saying: "Do they think we have forgotten Syria?"[6] A chance to get their revenge on the British by sabotaging their efforts on an issue connected with the same region in which the French had recently been so bitterly insulted, together with the opportunity to obtain from the Haganah classified information relating to the Middle East, imparted an aspect of "give and take" to the relationship which developed between the Mossad and the French Secret Police and Intelligence Service.

Respect and sympathy for the activity of the Mossad and the Haganah were strengthened by the fact that members of the Socialist Party, the cornerstone of French Governments in those days, saw Zionism as a socialist national liberation movement and felt class solidarity with the organizers of illegal immigration who were all affiliated with the labor movement in Palestine and many of whom were kibbutz members.

This class solidarity helped solve a problem which very nearly put a stop to the sailing of the *Exodus* at the last moment, when the truck drivers in the Marseilles region joined a wave of nation-wide strikes. The illegal immigrants were supposed to be transferred to the port of Sete in several dozen trucks, according to a strict and well regulated time-table. From the beginning, the trade union activists, all of them socialists and communists, were inclined to allow the illegal immigrants into the port, despite the strike. A donation of one million francs to the strike fund reinforced this positive attitude and "paid" for the free pass through the picket lines to the 170 Mizrachi brothers' trucks – 150 trucks for transferring the immigrants and a further 20 in reserve in case of breakdowns (Har'el testimony; Har'el 1964; Derogy 1972, 84–85; Einor 1985; Har'el 1985).

On 9 July, the *President Warfield* left Port de Bouc and sailed south west to the small port of Sete, which had been the port of departure for four previous illegal immigration ships. The advantage of this small port was that it was situated in the constituency of Jules Moch, the French Transport Minister and an old friend of the Mossad. Moch, who was very familiar with the port, gave advice on the best place for the ship to anchor – close to the exit and not too far into port, so as not to risk being blocked. The clerks at the port, the customs, border control and other authorities were activists in the local branch of the Socialist Party. The regional officer was a Jew with left-wing leanings, and a cousin of Jules Moch himself (Derogy 1972, 70–71).

As soon as news went out that the ship had arrived at the port of Sete and that thousands of illegal immigrants had embarked her, the British Embassy in Paris protested to the French Foreign Office, and received the reply that an order had been issued to the local authorities not to permit the ship to set sail and that all the passengers would be obliged to disembark. The British were assured that the French Foreign and

Transport Offices would enforce the two clauses limiting the ship's sailing license, which allowed her to cruise under pleasant weather conditions only, with no passengers on board.[7] The British Embassy in Paris was not content with promises which were issued too high up and too far away from the place where the action was taking place. They sent out an urgent missive to their consul-general in Marseilles, saying that if he suspects that the ship is about to sail, he must see to it that the local authorities prevent this from happening, on the pretext of bad weather – especially if there are passengers on board. For some reason, the missive, which left Paris on 10 July 1947, arrived at Marseilles only on 12 July 1947 at 10:05.[8] By which time the bird had flown the coop.

This chapter in the Exodus Affair – which accounts for the time at which the ship first entered the port of Sete on the evening of 9 July and up to her exit to the open seas in the early morning of Friday 11 July is almost undocumented, but it is quite obvious it contained features of illegal activity. The stories of the participants are soaked with an atmosphere of *A Thousand and One Nights*, and indeed, can the secret spiriting out of a ship bearing 4,500 passengers, in defiance of all the rules and regulations, be explained in any other way? The following are the main events, although here and there there may be a small inaccuracy (Ben-Amotz 1950, 31–53; Holly 1969, 191–203; Derogy 1972, 85–105; Roseman 1984; Ganuz 1985, 141–45; Har'el 1985; Leichter 1985; Peker 1985; Katzanelson 1985; Einav 1988; Hadari 1991, 165–68).[9]

The local Commissioner of Police agreed to the request that he and his men be present at the port at the very unconventional time of 3 o'clock in the morning. It took longer than planned to get the trucks ready and the exodus from the camps was delayed by about two hours. Thus the first immigrants boarded ship only at about five o'clock, which was still three hours before the official time at which the port passport control officials started their working day. The examination of the passengers' documents was far from thorough. The ship had a sailing license to Istanbul, whereas the visas presented by the passengers were to Colombia. Furthermore, the ship did not even have a license to carry passengers. Cases of incompatibility between identity papers and their owners were solved on the spot by using a few words of persuasion and explanation.

Embarkation took about six hours and was completed at around eleven o'clock in the morning. The British did not give up. An aircraft of theirs had been circling above the port since dawn, and their frenzied activity in Paris produced the dispatch of some French officials from Marseilles to the port of Sete. These made a check and forbade the ship to set sail – for safety reasons. Their demand that part of the ship's engines be handed over to them in order to ensure that the ship remains anchored in port, were met with a polite but firm refusal.

   This development caused concern. Was there going to be a repeat of the Spring 1946 La Spezia Affair, when the British succeeded in preventing the sailing from Italy of a Mossad ship carrying 1,014 immigrants? (Hadari 1991, 135–40). This would indeed be a harsh blow to the Mossad and the illegal immigrants alike. So the French would have to realize what was in store for them and be persuaded that it would be in their best interests to help the ship get away from French territorial waters as soon as possible, or at least to turn a blind eye. First of all, the papers – the passports with the personal visas to Colombia – were collected and destroyed as soon as the illegal immigrants climbed on board ship. From then on they became people with no nationality and no destination. Second, the ship's commander – Yossi Hamburger (later Har'el), the Captain, Ike Aharonowitz and Mordechai Roseman, disembarked and met with the port and district authorities in order to persuade them that by allowing the ship to sail out of port, they would avoid having to undertake responsibility for the welfare of 4,500 people – which would be the best thing for all concerned. Since the idea was to frighten the French, rumors were spread of possible epidemics on board ship, followed by a demand for food and soap to be supplied by the port authorities. In order to create a sympathetic atmosphere and to draw attention away from the issue at hand, the French officials were treated to a fine meal and excellent wine.

   Officially, there was no change in the authorities' orders forbidding the ship to raise anchor, also from all accounts, little was done to enforce these orders. The port's topography would have easily permitted total blockage of the ship's way out, had this been desired. Moreover, as Jules Moch wrote to his Prime Minister, Paul Ramadier at the end of July: "It was possible for the authorities to remove the immigrants from the ship by force, but this would have resulted in bloodshed, and no one was about to take responsibility for that. As soon as the ship succeeded in slipping out of the port at Sete, warships could have been sent out to stop her, but obviously it would have taken more than a warning shot to make her stop in her tracks. She would have had to be sunk in order to make her stop and this was out of the question."[10]

   Paris was concerned at the time with matters of great importance. The economic future of France and Europe was in the balance and the threatening shadow of the Cold War was getting ever closer. The Marshall Plan, which the European Foreign Ministers were meant to discuss at the summit conference which was about to open in Paris two days hence, required considerable cooperation between France and Britain and it would have been most inappropriate for one immigrant ship to spoil relations between these two allies. The Mossad people tried to recruit the help of their old friends, people who had always helped them in the past. But this time they met insurmountable problems – their friends were unable to come to the rescue. Beyond their replies that "this time we can't do it", there was a clear hint that it would be best to back down, in other words – to remove the passengers from the ship. To postpone one battle for the sake of the whole war. When it became obvious that this was the situation, Meirov ordered Hamburger to set sail with no further delay and not to wait for any official permission, which would probably never have been forthcoming anyway. Any further procrastination may very well have put paid to any practical opportunity to continue with the plans, once the ship's path was physically blocked.

One of the better known chapters in the story of the *Exodus* is the one which relates the ship's escape from the port of Sete. It was an odyssey of mishaps, bad luck, initiative and near miracles, which has been told countless times in a variety of versions. The most authentic description of the events, in the most down-to-earth and contained manner, which imparts to the reader the drama and the atmosphere better than all the superlatives related later on, was a cable from the ship on the morning of Friday, 11 July 1947 at 7:30:

> At six o'clock this morning we managed, under great danger, to escape from the port. The following are details of our action.
>
> The navigator was supposed to arrive at the vessel at two o'clock and maneuver us out of the port. We had everything ready and waited until three thirty. The navigator did not arrive. We decided to go out alone. As we were activating the propeller, we found that a foreign body – probably a cable – had become caught in it. We succeeded, after several attempts, to free the propeller – this lasted an hour. Very carefully, the captain began moving the ship. At the turn to the port entrance, we hit a sand bank. We struggled with the sand bank for about an hour and a half, until the captain's desperate efforts succeeded and he took us out to the open sea.
>
> I would point out:
>
> a. The excellent work carried out by the captain.
> b. The port's pilot came out in the morning and saw us stranded on the sand bank and didn't raise a finger to help us.
> c. The vessel remained completely undamaged.
> d. All efforts to escape were justified, despite the risks involved.[11]

The escape of the *President Warfield* came as a surprise to the British and as a bitter personal insult to Bevin. The ship sailed from Sete at the time when he, the British Foreign Secretary, was in Paris. The idea of refoulement had already been discussed several times in British Government circles and the decision to put it into operation was still an option. The fact that the first candidate for refoulement had succeeded in escaping from France under Bevin's very nose was a coincidence, but it is possible that it had an effect on his position, on the strength of his reaction and on the way he subsequently dealt with what was to become the Exodus Affair.

Bevin had arrived in Paris together with 15 other European Foreign Ministers in order to take part in discussions on the Marshall Plan between 12 and 15 July. This is the reason that the first references to the issue of returning the *President Warfield* to France were made on a ministerial level. Bevin discussed the issue of illegal immigration to Palestine personally with the French Foreign Minister, Bidault, at their meeting in Moscow at the beginning of May 1947.[12] This time, on the morning of 12 July, the talk was much more practical. After protesting the fact that the ship had been supplied with food and services while in a French port, and expressing his surprise at the way the ship, with her more than 4,000 passenger load, had managed to escape in defiance of the conditions of her license, Bevin demanded explanations as to how this had been possible and insisted that the necessary disciplinary measures be taken against those who had permitted the ship to escape, despite the promises of the French Government. He then went on to make his new demand, by making it clear to Bidault that the British Government "intended to make an example of this ship by obliging her to return to a French port with all her passengers". This new policy, he pointed out to Bidault, is based on French cooperation in having the ship return to France and all her passengers disembarked. Bevin was impressed that his French colleague was of similar mind.[13]

Bevin's persuasion tactics were now joined by mention of the friendship between the two nations, promises given by France in the past, the fact that the Palestine issue was currently being handled by the United Nations (i.e. it was *sub judice*). Even the welfare of the passengers themselves was mentioned – depicting them as victims of those who are trying to profit at their expense. "Jews in all parts of Europe are being encouraged to sell their possessions in order to purchase at extravagant rates a passage to Palestine .... It is no less in the interest of the immigrants themselves than in the desire to promote peace in Palestine that HM's

Government are using their utmost endeavors to put an end to this infamous traffic."[14]

In his desire to make the most of his stay in France, Bevin also had a meeting with the French Prime Minister, Ramadier – with Bidault's consent – who told him that he was hearing of the *President Warfield* for the first time. Bevin was outspoken and even threatening. He explained to the French Prime Minister that "in the case of Palestine, not only Jews, but Arabs were affected and I conceived that the indulgence shown to Jewish immigration by French authorities might well have repercussions in French North Africa." In order to reinforce this, Bevin reminded Ramadier of the measures taken by him, as British Foreign Minister, to ensure that British subjects avoid activities which are in contradiction of French interests and asked, sarcastically, "was it too much to ask that the French Government should reciprocate in the matter of this illegal Jewish traffic, which was in any case largely a financial racket controlled from New York?"

Ramadier insisted that France was not able to examine the sea-worthiness of foreign vessels, and that the passengers to Palestine were concealing their true destination. Bevin was confident that Ramadier had agreed with him that steps must be taken to eliminate the issue of illegal Jewish immigration into Palestine, which was a "potentially serious cause of misunderstanding between the two governments".[15] Nevertheless, a British Government official was impressed that Ramadier had shown less willingness to comply with Bevin's demands than had Bidault (Crossley 1947). In any case, in all his talks with the French leadership on the *President Warfield* issue, Bevin received no clear cut reply to his demand that the ship and her passengers be returned to France.

Britain set off on the wrong foot in her first attempt at implementing the refoulement policy. Bevin's stay in Paris as the *President Warfield* was setting sail for Palestine intensified his personal involvement in the affair, not in the best interests of the British Government, as his verbal negotiations with Bidault resulted in misunderstandings which were later hard to resolve. The French Foreign Minister had overestimated his colleagues' position and did not realize that he was virtually alone in his sympathetic attitude to Britain's requests. And the British wanted the best of both worlds. In Bevin's words to Bidault (both written and spoken), this is the sentence that stands out: "We intended to make an example of this ship by obliging her to return to a French port with all her passengers." To whom was he trying to teach a lesson? To the French the British said that the objective of refoulement was to inhibit the organizers of illegal immigration;[16] in internal correspondence, on the other hand, stress was placed on disinclining the French Government[17] and as a result, the Italian Government as well,[18] from cooperating with the organizers of illegal immigration. The return of the *Exodus* to the port from which she sailed, therefore, had a double, and even triple objective, and Bevin tried, in fact to rope in the French to act against themselves. This fact had not escaped the French.

Notwithstanding the fact that the French response – which did not satisfy the British – was received finally only when the *Exodus'* passengers were making their way westward – back to Europe – the British set about preparing the practical means for instigating their refoulement policies at a time when many details were still unknown. Due to the speed in which the events took place, many of which were not under their control, the British found themselves short of time and acted under pressure. And since this was the first time (and ultimately the last) that their new policy was being instigated, they were not saved the process of trial and error.

Bevin was sure that the action would be more effective and impressive and legally sound if the illegal immigrants were to be returned to France on the *Exodus* herself and not on British deportation ships. The unknown factor in this idea was the condition the ship would be in after being captured close to the Palestine shore, and whether or not she would be capable of making the return journey to France. And if she could, after using the ship's overloading as a propaganda lever against the organizers of the operation, it was clear that it would be impossible to send her back with the same 4,500 passengers on board. Thus, Bevin suggested that some of the illegal immigrants be placed on other ships and be transferred back to the *Exodus* as they enter French territorial waters.[19]

The man responsible for applying the program in the eastern side of the Mediterranean was the British High Commissioner in Palestine, Sir Alan Cunningham. He was asked to make every possible effort to have the *President Warfield* towed back with some of the immigrants on board.[20] The men on the spot in Palestine tried to dissuade London from fulfilling Bevin's plans. They had first-hand experience of the condition the illegal immigration ships arrived in once these had been forcibly apprehended, and were sure that it would be hard to make the ship herself turn back, and anyway she would sail behind the three other ships which had already been prepared to carry the illegal immigrants from Haifa. The High Commissioner had grave doubts as to whether any passengers could remain on the original ship, and he believed that the plan for returning them to the ship at mid-sea, close to the French coast, would be impossible to achieve. At the end of the communiqué in which

Cunningham outlined his reservations about the plan, he let the cat out of the bag. If indeed it was important for all four vessels – the *President Warfield* and the three deportation ships – to arrive in France together, the three would have to be sent to Malta, where they would await the *President Warfield*, since they could not be detained in Haifa.[21] His past experience and familiarity with the conditions in Palestine led him to the conclusion that having three deportation ships waiting, full of illegal immigrants, in Haifa's port was nothing less than a time bomb.

The High Commissioner was keen to have the illegal immigrants leave Haifa as soon as possible, with no delay, and tried to pass the buck to Malta. However, having no legal cover for detaining the immigrants, the British ships bearing them were not permitted to anchor at Malta. There arose an obvious conflict of interests between the various branches of the British administration. While the High Commissioner for Palestine desired to end his part in the affair as quickly as possible, so long as there was a question mark over the position France was taking in the matter, the people at the British Embassy in Paris were playing for time. The delays involved in bringing back the *President Warfield* might have helped in this objective. In their messages to London, they stressed that it was more important to have all the ships arrive in France *together* than to have them arrive *quickly*.[22]

The situation was tenuous and the changes swift. It was soon obvious that from the point of view of impressing the French Government and straightening the legal issues, there was no particular advantage to returning the immigrants on the ship on which they had sailed from France, and the most important issue at hand was the actual return of the passengers. Within a few days the time element also became of significant importance. On 16 July information came from the British embassy in Paris to London, that although the immigrants must not be returned to France too early, and certainly not before a decision had been taken by the French Government, they must also not be too far from the shores of France when the French decide to accept them back.[23] In view of the general technical difficulties involved in bringing back the ship, and especially in a convoy with the three deportation ships, the new evaluation caused the idea of bringing back the ship to be discarded, although it was still considered of psychological significance for the organizers of the "illicit traffic". Two days before the battle between the *Exodus* and ships of the British fleet opposite the shores of Palestine, it was decided in London that there was no need to return the ship if she could not be used as transport for the immigrants back to France.[24]

The idea of returning the immigrants to France in two waves was rejected because of the fear that the public outcry which would inevitably follow the first wave would probably cancel the French agreement before the arrival of the second wave. Either way, it was clear to the British that the French Government's agreement to receive the ship's passengers would be condemned by Zionist circles in France, but the matter would be forgotten soon enough, once it became an established fact.[25]

The fear that the Jews would act in France to reverse the Government's decision before the operation was completed, increased the necessity for correct timing between taking the decision and the arrival of the deportation ships in France.[26] The British were especially worried at having their plans leaked and published, since this could have resulted in Zionist pressure on the Government of France before a decision had been reached to accept the refugees back. The success of the operation therefore, depended on its being kept a secret to the last moment. The Secretary of State for the Colonies made it clear to the High Commissioner that "provided there was no leakage of information from French sources, it seems important to keep the destination of the convoy secret, if possible, until its final arrival in France."[27] The Secretary instructed him not to release any information on the destination of the ships, not even if questions are raised in London and Palestine, once it became clear that the ships were not on their way to Cyprus.[28]

The French did their best to keep matters correct and to cool the enthusiasm of the British, who were acting as if an agreement had already been reached in principle and only the details had yet to be settled. They explained to the British that no ministerial meeting had taken place following Bevin's request to Bidault the day after the *Exodus* had sailed from the port of Sete. The matter had been passed on to the French Prime Minister, and although Bidault and Bevin saw eye-to-eye on the issue of returning the *Exodus*, this did not constitute official French Government approval until Prime Minister Ramadier's authorization had been received. There was even a word of friendly advice to the British from the French Foreign Office, suggesting that it would be to their advantage not to begin discussions on the practical arrangements for receiving the immigrants, before the actual return had been approved by Ramadier. Premature discussions, it was suggested, might have revealed the practical difficulties involved in returning the immigrants, and have a derogatory effect on the nature of the decision.[29]

The British found themselves in something of a trap. The success of the operation depended on its swift execution but the French Government was prevaricating. Too much pressure might have brought about undesirable results. By bringing in the ships on the basis of a promise made to Bevin by Bidault, thus presenting the French with a *fait accompli*, would most likely cause a situation whereby the first time that France was cooperating – albeit unwillingly – in preventing the use of her ports for illegal immigration to Palestine, would also be the last.[30] Time was running out. The ship was scheduled to arrive at Haifa on Friday 18 July. Her passengers had to leave Haifa within 48 hours. And by Thursday 17 July, there had still been no reply from the French.[31]

6 · Seven Days on the Seven Seas

There is little doubt that anyone among the some 4,500 illegal immigrants on the ship that was to go down in posterity as the *Exodus 1947*, knew who the President was, after whom the ship had originally been named *President Warfield*. It was indeed rather a strange name and sometimes a confusing one. For example, when the ship got caught up in a storm at sea in late February 1947 on her way to Europe from the east coast of the United States, the coastguard informed the other ships in the vicinity that they were to rush to the help of the *President Garfield* (Holly 1969, 155). However, the ship had not been named after the American President James Abram Garfield, who served a six month term of office in 1881, but for Solomon Davies Warfield, former President of the Baltimore Steam Packet Company, for whom the ship had been built during the 1920s (Holly 1969, 8).

The name which the ship had borne ever since her launching on 6 February 1928, was about to disappear from the world. Once the illegal immigration operation into Palestine had been renewed, soon after the end of the Second World War, all the ships used in this operation were given Hebrew names. The renaming of the ships was no simple matter to a society such as the Yishuv, which attached enormous importance to the spoken and written word, no less than to symbolism. The Mossad took this task very seriously and established a special committee for this purpose, although it is no secret that in many cases the Mossad head personally conceived the ships' names. When, in December 1947, the time had come to choose names for the largest of the illegal immigration ships, the honor of naming them was given to David Ben-Gurion, "Prime Minister of the State in Making", who dubbed them *Kibbutz Galuyot* (Ingathering of the exiles) and *Atzma'ut* (Independence). Ordinary Mossad activists, Palmach members and the illegal immigrants themselves found themselves with no say in the matter.

The symbolism surrounding illegal immigration activity was deeply rooted in the Palestinian Jewish experience. Of the 64 Mossad ships used in illegal immigration during the three years following the end of the Second World War, only two were given names which raised associations relating to the Diaspora: *Mordei Hageta'ot* (Ghetto Resistance Fighters) and *Yehuda Halevi* (which sailed out of North Africa, bearing the name of the renowned twelfth-century Hebrew poet and philosopher). A further two were given names with universal meanings and connotations. One – *Arba ha-Heruyot* (The Four Freedoms), which sailed in August 1946, the fifth anniversary of the Atlantic Charter; and the other – *Exodus 1947*. Most of the names given to the illegal immigration ships were aimed at the Jews in Palestine – to reinforce their spirit and to make them rally round in support of the national struggle. Some names went side by side with the struggle against the British (for example: *Latrun* and *Rafiah* were named after the detention camps in which some of the Yishuv leaders had been detained, together with hundreds of Haganah members during the summer of 1946). In other cases they served as slogans, used to raise morale, such as: *Lo Tafchidunu* (You can't frighten us), *Le-Komemiyut* (To independence), *La-Nitzahon* (To the victory) and *Af-Al-Pi-Khen* (In Spite of that – in response to the expulsion of the *Exodus* immigrants to Germany). Some ships honored the founding fathers of the Zionist Movement, its leaders and supporters, or those people from the Yishuv who fell in the Second World War (Hannah Senesh, Enzo Sereni, Haviva Reik, Katriel Yaffe and Amiram Shochat) and those who had been killed in operations related to illegal immigration (the ship *Bracha Fold* had been named after the Palmach member killed in a skirmish with the British army in March 1946, and the *Shabtai Lojinsky* for an emissary who was killed in a traffic accident in Italy). Of the dozen Jews – 11 illegal immigrants and one American crew member – who were killed in clashes with the British off the Palestine coast, and the eight immigrants from the ship *Rafiah* who drowned at sea,[1] not one had the honor of having an Aliyah Bet ship named for him (Halamish 1988, 56–57).

A list of names to be given to future illegal immigration ships was sent by Mossad headquarters in Palestine to the Mossad in France during the last week of May 1947. The list included such names as: *Nitzolei ha-Tofet ha-Nazi* (Survivors of the Nazi inferno), *Atzma'ut Yehudit* (Jewish independence), *Ha-Noded ha-Nitzchi* (The eternal wanderer), *Shivat Zion* (Return to Zion), *Ha-Tnu'ah ha-Tziyonit* (The Zionist Movement), *Geula* (Redemption). A subcommittee was appointed whose task it was to propose additional names.[2] Nonetheless, the first ship to set sail after the arrival of the list bore a name that was not included in it. The process of choosing the name *Exodus 1947* had been rather unconventional. It was proposed by Moshe Sneh, head of the Political Department for Europe and of the Aliyah Bet department in the Jewish Agency Executive, who was staying in Paris at the time. The Mossad in Paris, who thought the name was perfect for such an enormous (by current standards) ship adopted the proposed name immediately (Zameret 1964; Slutzky 1972a, 1153).

On 11 July, the Mossad in France informed the Tel Aviv HQ that the *President Warfield* would from then on be known as *Exodus 1947*.[3] This information did not reach the ears of the ship's passengers. On the third day of the voyage, the crew broadcast an urgent message to the Mossad HQ in Tel Aviv: "Please advise us immediately as to our Hebrew name," and included a few suggestions to this end.[4] The immigrants suggested calling the ship *Mordechai Anielewicz*, after the commander of the Warsaw Ghetto uprising. The American crew members preferred *Roosevelt*, although it is unclear whether this was in honor of the late American President (which would have been compatible with her original, presidential, name) or in respect for his widow, Eleanor, who was a supporter of Zionism and much admired by the Jews of the United States. The ship's escorts from Palestine proposed the name *Ha-Meri ha'Ivri* (the Hebrew resistance) (Einav 1964; Roseman 1984; Peker 1985; Har'el testimony).

The reply from the Mossad's Tel Aviv HQ the following night was quite different and uncompromising: "Your name is going to be *Exodus 1947*, in Hebrew you will be known as *Yetz'iat* (*sic*) *Tashaz*. Both names are to appear simultaneously."[5] The Hebrew version of the name (Yetzi'at Eiropa Tashaz) had probably been determined in Palestine; from France, as mentioned, came only the name *Exodus 1947*. And of course the ship could not remain with such a foreign-sounding name, and a Hebrew name had to be found which would both conform with tradition and appeal to the Yishuv in Palestine.

The name, however, did not appeal to the Palestinian team escorting the ship. So unimpressed were they by it that they did not even take the trouble of informing the immigrants themselves of the name of the ship they were traveling on. The ship's sophisticated loudspeaker system broadcast various culture and entertainment programs to raise the morale of her passengers and to help pass away the time. Announcements were broadcast periodically and there were special notices regarding the impending battle with the British and the planned dash-for-shore. No mention was made of the ship's new name and most of the immigrants first heard it in the broadcast from the ship to the Yishuv, on the evening of Thursday, 17 July 1947 (Dror 1961, 616; Perlov n.d., 125).

When, then, were the ship's name and flags changed? Usually this was done as late in the operation as possible. In this case the changeover took place right at the beginning of the battle, since so long as the ship was outside of Mandatory Palestine's territorial waters, she was still officially a Honduran ship on her way to Istanbul. On Thursday morning, the commander of the British forces escorting the ship noticed that she was bearing her original name and flying a Honduran flag.[6] When she sailed into the port of Haifa on Friday afternoon, she was flying the Jewish national flag and there was a large banner at her center declaring that she was HAGANAH SHIP: EXODUS 1947. Her original name, *President Warfield* remained on the ship's prow.

When the name *Exodus* hit the headlines, it was thoroughly internalized by the press and the public alike. It's quite amusing to consider what the international media would have made of a ship with a name like *Lo Tafchidunu* or *Sh'ar Yishuv*, both of which are very meaningful in Hebrew but are totally untranslatable into any other language. Under the circumstances, the choice of *Exodus* was very expedient. Moshe Shertok (later Sharett), head of the Jewish Agency's political department, described it as "a stroke of genius, a name which by itself, says more than anything which has ever been written about it" (Zionist General Council 1947). In America, the name was well and truly absorbed and even President Truman soon heard rumors about a ship called *Exodus* (*FRUS* 1947, 1138–39). The French, too, tended to make use of the ship's new name, to the great consternation of the British, who always made a point of calling her the *President Warfield*. A British Foreign Office official was roundly reprimanded for mistakenly inserting the name *Exodus* into a report he had written.[7] On this particular issue, the Mossad people found themselves surprisingly on the side of the British. In their internal documents, they continued to refer to the ship as *The President*, even after the new name had been adopted. It would seem that such a presidential name represented the ship's elevated status as the flagship of the entire illegal immigration fleet.

The journey of the *Exodus* eastward from France to Haifa was a relatively swift and easy affair. It had taken *Knesset Israel*, with some 4,000 illegal immigrants on board, 19 days in November 1946 to reach Haifa from Yugoslavia, as opposed to the seven days *Exodus* spent on the high seas before the battle, arriving at the port of Haifa on the eighth. It was crowded on board, but no more so than on other ships. At the time, *Exodus* carried a record number of illegal immigrants, but she was also larger than all her predecessors. The close and crowded conditions on the ship were described in much the same way by the Palestinian escorts and the immigrants themselves. Zvi Katzanelson ("Miri"): "We received them and we began shoving them in, helped by officers and sailors and the rest of the crew" (1985). The immigrant, Yosef Leichter: "As soon as each of us was allotted his own space, he was expected to thread his way in with his parcel and stay there" (1985). Another immigrant, Yehuda Peker: "There were ushers there, who made sure that everything was in order, they sent some of the people away, so it wouldn't be too crowded, and ordered people to enter the holes ... not to wander around, not to linger in the alleyways" (1985). There were all sorts of logistical problems in organizing and settling so large a mass of people, but all in all, the space allotted to each individual immigrant was no smaller than that on other illegal immigrant ships. Even though several bunks got damaged during the loading and immigrants were housed in holds at the bottom of the ship, a telegram was sent out at nine p.m. on the day of sailing: "Everything is OK. The vessel is perfectly stable. We can still take on up to 1,300 more people."[8]

This message, like the use of food supplies as ammunition in the course of the battle with the British, show that there was no lack of food on board. The ship was loaded with enough supplies to last for 14 days, the kitchens were large, with good refrigerators and up-to-date cooking facilities. All these allowed the preparation of large quantities of food, which was varied, nutritious and tasty – compared with that on the other ships. Food distribution was carried out with speed and efficiency. There were, of course, cases of elbowing and queue jumping, but these were because of the passengers' past experiences and had nothing to do with any kind of food shortage. In addition to the solid food, the immigrants were supplied with hot drinks twice daily and at lunch time they were given soup. Each immigrant was given a one-liter glass bottle, which was filled daily with drinking water. Washing was done in salt water.

As mentioned, the immigrants were prepared in advance for conditions on board ship. Ushers maintained order. Traffic along the pathways between bunks was one-way only, in order to avoid traffic jams. Even the most elementary things had been taken into consideration. For example, people took it in turn to watch over the lavatories, to hand out toilet paper, to make sure that the bowls remained unblocked after use and to go in and clean the place from time to time. The clean-lavatory project was crowned with success. The British military physician, who came on board after the battle, found the ship in a much better condition than he had expected. Admittedly (he reported) it was badly overcrowded, but hygiene was satisfactory, and the passengers, especially the children, seemed clean. He was surprised, because it seemed to him that the ship's sanitary equipment did not appear sufficient for 5,000 passengers (Bett 1947). There were only thirteen lavatories on board the *Exodus*.[9]

There were problems. But this is not surprising in so large a community, of whom many were not only sailing for the first time in their lives, but for whom this was only the first time they had set eyes on the sea! One of the counselors with the "Dror" children's house reported:

> Our day to day life begins down in the cellar. Hundreds of people trapped in that narrow cellar. A motley crowd, unused to mutual consideration and certainly not to cooperation. If you told the children to lie down on the shelves, they would obey and lie down. But try telling something like that to one of the "individuals" – and these are the majority of the people here. They wonder around at their pleasure, stand for hours beside the small window, taking up the last of the air from the remaining passengers down in the cellar. Women hang their underwear out to dry on the edges of their shelves, thus blocking out the air for the rest of us, which is not pure anyway, and lots of other troubles of this sort (Habbas 1954, 272).

The counselor goes on to tell how the immigrants didn't always listen to their ushers, but when the Haganah people went down to sort things out, it did help, if only for a while. There were only half-a-dozen Palestinians on board ship. They were introduced to the immigrants over the loudspeakers system – each according to his nickname and task on board ship: "Amnon – Haganah appointed commander; Miri – in charge of food and water supplies; Gad – law and order and security; Uri – radio operator; Sima – first aid and child care. The ship's captain is Yitzhak, from Palestine – a member of Haganah."

The same broadcast also mentioned the American sailors and workers on board ship and the "enormous efforts invested by the Haganah, the Yishuv and the Jews of America" in acting out this "tremendous operation which involves the removal of thousands of Jews from Germany" (Habbas 1954, 224).

It is interesting to note that, while the men were introduced by their "underground" nicknames, Sima, the only woman in the team, was presented by her real name. The captain was also introduced by his own name, which might point to his not-quite-defined status on the ship. He was not an escort according to the accepted definition of the word, nor was he "simply" a captain, but a Haganah man. Whereas they were all – the Mossad people as well as the Palmachniks – members of the Haganah; Aharonowitz and the rest of the escorts with the exception of the commander, belonged first and foremost to the Palmach. The "lads" from the Palmach, who, during their activity in the illegal immigration operation, were under the command of the Mossad, maintained their own *esprit de corps* throughout. Thus, on 13 July the escorts on board the *Exodus*, according to naval tradition, sent a telegram to their friends in the Palyam (the naval branch of the Palmach), which read: "To all those raising a toast on the 13th – best wishes from the *President*'s people."[10]

The escorts were helped by the American crew members and the immigrants' secretariats in ensuring that life on board ship went on in as orderly and comfortable a way as possible. The ship had a sophisticated loudspeaker system, but there was no one among the escorts who could speak the language of the immigrants. When they were still in Sete, representatives of the movements were called to the microphone to broadcast their information to their people, in their language. Afterwards, a timetable was created, by which each movement was allotted a fair share of broadcasting time. There was even a handwritten "wall bulletin" published on *Exodus*, with news, information, poems, etc.

On the first day out of port, the ship's commander noticed the separate groups (minyans) of people at prayer. This was typical of the period following the Second World War. An atmosphere prevailed of "all Jews are comrades", one for all and all for one, and this went hand in hand with clannish sectarianism, separatism and deep loyalty to the group and the party. Where the Exodus Affair was concerned, this was generally commendable. No real feelings of tension were evident between the various groups while the ship was making her way eastward and the fact that people were divided into groups was helpful both from an organizational point of view and for the good feeling this gave their members.

Life on board ship went on in an orderly and well-organized manner throughout the seven day sea voyage, the internal radio programs and other cultural activities helped pass the time away pleasantly for the immigrants and the ship was well stocked with food, water and medical supplies. The British doctor was impressed that from a medical point of view, the ship was well prepared to cope with casualties. There was a first aid station on each of the decks and a hospital had been set up in the stern. These facilities were manned by male and female medics. He found a large quantity of bandages, plaster of Paris, morphine and plenty of additional equipment for looking after casualties, but very little else (Bett 1947).

Up to the night of the battle, the medical team had been employed mostly in supplying pre-natal care to the pregnant women and then helping them in childbirth. At ten o'clock on 12 July 1947, the ship sent the happy message to the Mossad in France: "Congratulations. It's a boy. Both mother and son are well."[11] The message to the immigrants was: "This morning a baby boy was born on our ship. Let us hope that this child will be a symbol of our unwavering desire to live. We wish the child who was born on the way, to succeed in planting his roots in the earth of our homeland" (Habbas 1954, 225). More babies were born on the short journey between France and Haifa. On 15 July, "one of the women died. Cause of death – complicated childbirth. The baby boy is alive and everything is being done to care for him." Thus the wireless message from the ship to Palestine.[12]

According to Sima, the nurse,

This was an event worth recounting, since it has in it all the tragic history of the Jewish people in our time. The woman had gone into labor the day before the ship set sail and she was admitted to hospital. When her husband learned of the ship's imminent departure, he went to the hospital at night and released her on his own authority. I tried to persuade him to remain behind with her – but he refused, afraid that this would be his last chance to immigrate to Palestine. It was a complicated and difficult birth. We found a thrombosis. And a small and weak baby came into the world …. The poor father felt himself guilty and the double sorrow gnawed at his heart. He begged us to at least save his son's life. But this was no easy matter. Most of the nursing mothers had lost their milk because of the overcrowding and sickness they had suffered. At last I found what I was looking for. At first, the woman refused to help, but I managed to persuade her, by awakening in her latent maternal instinct and by promising to do everything I could to help her. But, by evening, she too succumbed to sea sickness and all my efforts were in vain. A doctor [one of the immigrants], suggested I start feeding the baby with canned milk, the way they had done in Russia during the war. Yossi, the ship's commander, took special interest in the baby's welfare: "we must do all we can to keep him alive" – he would say over and over again. But – how? Who was going to want to take care of him? In the end I found a woman of about 60, a gynecologist from Russia, a good person, and she agreed to take responsibility for the child, and for this reason she was allowed to remain in Palestine and was not obliged to go through the hell of the return to Port de Bouc and Hamburg. (Habbas 1954, 52)

The baby was taken off the ship at Haifa, together with the woman who was looking after him and his father and taken to hospital. But he died just a few weeks later.

The death of the young mother was a painful and heartbreaking experience. "We are mourning the death of the first victim," one of the immigrants wrote in her diary. "A young woman died in childbirth. The baby is alive. The funeral was heartrending. The guard of honor consisted of the ship's crew. The body was covered in the blue and white flag. The Captain [in fact, the commander] said a few words in Hebrew, we all stood in silence for a minute, and the body was lowered slowly into the sea. Throughout the ceremony, the woman's husband stood supported by two sailors. The sight of his tears tore at our hearts" (Diary 1947a).

Most of the immigrants were still unaware that anyone had died, even as the funeral service was taking place. Only the following day they heard about it, from the ship's loudspeakers and from the wall bulletins.

Paula Abramowitz was the first victim of the Exodus Affair, and she would not be the last.

7 · *The Battle*

Until the middle of August 1946, the Mossad had not been disposed for a physical confrontation with British attempts at overpowering its ships. Apart from the actual sea journey and all the attendant suffering, the immigrants were not expected to participate in a physical struggle and even those who were captured and imprisoned at Atlit were released shortly afterward. When it became apparent that the British were planning to deport to Cyprus the immigrants on ships anchored at the port of Haifa during the first half of August 1946, the Mossad ordered that passive resistance be used while the immigrants were being transferred to the deportation ships. Immediately on release of the official British announcement, that all captured illegal immigrants would in future be deported to Cyprus, the Palmach HQ devised a comprehensive plan for resistance, most of which was approved by the authorized Zionist bodies. The plan included fortifying the ships and resisting being overtaken at sea; organizing the immigrants to oppose attempts on the part of the British soldiers to board the ships, by using stones, sticks, cans of food etc., but to avoid the use of firearms; dodging enemy ships and landing on a sand bank close to a Jewish settlement, where the immigrants could disembark; passive resistance on the part of the immigrants to being transferred to deportation ships at Haifa and on disembarking in Cyprus; damaging British deportation ships, by setting off small explosive charges, thus delaying their departure for Cyprus. Palmach HQ also came up with the idea of attacking Royal Naval bases in Palestine and at Mediterranean ports but the Zionist authorities limited this to causing damage to British vessels involved in chasing illegal immigration ships and transporting immigrants from Palestine to Cyprus (Allon 1953, 581–82).

The Mossad accepted the resistance program, although somewhat less enthusiastically than the Palmach. Usually it was the Palmach that pushed for stronger expressions of resistance, while the Mossad served as a moderating influence. There were several reasons for the differences in opinion between the Palmach and the Mossad. First, the two organizations did not see eye-to-eye on the emphases that had to be given to the objectives of illegal immigration. The Mossad's main concern was to bring Jews to Palestine – Holocaust survivors, citizens of Eastern European countries, where there was an imminent threat of an Iron Curtain blocking their way to Palestine, as well as North African communities. The Palmach, on the other hand, was more involved than the Mossad with the political implications of illegal immigration and their protest value.

Second, there was the delegation of work in the immigration operations and the definitions of tasks. The ship's commander, who was responsible for the immigrants' welfare and their passage to Palestine, was a Mossad man, whereas the responsibility for organizing resistance fell within the scope of the Palmach. Moreover, the Mossad people differed from the Palmachniks in several ways: a. age – the Mossad people were usually older than the Palmachniks; b. background – most of the Mossad people had themselves immigrated from Europe, while the Palmachniks were mostly Palestine-born, or had immigrated at a tender age; c. training and experience – a great many of the Mossad people had been involved in saving Jews before and during the Second World War, and were well versed in methods of conspiracy, whereas training received by the Palmachniks had been mainly military.

Still, it must be stressed that the Palmach people active in illegal immigration operations were under the sole authority of the Mossad, even if they were inspired by other sources and had moral obligations to their comrades. The Head of the Mossad summed up in retrospect the relationship between the members of the two organizations: "The two generations complemented each other in this vital operation. Activity was not always easy or harmonious, although in the final analysis, each generation made its own contribution" (Habbas 1954, iv).

A turning point was reached during the summer of 1946, not only in the history of illegal immigration, but in the overall struggle against the British. The blowing up of the King David Hotel in Jerusalem on 22 July was the final act of The Hebrew Resistance Movement, in which the three organizations – Haganah, IZL and Lehi – cooperated under a common command. Shortly thereafter, the Jewish Agency Executive decided to transfer the focus of the struggle for Palestine to the political arena; thus illegal immigration, which heretofore had been but one part of a wide front of struggle, remained, in fact, the only sphere of activity left to the organized Yishuv against the British. Paradoxically, however, since August 1946, the Yishuv had almost completely stopped taking part in illegal immigration activity. The demonstrations which took place in Haifa, on the day immigrants began being deported to Cyprus – during which three protesters were killed – were the last manifestation of mass efforts on behalf of illegal immigration. It was widely noticed that since the summer of 1946 most of the struggle against the British was being borne by the illegal immigrants themselves.

The poet Nathan Alterman, who followed the events closely, gave the issue expression in his "Seventh Column" poems in the daily *Davar*, the most widely circulated Hebrew newspaper of the time. His poem: "Division of Duties", which was published at the end of 1946, under the headline: "Resistance of the immigrants on the *Knesset Israel* was broken with smoke bombs" was particularly cutting in its criticism of the Yishuv. The poem describes a little illegal immigrant girl, choking on the fumes, desperately trying to reach fresh air;

> But then she remembered that I, the Yishuv!
> Had ordered: Halt! Don't move! …
> Do not go willingly! Fight it!
> Resist!
> … And maybe she'll make the same reckoning with me:
> What part was placed that day in her hands,
> And what part did I take on myself? …
> And she'll say, in the name of all her friends, the infants,
> That the Yishuv has no right to demand from her
> What it fails to demand of itself, and its children.

The poem ends by determining that the division of duties in the struggle was not done necessarily "according to division of strength" (13 Dec. 1946).

The daily *Ha-Aretz*, with its consistent stand against violence, identified in a late May 1947 editorial with the illegal immigrants on the ships *Ha-Tikvah* and *Mordei ha-Geta'ot*, who decided not to resist the British. "The Yishuv and all people of goodwill laud them for this decision … no matter what form the Yishuv's resistance takes against the rules of the Government, we cannot coerce them, the immigrants, into fulfilling it. They have done their part by the very act of illegal immigration" (26 May 1947).

The Palmachniks, on the other hand, were dissatisfied with the minor tone which characterized the resistance. They told Ben-Gurion exactly three months prior to *Exodus*' struggle opposite the shores of Palestine, that as far as they were concerned, illegal immigration was too small in scope, and resistance to the immigrants' deportation to Cyprus was altogether insufficient; response to British policy on illegal immigration did not have to be confined to the port of Haifa, but the British had to be beaten abroad as well, and the entire matter of illegal immigration had to be removed from the Mossad and placed in the hands of the Palmach (Ben-Gurion Diaries, 17 April 1947). The Palmach commander, Yig'al Peikovitz, had visited Europe shortly before, where he met Palmach sailors, who expressed similar sentiments. On his return to Palestine, he tried to influence the Yishuv leadership to increase the scope of illegal immigration and the role played by the Palmach in this, but to no avail (Allon 1947, 838).

Peikovitz at that time, was concerned by the decreased level of resistance shown by the immigrants during the spring of 1947. At first (27 May 1947), he sent a telegram to the Palmachniks in Italy and France, reminding them that "my order regarding unarmed resistance to the capture of our ships and the transfer [of immigrants] to deportation ships, still holds" (Gil'ad 1953, 637), and then sent them a long and detailed letter (Allon 1947). He believed that the almost entire drop in resistance on the most recent immigrant ships was misinterpreted, both by the Yishuv and by the British, and saw fit, therefore, to "remind you of my opinion, in order to make you understand our stand, that unarmed resistance must be exhibited, and that it must be as firm and as prolonged as possible". He listed the excuses for not exercising resistance as he had heard them from the ships' escorts: inactivity on the part of the Yishuv; a fear of casualties; the fact that resistance was virtually ineffective; the humiliation of being dragged off to the deportation ships and a lack of enthusiasm among the immigrants to take part in the struggle.

One after the other, Peikovitz rejected these excuses, stressing the vital importance of resistance on the immigrants' part, since this "is one of the last vestiges of our war on foreign rule, the Jewish people's fight for their existence". However, he went on, "wherever possible, we must avoid shedding the blood of our adversary, so as not to give him justification for murdering immigrants." Yet, casualties are sometimes inevitable and there was a demanding tone to Peikovitz's explanation to his subordinates that "yes, my comrades, with all my own personal sense of responsibility, I would say: there must be resistance, in spite of possible casualties." Of course, it would be better to have this resistance take the form of a program in which the immigrants are taken off the ship, as she is stuck on a sand bank, but "resisting capture by the British, whatever form this takes, is in itself a definite objective".

One might ask: "Why bother to resist if deportation to Cyprus is inevitable?" Peikovitz admitted that the British would succeed in overpowering all the ships and deporting all their passengers. Still, "First and foremost, resistance has a purposeful objective – to prevent, as far as possible, any further measures being taken against illegal immigration." Also, resistance has the power "to make the process of deportation as difficult as possible, since this, anyway, is one of the less pleasant tasks an oppressive administration has to fulfill. Now and then, resistance has to rekindle the support of our people in the Diaspora, who might be able to help us and to awaken the conscience of those nations of the world who have not yet lost theirs." Also: "There is an historical-educational, political and moral aspect involved here. It is inconceivable that Jews be dispelled from this country, without doing their utmost to resist." Finally, he repeated: "Resistance must be continued, therefore, under all circumstances. This letter is both an explanation and an order."

The letter almost certainly did not arrive in Europe before Exodus set sail (Aran 1985; Har'el 1985; Katzanelson 1985; Perry 1985), but its spirit was known to those emissaries accompanying the ship and they identified with it. Many of the immigrants anticipated a struggle and were ready and willing to take part in it, in the spirit of ha-Shomer ha-Tza'ir's order of the day.

And the ship? For months the teams from Palestine and America, together with the Mossad in America and Europe, assisted by local workers, had been working to reinforce her, to make her battle-worthy.

When it came to resistance, the *President Warfield* had several advantages. She was high, so much so that some of her decks were even higher above sea level than those of the British destroyers, a fact which would make it hard for the British seamen to storm her. The ship was powerful. Her nether parts were made of steel, an important advantage when being rammed by a war ship. She could dodge these ships thanks to her ability to work up a speed of 20 knots for a short while, and, being flat-bottomed, she was able to get up close to shore and hole up on a sand bank, where the British ships could not reach her. The *President*'s dodge and break-through program was based first of all on the hypothesis that the British would not try to sink the ship and on the certainty that they would never sacrifice one of their own ships in a chase after an illegal immigration ship, in other words – their ships would never reach the spot where the *President* could already be stuck on a sand bank close to shore, by which time she would have completed her task and her life. The team working on her had made careful checks of her dimensions and found that she was sturdy and that there was no danger of her overturning while digging into the sea bed close to shore (Aran 1985).

Special efforts were made, in preparing the ship, on reinforcing her, with the express purpose of preventing, or at least seriously hindering, British soldiers from boarding her. The ship was ringed with metal pipes, with holes 60 centimeters apart, whose purpose was to release steam in the direction of the British warships. Another pipe was meant to spray out boiling oil. The machine room, steam room, wheel house and radio room were covered with wire, in order to ward off an attack of smoke and tear gas grenades and reinforced in such a way as to prevent soldiers from bursting in. All the decks below the boat deck were covered with nets and barbed wire and other obstacles.

Her size and shape and her long journey from the United States to Europe and between the ports of Italy and France under the wary eyes of the British, made it impossible for her to ever reach the shores of Palestine unnoticed. Indeed, even as the immigrants were boarding her at the port of Sete, a British plane was circling overhead, and a short distance out at sea, a British Naval warship was lying in wait for her. On the first evening of her voyage, the *President* reported that a destroyer was "following us. She tried speaking to us. But we did not reply. For the time being, she's not doing anything. Only following us from a distance of five miles." The next day the ship reported: "The little bitch is still following us," and the same afternoon she was joined by "a four-engine airplane. The airplane is in contact with the destroyer." On Saturday evening the destroyer following the *President* since she exited the port of Sete was replaced by another destroyer, apparently because the Isle of Malta was a boundary for the various British Naval forces in the Mediterranean. On 13 July (Sunday) the *President* reported: "Today at 12 o'clock a cruiser joined our escort. The airplane has left. We are now being escorted by one destroyer and one cruiser."[1] On the morning of Thursday 17 July, they were joined by four more destroyers.[2]

So, the *Exodus* was not destined to sneak out toward the shores of Palestine, but to burst openly through the blockade, by dodging and swiftly nipping through, beaching herself on a sand bank and letting off her cargo of immigrants on the beach. But an alternative program had been prepared in the event that the British tried to overpower the ship. On the way to Palestine the crew had been busy sealing off the lower decks and the entrances with fences and nets. The ship's arsenal – piles upon piles of food cans, potatoes, bottles and other objects – was concentrated in various places on board. The ship was divided into sections, each of which was manned by a group, usually of members of the same movement, and each group had its own commander. They went through practice routines, each fighter taking up his post as soon as warning sirens were sounded.

Throughout the week of the voyage, the resistance and breakthrough plans were thoroughly processed and as the ship got closer to the shores of Palestine, more and more changes were made in the plans. It was planned at first that the ship should arrive from the south, and if she was ordered by a British destroyer to sail to Haifa, she would do so. Under these circumstances, she would sail at a distance of about six miles from shore, so as to be able, in a quick maneuver, to mount a sand bank within half an hour. The orders were to have all the boats and rafts ready for action, and if the ship should get close to shore, these vessels would be used in unloading passengers and transferring them to land. Those of the immigrants who were strong swimmers would jump off and swim to shore. The order was that life belts were to be supplied and ropes had to be prepared, so these could be stretched quickly from the vessel to shore. In the event of enemy disturbance, the ship would have to continue to follow orders from inland, although the possibility was considered that the operation would not take place at all, in which case orders were issued on hiding the ship's crews and making arrangements for escorting the immigrants to Cyprus.[3]

The escorts reckoned on Monday 14 July that the ship would be arriving at Tel Aviv on Thursday at eleven o'clock in the morning. Based on this assessment, a plan for disembarkation was made up, for Thursday 17 July between six and seven o'clock in the evening. From Palestine came the information that they were "preparing a beach head". But, to be on the safe side, they added: "In the event that you will be unable to get away, resistance must be exercised as usual."[4] Bad weather slowed the ship down and a day before the expected landing, the crew informed their counterparts in Palestine that "it is doubtful that we shall be able to land on Thursday." This delay caused considerable concern on shore: "Has the ship been damaged in any way yesterday?" "The machines are fine," came the reply. "The delay started because of a leak ... we were held up because we've been waiting for the concrete to dry."[5] That same day the ship's escorts announced a proposed amendment to their disembarkation program. The escorts, most of whom were very familiar with the Tel Aviv coast, proposed landing opposite the end of Nordau Street, north of the point determined by the Mossad, where they would come to a halt some 250 meters from the beach.[6]

From then on the plans went haywire and disagreement was rife among the escorts and people on land, as to the best time and place at which to land on the beach. For two days telegrams were flying back and forth from ship to shore and changes were made and remade (Exodus File a), but in the end a plan was finalized, which was in fact very similar to the original one, including these details: The ship would journey northward from Egypt at a significant distance from the territorial waters of Palestine, and turn right at full speed, opposite Tel Aviv, dodge the British escort and arrive at Tel Aviv beach on Friday 18 July at around nine o'clock in the morning. If she is attacked by the British ships, she will defend herself and endeavor to prevent British troops from boarding her and try to sneak her way toward Tel Aviv, after responding to the British demand that she set sail for Haifa. She will then board a sand bank near Tel Aviv beach and all her passengers will disembark – either by swimming, or rowing ashore in boats and rafts, or with the help of ropes. The beach will be full of local people, there to help the immigrants, and the immigrants will be able to mingle and get swallowed up among the crowds on the beach (Exodus File a; Diary 1947a, 16 July 1947; Aran 1985; Har'el 1985; Perry 1985).

From the perspective of 50 years, there is little relevance to the question, did this plan stand a chance? But that does not mean that we cannot wonder if the people involved at the time – the Mossad and the Palmach people on the ship and in Palestine, and the immigrants themselves – believed that there was a chance that the plan could succeed. Moreover, had all the necessary arrangements been made to ensure its success?

Among the immigrants there were those who believed that they would succeed in entering Palestine without being caught. Some of them were willing to swim to shore. Others, and it seems that they were the majority, did not harbor too many hopes that they would manage to escape and they packed their belongings, so as to have with them the bare necessities for the first few days in Cyprus (Diary 1947a, 16, 17 July). The ship's escorts, notwithstanding all their enthusiasm and determination to accomplish the disembarkation, for whose location, timing and character they were mostly responsible, did not give too much thought to its outcome, since they knew that once they landed, responsibility would be handed over to on-shore command.

And on land? Were practical preparations being made for disembarking the immigrants on the beach at Tel Aviv? A thorough and critical analysis of what has been written so far on the subject, shows that no real preparations were made in anticipation of the ship's arrival (Allon 1953, 529–613; Kol Israel 1964; Derogy 1972, 136; Slutzky 1972a, 1156). It was only at noon on Friday that the Yishuv joined in the struggle, after news arrived of the battle on board the *Exodus* and its toll. Why were no real preparations made on the beach and why did the Mossad's Tel Aviv HQ make last-minute changes in the original plan, if they had no intention of carrying them out?

On Thursday 17 July, at four o'clock in the afternoon, instructions were dispatched to the ship in the name of Haganah chief, Israel Galilee, calling for the immigrants to be disembarked the following night (Friday) at Bat-Yam, south of Tel Aviv. If the ship was unsuccessful in reaching Bat-Yam at night, she was to make it to Tel Aviv, as early as possible during the day, and a crowd would be waiting to try to bring the immigrants on to the beach. If the ship did not succeed in sidling her way into Tel Aviv, a further attempt must be made to sneak her into the Haifa area.[7]

Immediately after this, three telegrams were sent to the ship from the Mossad HQ, regarding the broadcast to the Yishuv. The first telegram provided technical instructions, such as time of the broadcast, the wavelength to be used, opening sentences and the correct distance at which the reader should be seated from the microphone. The second telegram listed the subjects to be included in the broadcast: the suffering of the immigrants and their passionate desire to get to Palestine; protest at the British Government's closed-gate policy in Palestine; a call for United Nations intervention; a call for public solidarity with the immigrants (at the same time, there were to be *absolutely* no instructions issued to this same public, nor must it be called on to take action); and an announcement that illegal immigration activity would continue. A further telegram was sent out immediately after this, with more details on one of the issues in the previous list: "Send a message to the United Nations demanding that they come to the ship to collect live testimonies, before the Committee leaves the country."[8]

As we have seen, UNSCOP did not affect the timing of the *Exodus*. The first hint of the idea to take advantage of the ship in making an impression on the UN committee may have been included in the message to the vessel from France, two days after setting out to sea: "It is imperative that you speed your voyage to Arnon [Palestine]. The sooner you arrive, the better."[9] About a year and a quarter before, during the visit of the Anglo-American committee, plans had been made to bring the ship *Wingate* to the beach at Tel Aviv and to remove her passengers with the help of crowds of Tel Avivians. The Palmach and Haganah were entrusted with sealing off the area and keeping the British forces out, but the ship was apprehended mid-sea, thus frustrating the disembarkation program. Nonetheless, there had been some incidents involving firearms that night, which came to be known as *Wingate* Night, and a female Palmach member was killed. These events increased the tension between the Yishuv and the British authorities (Slutzky 1972a, 874–76). Quite possibly, the presence of UNSCOP in Palestine affected the July 1947 decision not to use crowds in removing the *Exodus* immigrants on the Tel Aviv beach, in the spirit of the informal armistice between the organized Yishuv and the British authorities.

And indeed, no efforts were made to recruit the public to help the *Exodus* immigrants reach land in Tel Aviv. "Ha-Homa" bulletins, dated 17 July, informed the public of the arrival of a ship called *Yetzi'at Eiropa Tashaz* (Exodus from Europe 5707), but no kind of activity was required of them. Instead, they were asked to have their wireless sets turned on on Thursday evening and Friday morning, to wait for a broadcast from the ship (Slutzky 1972a, 1156). Before the broadcast, the ship's crew were given specific instructions "not to give any orders to the public, or to call the public to action". On 15 July the Mossad HQ had informed/ordered the ship: "You can broadcast to the Yishuv, but make no mention of the fact that you intend to come to Zelig [Tel Aviv]." At noon on Friday 18 July, when the ship was making her way to Haifa, following a night of battle, the Mossad repeated the instruction "not to broadcast any call which might be interpreted as orders" (Exodus File a).

This series of orders from shore may indicate that the Zionist leadership wanted to avoid any kind of provocative mass activity during the visit of UNSCOP in the country. This also reinforces the impression that the sides – the Mossad on shore and the ship's escorts – did not see eye-to-eye on the issue of removing the immigrants on the beach. Even though in the end the Mossad informed the ship that it agreed to the escorts' proposals regarding the location of the disembarkation, its timing and the use of crowds, it had, in fact, other plans and these were not revealed to the escorts, probably in an attempt to avoid any further argument. It is possible, too, that the order, which was changed and rechanged on Thursday afternoon, to call upon the United Nations committee to intervene closely, was the result of a decision taken by the Zionist leadership to relinquish the idea of disembarkation on the beach, in favor of all the fuss involved in transferring immigrants to deportation ships in Haifa, before the very eyes of the members of UNSCOP.

For the British, as well as for the Mossad, the *Exodus* was more than just another illegal immigrant ship. The British were determined that this ship was not going to break the blockade. They had to apprehend her, no matter what. Otherwise, how could they realize Bevin's promise/threat to Bidault that they intended to make an example of this ship by obliging her to return to a French port with all her passengers aboard.[10] The British had the element of surprise. They did not publish in advance their intention of returning the *Exodus* immigrants to Europe, and their plans for capturing the ship were kept strictly secret. These plans were aided immeasurably by their familiarity with the *President Warfield* from the days (between 1942–1944) that she had served under a British flag. The destroyers accompanying the ship on her voyage from France to Haifa were equipped with drawings of the ship and their crews were even aware of most of the preparations that had been made on the ship in anticipation of a battle near the Palestine shore. And they were prepared to thwart them (Report on Interception).

The preparations on *Exodus* for the possibility of being overpowered by British soldiers were based, to a great extent, on her height advantage. The destroyers' bow, which rose to about six meters above sea level, were only slightly taller than the foredeck on *Exodus*, and lower by two to four meters than the ship's other decks. The lower and middle decks on *Exodus* were very well protected by nets and fences, but the upper ones remained exposed, on the assumption that the British would have no way of accessing them. This assumption, as it turned out, was mistaken.

Lieutenant Commander E. A. S. Bailey, commander of HMS *Childers* was aware of the advantages *Exodus* had over the destroyers. His calculations showed that the bridge – the tallest construction on the destroyer – was the same height as the *President Warfield*'s boat deck. This deck was the number one objective for overtaking the ship, because this was where the wheel house was located. The destroyer's bridge was situated some two meters from its side and Bailey sought out a way in which a soldier, heavily loaded with equipment, could ford this distance in the short time it would take for the destroyer to come abreast of the immigrant ship. He had the idea of building a construction of boarding platforms, to stretch from the bridge to the destroyer's side, and from which the soldiers would jump onto the exposed, strategically significant upper decks of the *President Warfield*. These boarding platforms were built on to four destroyers and, once these had joined the other destroyers escorting the immigrant ship on Thursday 17 July, they made sure the people on *Exodus* did not see the side which had been prepared for battle (Report on Interception). And indeed the immigrants had no idea of the special arrangements made by their adversaries for storming and taking control of their ship.

On 14 July, after the ship had passed Malta on her way east, the British Naval ships were given an order to begin the process of verbally softening up the passengers. The British informed the immigrants – both in English and German – that, although they did not intend to permit them to land in Palestine, no one wanted to hurt them, but it was the duty of His Majesty's Navy to uphold the law, even if this required the use of force.

Therefore – as they said over loudspeakers from their destroyers – resistance was useless, and would only be harmful. The reply – so the British wrote in their reports – was in "American". On Thursday 17 July, at nine o'clock in the evening, the British ships warned the *Exodus* that they would apprehend her as she entered Palestine territorial waters and proposed that the crew sail her into Haifa of their own accord. The reply to this was a loud, masculine chorus of: "The Yanks are Coming". Unlike on previous nights, the British ships turned off their lights and remained in darkness from then on.

Our information on the tasks entrusted to the fleet escorting *Exodus* comes from a document which had been filed away in the British Archives, and opened for the scrutiny of researchers, despite being clearly marked "Secret (to be destroyed by fire when complied with)". The objective of the operation was the speedy apprehension of the *President Warfield* by placing as many British soldiers as possible on her decks in as short a time as possible. The soldiers' first mission was to capture the navigation bridge and to take control of the ship's course. The start of the operation was set for two o'clock in the morning of 18 July. The major part of the work was given to four destroyers: *Chieftain*, *Chequers*, *Charity* and *Childers*. The destroyer *Cardigan Bay* was ordered to prepare to pull people – soldiers and Jews – out of the water. The cruiser *Ajax*, which was too low and too slow to take part in the storming of the *Exodus*, was ordered to move in between the immigrant ship and shore and to prevent the former from dodging her way on to the beach (Report on Interception). In the course of the operation, the British fleet was joined by the destroyers *Rowena* and *Providence*, bringing to eight the number of battleships responsible for apprehending one illegal immigration ship.

At 01:52 the battle ships were given the order to take up positions for boarding the *President Warfield*. The order for the beginning of the operation was issued at 02:42. At that very moment, the *Exodus* was broadcasting the wireless message: "We are 20 miles west of Gaza."[11] The British ships, which had been in total darkness since nine o'clock in the evening, flooded the *Exodus* at once with giant beams of light from powerful projectors, while their loudspeakers called to "Halt the ship, you are entering territorial waters!"

Where was the ship at that moment? A mid-sea attack on a ship could have seriously embarrassed a naval superpower such as Great Britain, so that the people involved claimed, at the time and afterwards, that the action had taken place legally, and within the Palestine coastal strip.[12] However, internal British reports prove beyond a shadow of a doubt that the attack on *Exodus* began at a time when she was located far away from the territorial waters of Palestine, some 17 or even 20 miles away from shore, at a point from which it was impossible to see lights from any direction.[13] The British admitted to themselves that, in order to prevent the ship from landing on the shores of Palestine, it was necessary to begin placing forces on her while she was still outside territorial waters. There were those who proposed to limit criticism by claiming that they were acting in response to Jewish provocation.[14] Within a few days, an unequivocal directive was sent out to British ambassadors in the world capitals: "The initial stages of this operation did in fact take place outside territorial waters. You should not (repeat not) admit this and should merely decline to comment."[15]

As mentioned, since the end of 1946 discussions had been held in the Cabinet, the Ministries, Ministerial Committees etc. on the issue of intercepting illegal immigration ships mid-sea, but there was always a reluctance to decide on this step. And now, the organizers of "Operation Mae West" were not in the least troubled by the question of the legality of such an action and they simply went ahead with it. The Commander-in-Chief of the British forces in the Mediterranean had no doubt that in order to capture the ship, it would be necessary for him to start acting at a decent distance from the three miles line. No mention is made of this issue in the operation's plans for action.

Although illegal immigrant ships had already in the past been intercepted mid-sea,[16] the people on *Exodus* were surprised by the operation's timing and the location in which it began. The Palestinian escorts had indeed taken into consideration the possibility of the ship being attacked outside territorial waters, but they assumed – although this may have been wishful thinking – that this would be carried out at such a distance from shore that would enable Britain to claim that the ship had already entered territorial waters, and give them (the escorts) a chance to carry out their own breakthrough plan.

The alarm siren was set off at the beginning of the attack and wailed for a long time. Two destroyers sailed up to the immigrant ship on either side, each one with 15 soldiers ready to jump aboard the vessel. The *Exodus* slowed down at once. One of the destroyers "slipped" forward, thus missing the first attack wave.[17] One of the groups of soldiers waiting on the second destroyer failed to jump as planned, since the space onto which they were supposed to jump was well-covered with nets. Another group, consisting of six soldiers, succeeded in jumping toward the ship at 03:05 o'clock from the boarding platforms specially prepared for this purpose, and were smothered in smoke from smoke bombs, tear gas grenades and probably also overhead machine gun fire set off by the British.

The six soldiers landed inside a group of women and children, encountered weak resistance and beat their way, with coshes, toward the wheel house. The ship increased her speed to 13 knots, and commenced violent alterations of course. Within a few minutes the soldiers had taken control of the wheel house, after breaking through the roof with axes. The second officer, Bill Bernstein, was mortally wounded by a blow from an ax. The soldiers threw out the crew, grabbed the steering wheel and turned the ship westward, with the intention of bringing her to a distance of 30 miles from shore. But their control of the ship's course was short-lived. Within minutes, the crew members had disconnected the main steering wheel and Aharonowitz steered the ship with the help of the reserve wheel which had been installed in the ship's rear, for this express purpose.

The six soldiers found themselves facing a strange and dangerous situation. Under siege within the wheel house, surrounded by a furious crowd which was throwing all sorts of objects at them – and they were holding in their hands a "dead" steering wheel. They made use of all the fireworks and gas grenades in their possession and even fired two shots through the open hole at the top of the cabin, and had no choice but to await reinforcements. Which were slow to arrive.

Only at 03:20 a.m. was Lieutenant MacPherson, commander of the forces on the ship, able to reach the site of the action. He and three soldiers who came with him, found the air on board the ship thick with smoke and were attacked immediately with a shower of objects. While running to the wheel house, they were obliged to take refuge in the first cabin they came across, although this supplied doubtful cover. They were surrounded, attacked with tins and bottles and fists, not to mention being cursed and spat on. Two of the soldiers emptied two rounds of bullets over their attackers. They were saved by Grauel, the American Methodist minister, who took them to his cabin and went to find the captain. MacPherson had an important message to deliver to him. "Two Polish thugs" were put in charge of guarding the British officer and his men, "each having a concentration camp brand on their arm and telling us in no uncertain terms that they did not intend to be put in another concentration camp by us" (Report on Interception).

At that time, 03:30 a.m., there were only three officers and twenty soldiers on board the *Exodus*. From the destroyers it seemed that opposition on the ship was great. The operation's commander prepared 50 men on each of the destroyers with the boarding platforms and believed that if he could transfer two hundred men to the *Exodus* within a short time, control of the ship would be assured. Still, by 04:45, two hours after the operation had begun, only about 40 men had managed to board the ship, and by "cease-fire" time, this number would be no larger than 50, and this was after the destroyers had rammed the *Exodus* at least 20 times. The ship's crafty maneuverings and the narrowness of the boarding platforms were the cause of the small number of soldiers being able to board *Exodus*.[18]

The repeated ramming of the ship by the destroyers rattled the ship and caused her damage. There was great commotion on the ship. The British threw aboard a large number of smoke bombs and dozens, maybe even hundreds, of tear gas grenades. The fighters on board the *Exodus* set off American-made distress flares, which had a powerful flame and let off thick, caustic, yellow smoke and directed them toward the destroyers and the soldiers on board ship. The steam pipe proved useless, both because there was not enough pressure in it and because the soldiers jumped too high above it. The oil pipe was also a waste of time. True, the oil which spilled onto one of the destroyers made its deck and boarding platforms very slippery and hindered the soldiers' movements; but the wind blew the streams of oil back in the direction of *Exodus*, covering the fighters with a layer of black slime and made their deck sticky and slippery.

Not all the fighters succeeded in taking up their previously determined positions when the battle began and the alarm was raised. The youngsters took advantage of the ensuing commotion and many of them joined in the fighting, having previously been forbidden to do so, because of their age. Only three of the medical teams arrived at the scene of the battle – the physician, Dr Cohen, a member of the ha-Bonim movement in England; the medic, Avi Livni, an American volunteer and ha-Shomer ha-Tza'ir member; and Sima Schmukler, the nurse from Palestine (Habbas 1954, 53; Report on Interception). The ship's escorts from Palestine were all busy, each at his own task, and only one of them – Micha Perlson (later Perry)– took an active part in the fighting. Having received his military training in the Palmach, and being responsible for communications with the immigrants, he had been previously entrusted with preparing the people for battle. In the course of preparing for battle, the ship was divided into sectors, and a commander was appointed for each – an immigrant or an American. Perlson's area included the wheel house, which was to become the focal point of the battle.

The British reports stress the role played by the Americans in the fighting, since most of the verbal communication between the people on board and the soldiers was carried out through them, and also because many of the Americans – young men, healthy and strong, full of fighting spirit and a sense of mission – took part in the battle itself. Actually, most of the fighters were young members of the pioneer groups. The British were impressed that the fighters included many young people aged between 16 and 18, and this was the age-group of many of the wounded. Some of the fighters were younger still. The ha-Shomer ha-Tza'ir secretariat on board ship decided to bring in all movement members over the age of 14 to fight alongside their elders (Habbas 1954, 161–62).

The three victims of the battle represent a cross-section of the fighters. The American crew member, William (Bill) Bernstein; Mordechai Baumstein, aged 23, ha-Shomer ha-Tza'ir kibbutz member; and 15-year-old Zvi Yakobovitz, of the Dror children's home. At six o'clock in the morning the British doctor found Bernstein unconscious and mortally wounded, suffering from a fracture at the base of his skull. He and Baumstein needed head surgery, but conditions on board ship did not allow this and Bernstein died of his wounds on the way to Haifa. Baumstein and Yakobovitz had bullet wounds. According to the British, one of them had been holding an ax at the time he was shot, and the other appeared to be armed.[19] Since it is quite clear, as I am about to prove, that the people on *Exodus* had no firearms, it would seem that this latter claim stems from fact that the soldiers were overcome by fear at the commotion at the time they were engaged in battle on board the ship. The claim may also have been an attempt on their part to excuse the fact that they had resorted to the use of firearms, which they did not deny.[20]

At the same time as the battle was in full swing on the upper decks, people in the bowels of the ship had no idea what was going on. Ramming by the destroyers, sounds of splintering wood, water pouring in through holes in the ship, tear gas fumes and stinging smoke bombs all caused panic among those of the passengers who were not taking an active part in the operation: "Cries came from below from the thousands of people who knew nothing of what was taking place on deck, but felt as if the world was falling in on them. They called to put an end to the battle. But how? They asked that a white flag be raised. And the irony behind this pathetic but typical story is that although they all wanted to stop this débâcle – there was no one among them who was willing to contribute one white towel for use as a flag! ..." (Habbas 1954, 54).

Instead, "down below deck the men organized the women to shout and to demand an end to hostilities. From all around came the cry: Stop – stop – stop!" Two camps were formed – the fighters above and the home front, down below. "Every now and then a runner would come down and demand reinforcements for the battle – no one moved … . The first wounded started arriving from above. No one approached them, people barely moved aside to make room for them to get to the clinic" (Dror 1948, 31–32).

At the same time as the British were facing grave resistance on the top decks, which frustrated their plans and forced them to take cover from the barrage of objects raining down on them from every direction, the situation inside the ship was quite different. The soldiers, on their way to the machine and boiler rooms stepped between the immigrants undisturbed. But they were unable to take control of their objectives, because these rooms were locked and blockaded and surrounded by tight webbing against gas grenades and smoke bombs.

About two hours into the battle the commanders who remained behind on the destroyers were convinced that the attack had been a total flop. Only about 40 officers and men had succeeded in reaching the deck of the immigrant ship, and their colleagues, who remained behind, heard nothing and did not know what had happened to them. The groups of soldiers on board *Exodus* had no means of communication with each other and several of them had been taken prisoner. The main steering wheel was disconnected and the other one was controlled by the ship's captain. As far as the Commander-in-Chief Mediterranean was concerned, the situation was very close to failure.[21]

The number of soldiers on *Exodus* was insufficient to take control of her and it was almost impossible for any more to come aboard. The ship was sailing at a high speed and following an erratic course. On three out of the four destroyers the scaffolding had become completely useless and they had all been severely damaged. At the same time, the Jewish fighters were near exhaustion. Only 30 of them were still on their feet. They were tired and thirsty, the smoke making their breathing labored, their clothes were soaked in oil. The ship had holes in her sides from being rammed by the British ships and parts of her had broken off and collapsed.

Dozens of wounded people lay on the decks, some of them seriously, some even mortally. The medical team was unequipped to supply them all with the necessary treatment. Dr Cohen, who bore the main burden of caring for the wounded, was especially concerned about those in need of blood transfusions. He informed the ship's commander that if these did not get a blood transfusion within a short time, some of them might die. Hamburger decided immediately to cease resistance and the British officers on board the ship were requested to contact the destroyers and ask for medical assistance.

The operation's British commander, who had received no sign of life from his men since the onset of the battle, felt great relief when Lieutenant MacPherson made contact with the *Charity* at 05:15 and reported that resistance was dying. The commander was skeptical about the information that the captain was willing to sail his ship into Haifa and that they were in need of urgent medical assistance, and decided first of all to establish the truth. He ordered the *President Warfield* to stop, and when she did, the *Chequers* medical team was sent aboard her at 05:40. The doctor found three Jews mortally wounded and about 200 "cases" requiring medical attention, of which about 70 were in serious condition. There were also three wounded soldiers, two of whom were in need of hospitalization. A soldier who had fallen into the sea in the course of the battle, received medical attention on one of the destroyers.

Once the British medical team had boarded the *Exodus*, the imprisoned soldiers were set free, the wheel house began operating again and the ship set sail toward Haifa under the command of the American crew member, Berny Marks, who was introduced to the British as the ship's captain. At about nine o'clock the ship stopped once again in order to allow a further medical team to join the previous one, whose hands were full. By noon it seemed to the British that the Jews' spirits were reviving. The commander of the British forces on *Exodus* was concerned about what might happen on board, once the ship entered the port of Haifa, and asked for a reinforcement of about 40 additional hands. Rough seas made it possible for only 20 to come aboard. And thus, *Exodus* went on her way toward Haifa, which she reached close to four o'clock in the afternoon of Friday 18 July 1947, escorted by eight warships of the British Royal Naval Fleet.

The two sides in the battle between the British Naval ships and the *Exodus* were unequal and the results could have been anticipated. Both sides involved in the illegal immigration operations had unwritten "rules of the game", a "gentleman's agreement", almost. The British were willing to come to terms with symbolic resistance on the part of the immigrant ships, if this did not entail risk to human life, and made this fact known to the Mossad shortly before the arrival of *Exodus*.[22] Everyone involved in illegal immigration was convinced that the British would never sink an immigrant ship, and even though they did in the past happen to open fire during attempts to overpower immigrant ships, no one thought for a moment that this would have been done in an undiscerning manner and at a crowd of people, whether on board ship or during disembarkation. The immigrants and their escorts appreciated that when all was said and done, they could depend on the inherent decency of the British soldier and that if one had to have an adversary, a

British soldier was better than many others. The Jewish side was more afraid of *Exodus* people drowning during disembarkation, than of being shot at by the British (Aran 1985; Katzanelson 1985; Report on Interception, 27).

The first of the two eventualities for which the people on *Exodus* had prepared themselves – to dodge the British ships and push through to shore – was no longer considered, as soon as the battle had began earlier and further from shore than anticipated. The second eventuality – resisting the British as they were storming the *Exodus* – took three forms: the use of defense means, which had been installed when the ship was purchased and were constantly being updated and improved ever since, right up to the eve of battle; "artillery", consisting of objects – bottles, tins, etc.; and face-to-face battle. The boarding parties were confronted with a barrage of metal poles, tent pegs, screws, nails, buckets, bottles, and especially, food: Tins of preserves, crates of food, potatoes and so on. *Exodus* had loaded up before her departure with enough food to last fourteen days, and the battle had begun on the eighth day of the voyage. "We knew it was all over," said Katzanelson, who was in charge of supplies on the ship, years later, "we didn't hold back on anything" (1985). The British doctor who boarded the ship at the end of the battle said that "there was enough tinned food and potatoes scattered about the upper deck to feed *Chequers* for about a week or so." The soldiers collected the tins of food in order to send them to their families in England. At a time when England was in the throes of postwar food rationing, this wasteful use of food as ammunition angered the soldiers and increased their negative attitude to the immigrants.[23] The same Naval doctor recommended "that more could be made of this [Jewish wastefulness] in our propaganda" (Bett 1947).

And firearms? No mention was made of this in the orders issued by the British commander of the operation. The commander of one of the boarding parties ordered his men to use force only if the immigrants resisted and to resort to firearms as a means of self-defense, if this was necessary. In their summing up reports, the British repeatedly pointed out the great restraint demonstrated by their soldiers, especially when it came to opening fire. Thus, they reckoned, they avoided injuring many more of the Jews, although they did not hide the fact that their men opened fire on several occasions. They admitted that shots were fired twice in order to help their men jump over to *Exodus*; machine guns were fired toward the ship at the very beginning of the operation; and soldiers on board ship fired several times toward the immigrants. This is all according to British reports, which were written shortly after the events took place (Report on Interception). In retrospect, there were those who tried to present a different picture. Allan Bullock, Bevin's biographer, for example, claimed that the overpowering of *Exodus* was achieved without the use of guns (1983, 449).

It is quite clear, therefore, that the British did make use of firearms as they overpowered the *Exodus*. Did they indeed exercise restraint? Did they only shoot in self-defense, or was it also out of fear and not always where really necessary? These questions will remain open and have no clear-cut answers. The British point out the number of dead, three, as evidence of the fact that use of firearms was limited. The people on *Exodus*, who expected the battle to be fought according to the unwritten rules of previous illegal immigration operations, remember that the British shot a lot and indiscriminately. They believe that the large number of wounded (suffering from bullet wounds, concussion, cuts and fractures), indicates the brutality of the battle. Twenty-seven of the wounded (26 immigrants and one American) were subsequently admitted to hospitals in Palestine,[24] and several dozen others were transferred to the deportation ships. Some of these boarded on their own, others were carried on board on stretchers.

Almost certainly the Jewish side did not use firearms, although some British documents claim otherwise. The officer who took control of the wheel house, together with the first boarding party, claimed in his report of the same day, 18 July 1947, that when the *Exodus* people swarmed in trying to break their way through the hole in its roof, "two shots were fired into the wheel house". Quite possibly, these two shots that the officer heard came from another group of soldiers who were storming the wheel house at that exact moment, and, forced to take shelter on the way, fired two shots at the immigrants – according to the officer in charge of that boarding party himself.

No one on the *Exodus* was in the possession of firearms. They knew that a few pistols would make no difference in the long run, while a single shot on their part would give the British all the excuse they needed to open fire on them, for control to be lost of the situation and to break the tenuous "rules of the game". The Palmach HQ stressed repeatedly the orders for unarmed resistance, and in his letter on the eve of the ship's sailing, the Palmach commander warned again "when resisting, to avoid as far as possible, taking the life of the enemy, so that he never has an excuse to murder immigrants" (Allon 1947, 839). Even though this letter did not reach the escorts of the *Exodus* in time for her departure, their actions were compatible with its contents. A couple of days prior to the battle three guns were confiscated from American members of the crew, and tossed into the sea (Garcia-Granados 1949, 181; Aran 1985; Har'el 1985). The weapons taken from the British soldiers "captured" in the course of battle were also thrown into the sea, or laid aside with no use having been made of them and returned to the soldiers at the end of the battle.[25] The British finally admitted to themselves that, like their predecessors, the illegal immigrants on *Exodus* did not resort to the use of firearms.[26]

As far as the British commander of the operation was concerned, they were very fortunate that they succeeded in capturing the *President Warfield* and that the Jewish determination was broken while the British boarding parties were actually still at a distinct disadvantage. The Commander-in-Chief Mediterranean was sure that "this was by far the most difficult and dangerous boarding so far carried out by the Palestine Patrol".[27] He sent out a series of letters and telegrams to his superiors, in an attempt to persuade them not to consider a repeat operation like the one involving the *President Warfield*, in which two British Naval destroyers had been damaged, one of them had been put out of commission for three or four months. In a personal letter to the First Sea Lord, he wrote that the *President Warfield* affair had been "so very nearly a failure that I feel I must point out that only a little more resistance and a small development in physical obstruction will make boarding impracticable or at any rate very costly in casualties and damage".[28] The case of the *President Warfield* had, in his opinion, illustrated great advance in resistance techniques, which might yet be improved, while the British had already realized their full potential from a technical point of view, so that any future success would have been doubtful.[29]

In the wake of the difficult battle for the *Exodus*, the British decided that there would be no repeat of this operation of intercepting and capturing illegal immigration ships. Furthermore, they feared that resistance on the part of immigrants who knew in advance that they would be sent back to Europe, might turn out to be even more stubborn and desperate than in the past. Certainly it was worthless entering into violent clashes with the immigrants and the Yishuv for no purpose, in other words, when there was no chance of their implementing their refoulement policy. Shortly after the *Exodus* battle, the British informed the Jewish Agency that the immigrants who made their way to Palestine on the two ships *Bruna* and *Duciana* would be sent to Cyprus and would not be sent to their ports of origin.[30] These ships were not intended for return to Europe for two reasons. The British did not know for sure where they had set off from; and in the absence of the *Runneymede Park*,

Ocean Vigour and *Empire Rival*, which were used to deport the *Exodus* immigrants back to France, and with the *Empire Lifeguard* in dry dock after being sabotaged in Cyprus, the British did not have enough ships to transport immigrants for long distances and for any length of time (Cable 1947).

The decision on the two ships, immediately following the *Exodus*, was the order of the day and the British made it clear to the Yishuv in a broadcast on the "Voice of Jerusalem", that "this does not indicate the Government's future behavior". Both ships had been taken without resistance and the transfer of their immigrants had taken place peacefully.[31] Still the British continued to prevaricate on the question of intercepting illegal immigration ships, in light of their experience with *Exodus*. The Commander-in-Chief Mediterranean proposed taking other measures, rather than boarding the ships mid-sea, as a result of the heavy price of "Operation Mae West", like, for example, using verbal persuasion and menacing gestures to shepherd a ship to Haifa. If these measures should fail and an illegal immigration ship should still beach up on a sand bank, the only victims of such an operation would be those same Jews who insist on jumping into the water too soon (and not British soldiers!) and the illegal immigration ship would no longer be usable. He admitted that this would involve other problems – such as finding the illegal immigrants and transferring them from the place at which they landed to the port of Haifa as well as forfeiting the chance of sending them back to their port of origin, still – it should be remembered – it was not he who had to contend with these problems.

So great was his concern with regard to another *Exodus*-style confrontation, that, in advance of the arrival of the ships *Northland* and *Paduca*, both powerful and suitable for resistance, he gave the senior officer on the spot free reign to hold-over the overpowering of the ships, if he believed this might cause serious damage and casualties, or end in failure.[32]

The British were keen to know what had caused the Jewish will for resistance to collapse, at the very time when it seemed they still had the upper hand. They believed this was due to the following reasons: (a) All navigational equipment was lost with the wheel house and chart house, so that the crew did not know where they were, or even what course they were steering; (b) The condition of the wounded and their calls for help. "The knowledge that the mate was dying of cosh wounds had a scaring effect on the American crew"; (c) The severe damage to the ship's superstructure, particularly on the saloon deck (it was possible from outboard to see daylight through gashes on either side of the ship at this level) caused Jews (i.e. the immigrants) and some members of the crew to think the ship was in danger of sinking; (d) The party that patrolled the decks in the early hours between 04:00 and 05:00 gave the Jews, including those wired in by the steering engines, the impression that the Navy was in charge of the whole ship (Report on Interception).

Documents of the time, both British and Jewish, make no hint of the fact that the order to cease resistance came from the command on shore in Palestine. Throughout the battle, there was no wireless communication between the ship and shore. This was broken at the very beginning of the British attack and restored gradually only after the resistance ended.[33]

The people of *Exodus* knew that the balance of power was to their advantage and that the British were not succeeding in taking control of the ship, although what they did not know, of course, was how close the British were to failure and the extent of their own pessimistic evaluation of the situation. The decision to stop resisting and to sail of their own accord to Haifa was explained by the *Exodus* people in a live broadcast to the Yishuv at 07:30 in the morning. "On our deck there are one dead, five dying and 120 wounded. The resistance continued for more than three hours." After a plea to the members of the United Nations committee to come to Haifa, the broadcast ended on a note of apology almost: "Owing to the severe losses and the condition of the ship, which is in danger of sinking, we were compelled to sail in the direction of Haifa, in order to save the 4,500 refugees on board from drowning" (*Ha-Olam*, 24 July 1947).

In fact, the battle ceased for the following reasons:

a. The condition of the ship, which was badly gashed by the ramming of the destroyers. The water flowing in and the widespread damage to the upper deck, spread panic among the immigrants. However, checks made by the ship's captain and her commander revealed that the damage was not as bad as it had seemed and that the ship was not in danger of sinking. Probably the dramatic description of her sorry state, during the morning broadcast to the Yishuv, and the claim that she was no longer seaworthy was meant to increase the impression that the British had been very cruel in their actions against the ship. This was aimed less for the ears of the Yishuv than for those of the United Nations committee. The British control of the wheel house had not prevented the ship's crew from steering her with the help of the reserve wheel, and to maneuver her, at great speed, in a zigzag path. But lacking suitable navigating instruments – the improvised compass was not working properly in the stern of the ship because of the metal covering all around – it was difficult to make any moves requiring accuracy, such as bursting forth toward a defined and predetermined piece of coast.

b. The condition of the fighters. The British did not succeed in gaining control of the ship, but the Jewish fighters were exhausted. There did not remain so much as one man capable of continuing the fight after two exhausting hours of battle. They were all scalded by smoke and gas, soaked in oil, beaten and bruised, and many of them were wounded.

c. The overwhelming reason for stopping the battle was the condition of the wounded, as the British medical team noted. The cries of the wounded could be heard from all around. The American officer was unconscious. The youth, Zvi Yakobovitz, an orphan, was in critical condition. The cries of the boy's younger brother shocked everyone present, including the British doctor who was trying to save his life. When Dr Cohen came to Hamburger and told him that several of the wounded were in a very bad way indeed and if they didn't get blood infusions in the shortest possible time they were very like to die of their wounds, the ship's commander decided to put an end to resistance immediately and to request medical assistance of the British.

d. The decision was based largely on the concept of resistance held by the people on *Exodus*. It was quite clear that in the end the British would succeed in overpowering any of the ships and deporting the illegal immigrants on board. Still, as the Palmach commander wrote, the act of resistance had an important historical, educational, political and moral role to play. "It is inconceivable that Jews would be expelled from their country, without doing their best to prevent it – otherwise we would be, to ourselves and to generations to come, no less than toward the rest of the world, a nation of weak-spirited people who are quick to surrender" (Allon 1947, 840). With this in mind, the people on *Exodus* did their best to fulfill their obligation to resist, as they understood it.

The commander on the Jewish side, Micha Perlson, believed that "we did the most that we felt could be done. No more could have been achieved. Unarmed as we were, we could not have done more" (Perry 1985). Mordechai Roseman had no illusions that the British would not be able to capture the ship. But he still believed that they had a slight chance of success. As far as he was concerned the resistance did not end with the question of whether or not it would lead to victory, but whether it had any demonstrative value: "It was part of the overall concept behind the ghetto warfare. You don't fight only if you have a chance at winning, you fight because you believe in the justice of your ways." But, unlike the ghetto wars, the battle for *Exodus* was not a Massada-style battle, it was not a fight to the death (1985).

Many years later the ship's commander explained his decision to cease fighting: "My consideration was simple. Resistance – we had to resist, and we did. I accepted command of a ship bringing illegal immigrants to Palestine. I did not accept command of immigrants with the aim of turning them into fighters, and certainly not to bring in a group of casualties, who had already been through the Holocaust and who might die on the way between Natanya and Haifa, since I would be playing with their lives, for the sake of a point we had already made. Our resistance was in the act of leaving Europe and in physical resistance" (Har'el 1985).

The illegal immigration activists from Palestine and the immigrants themselves saw the actual exit from Europe as an act of resistance to the policy of the British Government. The illegal immigrants on board *Exodus* had left the DP camps in Germany, fully aware that they were destined for Cyprus, which they conceived of as "half way to Palestine", "a corridor to Palestine" and "the eve of Palestine". Being deported to Cyprus was not, in their opinion, a failure. Still, the escorts on *Exodus* couldn't help but feel a sense of failure, of not having succeeded in one part of their struggle. They had hoped that the ship would succeed in reaching shore, even though they knew that their chances of achieving this were slim. More than anyone, it was the ship's captain who believed in their chances of success. *Exodus* was the first illegal immigrant ship to be sailed the whole voyage by a Palmach captain, rather than a foreign seaman. And the captain, who was sailing for the first time on an illegal immigrant ship, was confident that, thanks to the ship's technical characteristics, her size and the plans for action, it would have been possible to break the siege more successfully than had been the case of the *Ulua* (*Chaim Arlozoroff*) five months previously (Aran 1964, 1985).

The break in fighting was seen by Aharonowitz as merely a temporary cease-fire, and on Friday, he proposed to his colleagues that they attempt to reach the shore at Kiryat Chaim (north of Haifa). This was one of the options telegraphed from the Mossad HQ to *Exodus* while she was on her way to the east, but Aharonowitz's colleagues did not consider the idea seriously when he raised it on Friday, following the battle. The stormy sea prevented the transfer of casualties to the British destroyers, which were less stable than the flat-bottomed *Exodus*. So, the same considerations as were instrumental in the decision to cease the battle in the early morning, were decisive later on: A swift flight to Haifa, where the wounded would be taken to hospital.

Moreover, it was imperative under the circumstances that *Exodus* sail to Haifa. This was not a specifically issued order, but was obvious from the call to the United Nations committee to visit the ship. On Thursday evening, the ship broadcast:

> Dear Sirs, we implore you to visit us, on the deck of our ship, to witness for yourselves the live testimony of 4,500 refugees. Please come and see with your own eyes – our ship, our suffering and the efforts we are making to reach the safe haven of our homeland. Witness for yourselves the cold-heartedness of the British, as they try to expel us from the shores of our homeland, in order to incarcerate us, behind barbed wire, in concentration camps, which cannot but remind us all the time of those concentration camps in which we were interred during the days of the Nazis in Europe.

On Friday morning the ship repeated the invitation to the UN committee: "We implore the members of the committee: Come to Haifa! See the evil!" (*Ha-Olam*, 24 July 1947). A message from shore to ship at one o'clock in the afternoon said: "In answer to your request, the United Nations committee is leaving for Haifa."[34] And the ship, too, had to make her way to Haifa.

Detailed descriptions so far published of the battle on *Exodus* off the shores of Palestine, relate an argument between the captain and the commander of the ship while the battle was raging. Aharonowitz, it would seem, tried to prevent Hamburger from issuing an order to put an end to resistance. These descriptions are inaccurate, even abusive. For example, the description (some of which is totally unbased) in the book *Parashat Exodus be'Or Hadash* (A New Light on the Exodus Affair; first published in French: *Le Loi du retour*) which tells how "Ike ran from his position by the reserve steering wheel to resist with all his strength the order to surrender. He was brandishing a gun, threatening even his friends."[35] Arguments the author relates to Ike Aharonowitz, as if they had been uttered on board ship, are quoted from an interview given to Kol Israel ("The Voice of Israel", Israel State Radio) 17 years after the incident, and even this deviates from the original. It would be only right to stick to the facts.

The commander and the captain had fundamental different concepts on the matter of resistance, however, the paradigm of conceptual differences between the Mossad and the Palmach, presented earlier in this chapter, is not sufficient to make this clear. Hamburger considered himself obligated to Yig'al Peikovitz's definition of resistance and, according to Aharonowitz there was no dispute on board on the issue of resistance, which had been agreed upon in advance with Meirov and Ada Sereni. Nor did Aharonowitz contest the necessity to cease resistance, in order to allow the wounded to receive medical care. Later, in *post factum* reports to the Palmach, he claimed that he had felt that it would have been possible to carry out the breakthrough plan (Aran 1985; Har'el 1985).

In order to understand the different concepts of resistance held by Hamburger and Aharonowitz, we must bear in mind the different experiences each of them had been through before the battle itself. Aharonowitz had boarded the *President Warfield* in the United States at the end of 1946. He was partner to all the many preparations the ship had to undergo, and a strong bond was formed between him and the ship which, for about nine months, had served as his home. Aharonowitz, who was a devoted activist, believed wholeheartedly in the ship and her crew's ability to break the British blockade and to reach the shores of Palestine, to prove that the blockade was ineffective, to bring to shore a large number of illegal immigrants and to attract large scale publicity both in Palestine and in the rest of the world. This was the first time that an illegal immigration ship had been placed in the hands of a captain who was a member of the Palmach – and what a ship! Aharonowitz was full of ambition to succeed, and this success was to be a huge one for the illegal immigration project, the Palmach and for him personally. In November 1946, when Ike Aharonowitz first boarded the *President* to begin his long voyage on her, Yossi Hamburger was commanding the illegal immigration ship *Knesset Israel*, on which three immigrants lost their lives during the confrontation with the British. He had been deeply impressed by the events on this ship. Alterman's poem "Division of Duties", quoted at the beginning of this chapter, faithfully described Hamburger's feelings, which he expressed to the poet after the battle on *Knesset Israel* in Haifa port.

Disagreements did indeed arise between the captain and the commander, on the voyage from France to Palestine, for example, the timing of the final preparations for the British attack. However, the bitterness surrounding the description of the argument between the two during the battle is based on a dispute which broke out between them years after the Exodus Affair was over (Aran 1963, 1964; Har'el testimony; Har'el 1964), and its effect became more powerful because of Leon Uris' book *Exodus*, and the subsequent Hollywood movie, which re-awakened a wave of interest in the original affair.

The ironic paradox of the Exodus Affair was, that the very decision to forego the demonstrative act of bursting through to shore, which stemmed from the need to save the lives of the wounded, was – due to Britain's policy as conducted by Bevin – responsible for the ship's widespread publicity and the impression she made on world public opinion. It was proof that "every cloud has a silver lining", or in the words of the dedication to the minister John Grauel, in the book the Palestine escorts gave him as a souvenir of their adventure: "To the memory of one failure. A few more failures like this one, and we'll have won, a few more such victories and our adversaries will be lost in the abyss of oblivion" (Habbas 1954, 12). This paradoxical process began even before the return of the *Exodus* immigrants to France. The visit of UNSCOP in Palestine, accompanied by dozens of media personnel from all over the world, and the presence of two of its members at the port of Haifa at the time of the ship's entry, spread the name *Exodus* world-wide. This was not a case of "forewarned is forearmed", but of knowing how to make the most of available opportunity.

8 · Where Now?

In Haifa, the people were transferred from the *Exodus* to the three deportation ships more or less peacefully. Here and there, people showed some resistance, but this was soon subdued. People were exhausted from the battle, the gas and smoke and from the journey itself. They were sure that they were about to embark on a short voyage to Cyprus, where they would await their turn to immigrate to Palestine. This is what had been made quite clear to them in the four-language (Hebrew, Yiddish, German and Czech) flyers they had been handed out by the British in Haifa (Exodus File a).

At six o'clock on the morning of Saturday 19 July, the fleet of deportation ships sailed out of Haifa. It was only on Sunday, when it became apparent that the ships had not arrived in Cyprus, that suspicions were aroused of something not being in order and rumors started spreading that the ships were on their way to France. These developments shocked all involved. For the illegal immigrants, who believed while they were still in Europe that the worst thing that could happen to them would be deportation to Cyprus, the news came as a terrible disappointment and completely unanticipated. But why did it come as such a surprise to the Mossad and the Zionist leadership, who knew for months of Britain's negotiations with European countries about returning illegal immigrant ships to their ports of embarkation? This activity was, admittedly, secret, but at the beginning of June news began reaching the Mossad from various sources that illegal immigrants would no longer be sent to Cyprus, but from then on, they would be returned to their ports of origin.

The first inkling of this reached the Haganah from a British source that told of an agreement to this effect between the governments of France and Britain. The recipient of this information added, in his own writing: "This information must be treated with caution."[1] A couple of days later an urgent message arrived about a secret memo sent from the British

Jerusalem HQ, stating that in the event of immigrants being apprehended, they will be returned forcibly to France or Italy, in other words,
their ports of origin.[2] Similar messages arrived on 5 and 6 June, one of
which even stated that the passengers on all captured immigrant ships
would, from then on, be sent back to the British zone in Germany and
not to Cyprus.[3]

The existence of this intelligence information is referred to in the
letter sent by the Palmach Commander on 21 June to his people in
Europe, in which he mentioned the possibility that one day the
authorities would decide to return the illegal immigration ships to their
European ports of origin and warned that "the deportation to the ports
of origin is a real danger, lurking at all times" (Allon 1947, 840).

Thus the writing was on the wall, but the people who were supposed
to make use of the information, misread it. At the end of June, they
reached these conclusions:

> Despite the decision to send the illegal immigrants to their ports of origin,
> the authorities are facing certain difficulties, some of which are based on
> external political considerations and some connected with the current
> circumstances – the UN committee; it's not the right time to put the decision
> into operation. It's possible, therefore that the order will be postponed. We
> are informed also that the recent relative quiet in the country is not presenting
> a suitable background for putting into operation a plan such as this.
>
> Furthermore, only two countries with Mediterranean ports – France and
> Italy – have so far agreed to accept illegal immigrants. In other words, the
> matter cannot be implemented in the case of ships sailing from other ports.
> This "difficulty" has also not yet been overcome by the government.[4]

Exodus, as we recall, sailed from France.

For the first few days after the deportation ships had left Haifa, the
Mossad and the Jewish Agency were fed contradictory rumors and read
confusing information in the press.[5] The reliability of this information
can be seen, for example, on the first page of *Ha-Aretz* dated 21 July 1947.
The headline announced that "the illegal immigrants were transferred
by ships to *North Africa*"; the subtitle related how "the illegal immigrants
did not reach Cyprus since the government wanted to return them to
their port of origin in *France*." And a tiny last minute addition informed
that "at 2.30 at night, Reuters reported that the army in *Cyprus* were
alerted to receive 4,500 people at 4 o'clock in the morning." Indeed, at
that time, the ships' destination was unknown even to the British themselves. A reply had not yet been received from the French Government,
and the possibility of the *Exodus* passengers landing on Cyprus had not
been finally discounted.

On Friday 18 July 1947, while the immigrants were being transferred to the deportation ships in the port of Haifa, Britain's ambassador in Paris, Duff Cooper, suddenly got cold feet. He sent off an urgent cable to Bevin, warning him that deportation of the illegal immigrants back to France would result in sharp criticism in the Communist newspapers and probably among the Socialists also. He feared that disembarking the illegal immigrants from British ships in a French port would cause widespread anti-British propaganda and this would be received eagerly by public opinion in France, since the French still remembered the German persecution of the Jews during the occupation. He made it clear to his superior that the man-in-the-street is a complete ignoramus with regard to Palestine and regards these illicit immigrants as the last vestiges of a persecuted race, wanting only to find refuge in their national home. Therefore, although he was aware that there would be no new discussions on the program to return the Jews to France, he dropped broad hints that it might after all be better to bring them to Cyprus.[6]

The following day, Bevin ordered him to inform the French Government that the *President Warfield* passengers had left Haifa and were on their way to France. "You should say," elaborated Bevin, "that this action is being taken on the strength of the verbal understanding reached between M. Bidault and myself. We hope to hear very quickly at which port the French would prefer the immigrants to disembark." At the end of the message, Bevin added a secret paragraph: "For your own information only, we shall have to decide by Monday at the latest whether the convoy is to proceed to France or to return to Cyprus. But the French should not be given any indication at this stage that we are contemplating the latter possibility in any circumstances."[7] That same day, the Foreign Office informed the British Ambassadors all over the world that if the French refuse to accept the ships, they may be obliged to return to Cyprus.[8]

This information was classified. A rumor was spreading at the same time, that the illegal immigrants were being brought to France, where they would remain only until their journey could be arranged to Colombia (*Davar*, 22 July 1947). On 22 July 1947, questions were raised in the British Parliament on the matter and Sidney Silverman MP asked the Secretary of State for the Colonies about the "present whereabouts" of the *Exodus* immigrants, "who have not so far reached Cyprus, and concerning whose ultimate destination conflicting rumours are circulating". Creech-Jones' reply was that they were currently on three British vessels on their way from Haifa to France. When asked to respond to the rumors that these people would be transferred further, to Colombia, he replied that whatever was going to take place in France was entirely in the hands of the French authorities.[9]

It would seem that in this case the Secretary was telling the truth. He was unable at the time to supply a calculated reply with regard to the continued voyage to Colombia. The French authorities had claimed to the British that the *Exodus* passengers possessed personal passports stamped with valid visas, issued by the Colombian consul general in Marseilles. Therefore, on 21 July the British ambassador in Paris was informed by a French Government official, that his Government would ask His Majesty's Government to send the ships to Colombia as soon as they have re-fueled in Villefranche. This was impossible to implement. First, the vessels were not equipped for a transatlantic crossing, and second, they were needed immediately in Haifa in order to transfer other illegal immigrants to Cyprus.[10] The French then asked for the return of the *President Warfield*, for repairs, to make her sufficiently sea-worthy to handle an ocean voyage. This suggestion was also rejected for practical reasons – the ship was not sea-worthy at all, and there were no suitable facilities in Palestine necessary for even basic repairs.[11] At this stage each side was still trying to place on the other the responsibility for carrying out the operation. The British Foreign Office was most concerned about France's determination to send the immigrants to Colombia, knowing that this would increase the chances that they would show violent resistance to being disembarked in France (Crossley 1947).

The Jewish Agency considered seriously the possibility of deportation to Colombia. Its line of action was: If the Colombians refuse to admit the refugees they should publicly state so; and if they agree, they should state that they will accept them only if they arrive of their own free will.[12]

The Foreign Office in Bogota denied absolutely the reports in the local press regarding the Colombian visas which had been allegedly issued to the passengers of *Exodus*. The British ambassador in Colombia wrote to London: "Unless the consul-general in Marseilles, who is a retired army general, is out of his mind, or completely corrupt, it looks as if a forgery on a grand scale has been perpetuated."[13]

In any case, the Colombian Government had no intention of accepting the *Exodus* passengers and its embassy in France demanded that the French Government investigate the matter of the Colombian visas and prosecute those Jewish organizations responsible for the fraud. France rejected this demand and proposed that Colombia should herself undertake the task of prosecuting those they considered responsible. The French Government officials who dealt with the matter believed that the visas had indeed been issued by the Colombian consul, but with the express intention that they be thrown into the sea as soon as *Exodus* left France. Allegations of corruption, raised by the British ambassador in Bogota, had more than a grain of truth in them.[14]

While the British were checking the feasibility of the illegal immigrants being deported to Colombia – only on 24 July did the Colonial Office inform the Jewish Agency in London that "they can bury the Colombian story and the people will remain in France" – the Jewish Agency wanted to know if physical force would be used in disembarking the illegal immigrants in France. The Colonial Secretary was evasive in his reply to Parliament, although the question was raised repeatedly. On 24 July the Colonial Office informed the Jewish Agency that no force would be used and that the ships' arrival in France would symbolize the end of Britain's role in the affair.[15] This was after the French Government had already determined its behavior toward the returning illegal immigrants – and made this decision public.

The French Government had reached this decision following two weeks of heavy British pressure and Zionist counter-measures, which began as soon as news arrived of the deportation ships' return journey to France. For each party, this was something of a "test case", which they believed would in time determine the fate of the entire illegal immigration operation. The British Foreign Secretary had already decided to make an example of *Exodus*, by forcing her and all her passengers back to France. As far as the Zionists were concerned, this was obviously going to be a decisive struggle. "It must be quite clear," said Moshe Shertok, at a meeting of the Jewish Agency Executive on 28 July, "that we are on trial here, as to whether the people disembark or not."

Everyone involved on the Jewish side was terrified that if the *Exodus* immigrants land in France, a fatal blow would be dealt to the entire illegal immigration operation. It would paralyze the determination of the Jews remaining in the German DP camps to setting out on the arduous path of Aliyah Bet and put an end to France's quiet support for this operation. Each side calculated its steps in accordance with its own estimation of the immigrants' resolution. The Mossad's, as we shall see later, was lower even than Britain's.

As the three deportation ships moved westward, the British Foreign Office was busy collecting opinions from various sources, in order to formulate a program for disembarking the immigrants on French soil. The High Commissioner for Palestine, Sir Alan Cunningham, who was experienced in the ways of illegal immigration and knew exactly what had taken place in Haifa on 18 July 1947, reckoned that the immigrants may show a strong disinclination to cooperate and that the use of considerable physical force may be unavoidable, including lifting individuals bodily, for trans-shipment.[16] The commander of the deportation convoy, Colonel Gregson, believed that it would be possible to remove the passengers peaceably, if they are prevented from receiving any propaganda from elsewhere. He even devised a plan of action: *Ocean Vigour* would drop anchor close to shore and the other ships would anchor at a certain distance from each other. Attempts would be made, at first, to remove the passengers from the *Ocean Vigour*, which in his opinion would be easiest to achieve. The others will have seen the first 50 passengers disembark, and follow suite.[17] The Foreign Office accepted Cunningham's evaluation. As far as they were concerned, the key to the operation's success would be the use of physical force to disembark the passengers and they held intensive, sometimes even aggressive, negotiations with the French on this matter.[18]

The Jewish Agency in Jerusalem, Paris and America tried, whether by way of official diplomatic approach, or "through friends", to persuade the French Government not to permit the use of force in removing the immigrants from the ships. The first instructions sent by Shertok in Jerusalem to Sneh in Paris went even further: The French Government should refuse to land the passengers, who must remain Britain's liability.[19] The French press published announcements by the Haganah according to which the refugees would resist disembarkation, thus forcing the French authorities to fight Britain's war against the refugees, which would be contrary to French policy.[20]

The Jewish Agency envoy in Washington was ordered to persuade the State Department to influence Britain to return to previous procedure, in other words, deportation of illegal immigrants to Cyprus. He was not requested to mobilize the Administration to act on the French front. After all, what could the Zionists have asked of the Americans on this issue? To influence the French not to take in Jewish refugees?

In France, the Zionists were aided by their long-standing friends (Derogy 1972, 66–67, 158). Venia Pomerantz (Ze'ev Hadari) had meetings with the French Interior Minister Edouard Depreux, Father Glasberg (a Catholic of Jewish origin), who held a senior position in the Interior Ministry at the time and had been in contact with the Mossad since the end of the war, and with Andre Blumel, who held the post of President of the Zionist Federation and the Jewish National Fund in France and had run Leon Blum's office when the latter had been Prime Minister. These people, and others, made sure of informing the Mossad and the Jewish Agency of communications between France and Britain and of the atmosphere within the French Government. The day before the decisive Government meeting, Leon Blum claimed favorable results from his intervention with Ramadier, and Jerusalem knew that the Interior Ministry was firmly opposed to landing the illegal immigrants while the Foreign Office remained "very weak".[21]

The Jewish Agency sent their telegrams by regular telegraph services and they offer a laconic and practical description of the events. The Mossad's telegrams, in Hebrew and coded, were dispatched through its independent communication network, and these supply us not only with the dry facts but also with the atmosphere at the time: "Enemy pressure on the locals is firm and constant. The locals are indecisive," they reported on 22 July 1947, adding: "We are making every effort with the help of our friends."[22] The following day they sent an "urgent" cable to Palestine with news about "the local government's decision not to force landing on anyone. Whoever expresses a desire to land – will be received in France. We'll keep on the look-out and hope no one decides to land."[23]

Exodus was the last item on the agenda at a meeting of the French Government, on 23 July at the Rambouillet Palace, the French President's summer residence. The debate, which lasted a couple of hours, has been described as stormy. The Foreign Minister left the meeting for a while to talk to the British ambassador. Duff Cooper had arrived at the Palace with the aim of helping Bidault persuade his colleagues to comply with Britain's request, so as to avoid spoiling relations between the two countries at a time when they were discussing matters of greater mutual importance than the *Exodus* (Derogy 1972, 159–60). Bidault told Cooper that the position of his socialist colleagues, and especially that of the Interior Minister, Depreux, had been influenced by Leon Blum.[24] Depreux, Jules Moch and the Labor Minister, Daniel Mayer, who were very sympathetic to the Mossad and its activity, were members of the French Socialist Party, which held the majority in the Government, whereas Bidault, was a member of the Christian Democrats.

The Government debate had Bidault on one side, claiming that the British request must be complied with, both out of friendship and in order to alleviate the suffering of the poor refugees by accepting them in France; and Depreux on the other side, informing the Government that he had no intention of sending so much as a single policeman to take people off the ships. These opposing positions were based not only on the fact that the two men belonged to separate political parties, one of them strongly influenced by a powerful ideological mentor, but – and probably mainly – because of the positions each held in the Government. The Foreign Minister was worried about the detrimental effect the affair might have on carefully nurtured French–British relations, while the Interior Minister was concerned about the distasteful task of removing illegal immigrants from ships and the subsequent need to house and employ them. The arrival of some 4,500 refugees would constitute a very heavy burden on the country, which already had a large number of refugees, and might pose a dangerous precedent.

When the meeting ended, François Mitterrand, Government Spokesman and Minister in charge of veteran soldiers and war casualties, read the decision:

> In this unfortunate situation, simple in legal terms, but complex when one considers the mass of facts, France intends to take a humanitarian stance. Of course there is no disputing the fact that we have undertaken not to direct anyone to Palestine. Still, although these emigrants have crossed French territory, we emphasize that we shall not accept direct responsibility for their sailing, since most of them have come from the various zones of occupation in Germany, and were in possession of valid passports, with Colombian visas. If the ships transporting them should return to one of her ports, France does not intend to close her ports to refugees, but she shall not force them to land on shore. She will adopt a humanitarian position toward them, and supply immediate aid to those who wish to stay on her territory. (Derogy 1972, 160)

Le Monde devoted its evening editorial to *Exodus* (23 July 1947). The French people's sympathy for the illegal immigrants on *Exodus* – who, as rumor had it, had sworn to resist landing in France – was explained thus: "Who can condemn the citizens of a country, which herself suffered five years of the German jack-boot, for pitying the suffering of those who had survived the gas chambers?" Protesting Britain's demand of France, the editorial asked, further, "is it not rather strange to ask us to take renewed responsibility in the Near East, so short a while after we ourselves were the victims of every effort to remove us from this part of the world?" This was also the attitude adopted by the French Foreign Office in its briefs to the press (*Ha-Aretz*, 27 July 1947), but not in official contacts with Britain.

The French Government decided to accept the illegal immigrants but not to force them to land, and determined that Port de Bouc would be the port at which the deportation ships would anchor. The Interior Minister, who was made responsible for receiving the ships, outlined a set of rules, which aimed at preventing the use of force on the part of the British. The ships would anchor some distance from the wharf and the illegal immigrants would be transferred to French boats on which they would be taken to shore. France also made it quite clear to Britain that all physical violence was to be avoided while the illegal immigrants were being removed from the ships, as were other coercive measures, such as withholding food rations (Derogy 1972, 162–64).

The French Government's decision to forbid the use of force when removing the illegal immigrants, actually determined the outcome of the operation. Unlike in Haifa, where they could use all the force they wanted and as would later be the case in Hamburg, here in Port de Bouc, the British found themselves with their hands tied. Unless they had French cooperation, any attempted force on their part was doomed to fail, since even if the British were to force the illegal immigrants to transfer from the ships to smaller boats, it would be impossible to complete the job of transferring them to shore. The British also feared that such activity could draw accusations of brutality; make them look ridiculous to the battery of news reporters gathered at Port de Bouc; and could harm French–British relations.

At the end of July, Britain's ambassador in Paris said to French Foreign Office officials, that he had never before witnessed such a complete lack of goodwill and cooperation between their two countries.[25] Duff Cooper was quite right in his outburst. France's refusal to permit the use of force against the immigrants on her land and in her territorial waters, made it possible for the immigrants to stand by their decision not to land. Once force was no longer an option, the conflict became more evenly balanced between the two sides, as the immigrants were "playing on home ground", so to speak. Many years later, one of them was to write: "When the power of the destroyers had run out, on shores not their own, the struggle took on another kind of power game: Against the stubborn, inflexible stupidity of our captors – stood the revolt, anger and the intransigence of our own 'no choice'" (Peker 1964).

9 · We Shall Not Land!

Distribution of the immigrants among the three deportation ships that Friday evening at the port of Haifa was absolutely random. Children traveling without families embarked mostly with their original groups, since they tended to remain close to their leaders. But kibbutzim and groups which had originally boarded *Exodus* as organized units, now found themselves split up and there were even cases of families being divided. No one paid much attention to this at the time, because everyone was convinced that their journey was to be a short one only, and that they would soon be re-united in Cyprus. The British reckoned that *Ocean Vigour*, the first ship to be loaded, took on mainly children, women, families and many of the infirm; *Runnymede Park* took on many young people who offered some resistance to the transfer; and *Empire Rival*, the last to be boarded, was considered at that stage to be the most problematic of the three (Gruber 1948, 84; Katzanelson 1961; Fayer 1964).

On her way eastward, *Exodus* received orders from Palestine that "at least one escort must accompany the transport to Cyprus". The remaining escorts, together with the American crew members, were ordered to remain hidden on board ship until the arrival of the cleaning teams.[1] In the end three escorts accompanied the immigrants with 25 American crew members. Perlson went aboard the deportation ship, as he was the escort responsible for liaison with the immigrants. Sima Schmuckler, the nurse, decided at the last moment to remain with the immigrants, because, "as nurse in charge of the baby [whose mother had died in childbirth, on board ship], arrangements had been made for me to disembark. But when I saw the old doctor [who had taken care of the baby until then], standing there on deck, her eyes glued, longingly, to shore – she had a daughter in Haifa – I couldn't bear it and suggested she disembark instead of me" (Habbas 1954, 52).

Zvi ("Miri") Katzanelson's decision to board a deportation ship was in keeping with a personal principle, according to which he would remain with the immigrants until they reached their destination. This at first was Atlit, then Cyprus (Katzanelson 1985). Perlson and Schmuckler boarded the *Empire Rival*; Katzanelson went on board the *Runnymede Park*. There was no Palestinian escort aboard *Ocean Vigour*.

As the voyage drew out and there was no sign of Cyprus on the horizon, the passengers on each of the ships began organizing themselves in their own way. *Runnymede Park*, the convoy's flagship, was first. Katzanelson, who had made the journey to Cyprus in the past, understood that things were "beginning to smell fishy" and began to work together with Mordechai Roseman (Katzanelson 1985; Roseman 1984). The relationship between the two was molded by personality, experience and status. Roseman had outstanding leadership qualities and he was a talented orator and many of the immigrants were already acquainted with him from Europe, where he had held positions with the Brichah organization and in the DP camps. He had also been head of the ha-Shomer ha-Tza'ir movement in Germany, and on *Exodus* he had served on the ship's secretariat and as a communication link between the immigrants and the Hebrew-speaking escorts. Katzanelson, a veteran illegal-immigration activist, who had been escorting these ships since the summer of 1945, did not see himself as a commander and chose to remain as inconspicuous as possible (to the British), while backing Roseman to the hilt (Katzanelson 1985; Exodus Diary 1968, 85). The fact that both men belonged to the same movement probably increased their mutual respect and trust and made cooperation between them much easier.

A secretariat was soon formed, consisting of representatives of the various movements. Roseman was the undisputed leader on *Runnymede Park*, both with regard to the immigrants and as far as the British were concerned. He headed a fact finding delegation to a meeting with the ship's commander. When the immigrants learned of their changed destination, their immediate reaction was to declare a hunger strike and a spontaneous decision was taken that there would be no landing in France. The people began reorganizing themselves into groups, whether according to the same pattern as had guided them on *Exodus*, or – because of their present random distribution in three different deportation ships – in new groups.

Perlson, who went by the nickname "Gad", took control of *Empire Rival* and made it known that the Haganah was responsible for the passengers. When news came that their destination was France, he ordered the passengers, in the name of the Haganah, "not to land!" (Perry 1985; Leichter 1985; Tubul 1985). Perlson was the commander of the immigrants on *Empire Rival*, but he had to make use of translators and go-betweens. His messages to the immigrants had to be translated into Yiddish and he left to others – immigrants and Americans – all communication with the British, so as not to reveal his identity.

The immigrants on *Ocean Vigour* were confused and frightened. The first food allocation had been chaotic, and the American crew members and group leaders did their best to get things under control. After three days at sea, the immigrants formed a seven-member secretariat – one representative of each movement and one member representing the non-organized immigrants. Once again the immigrants arranged themselves into groups of 30 and the secretariat delegated tasks – maintaining shipboard hygiene, distributing food and water, etc. (Schwartz 1965, 86; Ganuz 1985, 181). Two of the immigrants were appointed to liaise with the British. Nonetheless, the lack of a Palestinian escort on board ship proved to be a problem: "There's no one to ask questions and to confer with," an immigrant wrote in his diary (Ganuz 1985, 183). Still, when the British informed the *Ocean Vigour* passengers of their destination, about two days before their arrival at Port de Bouc, the secretariat decided unanimously that there would be no landing in Europe and that they would disembark only on the shores of Palestine. The decision was relayed to the immigrants in several languages and "people responded favorably" (Ganuz 1985, 201).

Thus, despite the different populations on the three ships, which we shall discuss in greater detail later on, and regardless of the presence or absence of escorts from Palestine, a uniform decision was reached on all three ships, absolutely autonomously: "We shall not land in France."

Meanwhile, arrangements were being made on shore for the arrival of the three ships at Port de Bouc. With the French announcement that "France was not about to close her ports to immigrants, but she was also not about to force them to land," the next stage in the three-sided British–Jewish–French struggle began, this time with regard to the text of the French announcement to the immigrants and the way in which it was to be relayed to them. France's refusal to permit the use of force in landing the immigrants made these details doubly significant as far at the British were concerned. They asked the French to word their announcement in such a way as to imply the threat of possible use of force, or at least not to suggest explicitly that disembarkation was going to be a voluntary matter.

This was the original wording of the French announcement:

> The French Government wish to make known to the immigrants who were on board the *Exodus 1947* that they will not force them to disembark, but

will give refuge to all who disembark voluntarily. Those who decide to disembark on French soil will enjoy there all the freedom that France, a traditional land of welcome for refugees, and whose citizens have always fought for the freedom of the human person, accords to those who seek refuge on its territory. At the same time their material needs will be met to the greatest possible extent. In consequence, those persons wishing to disembark are requested to present themselves to the French officials controlling the disembarkation.[2]

The British immediately responded with a demand that the "softening agents" be removed from the announcement forthwith: "French Government ... *will not force them to disembark*"; "will give refuge to *all who disembark voluntarily*. Those who *decide* to disembark ..."; and the whole of the last sentence.[3] The British asked the French to emphasize the positive aspect of their invitation – the offer of refuge on French soil, where they would enjoy all the freedom that France accords to those who seek refuge on its territory.[4] Colonel Gregson, who reckoned that it would be possible to land the immigrants without having to resort to force, arrived at Marseilles on board the destroyer *Cardigan Bay* one day before the deportation ships arrived at Port de Bouc. He, too, felt the French announcement to be too softly worded. This time British Foreign Office men on the spot saw eye to eye with Gregson, who, they all agreed, "knew his Jews".[5]

The French complied with Britain's request to change the wording – to the distress of the Mossad and the Jewish Agency, but it was soon clear that the changes had no practical significance. At first the French proposed broadcasting their message to the immigrants over loud-speakers, but the British ambassador insisted that a French official present it personally on board the ships, with the help of a translator.[6] In London, where the use-of-force option had not yet been completely discarded, they soon understood that the visit on board ship of a French delegation would be an obstacle which must be removed, or at least made as brief and to the point as possible, and without the press.[7] The Mossad and the Jewish Agency, on the other hand, were in favor of having the press present on the arrival of the ships and the visit of the delegation and "in the event of incidents", as Shertok put it at a meeting of the Jewish Agency Executive in Jerusalem – clearly this was what he was hoping for – "it would bring a lot of publicity" (28 July 1947).

The French appointed a committee – consisting of representatives of the Foreign Office, Ministry of the Interior, Ministry of Transport and Public Works, a Public Health Inspector and a Red Cross representative – to deal with the deportation ships and their passengers. While the wording of the announcement had been decided upon in the high quarters of the Quai d'Orsay in Paris, where the British knew very well which strings needed pulling, in practical matters, those within the jurisdiction of regional councils and the ministries of the Interior, and Transport and Public Works, the Mossad had a way of turning events to their advantage, thanks to the sympathy and personal connections which had been oiling the wheels of their activity in France over the last two years. The Ministry of the Interior representative on the committee was a Zionist sympathizer, who worked hand in hand with Marcel Pages, a senior ministry official and an old ally of the Mossad. It was Pages who was credited with issuing the collective entry visas from Germany to France in duplicate, so that they could be used at two border stations, thus doubling the number of *émigrés* entering France "legally". The minister responsible for the committee and its activity, Depreux, brought in his friend, Andre Blumel – with the approval of Prime Minister Ramadier and Transport Minister Moch. When the committee needed help with translation from French into Yiddish and Hebrew, the "friends" offered the services of a Mossad activist, who was appointed as official translator to the French delegation. This man was Hannan Sonnenborn (later Einor), known as "Ya'akobi", after his kibbutz, Ashdot-Ya'akov (Habbas 1954, 80–93; Derogy 1972, 164–69).

Another round in the campaign regarding the nature of the French delegation's visit, concerned Andre Blumel's invitation to be present when the ships arrived in France and to witness the relaying of the French Government's announcement to the immigrants. The Mossad saw this invitation as one more achievement in their efforts to prevent the immigrants from landing in France.[8] One day before the ships arrived at Port de Bouc, Shertok reported with satisfaction to the Jewish Agency Executive in Jerusalem, that "our people have promised that Blumel will be there" (28 July 1947). That same day, the British ambassador protested at the French Foreign Office's invitation, claiming that letting Blumel, whom he described as head of all the Zionist organizations in France, address the immigrants, was tantamount to encouraging them not to land.[9] This round was won by the British. Blumel did not board the ships.

Britain hoped that an impetus would be created by the French delegation's visit to the ships, which would cause the passengers to land willingly. The Mossad, on the other hand, saw in it a chance, perhaps the first one, to make contact with the immigrants. Many years later, an ex-Mossad man described it thus: "The main problem was how to say in the first sentence – 'Do not land!'" (Hadari 1964). As the deportation ships were on their way westward, both sides had been making great efforts, the one to get the message "Do not land" to the passengers; and the other, to prevent all communication between the passengers and the outside world. This hectic activity only goes to show how little faith both the Mossad and the British had – while the Exodus Affair was underway – in the immigrants' steadfastness.

The Admiralty ordered the commander of the flotilla escorting the deportation ships to prevent messages being transmitted over a loudspeaker system close to disembarkation point, to confiscate all wireless equipment on the ships and to prevent the transfer of written messages from shore to the passengers.[10] We shall recall that Colonel Gregson was confident that the immigrants would disembark quietly of their own accord provided no outside Zionist propaganda reached them. And the Zionists did indeed search for every possible channel to bring the message "Do not land!" to the immigrants' attention, publishing news items in newspapers and over the radio, in the hope that these would reach them in some way or other. On 23 July 1947, the Haganah in France published an announcement on behalf of the immigrants that "they have sworn not to disembark from the ships, no matter what", and that they "would resist with all their might any attempt at removing them".[11] Five days later, however, reports were published (*Ha-Aretz*, 28 July 1947, for example) that the Haganah had not yet succeeded in making contact with the immigrants!

Perlson, no less than his colleagues in Palestine and in France, was concerned lest the immigrants on the two other ships choose to disembark in France. He decided to send one of the passengers on his own ship to one of the other ships, to pass on the "Do not land" order. The young man pretended to fall overboard, intending to be picked up by the next deportation ship in the convoy. The operation, however, failed. He was picked up by one of the escort ships, and after he had recovered and undergone a thorough interrogation, was sent back to his own ship.[12]

Boats were used in another attempt at contacting the immigrants. These floated around in the vicinity of the deportation ships near Port de Bouc and were equipped with loudspeakers through which the command "Do not land" was broadcast constantly. There are many sources, both British and Jewish, to substantiate the fact that the French delegation visited all the deportation ships – the *Runnymede Park* was visited on 29 July 1947, the *Empire Rival* and *Ocean Vigour* on 30 July 1947 – *prior* to the arrival of the loudspeaker boats in the area and *before* the immigrants heard the command not to land (Reichman 1947; Dror 1948, 39; Perlov n.d., 223; Ganuz 1985, 201–202).[13] Against these sources, stand retrospect testimonies of Haganah activists who insist that the boat or boats were broadcasting the order not to land during the delegation's visit to the first or second ship (Habbas 1954, 57, 104, 121–22). A similar claim is made in the memoirs of a member of the Sixth Airborne Division, who took part in escorting the *Exodus* immigrants to France. According to him, the British were impressed that the Jews were reconciled to the fact that they were being returned to Europe and there would be no problems landing in France. Unfortunately, things started to go wrong. The Haganah succeeded in spreading its propaganda by using loudspeaker boats and infiltrating guests on to the deportation ships (Wilson 1949, 127).

His recollection conforms with the official line taken by the British in explaining their failure in the Exodus Affair, although on more than one occasion it contradicts their internal documents. The Haganah people – both the Mossad and Palmach – follow two trends in their recollections of the Exodus Affair. "Venia's story" in Habbas' book is typical. He recalls how, during the French delegation's visit to the first ship, "a loud voice in Hebrew rent the air: 'In the name of the Hebrew Haganah in Palestine, in the name of the Jewish Yishuv, do not disembark these ships.'" A couple of lines later, he adds: "But the immigrants did not need to get these orders from Palestine. They knew very well what had to be done" (1954, 121–22).

Plans for the French delegation's visit went ahead and did not take into consideration Britain's evaluation of the potential resistance to be expected of the immigrants, but in accordance with the rules, by which the flag ship, *Runnymede Park* was to be visited first. British and Jewish descriptions of the visit are quite similar.[14] Some of the immigrants were on deck as the delegation arrived at the ship, but they soon went down to the holds and one of them, Roseman, demanded of the delegation that they join them, to see for themselves the conditions people were forced to live under and to speak to them there. The French official read out the announcement in French, and it was translated into Yiddish and Hebrew, with "interpretations" in tone and emphasis. When the Frenchman asked if anyone wanted to say anything, there was silence as Roseman rose to deliver an impassioned speech, the essence of which was: We thank the French Government for the offer, but we will settle for no less than Palestine. The crowd burst into hysterical tears, and at the end of the speech rose as one and sang the Zionist anthem, Ha-Tikvah. An immigrant wrote in her diary, in Polish: "Our leader spoke so nicely, that we all cried … the 'Ha-Tikvah' that we sang had in it so much pain, suffering, torture and the hope that we shall overcome and achieve our aim and that we shall not land in France, because we must not do so. The French delegation was very touched at our firm stand, our unity and the fact that we have not given in" (Diary 1947b).

Roseman's speech was aimed at the immigrants, to encourage them and give them strength, and he told the translator that no translation was necessary. The translator, however, thought otherwise and translated most of the speech into French. The senior French Government official, François Collaveri, was deeply impressed by the contents of the speech; he was already moved almost to tears by the dramatic way in which Roseman delivered his speech and at the immigrants' reaction to it. The next day Collaveri admitted to a representative of the British Foreign Office that he had been somewhat carried away by the hysterical atmosphere on board.

It was clear to the French delegation and to the British escorts that the immigrants were unanimous in their refusal to accept the French offer. The British consulate in Marseilles was quick to report to London that "we fear passengers on the other vessels will react similarly. We are now in no doubt that the passengers will not disembark without use of force." [15] This report was distributed among all the members of the British Cabinet. In fact, in their *internal* communications, the British allowed themselves to analyze the situation realistically and without excuses and propaganda. They realized that the immigrants' reply was that no one would leave the ship and they were all determined to reach Palestine. "Whilst the collective reply was dictated, it probably reflected views of vast majority of immigrants." [16] But three weeks later, in a *public announcement* issued by the British Government, regarding the deportation of the *Exodus* immigrants to Hamburg, the Jews' rejection of the French proposal was explained away as the result of constant and ceaseless Zionist threats and propaganda. [17]

The visit aboard the *Runnymede Park* and its aftermath refired Britain's anger with France. In private, they still toyed with the idea of using force to remove the immigrants from the ships, but they rejected this idea as soon as it was raised, knowing that without French cooperation and so long as France insisted on accepting only Jews who had disembarked of their own free will, the matter was impractical. [18]

The following day, 30 July 1947, the delegation visited the *Empire Rival* and the *Ocean Vigour*. Whereas on *Runnymede Park*, Roseman had sole command of the situation, outwardly as well as inwardly, on the *Empire Rival* there was a delegation of authority. Perlson, whose every word was law, was swallowed up among the immigrants and made a point of being as inconspicuous as possible. Together with his people, he had prepared in advance the response to the French proposal. It was decided who would address the delegation in French; who would make a speech in Yiddish to the immigrants, and an athletic boy was sent to climb up the flagpole, where he waited for hours in order to raise the Jewish national flag, while the delegation was visiting. The visit on this ship took place up on the deck.[19]

On the *Ocean Vigour* the delegation took up its position half-way, at the entrance to the hold, above the stairs. Here, the immigrants' immediate reaction to the French invitation was the least organized of the three. They reacted with loud cries of "We won't land", "Down with England" and "We were taken from Palestine and to Palestine we shall return" and similar slogans. After a while the French delegation began mingling among the immigrants and, according to a report by a British Foreign Office official, some of the immigrants showed signs that they were willing to land, but these were met with protests and threats on the part of the other immigrants, until they agreed to go back on their intentions. According to the same report, at this stage disagreements were arising between the French and the British. The French official demanded the right to interrogate several of the immigrants separately, so as to find out if they really did want to land. Colonel Gregson thought differently. He wasn't interested in having a handful of immigrants landing in the dead of night; his idea was to create a momentum and he asked for the landing to be postponed to the following day, when the immigrants who chose to, could disembark in full view of all the others on all three ships.

In fact, the French official, Collaveri, was acting for the good of the Jewish side. He explained his apparent sympathy toward the immigrants on the first day as being the result of exhaustion and excitement; on the second day, when he was clear-headed and in control (according to a British Foreign Office official), he tried to communicate with the immigrants without the presence of the British. At the end of the visit, when he was asked by Gregson to prepare landing boats and medical teams for disembarking the immigrants from the *Ocean Vigour* the following day, Collaveri refused, saying he would not do this without first receiving orders from Paris. And again the British were furious at the lack of cooperation on the part of the French.[20]

Another stage in the Exodus Affair had come to an end. The immigrants on the three deportation ships all gave an answer which was equivalent in content, even if it differed in form and style, to the French invitation: We shall not land. The immigrants, their leaders and their escorts were greatly relieved when they realized that they would not be forcibly removed from the ships and that the Haganah was with them and acting on their behalf. It was clear to the British that the immigrants would not disembark of their own free will and they were obliged to face a new situation, one they had not experienced previously, had not anticipated and were not properly prepared for.

10 · A Floating Concentration Camp

For more than three weeks the deportation ships had been anchored opposite Port de Bouc – three "Liberty" ships, each about 440 feet long and 57 feet wide at their center. The *Ocean Vigour* carried 1,494 immigrants; *Runnymede Park* carried 1,409; and there were 1,526 immigrants on *Empire Rival*.[1]

Britain rejected criticism over the harsh conditions aboard the deportation ships, pointing out in return that together, the three ships were larger than the *Exodus*, on which the immigrants had sailed to Palestine.[2] Not only was this cynical, it was also mathematically inaccurate, since only a small part of each deportation ship had been allotted to living quarters for the immigrants, while the remainder was used for various purposes and by the crew. Overcrowding was terrible in the ships' holds and their only advantage over the *Exodus* was that here people were concentrated on one level and not stuffed into layer upon layer of shelves. And this made day to day life somewhat easier, as far as distribution of food, announcements, cultural and educational activity, etc. were concerned.

The truth is that the British were well aware that the ships were unsuitable for transporting such a large number of people over such a distance, and that they were especially unequipped for a long sea journey. About six months before, it had been determined by the Mediterranean High Command that 800 was the maximum number of passengers each of the "Liberty" ships (which had been adjusted to transfer illegal immigrants from Haifa to Cyprus) could bear at one time. The Commander-in-Chief Mediterranean had warned that additional passengers would cause unbearable overcrowding which would endanger the life and health of the passengers, and that safety equipment on these ships was insufficient for so large a mass of people.[3]

Nevertheless, it was not unusual to load up to 1,500 immigrants on each of these ships. In January 1947, the civilian crew aboard the *Ocean*

Vigour complained about being employed in the transfer of illegal immigrants in a vessel which was completely unsuitable and was not equipped with adequate facilities for this purpose.[4] And here the issue at hand was no more than the brief voyage from Haifa to Cyprus! Physical conditions on board the two other ships could not have been any better, since, of the three, *Ocean Vigour* was in the best technical condition and carried larger quantities of food and coal at the time of setting sail from Haifa to Port de Bouc. *Ocean Vigour* was equipped with hammocks on which many of the immigrants could sleep, whereas the British had ripped out all the bunks and other sleeping facilities on the other two ships following sabotage by the Palmach. On *Empire Rival* and *Runnymede Park* all the immigrants (as well as some on *Ocean Vigour*) had to sleep on the hard metal floors of the ships, and certainly there were no provisions made for a prolonged sea voyage.

Two holds were allotted on each of the ships – one large and one smaller – in which the immigrants were housed. The floors and walls of these holds – sometimes they were defined as cellars or cages – were metal, with steel netting covering the ceiling and supplying the only source of air and light. There was a heat wave during their first weeks in Port de Bouc, such as had not been known in the south of France for many years. A British Foreign Office official, who accompanied the French delegation on its first visit to the ships, wrote to his colleagues in London that it was terribly hot inside the ships and unbearably stuffy (Coulson 1947). There was a flight of stairs leading to the holds and the entire area of the immigrants' quarters was cordoned off. In order to move from the immigrants' living quarters to other parts of the ships – the crew and military quarters, kitchen, clinic and most important of all, the water taps and lavatories – it was necessary to go out of the compound through a wire gate, all under the alert eyes of the British soldiers. Overcrowding was very bad and the sanitary conditions were appalling, with long queues winding their way down the aisles – for food, water, lavatories. At night, people had to sleep with their legs tucked up to their chests, for lack of space (Diary 1947b; Exodus diary, 1968, 31 July 1947).

In their January 1947 complaint, the *Ocean Vigour* crew members pointed out that with the immigrants on board, the ship resembled "more of a military prison or floating concentration camp".[5] The definition "concentration camp" was repeated in descriptions presented by people who visited the ships immediately on their arrival at Port de Bouc.[6] The communist newspaper *L'Humanité* called the three ships "a floating Auschwitz" and another French paper, *Combat*, denounced the British for putting people who had survived the Nazi concentration camps behind the barbed wire fences of the allied forces.[7]

As soon as it became known that the ships were making their way westward and not toward Cyprus, the Mossad began looking for Palestinian emissaries who would go aboard the ships and join the immigrants. It was done because the Mossad had little faith in the immigrants and out of fear that, left to their own devices, they would be unable to hold out, or to offer sufficient resistance on board the deportation ships. Testimony to this attitude is the fact, that, as soon as it became known that the *Exodus* immigrants were making their way to France, the Palestinian escorts on Mossad ships traveling to Palestine were ordered to stay with the immigrants and not to try to disembark in Haifa, and to encourage the immigrants to resist with all their might any attempts to land them forcibly at their port of departure.[8]

Recruiting of emissaries and placing them aboard the deportation ships stemmed also from a sense of responsibility and shared destiny with the immigrants. In this respect, the arrival of the emissaries on board the ships had great moral significance. It is possible to find similarities in things said, years later, by the emissary Eli'ezer ("Yuzek") Limon, with regard to the way the immigrants felt when he arrived among them: "Here are fellows from Palestine ... they lack nothing, yet they have chosen, of their own free will to come and join us, and share our harsh conditions" (1985), and the words of Yitzhak Artzi, on the arrival of the Palestinian paratrooper, Abba Berdiczew, in Romania in 1944: "A young fellow from Palestine, left his family and home and came back to the 'valley of tears', in order to give us faith and strength and confidence" (Porat 1986, 417). The background and conditions in 1947 were very different from those in 1944, but there is great similarity in the gratitude and happiness expressed by the Jews of the Diaspora toward the Jews of Palestine for their willingness to share their fate. It was the horrors of the war years, the collective guilt and helplessness felt by the Yishuv in Palestine, that created this need on their part to stand beside the immigrants at this trying time for them all, way beyond the sense that "they are never going to make it without us."

At the end of July 1947, Meir Schwartz, a Mossad emissary in France, received an urgent order from Meirov to board one of the ships. The Mossad chief feared a catastrophe, unless there was at least one Palestinian emissary on board each of the ships, and the Mossad in France believed that the immigrants were going to disembark, which would put an end to Aliyah Bet. It was imperative, therefore, to go aboard the ships and get the people organized (Schwartz 1965, 83; 1986). The new objective – that of joining the *Exodus* immigrants – could have been harmful to the ongoing activity of the Mossad and the Palmach in France. The number of activists on the spot was already limited and each of these was concerned with his own appointed task or was waiting for the next immigrant ship. The Mossad, therefore, decided to look for other sources of manpower, which they found at a festival for Democratic Youth in Prague. The Haganah managed to recruit three members of the Palestine delegation to the festival, making sure that a strict political balance was maintained – one emissary, Eliezer ("Yuzek") Limon, from ha-Shomer ha-Tza'ir, another, Elhanan Vanchotzker (later Yishai), a member of the Mapai young guard and Moshe Gilbo'a, a member of the Scouts. On arrival in the south of France, the delegates were ordered by the Mossad representative there, Avi Schwartz, to board the deportation ships and to try to take command of the immigrants. Subsequent orders would be sent from shore (Limon 1985).

In the meantime, until the reinforcements arrived, a Palyam member, known as "Skandi", boarded *Runnymede Park* on 31 July 1947. He did this easily, by taking a ride "with the food shipment. I picked up a crate and climbed aboard and remained there. I looked like all the others, so that no one suspected me. Once the food boat was gone, I went down to join the immigrants" (Exodus Diary 1968, 31 July 1947).

The British were subsequently much more careful when loading food supplies on board the ships, suspecting that the Haganah were using this method for getting their activists on board. They stopped lowering ladders down to the supply boats and placed food supplies in large baskets which were raised and lowered with the help of winches, instead. On 5 August Limon, masquerading as a French boatman, complete with the traditional cap and striped vest, joined a supply boat. He jumped into the basket of food crates and arrived thus on board the ship.

I landed on deck, together with this basket, and the vegetables, I looked all around me and saw this picture: the ship's stern was empty, and this was three or four meters deep, and a rope several dozen meters long was stretched across and every two or three meters, stood a soldier and behind each soldier were hundreds upon hundreds of immigrants, all watching as the food supplies were raised on board. I stepped on the deck and began taking up crates, I moved them this way and that, I fiddled with the crates and looked around and decided that there was no choice here, and that I would have to simply go straight toward the soldiers and somehow get under the rope and mingle with the people.

So I walk up calmly toward a row of soldiers, they aren't looking at me, and bend down under the rope and pass it and push my way among the immigrants and I remember saying just one sentence: "Ich bin von der Haganah in Eretz Israel" [in Yiddish: I am from the Haganah in Palestine]. It was enough. So they took to me immediately, brought me down to one of the lower decks and tore the French clothes off me and dressed me in the regular raggy outfit.

Limon was surprised to find Perlson and Schmuckler on board (Limon 1985), and he met Vanchotzker, who had boarded the day before, after passing himself off as a doctor (Habbas 1954, 63–64).

Opinions have been divided ever since, as to the practical contribution made by the emissaries' presence on the ships. There was, of course the matter of moral support, which was appreciated, but there is still no consensus as to the effect these had on the immigrants' steadfast refusal to land in France. When "Skandi" met Katzanelson after boarding the *Runnymede Park*, the latter was "very happy and didn't understand what I was doing there. I explained to him what I had been sent for and he laughed and said that he did not need any help" (Exodus Diary 1968, 31 July 1947). "Skandi" soon saw that Katzanelson was right: "There is plenty of internal organization ... Mordechai [Roseman] is the man in charge here and he represents us with the ship's management and he seems to be doing perfectly well. Everyone does as he says" (Exodus Diary 1968, 2 Aug. 1947). About three weeks after his arrival on the ship the emissary felt that his presence was "a waste of time" (Exodus Diary 1968, 19 August 1947).

As it happened, therefore, the two ships already with Palestinian escorts, were reinforced with emissaries, whereas the Haganah were unable to board any emissaries on the *Ocean Vigour* (since this ship was more closely guarded than the others), which, for the first ten days of the ships' stay opposite Port de Bouc had no such escorts. It was only on 8 August, as coal was being loaded at the Port of Marseilles, that the emissary, Meir Schwartz, was able to steal on to the ship. We are able, therefore to compare the situation on *Ocean Vigour* prior to Schwartz's arrival with that following it and are fortunate enough to have two extensive descriptions of events on this ship – one is by Schwartz himself and the second by one of the immigrants.

The immigrant, Yitzhak Ganuzovitch (later Ganuz) pointed out the importance of the emissary's presence from the point of view of *morale*, because he "brought with him a spark of life", and by his presence "offers friendship and a sense of security" (1985, 236–37). The emissary himself, on the other hand, considered his presence on board to be of great *practical* benefit. He was of the opinion that the relatively large movement shoreward from *Ocean Vigour* stemmed from there having been no Haganah emissary on board and as soon as "people learned of the presence of a Haganah commander on the ship ... the rate of disembarkation was reduced significantly and [eventually] ceased completely." He believed that his presence had a positive effect on the immigrants, "most of whom did not know who the Haganah representative was, but it encouraged them enormously and raised their spirits no end" (Schwartz 1965, 84–87). As mentioned, there is no questioning the moral benefit of the emissary's presence, but his effect on the rate of disembarkation requires further examination.

A total of some 130 immigrants chose to land at Port de Bouc.[9] Most of these (about 100) decided on this move during the first few days after their arrival.[10] The number had risen to 120 by the middle of August.[11] A further ten disembarked before the ships set off for Hamburg.[12]

Those who disembarked were mostly "sick and disabled", as reported by the Colonial Office to Foreign Secretary Bevin in the middle of August.[13] Some of them were in advanced stages of pregnancy and the doctors diagnosed difficult labor, so that, unlike most of the pregnant women, who were able to give birth on board ship, these were advised to disembark and be hospitalized. Among those to disembark were several mentally ill people (correspondence described these as "lunatics"), as were other types who were suspected of spying, informing and theft (Exodus Diary 1968, 4 August 1947; Habbas 1954, 199–206).

Most of those to disembark from the *Empire Rival, Runnymede Park* and, after 8 August 1947, from the *Ocean Vigour*, did so with the permission of the Haganah personnel on board. There were those whose medical condition required that they disembark and they refused to do so unless express orders were received from the Haganah; and there were those who received immigration certificates to Palestine and were able to immigrate legally, but refused to desert their comrades and their struggle. And then there were those who disembarked all on their own, with no permission from anyone (Habbas 1954, 184–215). Some others of the immigrants tried to prevent this partisan disembarkation, sometimes even through the use of force and on occasions they even mistakenly beat up people who were disembarking with Haganah permission (Habbas 1954, 70; Leichter 1985; Ganuz 1985, 238–40).

The largest number of people to disembark did so from the *Ocean Vigour*. Some 80 people had landed by 8 August 1947, followed by only a handful after this date, and these were mostly given permission (Habbas 1954, 207–215; Schwartz 1965, 87; Ganuz 1985, 238–40). Some 30 people had disembarked from *Runnymede Park* by 17 August 1947 (Exodus Diary

1968, 17 August 1947), and from *Empire Rival* only six people disembarked close to the time the ships were to set sail for Hamburg (Exodus Diary 1968, 19 August 1947). A few others disembarked shortly before the three ships left for Hamburg.

How can we explain the difference in numbers of immigrants to disembarked from each of the ships? Clearly, during the first few days at Port de Bouc, the first immigrants to leave the ships were those who were troubled by health problems. Later, too, most of the dropouts were sick in one way or another.[14] In this respect, it was the *Ocean Vigour* which was the weakest of the three deportation ships. She had been the first to be loaded in Haifa, and she it was who had received most of the wounded from the sea battle, as well as various other sick people. This correlation, between the order of embarkation in Haifa, the health of the immigrants and the number of immigrants to land at Port de Bouc was maintained with respect to the other ships. The *Runnymede Park* boarded second in Haifa and had the second largest number of passengers to land in France, and the *Empire Rival* was third.

Another parameter for examining the differences between the ships was the number of immigrants on each belonging to an organized group. Here, too, the *Empire Rival* was the strongest and the emissaries on *Ocean Vigour* and *Runnymede Park* "vied" with each other over which of the two had a larger contingent of difficult cases and fewer steadfast immigrants (Exodus Diary 1968, 1 August 1947; Schwartz 1965, 87). *Runnymede Park* had more than 250 children over ten years old, and this usually meant that they were traveling with one or other of the pioneer youth movements and not with their parents and many of them were orphans. These youngsters were strongly united in their determination to firmly resist landing. In this respect, it seems that the *Runnymede Park* had the strongest-willed population, followed by *Empire Rival* and finally, again, *Ocean Vigour*, most of whose children were younger and traveling with their parents.

At the other end of the scale were the "individuals" – people who did not belong to any of the youth movements or kibbutzim, mainly people who were traveling with their families and who constituted the weak link. The emissaries on *Runnymede Park* and *Ocean Vigour* complained often about the "difficult material" they had to cope with on their ships – families with small children and elderly people.

On all the ships, immigrants from Morocco presented problems of discipline, physical violence and the wish to disembark (Habbas 1954, 210; Tubul 1985; Roseman 1984). The Revisionist Betar group was also problematic, insisting on conducting debates on IZL activity and later on threatening to actively resist attempts to take them off the ships once they arrive at Hamburg – blatantly defying Haganah orders (Schwartz 1965, 94–95; Exodus Diary 1968, 14 August 1947).

The religious passengers, too, caused difficulties (Habbas 1954, 190). On all three ships, there were altogether about 1,000 people requiring kosher food,[15] and these people never stopped making a fuss throughout the stay at Port de Bouc – especially those on the *Empire Rival* and the *Runnymede Park*. A certain amount of kosher food had been sent at the beginning of August in the food shipments supplied by the Red Cross,[16] and after a while the Rabbinate in Marseilles proclaimed all the food to be kosher (Exodus Diary 1968, 8 August 1947). The Agudat Israel people demanded that their food be "cooked specially", but they were still not satisfied ten days after this had been arranged for them, complaining that their food rations were smaller and that they were being discriminated against (Exodus Diary 1968, 8 and 17 August 1947). Meir Schwartz, himself a member of a Poalei Agudat Israel kibbutz, was especially sympathetic toward the consumers of kosher food on board the *Ocean Vigour*. "The supply of kosher food is very difficult," he wrote to shore, asking that "effort be made to obtain kosher meat" (Habbas 1954, 208). A few days later, he reported happily that "the kosher eaters were given eggs today," and added: "Please make a point of sending out fish or eggs for the kosher eaters" (Habbas 1954, 211).

Food played a major role in the lives of the passengers of the deportation ships. "In the morning," wrote one of the immigrants in her diary, "as breakfast begins to be served, everyone concentrates on that – what will we get today. Everyone has a wonderful appetite, but there's not too much food. Matters of food allotment take up most of our day-to-day lives. I don't want to elaborate on the fact that sometimes there are quarrels over the distribution of food" (Diary 1947b).

When they set off from Haifa the ships were not adequately equipped for a lengthy voyage. The crew were given vague orders to prepare for a week-long voyage with a full load of passengers, beginning on 17 July 1947.[17] The journey from Haifa to Port de Bouc lasted 11 days and the food on board was not only insufficient, it was of poor quality and worm-ridden. Much of the preserved food was in cans stamped with a seal saying: Not for use after 1945.[18] As soon as the ships arrived at Port de Bouc, a decent supply of food rations was resumed, which, according to the British, resulted in released tension and an easing up of frayed nerves among the passengers.[19]

Everyone appreciated how important a regular food supply was to the immigrants' motivation to remain aboard, rather than disembark in France. The British considered, then rejected, the idea of stopping the supply of food as a means of pressure,[20] while the Mossad and the Jewish Agency were getting themselves organized to supply the ships with sufficient quantities of food during their stay in Port de Bouc. Still, although the quantity and quality of the food improved greatly as soon as the ships arrived in France, food – the insufficiency thereof – remained a major issue in all the letters dispatched from the ships to shore. Perlson, whose letters were usually controlled, friendly and to the point, wrote to the Mossad on shore, at the beginning of August: "You are clearly unable to fully appreciate the way in which the food issue affects our ability to maintain any kind of regime, in keeping with our situation. Just bear in mind, that most of the people are ex-concentration camp inmates, families with small children and babies as well as a large number of pregnant women. I repeat: Do all you can to ensure a large supply of food. I mean mainly basic commodities: Bread, meat, pulses and grains for children, babies and pregnant women" (Habbas 1954, 185). Similar requests were made repeatedly over about three weeks from all three ships.

The level of autonomy allowed to the immigrants with regard to the supply and preparation of their food differed from ship to ship, the best conditions being on *Runnymede Park*, where the immigrants were charged with bringing the food on board and they had full control of the kitchen. On its way to the *Empire Rival* the food was examined by the British, who could not resist "taking" some of it; cooking on this ship was done by the immigrants. The conditions on *Ocean Vigour* were worst of all. The British had control of all stages of food supply and preparation, and they pilfered a lot of the food meant for the immigrants. Theft was reduced when immigrants were posted to oversee the unloading of supplies, but once the British realized that food transports were used as a means of communication – notes were hidden in food and immigrants were exchanging messages in various languages with people on the supply boats – they stopped allowing the immigrants to take part in the unloading process and in the end, even forbade them to leave the holds when food was being transferred from the boats to the ships (Exodus Diary 1968, 19 August 1947; Habbas 1954, 210–13).

Three days before the ships left Port de Bouc for Hamburg, the British allowed a man and his son, who had boarded the *Empire Rival* in Haifa to join his heavily pregnant wife aboard the *Runnymede Park*. The emissary promptly "interrogated" the man on events on board *Empire Rival* and compared the two ships thus:

> They are short of food. He saw the food here and was amazed. Over there people are really hungry. They cook three times a day but they are allowed

to be in the kitchen from 6 in the morning to 7.30 in the evening, after which they are sent out of the kitchen. They do distribute the food they receive but a lot is stolen [by the British], so that a fair amount is lost. The same amount of food as is consumed there by a huge number of people, is eaten by half that number over here. For example, they hardly ever get one loaf of bread to two people, always three or two loaves for seven people. Strangely enough, the worst thing here was – one loaf among three people – but that was only for a short while. In addition, the amounts of cooked food there are very small. Here, we cook porridge in all the pots, then cocoa, tea or coffee, etc. But that's not what happens over there, they cook coffee and porridge at the same time and in this way they reduce rations. Altogether, the food situation over there is pretty bad (Exodus Diary 1968, 19 August 1947).

On the *Runnymede Park*, too, there were days on which food supply was bad and this had an immediate negative effect on the atmosphere on board ship. In the middle of August the emissary informed his colleagues on shore that "food is insufficient and people are going around half starved and the worst thing is that they are complaining and this brings down morale" (Habbas 1954, 203). How much worse, therefore, was the situation on the other ships.

11 · Not by Bread Alone

Notwithstanding the importance of a decent food supply to the deportation ships, the Palestine emissaries and the immigrant leaders on board reckoned that not by bread along would man exist, and alongside requests for food, came endless demands for a supply of text books, exercise books and pencils, for use in their improvised schools. For several hours every day, hundreds of children received an education, especially about Palestine and the Hebrew language. In time the children were joined by a large number of adults.

This educational and cultural activity helped keep up morale among the immigrants and made it easier to "while the time away" while they were anchored at Port de Bouc. The weather was terrible – for the first few days there was an appalling heat wave and then, from mid August onward, it never stopped raining. Shipboard orchestras and choirs were formed and these made the atmosphere on all three ships so much more bearable. The emissary on the *Runnymede Park*, who was often short-tempered with the immigrants, was very moved by a Sabbath-eve party they held, in which they sang songs in Hebrew and Yiddish. "One of the people sang a solo and it was wonderful," he wrote in his diary, "altogether a very nice party, which made a deep impression on me. These same families, these same Jews, are able, after all they have been through, to be happy sometimes and to sing songs. It was mostly the children who sang" (Exodus Diary 1968, 2 August 1947).

For all the *Exodus* people, the shipboard Sabbath-eve parties were the highlight of their week. The tradition had been established on the first day of *Exodus'* voyage from France to Palestine and it continued on the deportation ships on the voyage from Haifa to France, throughout their stay at Port de Bouc, and right through to the end of their journey to Hamburg. An integral part of the Sabbath-eve parties on *Runnymede Park* was a speech by Roseman, who "preached Zionism" and "brought tears to Jewish eyes". The Palestinian emissary recorded in his diary the main points of Roseman's speeches, together with an apology that "the speech, as translated here [from Yiddish], cannot make the same impression as it did on the people who heard it, and it seems that it gave them strength to go on for another ten days, if not longer" (Exodus Diary 1968, 16 August 1947).

Shortly after the ships arrived at Port de Bouc, contact was made with them by the Haganah activists on the spot, who considered ongoing communications with the ships to be of utmost importance, and sought ways of maintaining it. Boats with loudspeakers sailed around the waters in which the ships were anchored, broadcasting information and encouragement – notwithstanding attempts on the part of the French (in response to continued requests by the British) at putting a stop to this.[1] Notes were placed in food crates and introduced into loaves of bread. Doctors and nurses served as go-betweens and various other means of communication were also used.

Shore to ship communication was totally dependent on available means of transferring written or verbal information. Ship to shore communication, on the other hand, was also dependent on the level of importance attached to it by the emissaries and their willingness to receive orders from shore. The best system of communication was that with the *Empire Rival*. For Perlson, the Haganah people were a source of authority and help in maintaining day-to-day life on board. He made many and various requests – for food, medication, clothing, books and learning equipment, and asked again and again to be given "orders as to how to behave in the event that we are deported elsewhere and not sent back to Palestine" (Habbas 1954, 185).

Perlson made the most of his connections with people on shore, to obtain public sympathy and to ensure that *Exodus* remained in the headlines. He sent out communiqués to the newspapers, a letter to the Secretary General of the UN and copies of letters which were passed on to the ship's commander. He also suggested that his colleagues on shore "lodge complaints with the Red Cross and the French Government, since the British were not allowing us to send letters. Every prisoner has this basic human right and we, who have neither stood any trial, nor been judged by any judge, are denied it" (Habbas 1954, 192–94).

The Mossad wanted to get the exchange of letters organized and directed their activists on board the ships to make letter boxes into which the immigrants could place letters to their relatives and friends. These letters would be collected and transferred *en masse* to shore. The system would replace the existing one, by which the immigrants used to place their letters in bottles and throw them into the sea, to be picked up at random by passing fishing boats. Still, the Mossad activists on shore pointed out: "We would ask you to be very careful about using these letterboxes, since the letters may fall into the hands of the 'bastards' [the British] ... you must take special care not to have any letters in the box, which might be of harm to us." The instructions also demanded that all the letters "end up with us" only.[2] In other words, the letters were not aimed at the senders' relations and friends, but were recruited for promoting *Exodus* propaganda, and eventually they were used in writing up the history of the Exodus Affair.[3] Many of these letters never reached their destined addresses (Leichter 1985).

As the flagship of the convoy of deportation ships, *Runnymede Park* was visited by many journalists. On one of these visits Roseman was asked about the attitude showed by the British to the immigrants and he replied that "apart from isolated incidents, the attitude is good and everything is fine". Not only was this reply correct – the British did treat the immigrants on *Runnymede Park* most fairly – it also carried a message, aimed at attracting the media's attention to the main front of the immigrants' struggle. In Roseman's opinion, this front had nothing to do with improving shipboard conditions, but was directly related to bringing them to Palestine. Therefore, he stressed that "there is only one place on earth where we would land peacefully, and that is Palestine." Nonetheless, he could not resist adding that "conditions are very bad". The following day he was reprimanded from shore for giving such an unwise message to the media, who made a point of publicizing the good treatment the immigrants were receiving at the hands of the British (Exodus Diary 1968, 5 August 1947).

Like Perlson on *Empire Rival*, the Haganah activists on shore were interested in spreading the news of the British ill-treatment of the immigrants. Perlson had sent a copy of a letter to the ship's commander regarding "the criminal behavior of the ship's authorities in their struggle to force the passengers to land in France," and he suggested that his colleagues have it published in the newspapers (Habbas 1954, 181, 231). This resulted in orders from shore to the other ships to send out similar messages to the press, relating the harsh conditions on board, which were reminiscent of "floating prisons, worse even than the German concentration camps". Similarly, the emissaries on board were asked to send out telegrams to the French authorities, demanding that they "forbid the British to hold us for any longer, and to force them to send us away from here" (Exodus Diary 1968, 16 and 18 August 1947).

As the weeks passed, it looked as if interest in the Exodus Affair was waning and the idea of a simultaneous hunger strike on all three ships was beginning to "cook". On 12 August 1947 *Ha-Aretz* published a strategically placed headline: "Are the immigrants about to announce a hunger strike?" Five days later, the three ships received orders to prepare for a hunger strike the following day. The main aim of this action was to re-awaken public opinion and put *Exodus* back in the headlines. However, its objective was also an internal one – to encourage the immigrants and to give them a sense of "getting things going". The strike began at midnight, between the 17 and 18 August 1947 and went on until the following evening. The Haganah activists on shore informed the ships that the strike was successful and had achieved its objectives. In Palestine, the strike did indeed make the headlines and editorials were written on it, but the press in America gave it modest coverage only. Most of the publicity achieved by the Exodus Affair in the United States came later, after the immigrants landed at Hamburg.[4]

The British did not relish having to contend with a hunger strike held against them by a group of Jewish Holocaust survivors and throughout the Exodus Affair – which was constantly exposed to the press – they feared it very much. Britain's report on the way in which their ultimatum was relayed to the immigrants on 21 August 1947, in which the latter were informed that if they refuse to land in France, they will be taken on to Hamburg, ends – with a silent sigh of relief – by pointing out that there were no obvious signs on the ships of an impending hunger strike.[5] Thus it is clear why they did their best to pass off the 18 August strike as no more than a "bluff".[6]

Nonetheless, there was a grain of truth in their claim that the strike was partial, and that the Jewish Agency had exaggerated in its reports to the media.[7] After all, the hunger strike did not intend to starve the passengers, it was an act of demonstration, whose main objective was a proud declaration to the British that the ships were refusing to accept a supply of food that day. Small children, the infirm and pregnant women were exempt from taking part and all the immigrants were given a "green light" to nibble surreptitiously, without the British getting wind of it, although the latter were aware that the "passengers made use of private food reserves".[8] Still, a large majority of the immigrants held a full hunger strike, which "greatly weakened them, since they were already weak" (Exodus Diary 1968, 18 August 1947).

The relationship which developed between the immigrants and the British responsible for guarding them differed not only from ship to ship, but at every stage of their mutual voyage. The length of the first leg of the journey, between Haifa and France, was no less a surprise to the ships' crews than it was to the immigrants. These former had been kept completely in the dark as to the task they were involved in and its implications. They did not have enough clothes with them (Gruber 1948, 114), and, like the immigrants, they too, suffered from the shortage and poor quality of food aboard ship. When they arrived at Port de Bouc, the food the immigrants were given was better than that of their guards, and these did not hesitate to filch some of it for themselves. Theft of food was done under the pretext of looking for letters, newspapers and other things which were smuggled in from shore to ship by way of the food supplies (Habbas 1954, 78, 189).

There was constant tension on the *Empire Rival* between the immigrants and their leaders and the British, which was mainly initiated by the Jewish side. Perlson and his people, always on the lookout for ways of "beating the British Empire", were barely out of Haifa, when they began vandalizing equipment and throwing into the sea anything moveable they could lay their hands on. And we have already mentioned that they lodged endless complaints with the ship's commander, both verbally and in writing, all liberally spiced with threats and warnings, and which they made sure were also dispatched to shore for publication. In mid-August they sent a notice to the press, concerning a "Nazi–British act on the part of the Major, commander of the deportation ship *Empire Rival*: On Thursday, 14 August 1947, a small library of English and French books was brought on board. Once they were on board, the ship's commander took them for 'censorship' reasons and after a careful check, he found they included four books on Jewish and Zionist issues. And he showed great wisdom and courage by burning them" (Habbas 1954, 240).

A Revisionist organization, known as "The Hebrew Committee for National Liberation" went one step further and informed the press that the British authorities on all three deportation ships at Port de Bouc, confiscated and burned all the books in Hebrew and Yiddish, including prayer books. "Others, too, burned Hebrew books. Then they burned people and then they themselves were burned. Those who follow in their footsteps should be warned."[9]

Did the British indeed burn books?[10] An immigrant on the *Empire Rival* recalls that it all began because a sick immigrant was ordered by a Haganah man to disembark ship, but other immigrants, unaware that an order had been issued, tried to prevent the man from leaving. A full-scale brawl ensued, and it became important for the reason behind it to be suppressed. It was decided to blame the matter on the British, and that's how they came up with the story of the burned books (Leichter 1985). There is no clear reply to the question of whether the publications related to something which actually took place, or whether they were aimed at placing the British in a bad light. It is equally hard to determine, from a perspective of time, the accuracy of memories. Meir Schwartz remembers that "his" Major (on the *Ocean Vigour*) showed respect for the Torah Scroll brought to the ship and did not insist on his right to search through it, in return for Schwartz' "word of honour" (1965, 91).

How does the attitude of the British toward the immigrants – meaning the attitude of people on the spot, as opposed to policies of government and the considerations of decision makers – come forth in records which were written at the time, not for propaganda purposes or historiography? Thus wrote an immigrant in a personal letter sent from a deportation ship: "Some of the soldiers are really nice to us and even give us chocolate and sweets ... some of them even play with the children and look after them. But when an order is issued against us, they fill it. That's the way of all soldiers" (Habbas 1954, 173–74).

On *Ocean Vigour* the Major took part in a children's party and his soldiers tried to make friends with the immigrants and even offered to organize a boxing tournament (Habbas 1954, 210, 213). According to the Palestine emissary on *Runnymede Park*, "the majority of the English soldiers treat us well" (Exodus Diary 1968, 3 August 1947). However, "some of them are really nasty and quite simply antisemitic, but out of so many soldiers, you must expect at least some to be like that" (Exodus Diary 1968, 9 August 1947).

Now and again a fist-fight or an exchange of curses would break out between the immigrants and the soldiers, and there were even cases in which people were tormented in their sleep, and cigarette ash, burning cigarettes, and potato peels were thrown into the hold. Water or coffee was spilled over people at night and there were hold-ups in water rationing (Exodus Diary 1968, 17, 18 and 20 August 1947). The longer they remained in Port de Bouc, the more blatant this treatment became. The soldiers – who themselves were virtually prisoners – were annoyed with the immigrants, whom they considered responsible for fouling up their plans and forcing them to prolong their stay for God knows how long, on board ship.

The soldiers were usually reluctant to enter the immigrants' quarters, a fact which disconcerted the senior officers on the fleet of deportation ships. The officers were upset by the way their colleagues on the deportation ships interpreted the orders given to them that force must not be used against the immigrants so long as these do not harm soldiers or cause damage to the ships. Thus the immigrants were virtually given a free hand in managing their affairs on board ship, free of interference on the part of the soldiers, even when the leaders forced their will on individual immigrants who wanted to disembark. According to the Commander-in-Chief of the British Fleet in the Mediterranean, it would have been better to give greater latitude to the guards on the ships, in order to persuade the immigrants to clear the ships.[11]

The lackadaisical attitude taken by the British toward the situation on the ships was the result, among others things, of the large number of authorities governing life on board the ships: there was the ship's captain and the civilian crew; the British soldiers, paratroops of the Sixth Airborne Division, under orders from the army; and the Naval crews on the deportation ships and on the war ships escorting them, who were under orders from the Navy. The Mossad and Palmach made good use of the cracks, openings and "dead areas" between the various authorities, as well as the fact that the British were naive and somewhat slovenly. The limitations involved in being anchored in the territorial waters of a foreign country – France – and this country's opposition to the use of force, meant that the British had virtually no freedom of action. Many of them detested the task they had been assigned, sympathized with the plight of the immigrants, but at the same time, had the feeling – mostly correct – that they were being taken for a ride.

Relations between the immigrants and the British improved after the ships left Port de Bouc, especially on the Gibraltar to Hamburg leg of the journey. There was no longer a need to persuade the immigrants to disembark, nor was it possible now to filch their food supplies, and the pressure was off with regard to notes and newspaper articles, people being smuggled on board and other kinds of subversive activity. At this stage, they were all in the same boat. The soldiers were quite open in expressing their sorrow for having to follow orders which hurt the immigrants and these were equally open in conveying their confidence that the soldiers would not follow orders to use force against them. Immigrants who were intending to actively resist disembarkation in Hamburg apologized in advance, explaining that this resistance was not aimed at the soldiers personally but at their government (Wilson 1949, 135, 137–38; Schwartz 1965, 92, 94).

The situation on the *Runnymede Park* was dialectically opposed. All the while the ship was anchored at Port de Bouc, Roseman worked at developing a civilized relationship with the British command, focusing his struggle not on improved conditions, but on the right to immigrate to Palestine. As the ships approached Hamburg, they came closer to the moment of truth, for which he had to assemble all his people's strength. Over-friendly relations with the British soldiers and appreciation for their humane behavior would have caused a decrease in tension and

1. The President Warfield on the eve of her maiden voyage, Baltimore port, 1928 [Central
    Zionist Archives, Jerusalem].

2. One of the truck convoys on which the illegal immigrants made their way from
    Germany to France, June–July 1947 [Haganah Historical Archives, Tel Aviv].

3–4. Boarding the President Warfield, port of Sete, 10 July 1947. The ship was re-named in mid-sea Exodus 1947 [Photo: R. Gendre; Ha'apalah Project Information Center, Tel Aviv].

5. Exodus in the port of Haifa, 18 July 1947. The hospital was located in the ship's stern [Photo: Herbert Meirovitz; Central Zionist Archives, Jerusalem].

6. Illegal immigrants, surrounded by British soldiers on board the Exodus, 18 July 1947 [Photo: Hans Pinn; Central Zionist Archives, Jerusalem].

7. On the way from Exodus to the deportation ships, port of Haifa, 18 July 1947 [Central Zionist Archives, Jerusalem].

8. Registering the wounded immigrants at the port of Haifa, 18 July 1947 [Photo: Herbert Meirovitz; Central Zionist Archives, Jerusalem].

9. Two of the babies born on board Exodus during the voyage from France to Palestine [Photo: Herbert Meirovitz; Central Zionist Archives, Jerusalem].

10. Individuals and families making their way from Exodus to the deportation ships. Despite the intense midsummer heat, many of the immigrants wore heavy winter coats. Past experience taught them to be always 'on the safe side' [Central Zionist Archives, Jerusalem].

11. A general over-view of the dock at the port of Haifa, Friday afternoon, 18 July 1947 [Central Zionist Archives, Jerusalem; courtesy of Beth Hatefutsoth, Tel Aviv].

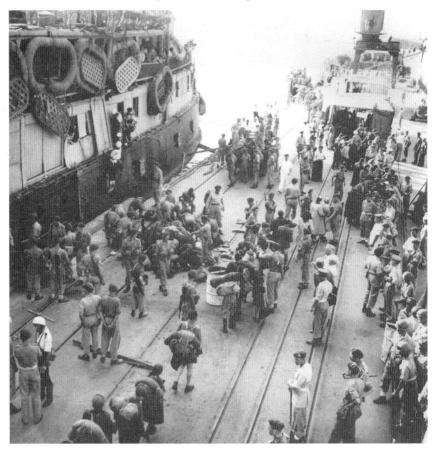

12. Checking personal belongings the immigrants were permitted to take with them on board the deportation ships [Photo: Hans Pinn; Central Zionist Archives, Jerusalem].

13. UNSCOP Chairman E. Sandstrom (in white hat) and committee member V. Simic (center) on the dock at Haifa, while immigrants are being transferred to deportation ships (Photo: Herbert Meirovitz; Central Zionist Archives, Jerusalem].

14. UNSCOP Chairman Sandstrom and member Simic disembarking one of the deportation ships after a short visit on board [Photo: Herbert Meirovitz; Central Zionist Archives, Jerusalem].

15. Haifa port, 18 July 1947, Deportation ship Ocean Vigour by the dock, and in the horizon (on the left) the Exodus, flying the Zionist flag (a blue Star of David and two stripes). In the foreground are the huts in which the immigrants were sprayed with DDT before being taken on board the deportation ships [Haganah Historical Archives, Tel Aviv].

16–17. Two of the demonstrations regarding the Exodus issue. Above: Jews from Belsen camp demonstrating at Hamburg while the Exodus immigrants are being disembarked there, 9 September 1947 [Photo: AP; Haganah Historical Archives, Tel Aviv]. Overleaf: New York Jews demonstrating on 24 July against the return of the Exodus immigrants to France and protesting against the casualties incurred when the British took control of the ship off the Palestine coast [Zionist Archives, New York; courtesy of Beth Hatefutsoth, Tel Aviv].

18. Imprisoned behind the bars of the deportation ship, the illegal immigrants watch the supply boats and call out to the reporters who every now and then came within the vicinity of the boats.

19. Forceful disembarkation of illegal immigrants from deportation ship Runnymede Park, Hamburg port, 9 September 1947 [Haganah Historical Archives, Tel Aviv].

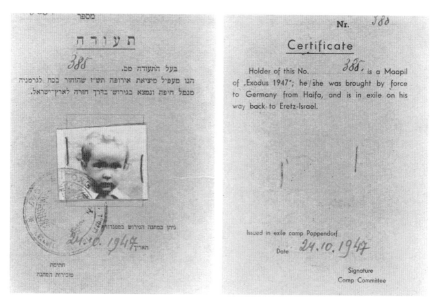

מספר

ת ע ו ד ה

385

בעל התעודה מס.

הנו מעפיל מיציאת אירופה תש"ז שהוחזר בכח לגרמניה

מנמל חיפה ונמצא בגירוש בדרך חזרה לארץ-ישראל.

ניתן במחנה הגירוש בפפנדורף

24.10. 1947 תאריך

תחימת

מזכירות המחנה

Nr. 385

Certificate

Holder of this No. 385, is a Maapil
of „Exodus 1947"; he/she was brought by force
to Germany from Haifa, and is in exile on his
way back to Eretz-Israel.

Issued in exile camp Poppendorf

Date 24.10.1947

Signature
Comp Committee

20a–b. On the eve of the transfer to the new camps in Germany, at the end of October 1947, the immigrants' secretariat issued 'certificates' to all Exodus immigrants [Courtesy of Ori Vashitz].

21. From the port of Hamburg the immigrants were transferred by train to prison camps in the British occupied zone in Germany [Haganah Historical Archives, Tel Aviv; courtesy of the photographer Ursula Litzmann].

22. The British placed a close guard on the deportation camps in Germany, not in order to stop inmates from escaping, but to prevent the entry of other displaced persons and Jewish emissaries from Palestine [Haganah Historical Archives, Tel Aviv; courtesy of the photographer Ursula Litzmann].

23. Immigrants preparing mattresses for themselves at the Poppendorf camp, September 1947. In the background are Nissen huts where the immigrants were billeted [Beth Hatefutsoth, Tel Aviv; courtesy of the photographer Ursula Litzmann].

24. First days in one of the deportation camps in Germany, September 1947 [Beth Hatefutsoth, Tel Aviv; courtesy of the photographer Ursula Litzmann].

25. Immigrants gathering around the ship's flag in a deportation camp in Germany [Central Zionist Archives, Jerusalem].

26. Exodus children playing in a deportation camp in Germany [Beth Hatefutsoth, Tel Aviv; courtesy of the photographer Ursula Litzmann].

27. Illegal immigrants dancing a tempestuous hora in expression of their joyful victory [Haganah Historical Archives, Tel Aviv].

harmed the immigrants' determination. Thus, all the way to Hamburg, Roseman made a point of inciting his people against the British soldiers (Habbas 1954, 293–94).

On the whole, relations between the immigrants and the British crews on the deportation ships were reasonable during the stages preceding their arrival in Hamburg. Here and there, there were instances of intransigence and even cruelty on the part of the soldiers, but the immigrants, who had already experienced an adversary far worse than the British, were able to appreciate the tender enemy they were facing and sent thanks to God that it was the British army they had to contend with and not the Russians or French or even Americans, not to mention the Germans (Roseman 1984; Leichter 1985).

12 · In the Shadow of UNSCOP and Terror

From mid-July to the middle of September 1947, three matters held the headlines of the Jewish press in Palestine: The activity, conclusions and recommendations of UNSCOP; the terrorist activity on the part of the two dissident organizations, IZL and Lehi; and the lengthy voyage of the *Exodus* immigrants. Toward the end of the second week in August the press began publishing news about growing tension and friction between Arabs and Jews. Compared with the other more burning issues, this seemed, at the time, to be only marginal. In retrospect, it is clear that, not only was the summer of 1947 a microcosm of the powers and processes which characterized the period between 1945–1947 and reached a peak during those months – it was also a time of change and transition. Since the summer of 1946 the struggle for a Jewish state in Palestine had taken place along diplomatic channels and was accompanied simultaneously by well controlled and restrained activity against the British Mandatory authorities. In summer 1947, the struggle was transferred to the international arena, while at the same time, preparations were being made for the next stage – a military confrontation with the Arabs.

The three main events of summer 1947 were mutually interactive. Clearly, our own main interest is with the points at which the Exodus Affair met each of the other two sides of the triangle and we shall open the discussion of the effect the events of summer 1947 had on each other, by examining the interaction between the Exodus Affair and the UN committee. Since much has already been written on the subject, we are bound to refer to the events not only as they took place, but also to the ways in which they were interpreted at the time and immediately afterwards.

In previous chapters we witnessed the early effects the United Nations committee had on *Exodus* and her cargo-load of immigrants during the voyage from France to Palestine. We saw how the Jewish

Agency, aware – as was Britain[1] – of the potential benefit offered to the Jewish struggle by the sight of immigrants being transferred from their ship to British deportation ships in the port of Haifa, asked the members of UNSCOP to come and witness it for themselves. The early morning battle on 18 July 1947 with its resulting damage and casualties made it politically imperative for the injured ship to limp into the port of Haifa in front of the UN committee members. The Jewish Agency, which, since the end of the war had been stressing the point that founding a Jewish state in Palestine was the only solution to the problems of Jewish displaced persons, was making, at that very time, great efforts to convince the committee to visit the Jewish DP camps in Europe. In addressing the committee in Jerusalem on 16 July 1947, Shertok begged its members: "Please pay a visit to the displaced persons' camps!" He made this plea after first telling them the story of the *Struma*, a battered illegal immigrant ship, which after trials and tribulations, had sank in the Black Sea in February 1942, taking all (but one!) of her 770 passengers with her. Shertok tried to draw a comparison between the *Struma* tragedy and that of the *Exodus* immigrants, when he said that "sinking the *Struma* did not put an end to the tragedy. It was only the beginning. And it goes on to this day" (*Ha-Aretz*, 18 July 1947).

On Friday morning, 18 July 1947, Shertok sent a message the UN committee chairman with the gist of the broadcast from the ship and asked for some of the committee members to make their way to Haifa and to be present as *Exodus* sailed into port (Exodus File b). The committee's chairman, Emil Sandstrom from Sweden, and the Yugoslav representative, Vladimir Simic, went to the port and watched for over an hour as the immigrants were transferred to the deportation ships (*New York Herald Tribune*, 19 July 1947). Also present was a large contingent of news reporters, many of whom were in Palestine to cover the visit of the United Nations committee and had followed the two members to Haifa. In other words, it was thanks to UNSCOP that *Exodus* received world wide news coverage, which would be one of her greatest assets throughout the affair. One of the reporters quoted the Yugoslav representative as saying: "It is the best possible evidence we can have", which became a key phrase in almost all the reviews and interpretations written on the Exodus Affair ever since.[2]

The idea of bringing the UNSCOP representatives to Haifa was a last-minute one, and had no effect on the battle and the ensuing ceasefire, as described in Chapter 7. On the contrary, it was a case of taking advantage of existing circumstances created by the battle, the fact of the casualties on board and the condition of the ship following the battering she received at the hands of the British destroyers. Indeed, the activity of UNSCOP had virtually no effect on the *Exodus* story until that meeting at the port of Haifa, and we must now examine the effect of the UNSCOP-*Exodus* mutual interaction during the next stages of the affair, in which the story of the *Exodus* immigrants deviated from all precedents in the illegal immigration operation, and was no longer a concrete example of the struggle of all illegal immigrants, but a unique odyssey. The issue on the one hand is, did the Exodus Affair have any effect on UNSCOP's discussions, conclusions and recommendations; and on the other hand, to what extent was the fate of the *Exodus* immigrants determined by the committee's activity and by the fact that the Palestine issue was then at the center of international political debates, as the moment of decision was approaching?

The assumption that the committee's members were so impressed by the Exodus Affair that it affected their conclusions and recommendations, was born in the summer of 1947 and was expressed on countless occasions. Golda Meir (for example) wrote in her memoirs: "Before the shocked eyes of the members of UNSCOP, they [the British] forcibly caged and returned to Germany the 4,500 refugees who had come to Palestine aboard the Haganah ship *Exodus 1947*, and by so doing I think that they actually contributed considerably to UNSCOP's final recommendations" (1975, 169).

Indeed?

UNSCOP's report included the following:

> During its stay in Palestine, the Committee heard from certain of its members an eye-witness account of the incidents relative to the bringing into the port of Haifa, under British naval escort, of the illegal immigrant ship *Exodus 1947*. In this, as in similar incidents, the Committee has noted the persistence of the attempts to bring Jewish immigrants to Palestine, irrespective of determined preventive measures on the part of the Administration, and also the far-reaching support which such attempts receive from the Jewish community in Palestine and abroad. (UNSCOP 1947a, vol. 1: 28)

The report also indicated clearly that the coincidence of *Exodus* arriving in Palestine at the time of the committee's visit served to illustrate the deep-seated distrust and resentment felt by the Jewish community in Palestine toward the British Mandatory Government as a result of its White Paper policy, by which only 1,500 immigrants a month were allowed into the country. Still, a close look at clause 119, quoted above, shows that in its composition there lurks an echo of the persistent British claim that the illegal immigration operation is a Zionist plot and not a spontaneous national movement. It stated that the committee had noted "the persistence of the attempts to bring Jewish immigrants to Palestine". And what about the determination of the Jewish DPs themselves to immigrate to Palestine?

Before setting off for Palestine, the committee had considered paying a visit to the DP camps in Europe. Fearing that a positive decision on this matter would be construed as pro-Jewish, whereas a negative decision would be seen as a victory for the Arab side, the committee chose to postpone any further discussion of this delicate issue until after it arrived in Palestine (Garcia-Granados 1949, 26). Then the decision was postponed once again until the end of the visit in the Middle East and its return to Europe (Unites Nations 1949, 228–29).

A large number of petitions were made to the committee during its stay in Palestine – for example, that it would act toward the release of prisoners and detainees; examine the methods used by the British Police in Palestine; and check the situation of the Jews in the Yemen and the plight of the Jewish refugees in Aden. These requests were all rejected by the committee, as being outside its jurisdiction. It even refused to address petitions demanding that it visit the deportation camps in Cyprus or to permit the testimony in Jerusalem of inmates of these camps. And then, the Middle East part of its work completed, the committee decided to appoint a subcommittee to visit the DP camps in Europe,[3] a visit which took place during the second week of August.[4]

The British were aware in advance that no good would come to their cause from such a visit and did not go out of their way to assist the subcommittee in its mission. The members encountered many difficulties in fulfilling their objective, which depended largely on the goodwill and cooperation of the British and American military authorities in the occupied countries (Garcia-Granados 1949, 216). The subcommittee visited several DP concentrations in Austria and Germany and were impressed that, since the visit of the Anglo-American Committee of Inquiry (some 18 months previously), there had been an intensification of sentiment in favor of immigration to Palestine. "Taken over all, it seems to us fair to say that practically all the persons in the Jewish assembly centers in Germany and Austria wish, more or less determinedly to go to Palestine" (UNSCOP 1947b, 25).

The importance attached, in advance, by the various parties, to the committee's visit to the DP camps in Europe, their intense activity – the Zionists for its taking place and the British to frustrate it – and the retrospective evaluations of its contribution to the final conclusions of UNSCOP, all lend extra meaning to the question – was the committee's vote on this issue influenced by the Exodus Affair? I doubt it. The Yugoslav representative, Simic, who had been present at the port of Haifa when the immigrants were being transferred to the deportation ships, and in whose name the phrase "it is the best possible evidence we can have" is customarily quoted – voted *against* paying a visit to Europe. Was he indeed so influenced by the incident in Haifa, that he felt any further evidence to be superfluous? If so, how shall we explain his anti-Zionist minority vote in UNSCOP? And how can we explain his country's abstention in the 29 November 1947 United Nations vote on partition?

In fact, the committee members acted according to the policies of their governments and within the authority of the committee as laid out in its letter of appointment. Emotional considerations probably served to strengthen the position of those of the members who already took a sympathetic approach to Zionism, when this was not in conflict with their government's policies, as in the case of the Guatemalan repre-sentative, Garcia-Granados.[5] There is a clear correlation between the voting trends of most of the committee members with regard to the visiting of Jewish DP centers in Europe; the committee's recommen-dations at the end of August; and their countries' vote at the UN General Assembly on 29 November 1947.[6]

UNSCOP's visit to the Jewish DP centers in Europe followed in the footsteps of the Anglo-American Committee, and a comparison would be interesting between these two committees, within the prism of the *Exodus* discussion. Bartley Crum, one of the American members of the Anglo-American Committee contributed an introduction to a book on the Exodus Affair, which was published shortly after the event. He wrote that "the *Exodus* story ... was a pivot on which world history turned .... When those years are written down, people will think of the *Exodus 1947* in the same terms as the Tea Party in Boston Harbor" (Gruber 1948, 13).

Such an emotional account is appropriate to a member of a body such as the twelve member Anglo-American Committee – six British and six Americans – in which personal persuasion and change of mind were possible. This happened, for example, to the Briton, Richard Crossman, in the course of the Committee's activity and, indeed, to Crum himself (Crossman 1947; Crum 1947). UNSCOP, however, was made up of representatives of 11 countries, all of whom were obliged to conform with the interests of their governments. The composition of the com-mittee was accomplished through careful thought *vis-à-vis* balance of power in the international organization and precise geopolitical division. Thus the committee included two pro-Soviet Slavs (Czechoslovakia and Yugoslavia), two pro-Arab Asian Moslems (India and Iran), two members from the British Empire (Canada and Australia), two people from Western Europe (Holland and Sweden) and three members from Latin America (Uruguay, Guatemala and Peru). The committee's members were aware of each other's basic positions. For example, once it had been decided to send a subcommittee on a visit to the Jewish DP concentrations in Europe, most of the representatives decided to send their alternates. But as soon as it became clear that the representatives of Guatemala and Uruguay would be participating in person, the Australian, John Hood, was quick to join, so as to prevent one of the pro-Zionist Latin Americans from being appointed chairman – because of their seniority (Garcia-Granados 1949, 212–13).

The conclusions, and especially the recommendations, of the two committees were totally different in nature. And paradoxically, it was the UN committee, whose members acted according to political rather than emotional considerations, that favored the Zionist cause much more than had their predecessors, who had been elected on a personal basis and were susceptible – or so it would seem – to persuasion and changes of mind, by exposing them to human dramas and moral allegations. In other words, with all due respect to sensitivity and emotional expletives, in the final analysis, practical decisions are made according to considerations which are much more down-to-earth and to the point. Thus, it was at the meeting at which a decision was taken to send a subcommittee to the Jewish DP concentrations in Europe, that the committee rejected Garcia-Grandos' proposal to send a subcommittee to Port de Bouc, to examine the situation there in light of reports about the deportation of the *Exodus* immigrants from Palestine to France and their refusal to land (*UN Weekly Bulletin*, 12 August 1947). The Swede, Sandstrom, admitted that he was torn between his personal feelings and his role as the committee's chairman, as he understood it, and apologized for being unable to intervene on behalf of the immigrants (Horowitz 1953, 183).

The relationship between *Exodus* and UNSCOP should also be examined on the level of diplomatic and political activity of the time. The Jewish Agency attached great significance to the United States' stand on the *Exodus* issue, as well as on the future of Palestine. The day after the fact of the immigrants' return to France had been made public, Shertok ordered Eliyahu Epstein (later Eilat), Jewish Agency representative in Washington, to do his utmost to prevail upon the State Department to press Britain into reverting to the former practice of deporting immigrants to Cyprus, pending a UN decision on Palestine.[7] But in the summer of 1947, it was no simple matter to prevail upon the

State Department on any matter concerning Palestine, since the United States was taking a completely noncommittal line, arguing that this was imperative to the UN decision on the appointment of UNSCOP. Thus, the Jewish Agency representative based his appeal to the United States' Government for urgent intervention on behalf of the *Exodus* immigrants on the very same UN decision, since – so he claimed – the behavior of the British in the Exodus Affair would make it even harder for the Jewish leadership in Palestine to curb the growing wave of violence following the ship's deportation.

The State Department official, Henry Villard, who was usually friendly toward Epstein, ignored his appeal this time, and his behavior reinforced Epstein's feeling that it was no use expecting any support from the State Department before the publication of the UNSCOP's findings – not on the matter of the special meeting of the General Assembly, nor with regard to the regular meeting of the General Assembly in Autumn 1947. It is interesting to note that Epstein asked to meet Villard to discuss the *Exodus* issue, but his conclusions from the meeting dealt with UNSCOP and the UN General Assembly. This shows what headed the Jewish Agency's list of priorities. As for *Exodus* – it seems we can learn from Epstein's conclusions that, here too, he had no great hope of American assistance.

There were other attempts at influencing the United States to act on behalf of the *Exodus* immigrants. Henry Morgenthau Jr (American Secretary of the Treasury in the years 1934–1945) and Franklin Roosevelt Jr raised the issue with President Truman – apparently on 23 July 1947 – and he promised to discuss with the Secretary of State, Marshall, means of influencing Britain on this matter. They got the impression that his attitude tended in favor, but he was still undecided. It appears that the President had indeed raised the matter with the Secretary of State, but beyond this there was no recorded activity on his part at this stage, even after intervention by Supreme Court Judge Felix Frankfurter.[8]

Outwardly, the American Administration had put a temporary freeze on the Palestine issue during the summer of 1947. For the Zionists, however, this period was one of tense waiting for the publication of the UNSCOP report and of intensive effort to persuade the UN member nations to support a solution which would include the founding of a viable Jewish state in Palestine. Thus, at a time when the State Department was trying to create the impression of detachment from the Palestine issue, *Exodus* supplied the Jewish Agency representative several opportunities to meet with senior officials in that Department. Nonetheless, although the official issue at hand was the fate of *Exodus*, the

meetings were devoted mainly to Palestine, UNSCOP and the forthcoming General Assembly of the United Nations (Eilat 1982, 154–63,
214–18).

During the early stages of the Exodus Affair, until the British
announced the deportation to Germany, the American stand was based
on the desire to distance the issue as far as possible from Palestine – that
the immigrants not be returned to Palestine and that events surrounding
Exodus have no detrimental effect on matters there, so long as UNSCOP
was convening and until a decision was reached by the UN on the
question of Palestine's future. It should be remembered, nonetheless,
that non-intervention on the part of the United States in the early stages
of the Exodus Affair, was in fact a continuation of the Administration's
policy of totally ignoring the constant British applications on the illegal
immigration issue, a line taken by the Americans before UNSCOP was
appointed, and which, at the time, was commensurate with Zionist
interests (Halamish 1986).

Exodus sailed from France in the midst of a world-wide diplomatic
assault on the part of Britain, accompanied by pressure on France and
Italy, aimed at putting an end to illegal immigration into Palestine. The
assault was supposed to have begun prior to the appointment of
UNSCOP, but was put off until after the special session of the UN
General Assembly in the spring. In all approaches made by Britain to
those member nations considered to have some connection with illegal
immigration to Palestine, reference was always made to the decisions of
the United Nations Special Assembly on the appointment of UNSCOP.
Britain's main contention in her request for assistance was the need to
prevent a deterioration in the situation in Palestine and in the Middle
East in general. In his angry appeal to the French Foreign Minister,
Bidault, as soon as *Exodus* sailed from France, Bevin mentioned UNSCOP
as one of the reasons behind his hopes that France would cooperate in
preventing the sailing of illegal immigrant ships.[9]

However, it was soon clear that Bevin was good at demanding but not
so good at fulfilling obligations. British policy on the Exodus Affair, of
which he was the chief architect, was plagued with incidents which
harmed the spirit of the UN decision to form UNSCOP. Time after time,
the British took unprecedented measures which clearly did not conform
with the spirit of the UN's demand "to refrain from ... any action which
might create an atmosphere prejudicial to an early settlement for the
Palestine question". Thus, the British were unable to use UNSCOP's
activity to their advantage in justifying their own policies, so they
continued striving to turn the tables. They admonished the Jewish

Agency for adopting such an irresponsible policy at so crucial a time as when the question of Palestine was in the hands of the United Nations.[10] From the way in which these things were presented, it would seem that the Zionists planned to make use of UNSCOP activity, and they were wrong in their assessment. They should have been aware of the fact that Britain was the one to determine the rules of the game, and that the *sub judice* status which ensued, in Britain's opinion, on all matters relating to Palestine, Britain would interpret according to her concepts, or rather, her interests.

The one-sidedness of the relationship between UNSCOP and *Exodus* was obvious during the French stage of the affair. While the Zionist leadership was hoping that the affair would contribute to the success of the Zionist cause on the UNSCOP front and in the United Nations in general, the closeness of events to the decision on the political fate of Palestine was of no benefit to the *Exodus* immigrants. Moshe Sneh summed up this state of affairs: "I am convinced that the immigrants of the 'Yetzi'at Eiropa' [*Exodus*] are going to save the Zionist struggle before Zionist diplomacy saves the immigrants" (*Mishmar*, 22 August 1947). The second part of this hypothesis turned out to be even more true during the "German" stage of the Exodus Affair, which took place at so critical a period in the history of Zionism. And we shall return to discuss this in due course.

The third side of the summer 1947 triangle consisted of terrorist activity by the dissident organizations. On Saturday night, 12 July 1947, two British sergeants were kidnapped in Netanya by members of IZL and held hostage against the lives of Avshalom Haviv, Ya'akov Weiss and Meir Nakar – members of the Irgun – who had been sentenced to death for their part in the Acre prison break-in (May 1947). The kidnapping placed the Haganah, as well as the Zionist leadership, in a considerable dilemma. The recently improved relations between the Zionist leadership and the British authorities, together with the hope that it would be possible to prove to UNSCOP and the whole world that the Jewish Agency was capable of imposing its rule on the public, made it imperative to end the matter as soon as possible. At the same time, the participants in the search for the two kidnapped sergeants could not help feeling that they were taking upon themselves a certain responsibility for the fate of the three IZL members, over whose heads hung a death sentence, and a rumor spread among the members of the Haganah that the organization was not, in fact, interested in finding the sergeants before it was absolutely clear what was to be the fate of the IZL men (Slutzky 1972a, 926).

On 18 July, the situation took on a more singular character. The British commander of "Operation Tiger" in search for the sergeants reported, that before becoming aware of the way the British were treating the *Exodus* immigrants, local attitudes to the army had been sympathetic and offers of assistance to the soldiers were commonplace. In the new situation, however, "all hope of help on the part of the public is unthinkable, for the time being anyway" (Slutzky 1972a, 927). A London newspaper even announced that the Haganah was stopping its activity against the dissidents because of the treatment of the illegal immigrants and Shertok decided not to deny this – although it was untrue.[11] And still, the British behavior in the Exodus Affair – first the bloody battle and then the deportation to France – made the search more difficult. The Haganah made excuses for their ineffectiveness in finding the kidnapped soldiers by claiming that the military administration imposed on the Netanya region was expelling Haganah patrols from the streets and that the deportation of the *Exodus* immigrants to France had produced a psychological climate which was discouraging to public cooperation. In his summary of the events of July 1947 in Palestine, the High Commissioner reckoned that the deportation had enormous influence on the Yishuv and reinforced, for a time, at least, the dissidents and their supporters.[12]

Among certain sectors of the public there was obvious sympathy for the dissident organizations, due to some extent to the uneasiness caused by the Yishuv's lack of response to the deportation of illegal immigrants and expectations of harsher action against the British. Haganah members asked "where is the struggle?" and from the ranks of the Palmach came the call for real resistance to deportation (Slutzky 1972a, 941–59). The political leadership's decision in the summer of 1946, to wage a limited and closely defined struggle came as a harsh blow to the Palmach, whose leaders together with the Yishuv's leadership were concerned at the affinity the young people were showing for the dissident organizations, as being the only ones seriously maintaining the struggle against the foreign rule.

And now, following almost a year free of demonstrations and military activity against the British, a row of protests and actions was waged during the first few days following the off-shore battle – before it was even known that the immigrants were being deported to France. The Yishuv's response, at first, was semi spontaneous. As soon as news spread of the battle and the casualties involved, there was a shutdown of shops and businesses in Tel Aviv. Later, the Yishuv's response was organized from above. On Sunday, 20 July 1947, several public rallies, marches and demonstrations were held in various places in the country – as the three victims of the battle were buried in Haifa. The National Council (ha-Va'ad ha-Le'umi) declared a shutdown of shops and businesses from 4:00 to 7:00 in the afternoon; restaurants were opened between 7:00 and 9:00 in the evening, but places of entertainment remained closed. The headlines in that day's *Davar* were more of an announcement than a news item: "Today, the entire Yishuv is demonstrating against the cruel attack on immigrants and in order to get the country's gates opened."

On the night between 20 and 21 July the Palmach attacked two radar posts in Haifa. One of them – on the French Carmel, had already been the target of an unsuccessful attack in the past. The Palmach forces, who succeeded this time in getting up close to the radar post, were discovered by British soldiers and one Palmachnik was killed. The other attack, on a new radar post in a military base at the edge of Achuza, was successful and the radar installation was blown up.[13] There had been no such activity since the summer of 1946.

What explanation is there for this extraordinary response of the Palmach and the Yishuv during the first days of the Exodus Affair, before it was even known that the immigrants were being deported to France? The off-shore battle between the British forces and the illegal immigrant ship and its passengers was indeed harsh and cruel, but there had been cruel and harsh battles in the past, at sea as well as in the port of Haifa, with loss of life even. But for over a year they had not resulted in responses as intense nor as decisive as now. It seems that what made *Exodus* stand out at that point was the broadcasts to the Yishuv, both on the eve of the battle and on Friday morning. This stirred up the indignation of the Yishuv and forged immediate emotional ties with the immigrants. "To this day, we are living out *Yetzi'at Eiropa*. The broadcast, which lasted several hours was tremendous and shocking," a young man wrote in a letter one month later (Ben-Dor 1949, 145).

The atmosphere in Palestine, the activity of UNSCOP and the actions of the dissident organizations, all served as background to the preliminary response which followed the *Exodus* battle. Since its revival after the Second World War, the illegal immigration operation had been conducted according to political considerations, which took into account both internal and external issues. For example, in October 1946, the Zionist leadership refrained from demonstrating against the forced deportation of immigrants on board the ship *Bracha Fold*, which the British had planned to send directly to Cyprus (but strong resistance on the part of the immigrants had brought about a change of mind), so as not to supply the British authorities with reasons to disrupt the elections to the 22nd Zionist Congress, underway at the time (Histadrut Executive, 26 Oct. 1946). In April 1947, three months before the arrival of *Exodus*, the Yishuv offered no response to the attack on the *Theodore Herzl*, in which three immigrants were killed; and another immigrant ship approaching the Palestine shore at the very same time received an order to make do with passive resistance only. The reason: The tense atmosphere in the country surrounding the execution in Acre jail of four IZL activists, and the fear that the army would open fire against demonstrators and immigrants (Sha'ari 1981, 64–65, 115).

Restraint was required on the eve of *Exodus*' arrival in Palestine, to prevent a deterioration of the relations between the British authorities and the Yishuv, and we have already discussed the implications this delicate situation had on the ship's plans to break through to shore and on the contents of her broadcasts to the Yishuv. But after the mid-sea battle and the visit of UNSCOP in the port of Haifa, and the attendant international media coverage, it would have been impossible not to react to the attack and its resulting casualties. On the contrary, the new situation actually demanded that the Yishuv demonstrate its sympathy for the immigrants and their struggle to reach their homeland. Moreover, all the protests and sabotage activity were also meant as a response to the increased activity of the dissident groups, to silence the agitation throughout the Haganah ranks and to harness the public's anger, without losing control of its reactions.

And on the other side, the evolution of the Exodus Affair had an effect on the behavior of the dissident organizations. It was not the first time that the IZL had kidnapped British soldiers and held them hostage in return for the lives of its members. A year previously, in July 1946, the hostages had been freed following an announcement that the two, who had been sentenced to death, had their sentence reduced to life imprisonment (Slutzky 1972a, 919). In January 1947, an Intelligence Officer and a British judge had been kidnapped and held hostage in return for the life of Dov Gruner, sentenced to death for his part in the Irgun attack on the Ramat Gan police station. The two were freed eventually, firstly because the execution had been postponed indefinitely, which was a partial achievement for the IZL; second, because of a fear that an over-zealous search by the Haganah would unearth the kidnapped Britons; and third, from a belief that executing the kidnapped judge Windham would have extremely negative implications on the attitude of the Jewish public toward the IZL (Slutzky 1972a, 920). The kidnapping of the sergeants in July 1947 had been different from previous such acts in several ways, not least of which was the fact that the atmosphere prevailing in the country following the use of force against the immigrants and their return to France had contributed to the determined decision of the IZL commanders to put into action their threat on the lives of the sergeants, in the hope that this time the Yishuv would accept such an act with understanding. The IZL took advantage of the last ten days of July to whip up feelings in favor of the execution.

On Sunday 20 July, the Irgun introduced itself to the Yishuv over the underground radio as representing a wide section of the public: "We know. Many members of the Haganah are now *comforted* by the existence of the 'dissidents'. They are saying – the IZL will get back at the British. Make no mistake. We shall get our revenge, and how!" (Kol Zion ha-Lochemet, 20 July 1947). After three days, the IZL was claiming that "from an historical perspective ... the deportation to France was beneficial," since it made the Jews in Palestine aware of the fact that "the British want to freeze us and in time to erase us completely from under the skies of our country" (Kol Zion ha-Lochemet, 23 July 1947). The IZL took up the case of the *Exodus* immigrants on the day the British sergeants were executed, in an attempt to muster public opinion in their struggle against the British: "We are calling you – the people of the motherland: Do not be a part of the disgrace; do not be a part of the betrayal. Do not stand by while the immigrants suffer. The desperate struggle of the people on *Exodus* is justified only if it is accompanied by the struggle of those already in Zion ... therefore, you must join the fight! .... Hit the enemy ... come together as one to fight the good fight, revolt!" (Kol Zion ha-Lochemet, 30 July 1947).

The High Commissioner was convinced by the beginning of August, that there was a strong contingent in the Haganah of people who admired the dissident organizations. A call by the Zionist leadership for a counter-struggle against these groups, therefore, may have blown up the Haganah from within.[14] But many in the Yishuv opposed the IZL's methods, and *Davar* appeared to have summed up a widespread sense of frustration the day following the deportation out of Haifa: "This uncontrolled and irresponsible activity on the part of the dissident organizations seems to be undermining the pure and tragic struggle of the 4,500 immigrant on *Exodus 1947*" (20 July 1947).

Notwithstanding reservations as to the methods the IZL was using, efforts were still being made to save the lives of the three Jewish men sentenced to death. In discussing the *Exodus* issue with State Department officials in Washington during the last week of July, the Jewish Agency representative also asked the United States to act toward having the death sentence on the three IZL members repealed (Halamish 1986, 212–14). A protest sent by the American Zionist leader, Abba Hillel Silver to the General Secretary of the United Nations in the name of the Jewish Agency for Palestine, pointed out that the imminent execution of three Jews, the mid-sea capture of *Exodus*, as well as the return of the immigrants to Europe, were contrary to the United Nations decision at the time UNSCOP was appointed (Exodus File b).

All instructions for activity in America regarding *Exodus* came from Palestine, and in every event clear directives were issued with regard to the illegal immigrants issue.[15] It was the Jewish Agency representatives in the United States who, on their own initiative, included the issue of the IZL activists under sentence of death. This caused much consternation to the ha-Shomer ha-Tza'ir party, who believed that including the "terrorist" issue would only weaken the case for the immigrants (Exodus File b). Initiative on the part of Epstein and Silver on the one hand, and the ha-Shomer ha-Tza'ir reaction on the other, indicate the complexity of the attitudes of various groups in the Yishuv and the Zionist movement toward the dissident organizations and their activity. At the end of July, with still a spark of hope left for saving the lives of the IZL activists, a certain self restraint could be seen among the opponents of the dissident organizations. The three were executed on the day the deportation ships arrived at Port de Bouc (29 July 1947). The following day, when it became known that the immigrants had all refused the French proposal, IZL announced that it had carried out its threat by hanging the two British sergeants. It was then, at the beginning of August, that all hell broke loose.

On 1 August 1947, *Davar* blamed the dissidents that "the crime of hanging the sergeants" would make it so much easier (for the world) to forget the heroism of the immigrants aboard *Exodus*, and the front page carried an article claiming that, as far as London was concerned, the act of hanging the sergeants had obliterated the suffering of the immigrants. At the end of August Shertok made some historic reckoning with the dissident organizations at a meeting of the Zionist General Council in Zurich:

> Terror is a knife in the back of the illegal immigration operation .... Never before have we seen heights of courage as those achieved by the passengers of *Exodus 1947*, never before have so many thousands of people shown such a height of moral courage, men, women and children, such martyrdom ... nor have we ever [had to] face the world in such abysmal shame and disgrace, as we did with the hanging of the sergeants. And the one stood opposite the other. And the two came together. And we know how the effect of *Exodus*

1947 in France and certainly in Britain and probably in the United States also, has been dwarfed by this outrageous act .... (25 August)

The execution of the sergeants at the height of the *Exodus* drama and while UNSCOP was in full swing came as a severe blow to the Zionist leadership, which was most concerned at the negative consequences not only on *Exodus*, but on the whole Zionist struggle. And the British fanned these fears. At a conversation with Golda Myerson (later Meir) on 31 July 1947, shortly after the booby-trapped bodies of the two sergeants were discovered, the High Commissioner said: "They [the dissident organizations] are damaging your cause. In London they are so furious with you that you will not get anything."[16]

The execution caused a negative turn of events from the Zionist point of view. The United States Administration with the media and public opinion underwent a change of attitude not only to the plight of the *Exodus* immigrants, but to the entire Palestine issue. Bevin was quick to exploit the execution in his own persistent and, so far, fruitless war on the American funding of illegal immigration to Palestine.[17] In private conversations Secretary of State George Marshall tied the British behavior on the *Exodus* issue with the hanging of the two sergeants,[18] and on 7 August 1947 he replied to Bevin's letter on illegal immigration, which had been lying on his desk for six weeks. Until August 1947, the Americans had been ignoring Britain's constant appeals on the subject, but this time they agreed with some of her claims, that illegal immigration was planned, organized and funded, to a large extent, in the United States.[19] On the same day – 7 August 1947 – the State Department sent out letters to the Treasury Department and the Attorney General, instructing them to study the matter and to find ways of responding to Britain's requests (*FRUS* 1947, 1136).

During the first days of August, the Jewish Agency representative in Washington reached the conclusion that there was no hope of American help on the *Exodus* issue. Any attempts at achieving public support for the immigrants were unsuccessful, because key figures, such as Bernard Baruch, a Jewish businessman and advisor to Presidents Franklin D. Roosevelt and Harry Truman, had their reservations about the execution of the sergeants. For the same reason, the American trade unions refused to send a telegram to the British Labor Party, in protest at the treatment of the *Exodus* immigrants. Jewish Agency attempts at prevailing upon the press to devote editorials to the *Exodus* issue proved virtually fruitless and when *The Herald Tribune* did publish an editorial on Palestine, it dealt more with terrorism than with the fate of the refugees on the deportation ships.[20]

By the end of August the negative effects of the execution were still evident on the American front. On 29 August Deputy Secretary of State Lovett discussed with Epstein the harm caused by Jewish terrorism to the Zionist cause in American public opinion (Eilat 1982, 215), and the fact that President Truman made do with an unofficial appeal to Britain to reverse her decision on deporting the immigrants to Hamburg, was explained by the media, among other things, "as a result of the escalating anti-Jewish feeling in England, because of the terrorists' execution of the two sergeants" (*Davar*, 31 August 1947).

In France, the scene of the *Exodus* drama, the execution caused negative vibrations:

> It was during the first few days of our struggle, when all public opinion was in our favor, that the news arrived that the two British sergeants had been executed in Palestine. One Minister said: You are weakening your struggle and your position. What is the essence of your struggle, immigration or hanging? If your method is hanging, this is a matter for gangsters and we want no part of such a struggle, even if you say that from a chronological point of view, it was the British who started. It was weakening the immigrants' struggle.[21]

Still, this did not result in any apparent change in government policy.

The execution did indeed have a disastrous effect on American, British and French public opinion, but how can we quantify this evasive and amorphous creature known as public opinion and gauge its effect on the decision making process? It is difficult to pinpoint the exact obstacles caused by the IZL activity to the political advantages achieved by the Exodus Affair, and we should turn now to examine the effect it had on the fate of the immigrants. Did it bear any weight in forming the British position on the *Exodus* question, in other words, did it contribute to the decision to deport the immigrants to Germany and to the British Government's intransigence on the issue?

MP Richard Crossman met his fellow party member, Bevin, at the beginning of August and discovered that the affair so infuriated the Foreign Secretary, that he said "he would not be surprised if the Germans had learned their worst atrocities from the Jews".[22] Crossman was impressed that the act hardened the Foreign Secretary's attitude toward the Jews. At the end of August, he said to David Horowitz in Geneva that he believed that "Jewish terrorism has had a prejudicial effect on British public opinion and destroyed any of its sympathetic elements. Even the shocking and tragic episode of the *Exodus 1947* failed to stir the public conscience, which still hasn't recovered from the anger over the murder of two sergeants at Netanya" (Horowitz 1953, 203).

Crossman's impression left its mark not only on the people of the Jewish Agency – with whom he had formed ties since taking part in the Anglo-American Committee and developing a pro-Zionist stance – but also on the way the period was written about, and it became one of the foundations of the thesis that the execution of the sergeants over-rode the Exodus Affair. Similar sentiments are expressed by the brothers John and David Kimche in their early 1950's book, *The Secret Roads*: "But the growing sympathy for the Jewish cause was to be extinguished by none other than the Jews themselves. In the midst of the upsurge of feeling for the *Exodus* refugees came the news of the hanging of the two British sergeants by Irgun terrorists; the news caused an immediate *volte-face* of British public opinion. Anti-Jewish demonstrations took place in Manchester and Liverpool, while the first reaction of the Government was a hardening of opinion against the luckless refugees" (1954, 189).

In his book *Cross Roads to Israel*, which was written in the early 1960s, Christopher Sykes wrote: "What little hope there was of an official change of mind in London regarding *Exodus 1947* vanished when, on the 31st of July, the bodies of two British sergeants were found hanging from a tree near Tel Aviv." According to this author, "once the decision had been taken not to land the refugees in Palestine or anywhere near it, and once the French authorities had collaborated with Haganah, there was nowhere else that the British authorities could send them except to England and after the outbreaks following the affair of the two sergeants, that would clearly have been an act of folly" (1965, 382–83).

Had the proposal to send the *Exodus* immigrants to England been seriously contemplated, when it became clear that they were adamant in their refusal to land in France – only to be rejected because of the hanging of the sergeants and the ensuing outbreaks of anger? Nicholas Bethell, who wrote his book *The Palestine Triangle* at the end of the 1970s after gaining access to documents in British archives, showed more caution in his definitions: "The atmosphere of these few days was calcu-lated to sharpen Bevin's already harsh attitude to the *President Warfield* passengers. On July 31st ... the question ... was, what was to be done with them. There could be no question of sending them to Palestine or Cyprus. There were therefore only two possibilities, a suitable British colonial territory or the British zone of Germany" (1979, 340–41).

Note: England is not mentioned.

Bethell's source was the cabinet meeting of 31 July 1947. The agenda included two Palestine-connected issues: "Jewish Illegal Immigrants from SS *President Warfield*" and "Kidnapped British Non-Commissioned Officers". Due to its importance – it was in fact the only debate of its kind specifically devoted to the *Exodus* – the entire transcript of the discussion is hereby included:

> The Foreign Secretary recalled that, in spite of our efforts to prevent it, the *President Warfield* had succeeded in sailing for Palestine from a French port with some 4,500 illegal immigrants on board. These Jews had secured forged Colombian travel documents; and the ship itself had sailed without proper clearance. He had taken the matter up immediately with M. Bidault, who had agreed that, if we were successful in intercepting the ship, her passengers might be returned to France. The *President Warfield* had been intercepted off the Palestine coast by a naval patrol and her passengers transferred to three other ships, which were now in harbour at Port de Bouc. The illegal immigrants had, however, refused to disembark voluntarily and it was clear that, without the cooperation of the French authorities, it would be impossible to compel them to do so. His Majesty's Ambassador at Paris had reported that the French Government were not prepared to afford such cooperation, and that further representations to them would be unlikely to produce any successful results. In these circumstances, he had discussed with the other Ministers concerned what alternative arrangements might be made for the disposal of the illegal immigrants. It had been agreed that there could be no question of sending them to Palestine or Cyprus and the Secretary of State for the Colonies was considering whether accommodation could be found for them in a British colonial territory, while he himself was looking into the question whether any might be sent to the British zone of Germany. Some of these Jews had in fact come from the United States Zone, and it might be possible to arrange for their return there. He had not yet been able to reach definite conclusions, and he proposed to consult with the Prime Minister before a decision was finally taken. No harm would be done by leaving the three transports at Port de Bouc for a few days; and there was a possibility that their passengers might decide eventually to go ashore peaceably.
> The Cabinet –
> Took note of the Foreign Secretary's statement.

Then:

> *The Secretary of State for the Colonies* informed the Cabinet that the High Commissioner for Palestine had not yet been able to confirm or deny the report that two British non-commissioned officers, who had been kidnapped some days previously, had been executed by the Irgun Zva'i Leumi.
> The Cabinet –
> Took note of the statement made by the Secretary of State for the Colonies.[23]

Allen Bullock's biography of Bevin suggests that it was the hanging of the sergeants which prevented the possibility of returning the illegal immigrants to Palestine or Cyprus. His sequence of events is garbled, since he presents the British soldiers' running haywire in Tel Aviv on 31 July and the outbreaks of antisemitism in England at the beginning of August as background to the Cabinet meeting which discussed the fate of the immigrants. But we know that the Cabinet meeting took place before confirmation had arrived of the sergeants' execution. Bullock's version also suggests that it was at that same meeting that the possibility was removed of bringing the immigrants to England, although the matter was never even raised at that meeting (1983, 449).

There is no doubt that at the beginning of August there were strong anti-Jewish and anti-Zionist feelings in England. Nonetheless, we have seen that the rejection of Palestine and Cyprus and the retaining of two alternative destinations – a British colony or the British zone in Germany – all this was done *before* news came of the execution of the two sergeants. Later on, we shall examine the process whereby Britain reached the decision to expel the immigrants to Germany and her stubborn refusal to budge from it. For the time being we shall make do with the following conclusion: The idea of bringing the immigrants to England was never discussed seriously at any stage of the Exodus Affair,[24] and in any case, the execution of the sergeants had no effect on the immigrants' destination.

By a strange trick of fate, a kind of coalition was formed between British historians and certain circles in the Yishuv – each for his own reasons – which indicates a circumstantial connection between the execution of the sergeants and the hardening of Britain's position toward the *Exodus* immigrants. At the beginning of August 1947, *Ha-Aretz* London correspondent, Robert Weltsch, reported (from a reliable source), that "there was not a single pro-Zionist remaining in Parliament, since last week cost us all our friends" (6 August). There is no doubt that the hanging made it easier for Bevin to implement his policies, as sub- stantiated by Hugh Dalton, who was Chancellor of the Exchequer at the time. The man had firm criticism on Bevin's policies with regard to disarming the Haganah, imprisoning the Yishuv leaders and the fact that Britain was "going to such lengths to try and stop all 'illegal immigrants'" – steps which he described as a "crescendo of stupidity". However, in hanging the sergeants, he wrote, "the Jews transgressed the bounds of my toleration .... After that I went *absolutely cold* towards the Jews in Palestine and didn't care what happened to them ...." (1962, 189–90).

Even if hanging the sergeants had no direct effect on the British

Government's decision making process regarding the deportation of the immigrants to Germany, it created a climate in which it was easier to defend those decisions and harder to arouse public opinion against them. For a national liberation movement, one of whose main objectives was to muster favorable public opinion and use it as a weapon in its struggle, this was a loss of valuable ammunition.

13 · From Catharsis to Apathy

Immediately after the booby-trapped bodies of the two sergeants were found on 31 July, the High Commissioner demanded that the Jewish Agency cooperate with the authorities in putting an end to all terrorist activity. He said to Golda Myerson: "Our patience has been stretched to its limits. You think only of the Jewish side, but I must consider the Arab and the British points of view and especially that of the soldiers."[1] He believed that the only alternative facing the Jewish Agency was to promise the Government full cooperation in rooting out the terrorists, otherwise it may be necessary to introduce Martial Law in the whole of Palestine.[2]

The activity of the dissident organizations and the methods proposed by the High Commissioner for rooting out the terrorists were strewn with danger to the Yishuv as well as to the Zionist leadership. By continuing their terrorist activity and undermining the authority of the elected leadership, on the very eve of the fateful decision on the political future of Palestine, the dissident organizations could have placed the Yishuv and the entire Zionist movement in a dangerous trap and shattered the foundations of their demand for independence. "Open cooperation" with the Mandatory Government in rooting out terrorism might have dragged the Yishuv into heated internal debate and even civil war. If the Jewish Agency were to issue a public call to wage war on the dissidents, it may well have revealed – both at home and abroad – its inability to enforce its will on the public.

For the Zionist policy makers the danger lurking behind the dissident organizations had a verbal aspect as well, which reached its peak during the summer months of 1947. Throughout the Exodus Affair, the IZL and the Lehi took advantage of the immigrants' misery to batter the elected leadership of the Yishuv and the Zionist movement, whom they referred to in their broadcasts as "pathetic leaders", "the traitorous leadership", "deserters" and "the ghetto council" (Kol Zion ha-Lochemet

1947, 30 July, 10 and 20 August). The Revisionist Party, who had by that time returned to the Zionist Organization, joined the verbal attack on the leadership. For example, at the time the deportation ships were making their way from Port de Bouc to Hamburg, they announced that "the British are not the only ones responsible for the immigrants' current situation. No less responsible is the Zionist leadership, whose policies paved the way to this holocaust" (*Mishmar*, 26 August 1947).

For the leadership, who had a longstanding and bitter account to settle with the dissident organizations, this was the last straw. This time, the top leaders and speech makers did not mince their words. Shertok defined the dissidents' terrorist activity as "a knife in the back of the illegal immigration operation – both in fact and from a political point of view." In other words, not only did their activity harm the immigrants and make their situation worse, it also prevented the possibility of achieving any political gains from their struggle. Furthermore, he said, whenever the moral flag of courage was raised and held against the world's conscience, causing emotional shockwaves which succeeded in pressuring the Government and whipping up inter-Governmental conflict, "something always happens, with some satanic accuracy, to humiliate us and sully our reputation, regress our position and release the world from any moral obligation toward us, to place the [British] Government in a positive light and justify arrests, executions, imprisonment and a war on illegal immigration" (Zionist General Council 1947, 25 August).

The Zionist decision makers agreed with the British claim that terrorism not only harmed the Zionist struggle, it also prevented the possibility of achieving increased immigration quotas. The British had considered making changes in their policies on immigration in the winter of 1947 – by increasing the monthly quota from 1,500 permits to 4,000. On Saturday 1 March 1947, just as the British Cabinet was on the verge of reaching a decision on this, the IZL blew up the British Officers Club in Jerusalem. They had not troubled to issue an advance warning to evacuate the place and 12 people were killed: five officers and soldiers and seven civilians. The Government immediately informed the Jewish Agency that as a result of this attack there would be no increase in immigration quotas (Jewish Agency Executive, 14 March 1947). At a meeting of the Jewish Agency Executive shortly after, the point was raised that "we were very close to receiving increased immigration quotas, but the terrorist activity had put paid to this possibility" (27 April 1947). In fact, these terrorist acts played right into the hands of the British and served as an *excuse* for a step they had already decided upon for different reasons, mainly that the British ambassadors in the Arab countries objected to increasing the quotas of Jewish immigration into Palestine and the fear of Arab reactions to such an act.

All the accumulated animosity toward the dissident organizations was released in full force after the kidnapping and hanging of the two sergeants. The crushing verbal outcry against them must be conceived against the background of two interweaving developments: The first – the Zionist struggle since the end of the war; and the second – the web of circumstances and events of summer 1947. The sense of horror and revulsion caused by the actual execution, and the feeling that this had harmed the immigrants' cause and undermined the propaganda value supplied by their struggle, were joined by fears that the act and its repercussions would have a negative effect on the UNSCOP deliberations and world public opinion. Moreover, the attack, with its signs of the sharpened verbosity which covers an inability to act, was also part of an attempt on the part of the Zionist leadership to prove its control of the Yishuv. And this fact had also to be seen and heard, to prove that the Yishuv was capable of handling its own affairs as an independent state. At this crucial stage, the Exodus Affair supplied the Zionist leadership with a golden opportunity to make hay while the sun shines. Maybe this time, in light of the heroic struggle of the immigrants, the Yishuv would understand the damage caused by the dissidents' acts and maybe now the time was ripe to denounce them and to cast them out once and for all.

For over a year, illegal immigration had been the most effective ammunition the organized Yishuv and its leadership could use against the dissident organizations. Summer 1946 had been a watershed in the history of the struggle against the British. The days of "The Hebrew Resistance Movement" were over. The Zionist leadership had decided to moderate the military struggle and to transfer most of the weight to the political arena. Thus, illegal immigration remained the Yishuv's only sphere of activity, which could be discussed openly. However, since the ships were almost inevitably apprehended and the immigrants deported to Cyprus, in the short run the operation might have appeared to be a failure. Thus it would have seemed that the only real subversive activity against the British was that conducted by the dissident organizations. The Palmach journal reckoned that this fact allowed the dissidents' "hollow boasting ... for being the only fighters", and made them more attractive to the youngsters in the Yishuv (Slutzky 1972a, 946).

Thus, since summer 1946, illegal immigration had been playing a particularly vital role on the home front. In the days when the dissident organizations were attacking the British and boasting of their successes, the illegal immigration operation was responsible for a closing of ranks in the Yishuv, for proving that it was not only the terrorists who were capable of beating the British. Illegal immigration was a positive, widely approved of issue, it was conducted under the auspices of the elected leadership, it had clear and defined boundaries and the other (British) side also maintained certain ground rules in its struggle to curb it. All this took place at a time when the Zionist struggle was being conducted mainly in the political arena, and forces were secretly being summoned for the decisive battle – the one with the Arabs. Not all the public were capable of understanding the tactical restraint needed at that stage in the struggle for the Jewish state and the Zionist leadership hoped to use the illegal immigration operation to its advantage in capturing the hearts of the country's young people and to persuade the public that national obedience was the order of the day.

In the summer of 1947 there took place a dialectic process, when the Zionist leadership made use of the trials and struggles of the immigrants to bond the Yishuv against the dissident organizations, while at the same time it was the sequence of events in the Exodus Affair, which contributed to reinforcing the dissidents, both in number and in prestige and to the increased sympathy toward them within certain sectors of the public. The British believed that it was Zionist propaganda that was responsible for this, while the Zionists were convinced that it was the result of British brutality toward the *Exodus* immigrants. Both these assumptions were not unfounded. There was indeed an increase in the open expression of anti-British sentiments at public gatherings and in the press. Even the weekly *Ha-Po'el ha-Tza'ir*, which usually reflected the more moderate stance of Mapai, wrote at the end of July, that "slowly but surely, the borders are being blurred between them [Bevin's Government] and the Nazi kingdom of hell" (23 July 1947). And the British agreed with the Zionists, that there was a direct connection between the forced deportation of the immigrants and the strengthening of the dissident organizations. They were aware that all the Jews were united on the immigration issue, political affiliations notwithstanding, and when immigrants are being expelled by force from the country, the public is more likely to forgive terrorist activity.[3] All the more so, when these immigrants are being returned to Europe, and then expelled not to Cyprus, but to Germany!

The Zionist leadership had been maintaining for a long time that the British attitude toward the immigrants was responsible for the escalating violence in the country and made it difficult for rational forces in the Yishuv to maintain a responsible and disciplined line. Representatives of the Jewish Agency often told the British that their war on illegal immigration may well destroy anti-terrorist sentiments in the country.[4] This was repeated firmly during the course of the Exodus Affair. Over and over again, it was impressed upon the British that their activity against the immigrants undermines the authority of the leadership and encourages terrorism. In their dealings with senior officials in London and Washington and with UNSCOP members in Geneva, the Jewish Agency representatives claimed that deportation of the *Exodus* immigrants to France, and their subsequent transfer to Hamburg, increased the Yishuv's opposition to the British and made it hard for the leadership to curb the increasing waves of violence. They complained that each time anyone with authority and responsibility succeeded in calming the population to any degree, the Government took measures, which inevitably achieved the opposite results.[5]

The High Commissioner was in full accord with the Jewish Agency on this point. He protested to the Foreign Office that its policies on the *Exodus* would ruin the level of goodwill which has been achieved during the past few weeks, and military sources in Palestine were furious at the fact that "just as things were beginning to sort themselves out, the British Government in London goes and unites the entire Jewish population against the British" (*Ha-Boker*, 3 August 1947). Nevertheless, and as if illogically, the British continued their headstrong fight against illegal immigration and even escalated their efforts, throughout the Exodus Affair.

It was not only the Zionist leadership that was in a trap that summer of 1947; the British, too, were in a labyrinthian situation. Although they were aware of the fact that their war on illegal immigration was the glue binding together the different factions in the Yishuv, they insisted on escalating their efforts. This was at a time when, in order to isolate the dissident organizations and to put an end to their activity – without having to resort to military force – they needed the cooperation of the Yishuv and its leadership, or, at least, a suitably sympathetic public climate. We have seen that the stubborn attitude taken by the British toward the *Exodus* immigrants made the search for the sergeants much more difficult, increased – according to the British themselves – public support for the terrorists, and made it virtually impossible to curb terrorist activity. But all these facts did nothing to soften the hard line they insisted on taking toward the *Exodus* immigrants.

The British, who knew of the dangers involved in their action, prepared an advance plan for suppressing the Yishuv's response to the deportation of the immigrants to their country of origin,[6] and reckoned that a stronger reaction should be expected if the immigrants were deported to Germany than if the destination was a tropical country.[7] But they were relieved to discover that the response was milder than they had anticipated and they concluded that the Jews were less interested in illegal immigration than they had been in the past.[8]

And there was some truth in this conclusion. Activity had been rife immediately following the arrival of *Exodus* in Palestine and before it became known that the immigrants were destined to be returned to France, and then, during August and September the Yishuv's reactions began faltering, exactly as the British were toughening their attitude to the immigrants, and the dissidents were escalating their activity. These swings in the Yishuv's responses were due in part to the fact that the Zionist leadership was having to maneuver itself with regard to *Exodus*, between political considerations concerning UNSCOP and the forth-coming United Nations debate, and the challenge of dealing with local dissident organizations.

Since the end of the war in 1945, the illegal immigration operation had been hounded by conflicting considerations of this sort and others. Still, none of them was strong enough to put an end to the operation, political dangers notwithstanding. While UNSCOP was visiting Palestine and even at the end of 1947, when the illegal immigration could have jeopardized all of Zionism's political achievements, ways were found for it to continue. Illegal immigration, which had its external objectives and was intensely important internally, was a major factor, one of the foundations of the Zionist struggle at the time.

In the days of "The Hebrew Resistance Movement", immediately after the war, with the echoes of war still audible, a significant proportion of the Yishuv population had been involved in the operation. The public's enthusiasm and willingness to take part in demonstrations and to welcome the immigrants as they landed on the beach, were way beyond the expectations of the leadership when they issued their call for action. This was a result of strong feelings of commitment and solidarity toward the Holocaust survivors, together with a sense of guilt originating in the days of helplessness during the war. The accumulated wrath and frustration against the British rule for forbidding the refugees access to Palestine, even transferring them to an obscure island in the Indian Ocean burst forth once the war was over. The illegal immigration operation was seen by the Yishuv not only as saving the firebrands that had survived the Holocaust, but also as proof, to themselves mainly, that the days of sinking ships like the *Patria* or the *Struma* and deporting immigrants to Mauritius were a thing of the past, never to be repeated.

The Yishuv's enthusiasm at the first waves of illegal immigration and the thrill of meeting the immigrants and hearing their stories did not last long. Between January and up to the summer of 1946, all illegal immigration ships were apprehended and their passengers imprisoned in Atlit. Beach landings had virtually ceased and the public was rarely required to help in any way. By August 1946 all public participation had ceased altogether. Since August 1946, the Palmachniks had been sensing a growing rupture between themselves and the public and they did not mince their words in criticizing the Yishuv's indifference and inactivity (Halamish 1988, 53–55).

We may recall how, as *Exodus* approached the shores of Palestine, her escorts began fearing (rightly, as it turned out) that the Yishuv was not prepared for a landing operation.[9] But even in the presence of plenty of objective reasons for lack of public activity (Haifa was under curfew at the very moment *Exodus* was pulling into port), the Mossad and Palmach activists were less than pleased at the Yishuv's behavior, as a Mossad member in France wrote: "Many people in Marseilles asked us: How do you expect us, the French, to fight your battles and oppose the British in carrying out their schemes, when people in your homeland have not even bothered to join the campaign and did nothing to prevent the British from deporting the immigrants" (Hadari 1949, 39).

Expressions such as these – and they were many and frequent – more than being a realistic description of what could be expected from the Yishuv under the circumstances, expressed the loneliness and alienation felt by those in the Yishuv who did rally round to take part in the illegal immigration effort.

The escorts and emissaries on board the three ships bearing the *Exodus* immigrants and their counterparts in France felt that the Yishuv had forgotten them and was leaving them to face the music alone. A "He-Halutz" emissary in Marseilles wrote bitterly to his colleagues in Palestine: "They all asked for one thing: That the Zionist movement and the Yishuv in Palestine stand by them, fight with them, and we promised them this. Was this a truthful promise? I doubt it, because even at Port de Bouc, we were a handful of people committed to the mission, without sufficient help from the Zionist authorities …" (Reichman 1947).

The question of how the Yishuv was able to stand by and leave the immigrants to bear the main brunt of the struggle on their weak shoulders was also asked outspokenly, as the Exodus Affair reached its peak. In his Seventh Column at the beginning of September, devoted to a baby who died on one of the deportation ships on the way to Hamburg, Alterman waged a fierce attack on the Yishuv. He was pondering and questioning whether the nation was pursuing to its limit "A life of boundless and immeasurable sacrifice, / Setting its shoulder to the times and their yoke" and told his fellow Palestinian Jews that "The nation may recruit [the child-immigrants] for duty / Only if it believes in its heart / That it is worthy of staring them in the face / At their funerals" (*Davar*, 5 Sept. 1947).

Similar sentiments had been expressed a few days previously by Yitzhak Ben-Aharon at a meeting of the Zionist General Council in Zurich: "The leadership has placed the major burden on the weakest of shoulders – those of the immigrant. The Yishuv was not an active part-ner in this struggle ... and expects of the immigrant ... to spend weeks and months aboard those prison ships ... while the Yishuv's battle disappeared and ceased altogether after the 29 June [1946 'The Black Sabbath']" (26 August 1947).

On the other side of the ocean, too, it was no easy task to call the Jewish public to action on behalf of the *Exodus* people. On 24 July a rally was held in Manhattan's Madison Square Gardens to express solidarity and outrage, and in memory of all the victims of the ship-board battle with the British and especially of the American crew member Bill Bernstein, and to protest the deportation of the immigrants from Palestine. The initiative for this rally came from Palestine, accompanied by repeated prompting. "We have cabled four times that some Jewish action would be taken," reported Shertok at a meeting of the Jewish Agency Executive in Jerusalem (28 July 1947). The rally was angry and emotionally charged, but the crowd was not large. The New York Police Department calculated that some 20,000 people took part. In Palestine the press pondered why the Jews of New York did not attend the rally in their thousands and believed that there were two reasons for this. First of all, it would have taken several weeks to organize a successful mass-rally in New York and this one had taken only two or three days to organize. "What's more, large rallies are no longer of any use. It does not mean that the Jewish public is devoid of feeling, but it has ceased to believe in the effectiveness of any action taken so far: Protest rallies and even political pressure" (*Ha-Aretz*, 8 August 1947).

The Mossad people in Palestine hoped to be able to awaken American public opinion by staging a mass funeral, "a funeral demonstration" for Bill Bernstein, whose body had been embalmed in order to transfer it to the United States. They believed that there was great educational value in allowing the mass of American Jewry to take part in the funeral. However, the Mossad head in North America, Ze'ev Schind, opposed bringing the body to America, because, after discussing the matter with people in the know, he had come to the conclusion that there would "not be an important rally".[10]

For two months *Exodus* never left the front pages in Palestine and usually held the headlines as well. Several editorials were also devoted to the affair. *Ha-Aretz* sent its London correspondent to Port de Bouc and he sent back emotional descriptions and first hand "color articles" on the events on board the deportation ships and on shore. Still, there were only a few "letters to the editor" on the subject. One of the readers complained that unlike *Ha-Aretz'* usually realistic position on Zionist policy, this time it was being carried away on a wave of commotion. "The descriptions you published of the *Exodus 1947* affair, the recent riots in Liverpool and Tel Aviv [attacks on Jews and their property, following the execution of the two sergeants] can only cause hatred for Britain within the Yishuv population, the kind of hatred which paves the way to terrorist activity" (*Ha-Aretz*, 10 August 1947).

A browse through the Yishuv's newspapers of those days can be misleading. The large number of writings on the fate of the *Exodus* immigrants and the fact that they were mentioned and praised at practically every public meeting, might give the impression that during the months July to September 1947, the Yishuv was being borne away on a collective catharsis of sympathy for the immigrants. The *Exodus* days were indeed the heyday of the illegal immigration operation and the adventure captured the hearts of many and renewed interest in the entire issue. Still, we should bear in mind that other matters also interested the public, except that not all of them received news coverage, if only because there was an element of secrecy attached to them. The Exodus Affair was a "good story", which took place at a time when there were few other printable stories to write about. Whenever another development occurred in the Zionist struggle, the *Exodus* story was pushed to the sidelines. As happened during the first few days of August, when three dozen people and three mayors were arrested in reaction to the execution of the two sergeants, and especially on 31 August and the beginning of September, when the headlines and most of the front pages were devoted to the conclusions and recommendations of UNSCOP.

On 11 August 1947, the President of the Va'ad Le'umi, Yitzhak Ben-Zvi, telegrammed the High Commissioner that the deportation of the immigrants to France was wreaking emotional havoc throughout the entire Yishuv (Exodus File b). In what way? After all, there had been no Yishuv activity on the *Exodus* matter following the initial wave of reaction, and things had reached such a state that in the middle of August the

Jewish Agency spokesman offered an explanation/apology, that "notwithstanding the tense atmosphere in the country, not for a moment has the Yishuv forgotten that we are in the fifth week of the immigrants' tragedy" (*Davar*, 17 August 1947). A few days later, David Remez, Chairman of the Va'ad Le'umi, held a press conference in which he reported that the Council had again discussed ways in which the Yishuv could express its solidarity with the illegal immigrants and their struggle to reach the shores of Palestine (*Ha-Aretz*, 19 August 1947). This proves that there was no public activity on the matter, and that this fact caused considerable discomfort. At the same time, this could also be proof of a need for lip-service to be paid to the immigrants and to other elements who demanded more public involvement than was forthcoming.

Why, then, was the Yishuv's involvement in the Exodus Affair so limited? Response was always impressive at times when the public was called upon to stand up and be counted – on the day of the sea-battle and at the funerals of the victims. But then there was a vague unwillingness to participate in lengthy and routine protest activity, whether from a feeling of fatigue, or because of skepticism as to the success of such activity; whether from indifference or because of a refusal to accept the authority of the elected leadership.

We must bear in mind just what the Yishuv – the Jewish community in Palestine – consisted of at the time. It was altogether a community of little over half a million people, including an ultra-orthodox community, which denied all ties with Zionism; a fairly large proportion of people who lived below the poverty line and a reasonable sized community of new immigrants, who had arrived in Palestine at the end of the war and during the subsequent two years. Many members of the Yishuv had served in various sectors of the armed forces, and there were those who had just recently returned from a lengthy term of service in the British army during the Second World War. As is the way of the world, people's opinions are made up from all sorts of factors, one of which is the struggle for day-to-day existence. And one must not disregard the fact that certain sectors of society were not carried away by the illegal immigration operation, or that their enthusiasm had waned with time. There were those who saw in the operation an illegal, unjust and expensive way of bringing people from Europe to Palestine – at first by way of a transit camp in Atlit, subsequently via Cyprus – at the expense of legally issued certificates. Those who had submitted requests for immigration permits on behalf of their relations, watched as the illegal immigrants jumped the queue, actually destroying the chances of their dear ones joining them in Palestine in the foreseeable future.[11]

Furthermore, the Zionist leadership did tend to choose a very "mealy-mouthed" kind of activity and made little serious attempts at drawing in the public to action. After all, their job was to navigate the Yishuv's responses not only through increased activity on the part of the dissident organizations and the considerations of the entire Zionist struggle, as already described, but also around the various concepts and positions held by sectors in the Yishuv as to the character the struggle should take. On the one hand, the militancy of the Haganah and the Histadrut's "activist" circles, and on the other hand the moderate *petit bourgeois*, who were not even successful in raising money for illegal immigration, as an act of civil disobedience.[12]

14 · The Last Weapon: Deportation to Germany

No sooner was it known that the deportation ships which had set sail from Haifa on Saturday 19 July, had not arrived in Cyprus, than rumors began spreading that they were on their way to France or North Africa, or Colombia even. The British announcement on 21 July that the ships were sailing to the port from which the *Exodus* had set off, put paid to these rumors, only to have another set of rumors take over, fiercer than the first batch, that France would not be the immigrants' final destination. On 23 July, the day on which the French Government decided to allow the immigrants entry into France, but not to force them to land, certain government circles in London made a point of spreading a rumor that in this case, the immigrants would be transferred to the British zone in Germany (*Ha-Aretz*, 24 July 1947). The press notice based on these rumors, was the first public indication that Germany was being considered as a possible destination for the immigrants. Intelligence of this sort had already been received by the Haganah beforehand.[1]

The short news item on 24 July, included several characteristics of British propaganda policy throughout the Exodus Affair. It contained a rumor, distributed by a senior person in authority, but "not to be quoted or referred to", and threateningly warning of an even worse fate if the immigrants refused to land in France. Responsibility here was placed squarely on the shoulders of the French, whose refusal to cooperate with the British was forcing the latter to deport the immigrants to Germany.

The rumor did not catch on immediately and it was almost a month before it became publicly official. In the meantime, various other rumors flew around as to the potential destination of the immigrants – if they do not land in France of their own accord. Many of the rumors were initiated and spread by the British as part of a deliberate smokescreen on their part. For example, on 31 July, at the end of the Cabinet discussion on the illegal immigrants, rumors were released that the Cabinet had decided to deport them to some tropical British colony; they would either be taken there directly, or they would be held for a while in the British zone in Germany. The Foreign Office spokesman made a point of announcing that the immigrants were currently as close to Palestine as they could ever hope to get.[2]

During the wait at Port de Bouc, the threat of deportation to Germany was aimed mainly at persuading the immigrants to land in France and inhibiting the French Government.[3] But it was not only logic and cold-blooded considerations that caused the British to spread rather then deny, these rumors. They too – and not only those who were taken in by the rumors – were more than a little confused. The three deportation ships had set off from Haifa before the French had given their consent for the immigrants to land, and before the British had formulated any alternative plans, in the event that matters got out of hand and the first attempt at refoulement proved unsuccessful. We have seen that even after they set sail out of Haifa, the Cyprus option still remained, in the event that the French reply turned out to be negative. The public announcement that the ships were making their way to France put paid to this and the British found themselves with no "desk plans" if France were to refuse to re-admit the immigrants, or – as happened – decided not to cooperate fully.

It is clear that Cyprus was ruled out, at a time when the British were explaining their escalated war on illegal immigration by pointing out that deportation to the Mediterranean island was not enough of a deterrent and anyway the detention camps were full to overflowing. The same reasons which propelled the British to return the immigrants to France, instead of sending them to Cyprus, were so much more valid during the next stage in the Exodus Affair. There was also the need to avoid the loss of face involved in bringing the immigrants to the eastern Mediterranean island, after they had been dragged all the way to the western edge of the sea and refused to land for three weeks and more. These reasons were expressed in internal British correspondence,[4] but could not have been used in explaining Britain's position to the world at large, so that explanation for the deportation to Germany was also based on the fact that Britain's policy of sending illegal immigrants to camps in Cyprus, where they would be eligible for inclusion in the regular immigration quotas, had only increased the flow of illegal immigrants from Eastern Europe via the Mediterranean coast countries.[5] However, the British were inconsistent on this and during the same week when the Cabinet had agreed that it would be unfeasible to send the *Exodus* immigrants to Cyprus, immigrants arriving in Palestine on other ships, were deported there. Which is the way matters remained until the end of the British Mandate in May 1948.

And if Cyprus was considered an unsuitable destination for the immigrants, how much more so was Palestine. Returning the immigrants to Palestine would have been seen as a step-back of a year or more in the struggle against illegal immigration, loss of face and self-contradiction, since Britain was fighting illegal immigration, first and foremost because Jewish immigration into Palestine (beyond the monthly quota of 1,500) was endangering – in her opinion – the situation in Palestine and the whole region. Under the circumstances, the Jewish side was aware of the fact that Palestine could hardly be a real destination for the *Exodus* people. The immigrants were indeed demanding to be returned to Palestine, but the Jewish Agency was asking Britain to "go back to earlier procedure", in other words, Cyprus.

The situation was already settled at the end of July. It was clear that the immigrants would not disembark of their own accord in France and they would not be returned to Palestine, or to Cyprus. Still, two weeks passed between the Cabinet meeting in which their fate was discussed and the time a decision was reached to send them to Germany. Why was the decision postponed to the middle of August and why was it reached on that date? At first the Foreign Office in London assumed or hoped that matters would calm down in time on board the ships anchored at Port de Bouc, and that their uncomfortable conditions would persuade the immigrants to disembark quietly.[6] Bevin and his staff in London thought it would be best to let things take their course, and waged a war of attrition against the immigrants. At the same time the ambassador in Paris, Duff Cooper, hoped to put an end to what he considered to be a diplomatic nuisance and a source of embarrassment. An article by Leon Blum, who defended the French Government and blamed Britain, helped Cooper to prod his superiors into action – to decide on a new destination and to move the ships out of Port de Bouc as soon as possible. His suggestion was that the Jews would have to decide within 24 hours whether their choice was immediate freedom in France, or deportation to another place, where they would be held captive, with no chance of getting to Palestine.[7]

Cooper's approach had been a link in the web of means used by all the elements involved in the Exodus Affair to pass the ball into his counterpart's playing field. But his proposal came too early. The Foreign Office in London made it clear to him that the Cabinet had not yet decided on an alternative destination and pointed out that defining a specific destination might indeed encourage the Jews to land, but might also encourage the French Government to persevere in their efforts to get rid of them.[8] A few days later London got the impression that if the

British Government were to inform the French Government that the only available alternative was the British zone in Germany, the former would consider sending an official to try to persuade the immigrants to disembark. Nonetheless, Bevin was sure at the time (6 August), that the ships should stay where they were for another week and there was no need to decide anything for the time being, but to make the most of every chance available to get the immigrants off the ships, once they had become too bored to remain.[9]

The British toyed with the hope that some ship-board epidemic would break out and the French would be obliged for the sake of public health to forcibly remove the passengers. While the ships were on their way from Haifa to Port de Bouc, the British released rumors that a sickness had taken hold of the immigrants but the Hebrew press in Palestine insisted that this was just an excuse for forcing people to shore in order to give them medical treatment (*Davar*, 28 July 1947; *Ha-Aretz*, 29 July 1947). One can notice a kind of disappointment between the lines of the document prepared by the Foreign Office in the middle of August, stating that the danger of an infectious disease had passed, and that only two cases of measles had been reported among the children on one of the ships (Alternative destination).

During the first half of August, the colonial option faded and finally disappeared altogether, while the German one was reinforced and actually remained the only possibility. But the British, who knew that the deportation of the immigrants to Germany would cause negative reactions all over the world, put off reaching any decision on the matter, while they continued to release partial and noncommittal information as sort of experimental balloons, to examine reactions and to soften public opinion in advance of the official notice.

And, in the absence of a clear British announcement, rumors were rife as to where the immigrants would be taken. Question marks became an irrevocable part of the headlines in the Hebrew Palestine papers: "The ships are preparing to sail. To Cyprus or to Kenya?" (*Ha-Aretz*, 7 August 1947); "Where will our immigrants be deported to? Australia? Hamburg? Argentina? Or some other hell hole in the southern hemisphere?" (*Davar*, 10 August 1947). It was hard to sort out the truth from among all the rumors and guesses. Thus, on 8 August 1947, *Ha-Aretz* had it from a clearly reliable source that the destination was to be – neither Palestine, nor Cyprus, but some place much worse than France. Based on this, the guesses were now coming thick and fast: Western Africa, Hamburg or a British colony in the western hemisphere? On 11 August the rumors in the press took on a much clearer and more defined turn. *Davar*, using its usual high-falutin style, still with a question mark at the end, asked: "Will England throw our immigrants back into Germany's Vale of Tears?" and in *Ha-Aretz*: "Danger of *Exodus* immigrants being returned to German camps this week."

By the middle of August it was time to decide. The Foreign and Colonial Offices came to a conclusion that a critical point had been reached with regard to attrition methods used so far. The thin flow of immigrants disembarking of their own volition had ceased altogether. Foreign Office officials made it clear to Bevin that, due to the stagnation at Port de Bouc, "it looks as if we should have to try our last weapon – a definite statement on an alternative destination, other than Cyprus or Palestine."[10] Harold Beeley, one of the senior officials in the Foreign Office, was certain at the time that the only chance of persuading the immigrants to disembark at Port de Bouc was by informing them of an alternative destination, with "Hamburg or some other port in the British zone of Germany [being] the only practical alternative". But even then the British were contemplating that it might turn out that as the time for the announcement drew near unforeseen and favorable developments may take place, that would "make the announcement of an alternative destination, such as Germany, unnecessary". Britain's heel-dragging on the issue shows a reluctance to announce that the immigrants were to be deported to Germany and it seems that, by prevaricating, Bevin was still hoping to be spared implementation of this difficult and unpleasant decision. In the middle of August, too, the British seemed to be swinging between clear deliberation and wishful thinking, still looking – as it were – for a miracle (Alternative destination).

Just as up until then they were hoping that in time things would work themselves out, by mid-August they were facing a race against time. The British soldiers together with the civilian crew who had spent over three weeks on board ship, were, in fact, no less prisoners than the immigrants themselves. The civilians had already caused serious trouble and there were signs that the soldiers, too, were running out of patience, especially those whose turn it was to go on leave. Employment of the civilian crew on *Ocean Vigour* was acutely problematic since their contracts, which had already expired, had been extended only to 24 August. If the ship did not set sail for the open seas before this date, the professional crew members would disembark, the voyage could not be made without them and replacements would have to be brought in from England.[11]

Furthermore, the three ships whiling away the time in Port de Bouc were badly needed back in Palestine. The British had it on good authority that seven illegal immigrant ships bearing a total of some 5,700 passengers, were about to set sail for Palestine shortly. It would take at least four weeks from the day the three ships with their cargo of *Exodus* immigrants set off for whatever destination and until their return to the port of Haifa. If the next large batch of illegal immigrants were to arrive in Palestine as expected, not only would it be impossible for the British to carry out their refoulement policy in the absence of the three deportation ships, it would also be impossible for them to transfer the immigrants to Cyprus. This in turn meant that there would be no way out of holding large numbers of immigrants in Haifa, an act which the British were eager to avoid at all costs. Re-equipping and preparing new ships for the purpose of transporting immigrants to Cyprus, or any other destination, would take at least six weeks, but there were no such ships available at all![12]

After the Colonial Office admitted in the middle of August that there was no region available in which a large number of Jews could be accommodated at such short notice, they were faced with a process of elimination, which left in the end only one option – Germany. Several elements gave Germany a definite advantage as a destination for the deported immigrants. From a practical point of view, the existing camps in Germany could house the returning immigrants, with little need for advance preparation. As for prestige, by sending the immigrants back to Germany, the British were sticking to their policy of refoulement. After all, the Jews would be returned more or less to the point from which they had set out.

In fact, the British had been considering this option while still in the early stages of forming their refoulement policy.[13] At that time they had thought that the return destination would be Italy, and were afraid of the difficulties involved in transferring the deportees from Italy to the British zone in Germany, through lands occupied by others. They even considered transferring the deported immigrants to the British zone in Austria. The France–Germany combination had advantages over Italy–Austria in that the British zone in Germany had a sea coast and ports. This, in turn, was behind the end-of-July idea of bringing the deportation ships to Germany, forcing the immigrants to disembark in a British-controlled port and returning them overland to France. In other words, even before Germany had become the only possible destination for the immigrants (in the middle of August), the British were considering the option of bringing them there – in order to overcome France's steadfast refusal to cooperate in forcing them off the ships as well as the immigrants' own refusal to land of their own accord. The idea was that this way the French would avoid having to forcibly land the immigrants and would need only to admit them into France after they had made the journey by train from Germany.[14]

Even when it was clear, in the middle of August, that the immigrants were being sent to Germany, the British did not relinquish the idea of returning them overland to France. It was not only public opinion that was meant to be appeased by this, but also the authorities in the British zone in Germany. These had been complaining that they had no room for any more refugees and that they had been promised that no more would be sent beyond the number already in the zone. The British military authorities in Germany reminded the decision makers in London that sending additional Jews to their zone would be in breach of British policy, which was "to keep Jews out of our Zone". The British commanders in the region explained that they were doing their utmost to prevent the entry of additional Jews and were even pleased to announce that they had succeeded in reducing the number of Jewish DPs to 12,000, and were constantly bringing this down by supplying them with immigration certificates to Palestine. They also feared that an addition of some 4,000 refugees would result in unrest among "our" Jews, who, for the time being, were being relatively quiet.[15]

The British Foreign Secretary apologized to his people in Germany that in spite of previous assurances, they were called upon to accept these refugees, "but I am reluctantly convinced that this is the only practical course open to us".[16]

Alongside Germany's many advantages as a destination for the deported immigrants, there were several drawbacks, and Britain was aware of them at every stage of the operation. Those who agreed to "neither Palestine nor Cyprus" were also voicing their differences against Germany. Even the ambassador in Paris, who put so much pressure on his Government to make up their minds on the next step, when he suggested announcing a destination which could also serve as a deterrent, took care to make it clear that he was opposed to deporting the immigrants to Germany. His explanation was double. From a practical point of view – once they arrived in Germany, they would begin anew their journey to Palestine; and from the point of view of propaganda – the negative effect the deportation to Germany would have on French public opinion.[17] The person who formulated the deportation-to-Germany decision did not hide from his Minister the fact that "sending these Jews back to Germany, the country in which they were persecuted, will have the worst possible effects from the propaganda point of view".[18]

Thus, at long last, in the middle of August, it was decided where to deport the immigrants: The British zone in Germany. And who fathered this decision? As is usual in situations such as this, the person required to reply to this question is exempt from having to name the real father from out of a whole row of people claiming paternity. Nevertheless, the decision is no orphan. Records point clearly at Bevin, who accepted it, in accordance with the opinion of the Committee on Illegal Immigration and the Ministerial committee on the subject.[19]

During summer and autumn 1947, Bevin involved himself very little in matters concerning Palestine. His agenda was taken up with the future of Germany, the Marshall plan and Britain's economic crisis. But even his biographer Allen Bullock, who claims that since announcing in February 1947 that the Palestine issue was being transferred to the United Nations, Bevin had not taken an interest in that country's military and civilian administration, admitted that the Foreign Secretary had been involved in the *Exodus* immigrants episode (1983, 448). In his book, Bullock stressed several times and quite rightly, that the statement so often attributed to Bevin on his intention to "make an example of this ship" relates to her return to France and not to the deportation of her passengers to Germany. According to Bullock, the deportation of the immigrants to Germany was not aimed at teaching anyone a lesson, but seemed to be the best answer available to a practical problem Britain had to solve (1983, 449–450). Still, the picture presented by Bullock is incomplete and as such, inaccurate, since at the end of July, Bevin informed his colleagues in the Cabinet that he was prepared to examine the possibility of sending at least some of the immigrants to the British zone in Germany "as a deterrent to the traffic".[20]

In explaining the reasons for deporting the immigrants to Germany, Britain tended to understate the educational, even vengeful, aspect of "making an example of this ship", and used all the means at her disposal to point out clearly to the rest of the world that everyone, except Britain herself, was responsible for the fact that there was no choice but to take the Jewish immigrants back to Germany.

Bullock, whose description of Bevin's part in the Exodus Affair reads like an apology and a vehement defense of the biography's hero, cannot resist describing his decision to return the illegal immigrants to Germany as a "blunder", except that he expands the circle of people responsible for the decision to include not only Bevin but Attlee and other senior ministers too (1983, 450).

But in the deliberations on the fate of the immigrants and in the process of formulating the decision to send them to Germany, we hardly ever run across the British Prime Minister, Clement Attlee. It was Bevin who navigated the Exodus Affair, with the help of reports from men on the spot and in full cooperation with the War and Colonial Offices. But let us not ignore the part played by the Colonial Secretary, Arthur Creech-Jones, in determining the direction the affair would take. He was instrumental in composing many of the clauses in the document outlining the decision to deport the immigrants to Hamburg and he was also the man behind the decision not to send the immigrants to any of the British colonies – because of a lack of suitable living accommodation in these places. He wrote to Bevin in the middle of August that if the French Government does not cooperate, the only place able to take them in would be Germany and "what feeling of distress attends these people should this solution be necessary is entirely their own responsibility".[21]

In retrospect, Creech-Jones tried to present himself as a better friend to the Zionists than they had believed, which is doubtful (Locker 1970, 189–90, 215). Anyway, even if he had wanted to, his ability to help them was limited, since it was Bevin who was the dominant minister on foreign affairs. Creech-Jones' weakness in the Cabinet sprung largely from the fact that he had held his position only since October 1946, whereas Bevin had been Foreign Secretary since the Labor party took over in July 1945. Bevin, whose relationship with his junior colleague was somewhat paternal, was the key figure in the Government, putting even his Prime Minister, Clement Attlee, in the shade.

Bevin and Creech-Jones saw eye-to-eye on the need to curb illegal immigration and to exercise a policy of refoulement, up to the point at which it was necessary to find an alternative destination for the deported *Exodus* immigrants who were adamantly refusing to land in France. When the attempt to return them to France failed, a conflict of interests arose between the two Offices involved. The Foreign Office was annoyed at the Colonial Office which had wriggled out of contributing its share in solving the problem and informed them that they should be prepared in case this situation was repeated in the future, and then the excuse of no suitable territory available in the colonies would not be acceptable.[22] After it was announced that the immigrants were being deported to Germany, the Foreign Office made it clear to everyone involved that if, in the future, an unsuccessful attempt at refoulement made it necessary to find a place for illegal immigrants, the Foreign Office would not agree to having them sent to the British zone in Germany and it would be up to the Colonial Office to find a suitable alternative.[23]

And this was not the end of British internal conflicts. By the middle of August, with the deadlock at Port de Bouc and fears of a worsening situation in Palestine, the High Commissioner came up with the idea of sending the immigrants to England.[24] At the beginning of September,

while on home leave in England, he attempted to get the deportation to
Germany rescinded. "Whitehall sources" explained that the High Commissioner's protest came from humanitarian as well as political
considerations. According to these sources, Sir Alan emphasized that it
was not too late to re-route the ships to another destination, which had
less painful and drastic associations for the Jews. Furthermore, the
sources denied that the High Commissioner had threatened to resign, as
the British press had hinted. They claimed that Cunningham's main
objective had been to save the Government from its own decision.[25] In
Palestine the news item was banned for publication by order of the censor,
although its content was known to the Jewish Agency, and Golda
Myerson sent the High Commissioner her thanks and hopes for the
success of his efforts.[26]

It just so happened that during the week between the decision and its
publication, rumors which had been rife for a month finally evaporated.
The place held by rumors and guesses was now taken up by articles and
stories on the harshness of ship-board life and the 18 August hunger
strike; and speculations on the results of UNSCOP whose conclusions
were about to be published. This dearth of information did not stem only
from a lack of interest in a subject which seemed to have reached deadlock, but also because having decided to keep their options open as to
what would happen and when, the British were no longer spreading
rumors. It was clear to them that the official announcement on the deportation would make the matter irreversible, so that in the interval between
reaching the decision and making it public they still hoped to be saved
from having to make the announcement. Thus it was decided to keep
the matter secret until 48 hours before the ships were due to leave Port
de Bouc.

The British hoped to create a situation whereby if they had to
announce the deportation, they could present the ultimatum as the immigrants' last chance to disembark in France of their own free will. They
also hoped that these circumstances would prod the Jewish Agency into
agreeing to persuade the immigrants to land.[27] And in the meantime, the
decision was kept a deadly secret. The British knew that if the Zionists
got wind of it, not only would they refuse to persuade the immigrants
to land in France, they would do their utmost to prevent such a landing.
And the decision was kept secret from the French, for fear they would
leak it to the Zionists.[28]

France and the Jewish Agency finally learned of the expulsion to
Hamburg only half an hour before it was announced publicly. The British
offered to help the Jewish Agency bring their representative to Port de

Bouc, where he could board the ships and persuade the immigrants to land. Berl Locker in London and Golda Myerson in Jerusalem flatly refused this offer, insisting that it was the job of the Jewish Agency to bring Jews to Palestine and not to persuade them to settle in other countries.[29]

The British were in two minds on how to inform the immigrants of their new destination. The Foreign Office stressed to its people in the south of France the importance of allowing each individual the "opportunity of taking in the sense of our announcement without the intermediary of the leaders". And the message from London to Marseilles insisted that the announcement be made at each hold and that it should be backed up by leaflets, distributed among the immigrants.[30] The men on the spot tried to learn something from the French delegation's visit to the ships at the end of July, and decided that if they were to avoid an outbreak of mass-hysteria, they should make the announcement in person to representatives of the immigrants – one from each hold – and they would then pass it on to their people. It would then be given out in writing, in order to prevent distortion.[31]

How long should the immigrants be given to consider their reaction to the announcement? At first this was to be 48 hours, then 36 hours, from 11:00 on the morning of Thursday (21 August 1947) to the following night, one hour before midnight. In the end, departure time was brought forward to 6 o'clock in the afternoon, to avoid an outcry if the ships were to set sail after the beginning of the Sabbath.[32]

The message presented verbally to the representatives and subsequently distributed in writing, in English and in French, was clear and laconic:

> To the passengers on the *Runnymede Park, Empire Rival, Ocean Vigour*.
> This announcement is made to you on behalf of the British Government.
> Those of you who do not begin to disembark at Port de Bouc before 1800 hours tomorrow, August 22nd, will be taken by sea to Hamburg.[33]

As usual, the announcement was first made on *Runnymede Park*. The British consul-general in Marseilles and Colonel Gregson explained the situation to the leaders, while the leaflets, in English and French, were handed out to the immigrants. Just to be on the safe side, someone from the consulate wrote the announcement in German in large letters on a blackboard. The leaders did not react to the announcement; the immigrants began singing the Zionist national anthem.[34] One immigrant wrote in her diary: "We have just been informed that if, by six o'clock, we do not disembark, we shall be taken to Hamburg ... once again,

Mordechai [Roseman] spoke nicely and raised our spirits. We must be strong, hold on and not give in" (Diary 1947b). The emissary was also impressed with Roseman's speech, which said that anyone who wanted to could disembark, but everyone would spit in their face, as would the entire Jewish race. "Our war is the war of a nation fighting for its existence and its right to survive, and we have no way to go back. Those evil murderers want to destroy us and to send us back to the hell from which we came. We cannot reconcile ourselves to this and they will have to force us off the ships. We have no way, and no desire, to return to that country … we must hold on to all our bottles and, altogether, to keep everything which may be used as a weapon of resistance" (Exodus Diary 1968, 21 August 1947).

Next to receive the information was the *Empire Rival*. "The passengers did not respond," reported the British consulate.[35] And this is how one of the immigrants described it in a letter to his friends in Palestine: "An official of the British embassy in France arrived on board our ship in order to prove to himself first hand what kind of impression the announcement would have on the passengers. I think he was disappointed by the stoicism of those 'lunatics', who do not seem threatened by anything." Like Roseman, the writer, Yosef Leichter, was a member of ha-Shomer ha-Tza'ir and there is considerable similarity between the words spoken by one on *Runnymede Park* and written by the other, on board the *Empire Rival*. Leichter went on to write: "Who do they think they are threatening? Survivors of Auschwitz, Maidanek, Treblinka? The fighters in the forests, the ghetto fighters and fighters on all fronts against the Axis Empire? … For us, all roads lead to Palestine and we'll get there even if we have to go via Hamburg" (Habbas 1954, 176).

"What a nerve!" wrote the Haganah emissary on *Ocean Vigour* to his colleagues on shore, "I get a notice from the Major that he wants to see six of the leaders immediately. I got together six of the ordinary people and detained them for an hour. Because if they can keep us waiting four weeks – we've got plenty of time" (Habbas 1954, 215). Colonel Gregson and the consul in Marseilles passed on the message, but they did not dare enter the holds, so they just threw the leaflets in, "but these were received with laughter". The immigrants' immediate response was: "We want to go only to Palestine, we have nowhere else, and those who took us from there by force, must take us back" (Ganuz 1985, 247–48). The British left angry (Habbas 1954, 215). They were impressed by the democratic way in which the immigrants had reached their decision. After receiving the announcement, the representatives asked permission to consult with the passengers and to hold a vote. Half an hour later, they sent up one representative, a doctor from Poland, who made his speech in German: "We have put it to the vote and have decided not to disembark. We have no quarrel with the British nation and especially not with the British crews and officers on this ship. We believe in British democracy. We shall maintain order and shall not disembark in France."[36]

The British allowed the press to board the deportation ships shortly before their departure to Hamburg, but were not happy with the visit. The immigrants prepared flags combining the Union Jack and a swastika and waved these at the reporters, crying: "Down with Fascism and England!" (Diary 1947b; *Ha-Aretz* 25 August 1947; *Davar*, 25 August 1947). Notwithstanding this rather unfortunate experience, Bevin ordered to have the *Reuters* correspondent, Boyd France, accompany the flagship *Runnymede Park*, on the journey from Port de Bouc to Hamburg. France sent out authentic reports on the mood of the immigrants on board. On 25 August 1947, all the Yishuv papers bore quotations from "one of the immigrants' leaders" – clearly Roseman – calling his people to prepare for a decisive fight when they reach Hamburg. "Cowards and traitors are allowed to land at Hamburg, but we, who are not afraid, shall remain on board ship and resist to the end." That day's evening edition of *Davar* carried the headline: "The immigrants on all three ships will resist actively attempts at landing them at Hamburg."

Immigrants and Palestinian escorts alike found it hard, in retrospect, to remember the exact moment at which they became aware that they were being deported to Hamburg. A review of documents of the time shows that this memory lapse began on the actual day of the announcement, 21 August 1947. According to reports, the immigrants' reactions were "muteness", "silence" and "singing the Zionist national anthem". But this is not the whole picture. One immigrant on *Ocean Vigour* remembers that "a shudder passed through us all when we heard about being returned to Hamburg. Sounds of weeping came from the edge of the hold ... and smothered groans engulfed the stuffiness all around ... a sense of depression took hold of the ship, together with a silent muteness, shocking ... the depression lifted slowly, and was replaced with a sense of apathy, as if nothing had happened" (Ganuz 1985, 247–48).

After all, rumors had been flying around the ships for some while of potential destinations for the immigrants (including Hamburg). True, this time it came as an official British announcement. But in Haifa, too, the British had informed the immigrants officially that they were being taken to Cyprus and this had turned out to be untrue. So that at Port de Bouc, on 21 August 1947, the immigrants believed that they "were being lied to, just as they had been lied to in Haifa when they were told that they were being taken to Cyprus, and they were taken to France. Thus, people think they are being taken somewhere else and not to Hamburg" (Exodus Diary 1968, 21 August 1947). Even the emissary who wrote this was full of doubts as to whether they were indeed going to Hamburg (Habbas 1954, 205–206). Immigrants and Palestinian escorts alike did not know if this was "a threat or a final decision" (Habbas 1954, 176), and were sure, or wished, that this was no more than a "trick to break their spirit and get them to land in France" (Exodus Diary 1968, 21 August 1947). The skepticism with which this announcement had been received was so obvious that a member of the British Navy could see it, even without understanding the verbal meaning of the response.[37]

Even the Mossad people on shore were unconvinced about the authenticity of the British announcement. "It is quite possible that the British aim merely to threaten you with a journey to Hamburg, in order to get you to disembark," they wrote to the ship, as soon as Hamburg was announced.[38] Several hours later, a Haganah message from Palestine was relayed to the ships, also doubting the decision to send the immigrants to Germany.[39] It seems that a great many people found it hard to believe that of all the places on earth, the British would choose to send Holocaust survivors back to Germany.

15 · A Change of Scene

A new wave of protests broke out when the rest of the world got news of Britain's intention to deport the *Exodus* immigrants to Germany, sharper even than its predecessor, which had followed their return from Haifa to France. Altogether, some 200 letters and telegrams were received by the Foreign and Colonial Offices and the Prime Minister, protesting the way Britain was dealing with the Exodus Affair. These came mostly from Jewish and Zionist organizations in England and other countries and a considerable number of them were a double protest – the first having been at the end of July. More than half of the protests were sent only *after* the immigrants had landed in Hamburg.

On 22 August 1947, a telegram arrived from Bern, Switzerland, addressed to the Foreign and Colonial Ministers. The writer, Mrs Vera Weizmann, justified her "last moment" appeal to them by the fact of her being a "woman and mother of two sons who fought in the last war in the British army and RAF for freedom, justice and equal rights for all human beings. One of them never returned." She believed that the *Exodus* people truly wanted – and not because of Zionist propaganda – "to flee from places of their tortured memories … to survive among their own people …. They have nowhere else to go and if life cannot offer them this refuge then life itself loses its meaning." Deporting them to Hamburg seemed to her an act of reprisal and "reprisals never bring any good".[1]

In the White House, too, and in the State Department in Washington, there was a growing pile of letters protesting Britain's behavior toward the immigrants,[2] and anti-British demonstrations took place in several cities in North America, initiated by the Zionist Emergency Council. Attendance at these demonstrations, however, was unimpressive.[3] There were no mass rallies this time of the kind which took place in New York on 24 July 1947, nor even more modest ones like that organized by the "American Friends of Haganah" in mid-August, when the Methodist minister, Grauel, returned home. This demonstration, in which some

3,000 people participated, called on President Truman and Secretary of State Marshall to protest against British policy *vis-à-vis* the Exodus Affair and to demand that the British Government return the immigrants to Palestine and open its gates to free Jewish immigration (*Ha-Aretz*, 17 August 1947; *Davar*, 18 August 1947). After 21 August, most of the responses were routine and lukewarm and consisted mainly of letters and telegrams, sit-down strikes and small demonstrations.

In the United States too, appeals to the President, the State Department and the British embassy in Washington came mainly from Jews and Zionists. One of the exceptions was a letter received by the Secretary of State from Bartley Crum, former member of the Anglo-American Committee, who claimed that the decision to deport the immigrants to Hamburg was in defiance of the Potsdam Agreement and that the United States should force Britain to fulfill her commitments.[4]

The limited scale and subdued nature of the protests abroad is reflected in Golda Myerson's speech at a special meeting of the Va'ad Le'umi in Jerusalem during the last week of August: "The most shocking thing is not what is happening to the thousands aboard those ships, but the fact that not a single country has come forth to cry out against this horrible injustice. We have still not heard of anyone apart from Jews who have joined the hunger strike. We have heard of no intellectuals or religious leaders, apart from Jews, in any corner of the world, who have joined us" (*Davar*, 27 August 1947).

In fact the British, too, were surprised at the relatively moderate official and public response to the news of the deportation to Hamburg. They had expected stronger criticism. On 14 August the British ambassador to the United States informed his superiors of rumors circulating in Washington to the effect that the British were considering sending the *President Warfield* immigrants back to the British zone in Germany, and he felt the need to point out that forcing these people back to the country which had just recently been the site of the worst anti-semitic atrocities, would no doubt cause a wave of American condemnation, which would deviate this time from the usual circle of Zionist propagandists. Moreover, the ambassador warned that the deportation might have negative repercussions on Anglo-American relations, which were at a delicate stage.[5] Bevin made it clear to the ambassador that Britain had already taken into consideration any potential ramifications to the deportation and he was indeed anticipating a loud outcry from that quarter; still, there was no choice, but to send these people back to the British zone.[6]

A year earlier, the British had diligently taken into consideration any

American reaction to British policy on illegal immigration to Palestine. For example, at a Cabinet discussion in the summer of 1946, before a decision had been reached to deport illegal immigrants to Cyprus, the then Secretary of State for the Colonies, George Hall, warned that resolute activity against illegal immigration (e.g. the return of immigrants to their port of embarkation, or deporting them to another destination, such as Cyprus or other suitable areas), "should also seriously damage our chance of getting co-operation from the United States in a long-term solution of the Palestine problem".[7] A month before, the Cabinet had followed the recommendation of the Secretary of State for the Colonies to reject the High Commissioner's proposal to suspend discussions with the Americans on the immigration of 100,000 Jewish DPs to Palestine, pending the return of five British officers kidnapped in Tel Aviv. Hall believed that suspension of talks with the Americans at that stage would receive a negative reaction in America.[8] The American Congress was about to discuss a loan to Britain and Prime Minister Attlee informed the Cabinet on 8 July 1946, that the American Secretary of State had advised Britain to issue an encouraging statement on the Palestine issue – in order to make the Congress debate easier. The Cabinet rejected this advice,[9] but the fact that it had been offered at all and brought by the Prime Minister before the Cabinet, tends to illustrate that the mood at the time was different from that of summer 1947.

In what way, then, did the summer of 1947 differ from that of 1946? This can be examined in light of historian Elizabeth Monroe's determination that, where the British were concerned, the Palestine issue was not, in itself, a matter of life or death and their policy on the issue following the Second World War was guided mainly by considerations such as the possible effect they would have on American–British relations at a time when Britain could not have survived without the financial and strategic support of the Americans (1961, 22). Britain's political and economic dependency on America had not diminished by 1947 – on the contrary. The difference was, however, that during the summer of 1947, Britain did not fear that the Palestine issue, and especially the Exodus Affair, could harm those relations. Thus, in all communications between the United States and Britain on the *Exodus* issue, not a single hint was given by the former that she had any intention of raising any kind of "stick" or of withholding the "carrot". And this refers not only to the contents of the communications, but also to their style and the way in which they were conducted. In 1945 and 1946 the Americans made sure to make public their stand on the Palestine issue. This public stand was, in fact, part of a policy which was aimed, outwardly, at putting pressure on Britain and inwardly, at influencing the Jewish vote in the autumn 1946 Elections to Congress.

A different tactic was adopted in summer of 1947 and communications were made quietly and through diplomatic channels. Furthermore, until the announcement on the deportation to Hamburg, communications had been unofficial in character and only after learning of the British decision to send the *Exodus* immigrants to Germany did the American Administration begin acting on a diplomatic level in Washington, London and Paris to rescind it. The day after news came of the deportation, the State Department ordered the American embassy in London to begin acting at once, in a personal and friendly way, to dissuade Britain from taking this step (*FRUS* 1947, 1139–40).

At the end of the Cabinet meeting on 22 August 1947, President Truman asked the acting Secretary of State, Lovett, about the ultimatum issued to the *Exodus* Jews and stressed the emotional upheaval this was causing in the United States. Lovett reported to the President on the State Department's communications with the British Foreign Office and explained the State Department's heretoforth informal activity on the issue: "A formal note would have had an almost certain effect of freezing the British in their position because of Bevin's great sensitivity on this point and because the British could with some justice say that we were interfering in the exercise of their powers. The informal approach was felt to be far more productive and was accordingly taken by us." The President was in full accord with this and asked Lovett to continue "our best effort to modify the British procedure" (*FRUS* 1947, 1138–39). As a result, another telegram was sent to the American embassy in London, stressing the negative effect the deportation would have on American public opinion and pointing out that protests against Britain had been piling up both at the White House and the State Department. The practical instructions were, to take up the matter at once with British Government at a high level in a more formal manner than that suggested in the previous telegram (*FRUS* 1947, 1140).

This, as we know, turned out to be fruitless. Once again the British repeated their routine reply, that they had been unable to find an alternative destination for the passengers and that the only place with suitable facilities was the British zone in Germany. The blame for the resulting situation was placed on France. As for the Jews themselves, each of them had been given the option to choose between landing in Port de Bouc, and going on to Hamburg. Bevin knew very well that the Americans would find the matter repulsive, but he was convinced that there was no choice and that Britain would simply have to face the music.[10]

Still, the British tried to wriggle out of this embarrassing situation by proposing that from Germany the immigrants be sent overland to France. The official request to the French on that matter was made only after the convoy of deportation ships had left Port de Bouc. At the same time, they appealed to the United States for help in persuading the French to agree unconditionally to the proposal. Britain's intention was to obtain American support in returning the immigrants to France, even forcibly.[11] On 30 August 1947 the State Department ordered the ambassador in Paris to inform the French Government that although they had no intention of discussing the legal aspects of the matter, the American Government would appreciate any action taken by France to ease the situation, due to the humanitarian aspects involved. In other words: Letting the immigrants into France (*FRUS* 1947, 1142). It seemed for a moment that the Americans had fallen into the trap set for them by the British. But they were quick to realize in Washington that the instructions which had been sent to Paris had been composed in such a way as to be too much in line with the British request, and the State Department found it necessary to tone them down a couple of days later and to make it clear to the ambassador in Paris that there was nothing in the instructions that could hint at support for the British proposal that France accept the immigrants unconditionally, or, in other words, even against the refugees' will (*FRUS* 1947, 1142).

The British then came up with a new idea: to get the French Government to renew their proposal that the immigrants disembark of their own free will at a French port, for example, Cherbourg (on the Atlantic coast). They believed that the immigrants would take this proposal seriously if a French official were to board the ships to confirm that France was indeed willing to accept them. Britain asked the Americans to authorize their ambassador in Paris to support this proposal and the acting Secretary of State instructed his Paris ambassador to discuss the matter with the French Government. The Americans found this proposal very tempting, and it seems that until the last moment they clearly believed that the problem could be solved by landing the *Exodus* immigrants at a French port before the ships had entered Germany's territorial waters.[12]

Here we should pay attention to the small difference in concept on each side. The British had pointed out to the Americans that landing the immigrants at a French port would make it possible to avoid the *expected hardships involved in transferring them from Germany to France*. Britain, who had already been censured for deporting the immigrants to Germany, offered solutions for overcoming the hardships of the next stage of the affair. As far as the Americans were concerned, the advantages of the proposal were that it would *prevent the need to land the immigrants in Germany*.[13] The Americans had aspirations that the ships would not arrive in Germany, fearing agitation of the Jewish DPs in the American zone. When it turned out later that landing in Hamburg was inevitable, and that their apprehensions did not materialize, the Americans lost interest in the subsequent fate of the immigrants and washed their hands of the whole affair.

Why, after a whole month of non-interference in the Exodus Affair did America decide to take a stand on the deportation to Germany? The fact is that America's appeal to the French Government was completely in keeping with its policy throughout the affair. At the end of July and during the first two-thirds of August, the United States treated the matter as being Britain's problem. America preferred to avoid taking a stand which might be interpreted as interference in Britain's ongoing policies – so long as UNSCOP had not completed its work and the United Nations had not determined the future of Palestine. Indeed, even at the end of August, the United States flatly refused to intervene between the British and the Jews on the *Exodus* issue.[14] America's appeal to France was made at the request of the British, at a time when the only options available consisted of landing the immigrants in France or in Germany. It would have seemed at that point, therefore, that the matter had nothing to do with Palestine, while, on the other hand, American interests were at stake.

As soon as they learned of Britain's intention to deport the immigrants to Germany, the Americans were motivated not only by a fear of an angry response in their own country,[15] but – and perhaps, mainly – by the fact that most of the *Exodus* people had originated in the American zone in Germany and returning them to that country might have caused agitation among the many DPs still living there. The American occupation authorities were concerned at the situation in the DP camps and mentioned it several times to their Government.[16] They had learned from experience that this "trick" of Britain's could very well result in an increase of the DP population in the *American* zone. And after all, like the British, the Americans, too, were interested in reducing this population, not increasing it.

America's fears regarding the return of the immigrants to Germany also contained echoes of the Cold War. It was still unclear which of the sides (American or Soviet) was favored by the Zionists, and the State Department were very wary of the Jewish DPs. This Department, and the Pentagon, both of whom were not exactly strongholds of Zionist supporters, were concerned at the communist influences absorbed by the Jewish DPs and suspected that once these succeeded in immigrating to Palestine they might strengthen the Soviet fifth column in the Middle East (Eilat 1982, 157, 161–63). America's phobia of all matters communist peeps out of a telegram sent by the American consul general in Jerusalem to the Secretary of State on 21 July 1947, in which he mentioned innocently that the port from which *Exodus* had sailed was controlled by French Communist organizations.[17] We should be reminded that in their crusade against illegal immigration, the British often made a point of mentioning the dangers involved in letting Jewish immigrants into Palestine, for fear that they might be Communist agents.

All in all, the role played by the United States in the Exodus Affair was very small and this, too, tended to be under duress. At first, there was no American intervention at all, for reasons which could be defined as *sub judice*, and in accordance with their traditional tendency to ignore Britain's appeals on the matter of illegal immigration to Palestine. When, at the end of August, the Americans wanted to rescind Britain's decision on deporting the *Exodus* immigrants to Germany, they were unsuccessful – because the efforts were "too little and too late". Too little, because the efforts were limited in their objectives, lacked determination and were completely isolated from the wider context of the ties between the United States and Britain. Too late, because the British Foreign Secretary had already placed his Government in a situation from which there could be no retreat without a serious loss of face.

The United States had determined her moves in the Exodus Affair without taking into consideration Zionist pressure, and often in conflict with the objectives of the Zionists. At no stage of the Exodus Affair had the United States tried to get the immigrants into Palestine, or even Cyprus, and at the final stage, the help they offered involved arranging the immigrants' entry to France. The Zionists ability to influence the Administration's position on the issue was limited not only because the event occurred such a long time (about a year and a quarter) before the elections, but more because at the early stages the United States took a strictly non-intervention stand, and at the final stage American and Zionist interests contradicted one another.

The Jewish Agency's initial response on the decision to expel the immigrants to Germany was presented by its London representative to a Colonial Office official as soon as information had been received of the fact (about half an hour before it was made public). He indignantly rejected Britain's proposal that the Jewish Agency cooperate in securing the landing of the immigrants in France. He also protested the claim in

Britain's announcement that it was under the influence of persistent Zionist threats and propaganda that the French Government's offer was rejected by the immigrants. As soon as he left the meeting, Locker sent a telegram to the Colonial Office, repeating the Jewish Agency's refusal to persuade the immigrants to land in France, and warning that the deportation to Germany would make things very difficult for those forces among the Jews in Palestine who were struggling against violence and disorder.[18]

From midday on the 21 August, the Jewish Agency was busy in behind-the-scenes encouragement to get people to send out as many protest telegrams as possible, but this time the Jewish Agency did not appeal, as it had in July, to people in high places to make use of their connections in the American Administration. Altogether the Jewish Agency's responses – both the outspoken ones and the diplomatic ones – were not particularly vigorous. Nachum Goldman, for example (a member of the Jewish Agency Executive), wrote to Emil Sandstrom, UNSCOP's chairman, saying that deporting the immigrants to a country responsible for the murder of six million Jews would arouse furious indignation among Jews throughout the world and was likely to result in a further aggravation of the condition in Palestine. Goldman claimed that forcing the immigrants off the ships might give rise to more bloodshed. Still, he made no specific practical request.[19]

Why did the Jewish Agency not ask for UNSCOP intervention at this stage of the affair? This could be because the Jewish Agency had learned from past experience that the committee had no authority to interfere in the Exodus Affair and that neither the committee nor its chairman had any intention of taking action on the matter (Eban 1977, 80). Still, the letter's vague and restrained tone was in keeping with the fact that the committee was in the process of summing up its report and the Jewish Agency was not interested in drawing its attention from this very important task.

For the same reason, the telegram the Jewish Agency sent on 24 August to all the UN member nations, including the Moslem states – Afghanistan, India, Iran and Turkey, and excluding Britain and the Arab states, did not contain a request for specific action beyond imploring them to intervene in an effort to prevent the perpetration of a crime against humanity by a superpower against a helpless group of people whose only wish is to secure their freedom and basic human rights.[20]

The Jewish Agency's request, that the United States impress upon the British Government not to deport Jews to Germany, was also formulated in the negative with no specific request for action. Moreover, the meeting held by the Jewish Agency representative in Washington with the acting Secretary of State, Robert Lovett (Marshall was out of town), with the specific objective of discussing the fate of the *Exodus* immigrants, dwelt on all aspects of the Palestine issue and the problems of European Jewry. Epstein initiated this course because he wanted to feel out the State Department prior to the forthcoming vote on Palestine in the UN General Assembly. *Exodus* was mentioned only once, toward the end of the report he sent the following day to Jerusalem.[21]

About two hours before the ships were due to sail out of Port de Bouc on Friday 22 August, when it was clear that Britain had every intention of carrying out her decision, the Jewish Agency people in France, aided by their local friends, made a last minute bid to get it canceled. At 4:20 in the afternoon Leon Blum telephoned ambassador Cooper on behalf of the Jewish Agency and informed him that should the British Government promise to allow the *Exodus* immigrants to travel to Palestine within a certain period of time, the Jewish Agency would advise them to land in France. To Cooper's question as to whether the intention was three to four years, Blum replied that he was talking about two or three months. The ambassador promised to discuss the matter with his superiors, but said he was pretty sure that the idea would be rejected, since it meant giving precedence to law-breakers over legal immigrants, who were waiting patiently for their turn to come.[22]

A meeting took place shortly afterwards between the ambassador and Marc Jarblum, initiated by the latter, at which the proposal was raised, in greater detail this time, and based on a precedent in which a ship – whose name he could not remember – was intercepted by the British near the shores of Italy. The passengers had refused to land and Britain had allowed them to enter Palestine at the expense of the monthly quota. If the British were to repeat this and allot half of each monthly quota to the *Exodus* immigrants, they would all be able to enter Palestine within six months. The ambassador had no recollection of such an incident and he made it clear to Jarblum that he did not believe it would be repeated. Nonetheless, eager to find a solution, he promised to ask his Government to allow the refugees who agreed to disembark in France to apply for an entry permit to Palestine, after which they would await their turn like all the others and would not be punished for trying to break the law by sailing on counterfeit documents. The ambassador considered this to be an act of generosity on the part of His Majesty's Government, but Jarblum thought it was not good enough. They finished their conversation at 5:30 by which time, as the ambassador wrote correctly, it was too late to reverse the decision.[23] The ships were due to sail at six o'clock.

The Foreign Office approved the ambassador's stand,[24] but reminded him (perhaps as a reprimand for his last proposal) that allowing illegal immigrants to jump the queue was not in keeping with "our principles", which were expressed in the decision to send the *President Warfield* passengers back to France.[25]

In London, Foreign Office staff were also unable to recall Jarblum's Italian story, but we know that the incident he was referring to was the La Spezia Affair (mentioned in Chapter 5), where the British finally agreed to allow the 1,014 immigrants into Palestine at the expense of the certificate quota (Hadari 1991, 135–40). People involved on the Jewish side of the Exodus Affair sometimes found themselves toying with the possibility that this story, too, would have a happy ending, just like its predecessor. But we must remember that not only did the La Spezia Affair happen before the refoulement policy was implemented, but also before the British began deporting all the immigrants they captured to Cyprus.

In Palestine, the news of the deportation was made public in an official announcement, which included:

> Pending the United Nations decision on the future of Palestine, the Mandatory Government is responsible not only for maintaining law and order in that country, but also to ensure the fact that nothing is done which could be interpreted as *de facto*, prior to the UN decision. The policy on immigration is of major importance with regard to the Palestine question and there is no justification for the Mandatory Government to increase the existing monthly quota of 1,500 Jewish immigrants in the intermediary period. The organizers of illegal immigration are trying to increase the quota, in order to mis-balance the number of Jewish inhabitants in the country, thus deteriorating the already tense and delicate situation, which has caused bloodshed among Arabs as well as Jews. It is the job of the Mandatory Government to fight the illegal immigration movement with all the means at its disposal. The transfer of illegal immigrants to Cyprus has only served to encourage the organizers of this movement. Thus, in the case of *President Warfield* the Mandatory Government has put into effect its prerogative of returning illegal immigrants to the country from which they set sail for Palestine.[26]

In Jerusalem, the Jewish Agency responded to this in a manifesto published on 24 August. Several versions had been tried before the final one was approved.[27] The published version left out several points included in previous ones, for example: The testimony of the American minister who had taken part in the *Exodus* voyage to Palestine; the story of *Struma* and *Patria*; and the burning of Hebrew books on the deportation ships. These were replaced with an extended response to the complaint that the organizers of illegal immigration "were deteriorating the already tense and delicate situation, which has caused bloodshed among Arabs as well as Jews". Previous versions had dealt with this superficially, and went on immediately to the subject of "spilling the blood of the refugees on *Exodus 1947* and other ships, by the armed forces of His Majesty's Government". In the final version, no blame was aimed at Britain, nor was any mention made of attacks on Jews in various English cities (following the execution of the two sergeants). However, what was said was this:

> In order to justify the deportation of the immigrants in the middle of July, the Government is exploiting incidents which took place in Palestine in the middle of August – attacks by Arab murderers and robbers on a number of Jews, which have nothing to do with the matter at hand. Not a single Arab in Palestine made the connection – as did His Majesty's Government in its announcement – between these incidents and the problem of immigration. On the contrary, these incidents only served to prove how much the masses of Jews and Arabs want peace, as could be seen from the declarations made by leaders of the two communities and the peace meetings of Jews and Arabs at the border neighborhoods where the incidents took place.

The British announcement touched a very sensitive nerve indeed, and exactly because of the grain of truth in it, efforts were made by the Jewish Agency to get it off the public agenda. On 18 July 1947, *The Times* of London pointed out that the line taken by the Jews in their testimonies before UNSCOP involved presenting the Palestine issue as a confrontation between the Jews and Britain, while the British line maintained that this was a Jewish–Arab problem. The Zionist leaders also realized – sooner or later – that the main issue involved the relationship between Jews and Arabs, but tactical considerations forced them to play this down as far as possible, at least until after the UN decision on the future of Palestine. Thus, in the final version of the response to the deportation to Hamburg, there was an obvious effort not to escalate the Jewish–British conflict and to deny the existence of a Jewish–Arab conflict.

The process of wording the response to the announcement on the deportation of the *Exodus* immigrants to Hamburg reflects changes which had taken place in the order of priorities on the Zionist agenda. At that stage, an awareness was taking hold slowly but surely, that the real and most important struggle was not over the fate of the immigrants but over the political future of Palestine. Thus it was necessary not to deepen the conflict with the British and to keep as low as possible a profile on the tension between Jews and Arabs. This awareness was still not shared by everyone and was expressed mainly behind closed doors. Different things were said in public, not only because of different points of view, but also from tactical considerations.

A chance to review the situation both openly and behind closed doors was presented by the meeting of the Zionist General Council in Zurich between 25 August and 2 September 1947. The immigrants were making their way to Hamburg at the time and UNSCOP was busy polishing up its report, which was signed on 31 August and published the following day. At open sessions of the Council, speakers applauded the illegal immigration operation and praised the courage of the *Exodus* immigrants. Shertok placed illegal immigration at the center of the Zionist struggle and at the final plenum it was decided: "The Zionist General Council sees the illegal immigration to Palestine [Ha'apalah] as being a main foundation of Zionism's political struggle against the designs of the White Paper and an essential element in the operation of rescuing the Jewish masses" (Zionist General Council, 1947).

In addressing the public, Ben-Gurion, too, was outspoken in his praise for that "enormous and magnificent drama, the drama of illegal immigration",[28] but behind closed doors, where he felt "things could be expressed clearly", he said that the central and most vital issue, both to the Yishuv and to Zionism, was the question of security and the need to create a Jewish armed force, because "it is on this that all our future depends ... and it is in accordance with this issue that we must determine all our Zionist strategy, externally as well as internally." Ben-Gurion tried to shake his colleagues into facing things as he saw them: "The Movement is concerned with other things altogether, such as the UN Committee of Inquiry and sees in these a central issue. These are called political issues and they are dealt with constantly. And I am sorry to have to disagree with our public opinion and to place something else at the center of our interests – the security issue, on which, at the moment, hangs the success or failure of Zionism."

He believed that the danger came from the Arab front. "At the moment we are facing not robbery and terror and attempts at disturbing us in our work, but the intent to uproot the Yishuv and to destroy in a single blow the entire Zionist 'danger', by annihilating all the Jews of Palestine."[29]

Ben-Gurion was ahead of his colleagues and adversaries in visualizing the next phase in the struggle for the creation of a Jewish state. At a meeting of the Political Committee of the 22nd Zionist Congress in December 1946, held behind closed doors, he had presented the security issue as being of primary importance to the Yishuv (Ben-Gurion 1950,

135–37), although at the Congress plenum, he presented illegal immigration as "the central front" (Zionist Organization Executive, n.d., 63–64). At that time Ben-Gurion made himself responsible for security and since then spent most of his time and energy on that matter. In his orders to the Haganah commanders (18 June 1947) exactly one month before the battle on *Exodus* near the shores of Palestine, Ben-Gurion outlined two enemy fronts – British and Arab – which leaned heavily on each other. On the Arab front, the Haganah was to be a decisive factor. The struggle between Zionism and Britain, however, "is basically *political* and not *military*", and "even military activity, necessary from time to time in this political struggle, is aimed only at reinforcing the political strife" (Ben-Gurion 1975, 13–14. Original emphases). This list of priorities and the definition of the Haganah's role on the anti-British front together dictated Ben-Gurion's stand on the response to the deportation to Hamburg.

In the last week of August, Ben-Gurion was visited in his hotel room in Zurich, by Meirov, head of the Mossad, Hoffman, head of the Jewish Agency delegation in Europe, and Daniel (Kurt) Levin – the man appointed by the Jewish Agency to be responsible for the British zone in Germany. The three disagreed on the question of what kind of action should be taken in the Hamburg port area and how the immigrants themselves should behave when they were being disembarked. Hoffman was convinced that attempts should be made to prevent the forced landing of the immigrants. Levin, on the other hand, disagreed and insisted that the immigrants had been through enough and that the struggle should not take place on their backs.[30] Hoffman and Meirov were in support of an extreme reaction in the port region, which would bring about a serious clash with the British. Their plans included acts of arson in the port and bringing in thousands of Jews from the British and American zones to the port of Hamburg, in an attempt to prevent the *Exodus* immigrants from landing on German soil. Levin believed that once the immigrants had been brought to the two camps prepared for them by the British near Lübeck, it would be possible to spirit them out within a few weeks to Belsen and from there to take them to Palestine with the help of legal certificates issued by the British for the Jews in their zone in Germany. Ben-Gurion agreed unequivocally with Levin and explained his opposition to the extreme action proposed by the other two by pointing out that the *Exodus* immigrants had already done enough and it would be unfair to involve them in activity which might end in bloodshed.[31]

In fact there were other reasons for Ben-Gurion's decision against extreme action in Hamburg. At the very time when the immigrants were making their way from Port de Bouc to Hamburg, the entire illegal immigration operation had reached a watershed. So long as international elements had to be convinced of the connection between solving the Jewish DP problem in Europe and the foundation of a Jewish state in Palestine, the illegal immigration operation had a vital political role to play. It was thus in the time of the Anglo-American Committee and also while UNSCOP was gleaning its information. But in those fateful days at the end of August and early September 1947, when all eyes were turned to Geneva, everyone knew that the issue at hand was a proposal to partition Palestine and to found a Jewish state in part of it. Later, following publication of the report, when the political arena had been removed to Lake Success, a change took place in Zionism's list of priorities, and illegal immigration was pushed slightly to the sidelines and it would not have been right for *Exodus* to complicate the positive sequence of things.

These political motives were also what guided the Zionist leadership in determining the restrained character of the response in Palestine to the deportation to Germany. On the day the ships set off from Port de Bouc, a protest rally was held in Tel Aviv, in which some 5,000 people took part (*Davar*, 22 August 1947). A public day of fasting, initiated by the Chief Rabbinate and religious in character, was held a few days later, to express solidarity with the immigrants. Also, Jerusalem sent out very mild instructions to all the towns and villages in the country as to the way in which people were to conduct themselves on the day the immigrants were removed from the ships in Hamburg. Work would be halted for two hours; public meetings would be arranged; flags would be lowered to half mast with a black ribbon tied around the post.[32]

Chaim Weizmann, who had not held any official position since December 1946, and who was in London at the time, feared the potentially negative repercussions this final phase of the Exodus Affair would have on the political process. Weizmann was not indifferent to the immigrants. Presumably he had been consulted on the telegram his wife had sent to the British Government. At a meeting in Basel to commemorate the fiftieth anniversary of the World Zionist Organization, Weizmann, "emotional and weeping ... honored the immigrants of *Exodus 1947* and their brave stand. The crowd stood on its feet and listened in silence to his speech" (*Ha-Aretz*, 2 Sept. 1947). A few days later, when it was a matter of days, maybe even hours, before the immigrants were forced off the ships, Weizmann tried to set up a meeting with Bevin (to thrash this out), who refused, preferring to avoid a discussion on the UNSCOP decision, and suggested that if Weizmann was interested in the boats, he would be better off discussing the matter with the Deputy Secretary of State for the Colonies (the Secretary himself was out of London at the time).[33]

Weizmann was acting as a private person, in order to dull the sting of the conflict with Britain. He believed that the Zionist Executive had been mistaken in its policy toward England and thought it would have been much better to develop a more or less normal relationship with Britain, so as to create a broader and more satisfactory basis from which the UNSCOP report could be implemented. His main fear was that Britain would avoid all involvement on the matter of the UNSCOP decision and might succeed in persuading the United States to follow suit, which would result in a dangerous vacuum. Weizmann was convinced that intransigence with regard to the *Exodus* immigrants would only worsen the relations between the Zionists and Britain and supply the Foreign Office with the opportunity to wash their hands of the whole Palestine question. For this reason Weizmann was interested in having something done to avoid a scandal in Hamburg, even if this meant sending the ships back to France, which he considered preferable to an international fiasco in Germany.

Weizmann found himself alone in London, as the ships approached Hamburg (the Jewish Agency Executive were in Zurich at the meeting of the Zionist General Council), and he felt free to approach the Government as he saw fit. He was invited suddenly to the Colonial Office on 6 September, where he warned the Government of the outcome of their decision to land the immigrants in Hamburg (*Ha-Aretz*, 6 Sept. 1947). The Deputy Secretary of State for the Colonies proposed returning the ships to France, if the Jewish Agency would commit itself in writing that it would advise the immigrants to disembark of their own accord. As there was no one in London with the necessary authority and he had been unable to get the green light from the Jewish Agency in Zurich, Weizmann appealed to Leon Blum and asked him to try to influence Bevin on the one hand and to advise the immigrants to disembark peacefully in France, on the other.

Ben-Gurion was furious at Weizmann's intervention. In an angry letter to the Executive in London, he expressed concern at the "strange news which reached me yesterday", and went on to describe in great detail the sequence of events, weaving a note of disdain for Weizmann firmly into the fabric of his message. He repeated his absolute disapproval of Weizmann involving himself in any kind of political activity either in England or in America.

Shertok, too, who had none of the bad feeling which characterized the Weizmann–Ben-Gurion relationship, was worried that the "British were exploiting Weizmann". Ben-Gurion was worried that things were being done not according to the decisions of the elected Zionist institutions and warned his colleagues that "any independent activity in London, unauthorized by the entire Executive, could blow up the Executive and perhaps even the Zionist Organization." Once it was decided what form the response in Hamburg would take – demonstrations, but no violent confrontation – Ben-Gurion considered the matter closed and concluded. He had no desire to open a Pandora's box of arguments, disagreements and – worst of all – partisan action from any quarter. What he wanted was a controlled and restrained response, one which would illustrate the responsibility and authority of the Zionist leadership, its unity and the fact of its rule over the public. Ben-Gurion believed that in all these respects, any interference on the part of Weizmann could have been harmful both internally and externally.

Ben-Gurion was walking a tight-rope. He agreed with Weizmann's assessment that the most important item on the agenda was the implementation of the UNSCOP report and that no obstacles should stand in the way of realizing the committee's majority recommendations. But not only did Ben-Gurion disagree with Weizmann on the importance of Britain's stand at this stage of the political process; as leader of the Zionist movement, who had to take in the picture as a whole, Ben-Gurion had to navigate the response on the deportation to Hamburg along the golden road between a spectacular act that certain circles in the Yishuv and the Haganah wanted, and completely and openly abandoning the struggle for the *Exodus* immigrants, in return for securing the UNSCOP recommendations.

The "Hamburg Chapter" in the Exodus Affair began on 21 August 1947 and ended on 9 September, when the last immigrant was removed from his ship on to German soil. The conclusions and recommendations of UNSCOP were made public between these two dates. As it had been in the early stages of the affair, so too in this chapter, the fate of the *Exodus* immigrants lay in the shadow of UNSCOP – especially after the first of September. At the final stage of the Exodus Affair, the Zionists had in effect almost ceased all effort to rescind the decreed deportation to Hamburg. No effort was made to harness the UNSCOP report in favor of the *Exodus* immigrants, the like of that made by American Congressman, Emanuel Seller, who wrote to the British ambassador in Washington on 2 September 1947, that "it would be an act of mercy if your Government would turn the ships back toward Palestine and allow these refugees to enter the Holy Land, now that the United

Nations Special Committee has asked that the doors to Palestine remain open."[34]

Of all the Jewish Agency Executive, Golda Myerson alone remained in Palestine at the time. When Shertok, in Geneva, learned that emotions in England were rising against the deportation decision, and that the Cabinet was supposed to discuss the matter anew, he cabled her: "Important nothing happens Palestine spoil chances".[35] What exactly did Shertok mean by this? He was certainly referring to the dissident groups, fearing that they would conduct another act of terror at the worst possible time. But what "chances" was he talking about, now that Palestine and Cyprus were both out of the question? It is possible here to observe the gap, not to mention the contradiction, between improving the fate of the immigrants and achieving the objectives of illegal immigration. If the objective was to prevent at all costs the need to land the immigrants on Germany's contaminated soil, then the only available option was to land them in France, and perhaps in England or some other European country. But such a finale to the affair would entail a full-scale fiasco from the point of view of the Zionist struggle.

And so, in the final week of August, as soon as the Jewish Agency got wind of Britain's approach to the Government of Denmark with the request that the immigrants be permitted to land on Danish soil, a telegram was sent asking the Danes to "adopt the same attitude as proclaimed by the French Government, namely, admit only those prepared to settle in Denmark of their own free will, without compulsion or intimidation". Furthermore, the Danes were asked not to lend themselves "to be a party to forcing those sorely tried people to land anywhere save in the country of their free choice".[36] Denmark, however, rejected Britain's appeal (although this had nothing to do with the Zionists' request), believing that there was no point in inviting the immigrants to a European country after they had refused the French Government's invitation. Nor did Denmark hide the main reason for this rejection, which was economic hardship (*Ha-Aretz*, 29 August 1947).

16 · "Each and Every One of You Is Dear to Us"

On their last night in Port de Bouc, a Haganah boat sailed between the deportation ships, repeatedly broadcasting the message: "Do not land!" over loudspeakers. After three weeks of adhering steadfastly to their decision not to land in France, this was for the immigrants not so much an order as an expression of solidarity, a message that they were not alone, that their fellow Jews in Palestine were firmly behind them. Boats bearing people from Palestine, sending out calls of encouragement to the immigrants, circled the deportation ships several times while they were anchored at Port de Bouc. An especially deep impression was left by the visit of Moshe Sneh on 8 August. Sneh was convinced at the time, that the immigrants were about to be sent to Kenya, and he told them not to lose spirit, because "the Jewish nation will not rest until you are all allowed to immigrate to Palestine, just as the people of Mauritius did in the past and the deportees to Cyprus are being allowed to. No matter where they send you to – we shall bring you home!" (Habbas 1954, 294).

The presence so close to their ships, of the former Haganah commander and so senior a member of the Jewish Agency Executive, had an enormous moral significance for the immigrants. But Sneh's promises offered little comfort, since those illegal immigrants he mentioned, who had been deported to Mauritius in 1940, had had to wait almost five years before being allowed back into Palestine. Mauritius remained a traumatically painful memory and as soon as rumors were circulating at the end of July that the Cabinet had decided to deport the immigrants to some tropical British colony, the Jewish Agency applied to the Foreign Secretary with a request not to do this, and reminded him that of 1,580 immigrants deported there, over 100 had died as a result of the harsh conditions.[1]

The emissaries on the deportation ships were desperate for instructions as to how to behave if they were transferred to a destination other than Palestine or Cyprus, and "Do not land!" did not constitute an adequate reply to their repeated requests. Nor were those instructions which did eventually get through to the ships, following news of the intended deportation to Hamburg, sufficiently unequivocal: "If they really bring you to Germany, try to make it obvious that you want to go to Palestine, but avoid any casualties on your side. They will certainly resort to force to get you off the ships. Try to preserve your strength and your health. Each and every one of you is dear to us. And we are counting on your strength in Palestine."[2]

The ships set sail out of Port de Bouc early in the evening of 22 August and from that moment on, all communications with them were severed and no orders or instructions could be transferred to their passengers – not even at Gibraltar, where they were placed under very heavy guard and continued to be incommunicado. Thus, it was up to each of the three ships to give its own interpretation to the order "try to make it obvious that you want to go to Palestine", in accordance with the character, experience and outlook of their leaders.

And, as we know, the emissaries and immigrants had evolved their own style of management and behavior on each of the ships, as well as the division of duties between them. Roseman was the uncontended leader on *Runnymede Park* and, from the beginning, he had worked closely with an elected secretariat. Perlson was the senior commander on *Empire Rival* and the secretariat he formed, only about two weeks after arriving at Port de Bouc, was more educational than practical. The immigrants had enormous confidence in Perlson and their obedience was a priori, for the simple reason that he was from Palestine and represented the Haganah. They called him Gott (in Yiddish – God), playing, intentionally, on his underground nickname – "Gad". The immigrants on *Ocean Vigour* handled their own affairs, aided by American crew members until 8 August 1947 when an emissary arrived on board. He joined the secretariat, which had been elected on the way from Haifa, and from then on, there was full cooperation among the immigrants, the Americans and the emissary from Palestine, who enjoyed a status higher than that of first among equals.

Each of the three deportation ships therefore, differed not only in passenger composition (age, family status, political affiliation) and in the extent to which the British were able to control the immigrants' lives, but also in leadership patterns. Apart from the fundamental decision: "We Shall Not Land!" which the immigrants had all arrived at independently on each of the ships while still on the way from Haifa to France, the character of their leadership definitely influenced their lives during the stay at Port de Bouc, and more so on the form their resistance took when they arrived in Hamburg.

The immigrants had great respect for the young people from Palestine, a respect which increased during the voyage from France to Palestine and became greater still during their stay at Port de Bouc. On the deportation ships – unlike on *Exodus*, where the immigrants and the escorts had been quartered separately – they all lived side by side 24 hours a day, and the emissaries and escorts found themselves highly admired and elevated to role model status. Shortly after landing in Hamburg, children of the Dror youth movement wrote: "Every day we saw – even if from a distance – how people of the Haganah were acting on our behalf. They were so tireless and devoted, they did everything they could to ease our suffering. We felt confident that as long as these people are here with us, nothing was beyond our ability" (Dror 1948, 43). One of the immigrants wrote in his memoirs: "No need for concern. The Haganah are with us. They are the personification of strength, ability and talent. They spread their wings above us, like the wings of an eagle in the sky, protecting its young. The Haganah are our security. They will not disappoint us" (Ganuz 1985, 144). Another wrote to his friends: "Led us [to Palestine] Jewish lads, the epitome of humility and honesty. We have not reached their level ... these are the young men of the Haganah from Palestine – I have nothing but respect for them" (Habbas 1954, 165–66).

Perlson was new to illegal immigration. He had arrived in France shortly before the *Exodus* had set sail and this was his first such voyage. He knew neither Yiddish nor any other of the languages spoken by the immigrants and his attitude to them was somewhat patronizing. He worried about them and was intensely sympathetic to their special needs – both material and spiritual – but he did not have a very high opinion of their staying power. In time, there were swings in his assessment. He tended to sum up the situation according to the number of actual and potential "drop outs", and at times when the immigrants were showing no tendency to land, Perlson would report that "everything is alright". But as the exhausting sojourn drew out and several of the passengers began expressing a desire to land, he wrote to the Mossad head that "if this waiting goes on much longer, it might be better to let off all those people who don't want to remain. This way we'll know that we are left with a group of people united in their determination and willingness, even if the number of people disembarking is as high as 20–25 percent" (Habbas 1954, 194).

On *Runnymede Park* Roseman, too, was concerned at the signs of weakness shown by the soft margins of his immigrant population. Perlson had reckoned that around 5 percent of the total population of his ship, or about 75 people, would be tempted to land (Habbas 1954, 190). If they were obliged to wait much longer, the number of people wishing to disembark might reach 25 percent, a situation he considered serious. Roseman, on the other hand, reckoned that within ten days or a fortnight a total of 400 people will have disembarked from his ship, or about a quarter of the immigrant population (Exodus Diary 1968, 13 August 1947); but this did not bother him too much. In the middle of August he told the immigrants: "It could take another week or ten days, a fortnight, a month even, and we'll still be here. Maybe 10–20–30–200–300 will disembark, but the remaining one hundred will stay on to the end, even if they have to be taken off dead" (Exodus Diary 1968, 16 August 1947).

This last was probably an attempt on his part to impress his audience. Roseman was no Elazar Ben Ya'ir and this was no Massada. His real attitude to the struggle, as well as his orders as the ship approached Hamburg, and the way he behaved during the landing, were totally pragmatic. The numbers he mentioned were also probably a show of bravado, which did not reflect his real assessment of the situation. Indeed, like Perlson, Roseman was confident that he had at his disposal a strong kernel of immigrants who would remain on the ship "to the bitter end" and they both believed that the struggle would ultimately benefit by the removal of the weaker elements from among the immigrants.

Perlson and Roseman did not see eye-to-eye in their assessment of the immigrants' willpower. The matter was complex and not clear cut. The composition of its immigrant population meant that *Empire Rival* could be considered a "strong ship". Only a small number of her passengers landed and there was a fairly large and united group of dependable activists. Still, Perlson never stopped being afraid of a mass landing. His constant struggle with the British over improved conditions on board, together with repeated demands of his colleagues on shore for food, clothing, blankets, books and school equipment, were to a great extent the result of a firm belief that a constant supply of these were the be all and end all of a successful struggle – in other words, would keep the immigrants on board.

Roseman took another approach, not only because the two were of different status and their jobs were not the same, but also because their backgrounds were different. Roseman was seven years older than Perlson. He had spent the war years deep in the Soviet Union and between 1944 and 1947, he had been an activist in the "Brichah" and in the DP camps. He knew the immigrants inside out, spoke their language and understood them. He, too, was aware of the importance to their morale of food and physical conditions. Still, during their stay in Port de Bouc all the energy he had extended in the struggle with the British had been turned toward a front which he considered to be the most important of all – the right of the immigrants to enter Palestine. The autonomy he had over all matters concerning food rations and distribution had been achieved through proper negotiations with the convoy commander and because he had been able to prove that he could control his people. The situation changed when the ships left France for Hamburg and with it, his approach. He began fanning the flames of hatred for the British, as the moment of (forced) landing drew near and he went to extremes of demonization: "Tomorrow or the next day, the Devil will take up his evil work again, he will do his utmost to hurt us and shatter our hopes …." (Habbas 1954, 294).

During the time they were anchored in France, official visits to the ships had been conducted according to rules of etiquette, which required that the first visit be to the flagship. Thus the first on the list of official visits and announcements had always been *Runnymede Park*. This order was changed when the ships arrived in Hamburg, where operational considerations determined the landing sequence. The British had always considered *Ocean Vigour* to be the weak link among the three ships and decided that this ship would be the first for disembarkation. They thought it would be better to go from the light to the heavy and hoped that, if they were to see their brethren disembarking easily from *Ocean Vigour*, the other immigrants would choose to follow suite (*Ha-Aretz*, 26 August 1947).

Ocean Vigour was the most democratic of the three ships and M. Schwartz preferred, whenever possible, to let the immigrants make their own decisions. An example of this democratic form of decision making was the trial by peers which those people who had been involved in fist fights were made to face (Schwartz 1965, 93–94). Still, he kept to himself the final decision on what form of resistance they would show to being forced to land in Hamburg. He did, however, hold discussions on the matter with the secretariat in order to hear other opinions. They were mostly in favor of passive resistance and were opposed to active resistance, which they believed to be totally hopeless and would only have caused further casualties. Anyway, the people were exhausted and weak because their food rations, never large from the beginning, had been reduced over the past few days (Schwartz 1965, 94–95).

The emissary on *Ocean Vigour* recalled that most of the ship's secretariat supported passive resistance and only a handful of Revisionists demanded active resistance. One member of the secretariat claimed a different balance of power, alleging that "he [the emissary] insists that our resistance be passive, to the great consternation of a large proportion of the secretariat, who demand the right to resist the British with all the means at our disposal and not to land on the shores of Germany" (Ganuz 1985, 280). Whatever, it would appear that some of the immigrants were more extreme and more militant than the emissary, who did his best to maintain reason. Some of them wondered if this "was really an order from the Haganah – that we disembark like that, without putting up a struggle – like a herd of sheep?" (Ganuz 1985, 279).

How can the emissary's moderate stand be explained, as opposed to the militant one of much of the secretariat and some of the immigrants? First of all, he had received the last order from Port de Bouc, saying clearly that further casualties were to be avoided. Second, after almost a month in their company, he had a pretty modest opinion of their staying power. Add to this the dismal failure of the hunger strike, which had been announced on this very ship on the first day of the Selichoth prayers of the month of Elul, with the aim of showing the world and the British how well organized the immigrants were, and united, no matter what (Schwartz 1965, 95). The strike had been stopped earlier than planned because of the heightened emotions on the ship when the immigrants were given back the bags that had been taken from them in Haifa. Many of the bags had been lost or were on another ship. Their fear of losing what little property they had managed to save from the Holocaust or to accumulate in the days following it had caused the "already bad mood to get worse. People were hungry and dead tired, so we decided to cease the hunger strike" (Schwartz 1965, 96).

The secretariat on *Ocean Vigour* consisted mostly of youth movement and kibbutz members, and any militant stance on their part was not really representative of the immigrants, many of whom were family members or elderly folk. And don't let us forget that these people had just spent almost two extremely unpleasant months at sea. And, as if to crown it all, a baby had died several hours after being born on board ship and buried at sea with full ceremonial honors (*Davar*, 2 Sept. 1947). This was an experience which affected all the immigrants and made them even more depressed (Schwartz 1965, 92–93; Ganuz 1985, 258–61).

As the time for landing drew near, the emissary put an end to discussions and arguments and issued his instructions/commands to the immigrants – they were to offer only passive resistance to being removed from the ship. He found himself having to work his way through opposing points of view. On the one hand, some people wanted to disembark forthwith and these were warned: "No one is to disembark without being carried off by at least four to six soldiers!" All men, women and children were to remain in the hold and to make no preparations for landing. On the other hand, he was fully aware of "the hot-heads among the Revisionists, those who had been demanding active resistance and were liable to force us into activism, through some irresponsible act ... I had to keep my eyes open on two 'fronts' so as to maintain internal order. We chose people from the kibbutz groups and others we could trust to stand as guards, and it was their job to prevent irresponsible acts by that raucous bunch." The immigrants were reorganized into groups; damp blankets and water were made available to put out tear bombs. There were also wooden coshes, "just to be on the safe side" (Schwartz 1965, 95–96).

Landing was planned for the afternoon of 7 September, but a heavy fog held up *Ocean Vigour*'s entrance into port, so that disembarkation began first thing on the morning of Monday 8 September.[3] The previous evening the immigrants had been told to get themselves ready for landing the following morning, but they were in no hurry to obey this order. The first to land were the immigrants who had been hospitalized in the ship's hospital and they made no fuss whatsoever. Then there was an interval. The British held some internal consultations, and decided to inform the immigrants, over the loudspeakers, that it was time to move. The response was a meager stream of people making their way slowly and quietly down the gangplank – until 08:45.

Resistance began at about nine o'clock. It seemed to the British that a group of young inciters in one of the holds was blocking up the gangway and no one could get through. The soldiers tried to push people up the stairs. As soon as it became clear to the commanding officer that the use of force would be necessary, he asked to have reinforcements sent in from shore. Apparently, those soldiers who had been with the immigrants since Haifa, were unable to bring themselves to use force on them. About a hundred of the soldiers already stationed in Germany climbed aboard and got straight to work: "The paratroops are trying to catch children and young people but these are able to kick and scratch their way out. The metal coshes are then put into action and blows are showered on everyone in sight. Children bite at the paratroops' hands trying to work themselves free. It takes two or three paratroops to drag each kid, twisting their arms behind their backs, beating them on the head and back and bending their legs. Bleeding heads" (Ganuz 1985, 283).

Another, less violent but effective method of removing the immigrants from the ships involved making a grab for their meager belongings. The immigrants would then jump up and run after the only treasures left to them on earth.

The sight of the immigrants being brutally removed from *Ocean Vigour* made the port a depressing place to be in. Add to this the rousing military marches and dance music being played over loudspeakers on the pier, recalling horrific memories of concentration camp days. Even Auschwitz was named in the reports as an object for comparison. Many of the spectators were red-eyed from weeping. A group of newspaper reporters organized a letter of protest to President Truman, denouncing the British brutality in handling the immigrants (JDC 1947a). They even sent out a protest to the relevant authorities, who issued new orders to the soldiers, forbidding cruelty, unnecessary violence and demanding "minimal use of force" (*Ha-Aretz*, 19 Sept. 1947).

On the following day, Tuesday 9 September 1947, it was the turn of *Empire Rival*. By eight o'clock in the morning all the immigrants had disembarked and no one on the wharf had the faintest idea of what was going on.[4] Someone expressed his surprise to one of the immigrants, that after such stubborn resistance in France, they were disembarking in Hamburg "like lambs" (Leichter 1985). So peaceful was the landing of the passengers on *Empire Rival* that the Jewish Agency spokesman in London felt obliged to issue a statement denying the news that there had been no resistance on the part of the *Exodus* immigrants to landing at Hamburg. He insisted, instead, that there had been "firm resistance from all the immigrants, but they were eager to prevent bloodshed" (*Ha-Aretz*, 10 Sept. 1947). The coverage of the *Empire Rival* landing in the press in Palestine was reduced to an item claiming that a bomb had been found on board the ship. The placing of bombs on illegal immigration ships was indeed a matter of routine, but in this case, things were not quite so simple.

Explosives had been placed on board the deportation ship *Empire Haywood* the first time illegal immigrants were being deported to Cyprus, in the middle of August 1946. There was an explosion and the ship had been held up for a few days (Gil'ad 1953, 690). The Palmach subsequently turned this "habit" of sabotaging British deportation ships into a tradition – even a standing order. And this attitude was shared by the Palmachniks at Port de Bouc and aboard the deportation ship *Empire Rival*. They obtained explosives and delay detonators and transferred them to the ship. Some members of the Mossad knew of this, although it was kept secret from the organization's leaders (Biber testimony; Biber 1964; Livyathan testimony; Einor 1985; Braginsky 1965, 384). Perlson made no mention of it in his letters to the Mossad activist responsible for communications with the ships, and certainly not to Mossad head, Shaul Meirov. He did not so much fear the evil eye of the British, who – if the correspondence between the ships was anything to go by – could be easily deceived. He was afraid, however, that if the Mossad leaders got wind of the plan, they would put an end to it. Also, don't let us forget that the unofficial delegation of tasks between the Palmach and Mossad decreed that the matter of resistance was to be handled exclusively by the Palmach, notwithstanding the fact that in everything concerning illegal immigration, they were under the command of the Mossad.

The complex relations between the Mossad and the Palmach and the scale of loyalties involved, are laid out clearly in a note sent to Perlson, probably by Nissan Livyathan (the senior Palmach commander in the south of France at the time). "Since time is short, I am interested in dealing with one issue only. We have decided to go ahead with the sabotage, without authorization from the Mossad. Since sabotage is commensurate with resistance. On this matter, we receive our orders only from the Division [Palmach] and there is a permanent order to sabotage all deportation ships wherever they are. Thus, I hereby give you an order to sabotage the ship, in the event that you receive the material. The explosion has to take place after the passengers have disembarked."[5]

This need to sabotage British naval vessels involved in the war on illegal immigration was so deeply ingrained in the Palmach and so taken for granted that they missed no opportunity to go into action. Of the three deportation ships, only the *Empire Rival* could be taken into consideration in this case. It was the only ship that had a Palmach member on board with sabotage training. At the end of August, while the ships were anchored at Gibraltar, the Haganah members on *Empire Rival* planned to use their explosives to blow up the British Naval ship *Ajax*. They had chosen this particular ship because they had a long account to settle with her: This was the ship that had been following *Exodus* on her departure from Sete on 11 July; was close by, watching on, during the mid-sea battle; accompanied the deportation ships all the way from Haifa to France; watched them as they anchored at Port de Bouc; and rejoined them until the exit from the Mediterranean at Gibraltar. The job of blowing up *Ajax* was given to Vanchotzker, who was supposed to swim up to the cruiser and to attach the explosives to her airscrew. It is almost inconceivable how so complicated an operation could have been carried out with such primitive means and without the minimum conditions necessary. In any case, the British had posted such a heavy guard on the deportation ships and this, together with the strong overhead lighting and deep water mines, convinced the "command group" on *Empire Rival* that the plan was hopeless and it was dropped (Yishai 1964; Perry testimony; Perry 1985; Limon 1985; Mills 1985).

Once the Gibraltar idea was dropped, plans were formed for blowing up *Empire Rival*. All the work of placing the explosives deep in the ship's bow was carried out by the emissaries and did not involve the active participation of the immigrants. These were not even told the meaning of the rumpus in the corner of the hold, but many of them caught on and understood what was going on. They did not all like the idea of placing a bomb on their ship, and people discussed the matter among themselves. At first they were concerned at the possible dangers involved in blowing up the ship, and the name *Patria* was mentioned. The *Patria* had been meant to sail illegal immigrants from Haifa to Mauritius at the end of 1940, and the Haganah had placed explosives on her to prevent her from sailing. But, instead of causing the ship minor damage, the explosion blew out a huge hole and she sank quickly in the port of Haifa. Over two hundred immigrants were drowned (Ofer 1990, 31–39). Then, the people on *Empire Rival* were not at all pleased at being ordered to disembark quickly and peacefully at Hamburg. Still, they made no protest and they accepted the word of the Haganah as law, just as it had been throughout the long journey (Perry 1964; Perry testimony; Leichter 1985; Tubul 1985).

The explosives were old and unfamiliar, and no one knew how long the two detonators could be delayed. Thus, it was imperative once the bomb had been placed, that the passengers disembark quickly. Experience of more than a year in deporting illegal immigrants to Cyprus had taught the British that ships had to be searched after the passengers had landed, and the swift landing of the *Empire Rival* passengers was suspicious. And, of course, the landing sequence had been determined according to the way the British estimated the level of resistance on each ship. And now the *Ocean Vigour*, whose passengers were considered the weak link in the entire operation, was presenting fiercer opposition than expected, while the *Empire Rival*, whose passengers had always been so hostile toward the British, fought with the soldiers, damaged the ship and were obviously very well organized – here they were disembarking quickly, quietly and without a sign of resistance. What wonder, then, that a thorough search of the ship was called for immediately?

The box of explosives was soon found and one of the detonators was pulled out. It was then placed in a hall in one of the port warehouses. The British called for a press conference at two o'clock on 9 September 1947, with the aim of defiling the Haganah as much they could. However, about half an hour before the reporters began arriving at the conference hall, the second detonator went off and a huge explosion shook the port (*Mishmar*, 11 Sept. 1947; Habbas 1954, 73; Perry testimony). Fortunately, the incident involved no casualties, but it did not pass without bringing about some response, and an internal Jewish one, at that.

David Ben-Gurion, the Chairman of the Jewish Agency Executive, demanded that the Mossad head conduct a thorough investigation of the bomb incident and deliver him the results. There were certain aspects of the affair which he considered to be extremely serious. One had to do with a matter dealt with in the previous chapter – Ben-Gurion's opposition to an extreme action in Hamburg, emanating from his overall view of things and his fear that a violent confrontation with the British, whether in the port of Hamburg or anywhere else, might very well cause damage to the entire Zionist struggle. Ben-Gurion was also troubled by what he saw as a breach of authority. It was clear to him that the bomb incident had been in contradiction of agreed upon decisions, and his anger at this breach of authority increased because this was a crucial point in the struggle for the state and the act could have sabotaged his efforts at presenting a united, legitimate and authoritative Zionist leadership, with no rents, no appellants, nonconformists or dissidents. Who, then, disobeyed orders? Was it the Palmach? Or could it have been the Mossad emissaries? Or could Ben-Gurion have suspected for a moment that Meirov himself had acted against his boss' orders?

Ben-Gurion summed up the incident in his diary on 17 December 1947, at the height of the controversy surrounding the sailing of the *Pan York* and *Pan Crescent* (the two giant ships known as the "Pans"), which were about to set sail from a Black Sea port with a cargo of some 15,000 illegal immigrants, bound for Palestine. This was just after the UN decision on the partition of Palestine and Ben-Gurion was eager to prevent their sailing, since this could have endangered Zionism's enormous political achievement. At a meeting of the Mapai secretariat on 9 December 1947, Ben-Gurion expressed his frustration at the fact that the Mossad was acting against his own position – "it's about a year and a half that I have been discussing with people involved that we must introduce changes in our activity … and every time I chanced in Paris, I raised the subject with Shaul [Meirov]. But they did things their way."[6] When it seemed that the Mossad people in Europe were going ahead with the "Pans" program despite, or at least not in accordance with, orders from Palestine, Ben-Gurion threw at Meirov that he and his men could bring about a tragedy of historical proportions, with their hasty actions. He was outspoken in his demand that Meirov reinstate himself as leader of the Mossad and put a stop to the wave of uncontrolled behavior on the part of his men. Could it have been against this background, in the midst of the controversy, that the attempted bombing of *Empire Rival* returned to haunt them three months later? Possibly it was only then that Ben-Gurion asked Meirov to look into the matter, and possibly the matter may have been examined earlier, but Meirov did not present his findings to Ben-Gurion before the middle of December, since it was only then that he returned to Palestine after the disembarkation in Hamburg.

Meirov insisted to Ben-Gurion that he had issued a clear order not to sabotage the deportation ships, so Ben-Gurion concluded that Perlson had defied the Mossad head's orders (Ben-Gurion 1982, 51). The matter is complicated and interpretations have, so far, made it no easier to clarify. When and how did Meirov issue the order "no sabotage", and to whom? The Palmach and Mossad activists involved in the plans to transfer the explosives made a point of keeping the Mossad leaders in the dark, with the aim of preventing these from ordering the cancellation of the operation (Biber testimony; Livyathan testimony; Perry 1985). The message in the note sent from Port de Bouc to Perlson: "We have decided to go ahead with the sabotage, without authorization from the Mossad", should read: "Without asking for Mossad approval", rather than "in defiance of Mossad orders".

It is almost certain that Meirov did not issue a "no sabotage" order to Perlson, either in a direct or in a roundabout way. The only reservation in the orders issued to the ships before they sailed out of Port de Bouc was "make sure you have no casualties". We should bear in mind also that Meirov had been fully in favor of extreme action at the port of Hamburg and that it was only at his meeting with Ben-Gurion at the end of August that this idea was rejected. Even if Meirov received information on the explosives aboard *Empire Rival* – after the ship had left Port de Bouc – there was no way he could had given Perlson a "no sabotage" order, either immediately on receipt of the information, or after his conversation with Ben-Gurion (in which he accepted Ben-Gurion's moderate resistance approach). Contact with the ships had been discontinued the moment they set sail out of Port de Bouc.

The issues are complex and in order to unravel them one must overcome two obstacles. The first one – a dearth of documentation of the time, whose contents, or their "silence", are able to shed light on the matter.[7] The second – the nature of testimonies recorded from memory, which are often inaccurate; in many cases contradictory; and frequently evasive, as explained by one of the heroes in the affair about forty years later:

"Well, this was something we didn't really want to discuss for years" (Livyathan testimony).

Since the passengers on *Empire Rival* had all landed by 8:00 am, the British decided to bring forward the landing of the *Runnymede Park* passengers to the same day, 9 September 1947 and to get through "Operation Oasis" as soon as possible. At first the immigrants were informed in several European languages that they were to disembark from the ship. Their reply was a loud chorus of raucous singing and they showed no inclination to land. About five hundred immigrants congregated in the first hold, encircling the walls and waiting for the soldiers. The soldiers went up to them and grabbed hold of a few, who put up a fierce fight, aided and abetted by their fellow-passengers, who began throwing things at the soldiers. Once the first group had been taken off the ship, many of the immigrants disembarked peacefully, helped by the soldiers. A group of about one hundred immigrants remained in the hold and these were very adamant in their resistance – especially the children. It took two or more soldiers to remove each one of them.[8]

The second and third holds were inter-connected and these housed some nine hundred immigrants, including the leaders. Notwithstanding Roseman's control of his people and in spite of prior arrangements, things got somewhat out of hand. As soon as the British started dragging people out, they encountered a shower of bottles and all sorts of other objects from all sides. Roseman called on his people to stop throwing bottles, but the soldiers did not understand this and thought he was inciting them to fight on. Therefore they attacked him (Diary 1947b). As things heated up, the fight was joined by immigrants who had not intended previously to resist and in the end about 90 percent of the passengers in the two holds had to be dragged off the ship. Spontaneity was not to the benefit of those who had planned to show passive resistance. Someone decided to use the old familiar – and time-tested – ammunition, the Zionist national anthem, "Ha-Tikvah". People straightened up immediately and stood to attention. The British soldiers burst through the ranks and grabbed at the immigrants and dragged them physically off the ship.

The British, who knew how highly the immigrants valued their meager possessions, took the advantage of the fact, just as they had on *Ocean Vigour*. The immigrant diarist described it thus:

> A few people disembarked of their own free will, but most of the people put up strong resistance. The greatest heroes were the children, who went wild and did not let the British take them off. I remained almost to the end with the children. An English soldier came up to me and told me to disembark,

I told him I would not. Then he gave me a hard push in the back and I hit him. He pulled at my hair but then let me go. I remained. But some time later he came up to me again. They had found some other way. One of them started pulling at my things and when I wouldn't let go, he began beating me across my hands with a cosh. I had no choice, I had to disembark. If it were not for my things, I would have put up a fight. But I could not give them up. (Diary 1947b)

The British made use of coshes and water hoses. More than twenty immigrants, including 15 men and seven women, required medical attention,[9] and it is impossible to estimate how many more had suffered only light wounds. It is hard also to evaluate whether or not the protests of the journalists had any influence on the force used by the British. One change was felt, to the relief of all present: this time, there was no piped music as the immigrants were being removed from the ship.

The following day, the newspapers reported on the fierce resistance shown by the immigrants and of the desperate fight between them and the soldiers. *Reuters* reported that "women, children and old people fought wildly, just like the youngsters". The diarist gave her own inter-pretation: "We did something for the world, for the honor of the Jewish people; and that was the idea. It was obvious that, when the British really wanted us to, we would disembark from the ship."

The *Ha-Aretz* reporter, Robert Weltsch, had a different view of the resistance: "Although a certain degree of resistance was quite under-standable in principle, I myself am sorry to admit that this kind of stubborn resistance seemed to me to be futile in face of so powerful a force and it could have ended in loss of life, had the soldiers not practiced restraint." He was critical of Roseman for being too strict and for ordering the children on board to "fight to the death". Weltsch admired the way in which the immigrants disembarked, singing, from *Empire Rival*. "The determined impression they made was no less powerful than the one made by the fight put up by the passengers on *Runnymede Park* and this time there were no casualties" (11 Sept. 1947). But how does one measure impressions, in cases like these? The fact is that the disembarkation of *Empire Rival* had almost no press coverage, and the impression this left forced the Jewish Agency spokesman in London to deny reports that the *Exodus* immigrants were showing no resistance to being disembarked in Hamburg.

The inmates of DP camps in Germany had been following with great interest the adventures of the *Exodus* immigrants, ever since the large exodus to France at the end of June. At first this interest was tinged with jealousy and accompanied by great joy and high hopes. The return to France and subsequent expulsion to Germany caused confusion and even desperation among the camp inmates. Spontaneous demonstrations broke out in several of the camps and towns in the American zone as soon as news arrived of the return to France. In Frankfurt a protest was presented to the British consul, via the American commander of the zone, and on 23 July 1947 about 10,000 people turned out to demonstrate and march from the offices of the Central Committee of Liberated Jews in Munich, toward the British consulate (*Ha-Aretz*, 19 August 1947; JDC 1947b).

Ten days before disembarkation at Hamburg, the Palestinian emissaries in Germany still had no clear instructions as to how to act in Hamburg and in the "Bastard Zone" (the British zone, in Mossad correspondence). In spite of the pessimistic assessment that "our forces here are too weak to act",[10] a spontaneous demonstration took place at six o'clock on the morning of 7 September 1947 at the Belsen camp, in which practically the entire camp population took part. The people wanted to express their solidarity with their fellow immigrants, on the day on which they were to be disembarked at Hamburg. A more formal demonstration took place that afternoon, in which Marc Jarblum, Joseph Rosensaft – President of the Central Committee of Liberated Jews in the British zone, and his deputy, Norbert Wollheim, and Dr Barou from the World Jewish Congress, took part. Press reporters and photographers, on the lookout for some sort of action, fabricated an attack by the demonstrators on an effigy of Bevin, which was subsequently set on fire (JDC 1947a). On the day the immigrants were taken off *Empire Rival* and *Runnymede Park*, several hundred Jews, who had been brought in from Bergen Belsen, demonstrated at the port of Hamburg. A group of them succeeded in entering the port but avoided confrontation with the British, in respect of Ben-Gurion's orders (Habbas 1954, 129–32; Yahil 1981, 45).

The landing of the *Exodus* immigrants at Hamburg was widely covered by the British press, as was the information that certain terrorists were planning to drop bombs on London (*Davar*, 8 Sept. 1947, afternoon edition). In France, 17 members of the Stern gang (Lehi) were arrested, and six homemade bombs were seized. The terrorists had planned this attack on targets in London in reaction to the deportation of the *Exodus* immigrants to Hamburg. In Palestine the headlines relating to this incident ended with a question mark, as if the editors found it hard to believe the news from London: "More deceit by Lehi?" (*Davar*, 8 Sept. 1947); "Dissidents conspire to bomb London from a plane they bought in France?" (*Ha-Aretz*, 8 Sept. 1947). And as a kind of repeat performance, while the Zionist leadership was trying to maintain a low profile on the response to the immigrants' landing in Hamburg, "Kol Zion ha-Lochemet" broadcast (on 10 Sept. 1947) that "the shame of the deportation to Germany must be avenged with the blood of the barbarian enemy ... the enemy will pay for the blood, the suffering and the tears of our brethren." In Paris, Peter Bergson blamed the Jewish Agency for "betraying the *Exodus* immigrants by ordering them not to use force in resisting their removal from the deportation ships" (*Mishmar*, 11 Sept. 1947).

17 · They've Done It Again

All the pent-up anger and frustrations of the last two months reached a peak during the forced landing at Hamburg and the immigrants went berserk on the trains taking them from Hamburg to Lübeck, sabotaging everything they could lay their hands on (Ganuz 1985, 286; Leichter 1985). From Lübeck they were taken to two camps which had been hastily arranged to accommodate them, two kilometers from each other, Poppendorf and Am Stow. The Poppendorf camp consisted of a series of corrugated iron roofed Nissen huts of various sizes (56 16×35 foot huts and 14 larger ones) and 125 eight-foot tents, each of which was to house 5–6 people. Each immigrant was supplied with a metal camp bed and a mattress which was no more than a sack, haphazardly filled with rough straw. And one blanket. The huts had been repainted on the outside, but rat holes were visible in the floors and walls. The 2,700 camp residents were supplied with five primitive washrooms. The improvised lavatories were open to the elements, with no internal divisions between one stall and the other. Weather conditions in mid-September in northern Germany were hardly ideal for spending nights in a tent, which meant that an additional 700 people had to crowd into the Nissen huts. Most people slept two to a bed on three- or four-storey bunks. The larger huts, which were originally designed for 60 people each, housed up to 130 people. During the day, in pleasant weather conditions, it was possible for the immigrants to spend time indoors, but the cold nights made the huts virtually uninhabitable.[1]

Two kilometers from Poppendorf, the Am Stow camp provided slightly better conditions. Here the immigrants were housed in wooden army barracks, 16 to a room on two-storey bunk beds. Most of the rooms were equipped with tables and chairs, but here too, the beds were lopsided and old potato sacks filled with straw and weeds served as mattresses. The water facilities in both camps were inadequate and no heating facilities were supplied. Nor were there any pavements between the huts and on rainy days people sloshed around in deep mud.

Poppendorf camp, which had been a prisoner of war camp, received 2,717 immigrants from the *Ocean Vigour* and *Runnymede Park*. Am Stow, which had previously been a British transit camp (which would explain the improved living conditions) took in 1,484 of the immigrants from *Empire Rival*. The local Joint Distribution Committee figured that the immigrants had been placed in accordance with their behavior during disembarkation at Hamburg and that the people from *Ocean Vigour* and *Runnymede Park* were sent to Poppendorf, the worse of the two camps, as punishment for their bad behavior. A guess just as good is, that the British had learned from their experience on the deportation ships that it was better to keep the *Empire Rival* immigrants apart from the others, since they had proven themselves to be demanding and trouble makers.

Preparations for the arrival of the immigrants in Germany were conducted by the British under conditions of uncertainty and were guided by a system of various considerations, many of which contradicted each other. On the one hand, they were obliged to supply the immigrants with reasonable housing facilities, since the main excuse for bringing them to Germany was that this was the only place on the face of the earth, except Cyprus, where such a large number of people could be housed in a short time. The wave of universal interest – brief but intense – in the immigrants, which arose during the days following the disembarkation in Hamburg, obliged the British to abide by their declarations. Nonetheless, they had to make sure that the immigrants were not supplied with living conditions which were too good, so as not to spoil the plan to return them ultimately from Germany to France.

The idea to return the immigrants via Germany to France, it should be remembered, had already raised at the stage when preparations were being made for the official announcement on the deportation to Hamburg. As during the second half of July, while the immigrants were making their way from Haifa to France, this time too, even before France had replied to the British on their approach, the latter already related to the possibility as given and planned their next steps accordingly. When the French reply arrived on 27 August 1947, the British Foreign Office was glad to learn that the French Government had made no mention of refusing to accept people who had been forced off the ships at Hamburg. Still, the French made it clear that they would take in only volunteers, in other words, this element of volunteering – which had caused the failure of the refoulement efforts since Port de Bouc – held fast.[2] Bevin did not feel that "the French Government's decision to allow those of

[the] passengers who so desire to enter France calls for any special expression of appreciation by His Majesty's Government". He considered the decision to be "after all, only a partial and probably ineffective fulfillment of Monsieur Bidault's original promise to me".[3]

The French made three demands. First, that the immigrants be required to express, of their own free will, their desire to go to France. Second, this agreement on the part of the French Government to solve the immediate problem must not serve as a precedent for the entry of other displaced persons from Germany in the future. And third, the *Exodus* immigrants would be entering France at the expense of the special quota determined for Jewish immigrants wishing to stay temporarily in this country. This meant that the total number of Jewish immigrants in transit in France, including the returning *Exodus* passengers, was not to exceed 8,000 people.[4]

The French also included in their reply a list of measures to be taken in order to ensure that those entering France according to this special arrangement are indeed the original passengers of the *President Warfield* and insisted that the immigrants undergo full medical examinations and thorough disinfectation in the British zone before setting out for France. And finally, they made it clear that the return of the refugees was not a question of days but of weeks. The holiday camps belonging to Entraid Français, which were to house those volunteering to go to France, would not be ready before the end of September and the French railway services would have to be informed of their arrival at least a week in advance.

And so, beyond their ability to forcibly remove the immigrants from the ships at Hamburg, and even though they were the official "landlords" in Germany, once again, the British were not in control of the situation. Every step they considered taking had to be tested against the demands placed by the French, and one after another of their actions was thus disqualified. If it had been left to them, the British would have sent the illegal immigrants to France straight from the wharves at Hamburg.[5] They would have saved themselves all the trouble of isolating the immigrants and all the problems entailed in this. But the lack of direct transportation from the port of Hamburg to France and the latter's inability to take in the immigrants immediately,[6] made the idea out of the question.

It was imperative to keep the immigrants in isolation until such a time as they return to France, and to ensure that they were not joined by other DPs. British soldiers guarded the trains bearing the immigrants from Hamburg to the camps and there were no German policemen aboard.[7] The camps were placed under heavy military protection, and despite promises to the contrary, German policemen were also posted alongside the British soldiers. These were detention camps in every sense of the word. They were surrounded by barbed wire, roadblocks and watch towers and huge spotlights lit up the night.[8] Anyone wanting to visit the camps had to obtain a special permit, to pass through a triple barbed wire fence and an armed British guard. Radios and newspapers were forbidden on camp. The camps were only slightly better than heavily guarded military prisons (JDC 1947a), except that in this case the heavy guard and isolation was aimed not at preventing the escape of the *Exodus* immigrants – on the contrary, the British were actually in favor of this[9] – but to prevent the entry of other displaced persons and especially to frustrate the attempts of emissaries from Palestine at entering the camps and arousing the immigrants.

The British were no longer afraid of violent outbreaks, once the immigrants arrived at the camps, worn out and hungry. They were now worried that, exhausted from their long journey, the immigrants would be unwilling to move on to any other place, once they discovered that conditions in the camps were not quite so bad as they had been lead to believe.[10] Knowing the living conditions in the camps, the British hoped – as they had when the deportation ships arrived at Port de Bouc – that a period spent among the forests of Poppendorf would cause a large number of immigrants to volunteer for transfer to France, and that it would be wise to let time take its course. The timetable set by the French increased the time spent under guard and isolation to the end of September, but did not increase the immigrants' willingness to return to France.

The unexpected arrival of 4,200 people in the British zone caused problems in supplying food and equipment, and the British were obliged to ask for help from Jewish organizations and the British Red Cross.[11] The military authorities had planned on supplying the returning immigrants with the kind of food rations usually given to refugees – 1,500 calories a day – and the Jewish voluntary organizations were to see to the necessary supplements. The dilemma, as we shall remember, was that if people were to find out that they could remain on the camps indefinitely and be supplied with fairly large (calorie wise) quantities of food, they were most unlikely to be tempted to go back to France.[12]

In their preparations to receive the returning immigrants, the British authorities were geared to the short run. They were sure that within a number of days their part in the affair would be over and the immigrants would return to France and those who refused to do so would be placed in the care of the International Refugee Organization. But this organization, too, refused to fulfill the task designated to it by the British and sent out instructions from its center in Geneva to its workers in Germany, not to offer help to the returning immigrants until all security precautions were removed from around the camps.[13]

It was then that London began considering the possibility of transferring those people entitled to aid by the IRO to the camp at Hohne or any other place where they could join an existing community of Jewish DPs. The reply from Lübeck was that this idea contradicted Britain's ongoing efforts to reduce the permanent Jewish population in the zone's camps. Furthermore, an unlimited supply of care and food for these people would greatly endanger the agreement the authorities had with Joseph Rosensaft, whereby no more Jewish DPs would be permitted to enter the camp at Hohne illegally – an agreement that Rosensaft made a point of honoring. There was also the fear that letting in the *Exodus* immigrants would encourage a large flow of DPs to enter the British zone, especially to Hohne, in the future.

But all these discussions were no more than hot air, because the immigrants refused to accept the status of displaced persons. By 12 September 1947 only about ten people had applied for help from the IRO, and London more or less gave up and accepted the fact that the immigrants would remain under British auspices, would continue to live in their special camps and would be free to transfer to France or to move around the British zone in accordance with the accepted rules in the region. They would be eligible to apply for immigration certificates to Palestine and would wait their turn with the rest of the Jewish DPs in the region. To this Lübeck replied that as soon as these people realized that they were being allowed to remain in the camps for an unlimited period of time and to receive a daily food ration equaling 2,750 calories – almost twice the amount in the basic rations supplied to other DPs in Germany – there was virtually no chance that they would respond favorably to the French offer.

After the proposals and suggestions from the Foreign Office in London were rejected, one after the other, the British forces in Germany came up with an idea of their own. They reckoned that if the immigrants were faced with the choice of either transferring to France or integrating in the German economy, where they would be obliged to make it on their own, their response could be very different indeed. The idea was not to release them haphazardly into the German population, but to follow the usual procedure for dealing with DPs. This entailed finding accommodation in a locality where they could also join the local workforce. They would then be given rail warrants to the nearest station and a haversack containing food rations for two days – and sent on their way. On their arrival at the chosen destination, they would be issued with ration cards by the German authorities, who would also arrange for their employment.[14]

Following this proposal – which arrived from Lübeck accompanied by the pessimistic assessment that only a negligible number of volunteers could be expected to join the France project, and the news that only about ten had registered with the IRO – an urgent meeting was held at the Foreign Office in London to determine further activity. The meeting was also attended by Colonel Gregson, commander of the deportation convoy, who was very familiar with the immigrants and made it clear to his fellow participants that even dispersal among the German population would not induce them to return to France. Furthermore, the Foreign Office pointed out to the authorities in Germany that this new tactic of theirs did not conform with the earlier line of propaganda, whereby the refugees were being sent to the British zone in Germany because, apart from Cyprus, this was the only place where they could be adequately housed. An act such as this – sending the Jews against their will into the German population – "would involve us in further odium without ensuring us any corresponding advantages". Moreover, dispersing these people would almost certainly require further use of force – and there was no way this could be justified to world public opinion. The Foreign Office insisted that the British authorities in Germany must not supply Jewish propaganda with any more ammunition, which would only backfire against them.[15]

At the end of September it was time to inform the immigrants of their imminent return to France. After a long delay, the French expressed their willingness to accept those who chose to return, and the British had already reconciled themselves to the fact that the chances of such volunteers stepping forward were negligible. They decided to use food as a lever by which to persuade the immigrants to return to France – volunteers will continue to receive the present generous ration of approximately 2,800 calories a day. Those who choose to remain in Germany will revert to the same basic food rations allotted to all the other DPs.[16]

The immigrants burst out laughing at this announcement, and quickly wandered away (*Davar*, 26 Sept. 1947). The next day, they held a demonstration at the Poppendorf camp, in which they paid tribute to the *Exodus* casualties, whose legacy was to "continue with our struggle, until we reach our homeland". They sang "Ha-Tikvah" and the Jewish Partisans' song. At Am Stow camp the immigrants turned violent and tore down the registration tent, where volunteers could sign up for transfer to France (*Ha-Aretz*, 28 Sept. 1947; *Davar*, 28 Sept. 1947; Habbas 1954, 247–48).

After three weeks only three people had accepted France's new invitation. A further six applied to IRO for aid.[17] The *Exodus* immigrants continued to outwit the British, who, after having taken all the steps to separate, select and guard them, were now forced to "swallow" a further 4,200 Jews in the their zone, which they had so wanted to empty.

This new situation had its economic repercussions as well. Whereas the financial upkeep of the deported illegal immigrants in Cyprus was the responsibility of the Government of Palestine, and most of the expense of maintaining the DPs in Germany fell on the IRO; the main burden of keeping up the *Exodus* immigrants fell on the shoulders of the British tax-payer. The Colonial and Foreign Offices argued among themselves over which of them was to bear this burden. The Foreign Office claimed that in accordance with the principle that it was the Government of Palestine which was financially responsible for discontinuing illegal immigration, it was only proper that they should also bear the cost of keeping the ex-*President Warfield* Jews in Germany. The Foreign Office then reinforced their claim by pointing out that their people in Germany had been opposed to bringing the immigrants into the zone in the first place, so that General Clay (the zone's commander) was right in insisting that it was not up to him to pay for their upkeep. The Colonial Office replied in kind: The Government of Palestine had also opposed bringing those Jews to Germany.[18]

As for the future transfer of the *Exodus* immigrants to Palestine, both offices agreed that their fate was to be that of the Cyprus deportees, whose return to Palestine was arranged by the Colonial Office.[19] The Foreign Office begged the Colonial Office not to postpone the inclusion of the *President Warfield* immigrants in the plans for evacuating the Cyprus camps, for fear that they would then remain outside the program for good, as a result of a possible last minute change of mind, which might occur if the Cyprus plan turned out to cause serious Arab opposition.[20]

Still, considerations of financial viability were pushed aside by considerations of prestige. Against the endeavors of the Foreign Office German department to get the *Exodus* immigrants out of Germany as soon possible, stood the ambition of other government elements – both in the Foreign Office and the Colonial Office – to teach those illegal immigrants and their patrons a thorough lesson. And thus the British left the *Exodus* immigrants out in the cold on all counts. On the one hand, they refused to allow them immigration certificates from the quota allotted to the DPs in the British zone in Germany, while on the other they excluded them from the quick evacuation of the Cyprus plan.

But in the end, the *Exodus* immigrants had a better fate than many of the other illegal immigrants. About half of them had left Germany, one way or another, by the date the State of Israel was founded, 15 May 1948. Not all of them managed to make their way directly to Palestine and after leaving Germany, many of them had to spend time in camps in the south of France. Still, within a few months, they had all arrived in Israel and the last of the *Exodus* people left Germany exactly one year after they had been removed by force from the deportation ships at Hamburg. At the same time, some 15,000 deported immigrants were still waiting in the camps in Cyprus, some of these had set out on their way to Palestine even before July 1947 (Sha'ari 1981, 148, 165, 364).

The *Exodus* immigrants, therefore, spent between several weeks to several months on German soil. Their living conditions, the ways in which they organized themselves, the methods used by the JDC for taking care of their needs, the Yishuv's attitude to them and the factors which determined the pace of their ultimate arrival in Israel – all these will be discussed in the next two chapters.

18 · All Jews Are Comrades

From the moment of their arrival in Germany the *Exodus* people insisted on their special status and kept themselves apart from the other DPs. In Hamburg and in the detention camps they introduced themselves as exiles from Palestine. When they were asked where they were from, the reply was inevitably *Exodus 1947*. They gave their place of birth as Haifa and their nationality as being Palestinian. They did not identify themselves by name so as not to be split up again and sent back to the camps from which they had set out. They chose random names of famous people, such as Greta Garbo or Charlie Chaplin. They even used garbled names of politicians, jokingly mixing up family and first names. Thus there would be among them a certain "Adolph Bevin", or one "Hermann Attlee", etc. They were inspired by the appearance of the British-appointed interpreter – "one of us" – who told them in Yiddish that all the Jews are to register under false names (Habbas 1954, 73–74; Levin testimony; Yahil 1981, 145–47).

Their seclusion and the jealous guarding of their special identity constituted first and foremost a link in the immigrants' struggle with the British. However, their insistence on exterritorialism had an internal aspect too. They refused to take part in any of the institutions set up by and for the Holocaust survivors, and developed their own way of life, different from that of the other DPs. Their elected representation was given the Hebrew definition "mazkirut" (secretariat) rather than the Yiddish "komitat". Those responsible for discipline on camp were known not as the camp police but as "sadranim" (stewards) (Yahil 1981, 145–47). Whether directly or not, always maintaining their self-esteem, with a touch of condescension even, they made sure everyone knew how united they were and what placed them apart from other DPs who had not gone through the agonies of *Exodus*.

Several days after their arrival at Poppendorf, the immigrants were rejoined by the leaders from *Runnymede Park* who had been arrested during the disembarkation at Hamburg. At the "welcome home reception" Roseman told the immigrants what they now had to do: "Today, the most important thing is to avoid being dispersed. We, the people of *Exodus 1947*, have been through so much suffering together, that we feel like we are all one big family. We have almost forgotten our political differences and the kibbutz movements we belonged to, and we can now get to work together as one" (*Mishmar*, 14 Sept. 1947).

In many ways the Exodus Affair was a microcosm of the processes and events typical both of the Yishuv and the community of Holocaust survivors at that time. Thus, Roseman's speech contained echoes of the "Unity" slogans used at the end of the war by ex-partisan Abba Kovner and his comrades, who formed a non-affiliated framework under the name "East European Survivors' Division". And as the emissaries from Palestine had been blamed for causing factionalism among the Holocaust survivors in Summer 1945 (Shapira 1986, 277–301), so too were the emissaries who penetrated the *Exodus* camps blamed for introducing party politics and threatening the immigrants' unity and moral. As Vanchotzker, one of the emissaries who boarded *Empire Rival* at Port de Bouc put it: "There was no atmosphere of party politics throughout the voyage. There was only one 'party', the Haganah. It was the Haganah's opinion which was most readily accepted and the Haganah's considerations were decisive. Everyone believed in the Haganah's purity and accepted its outlook. The arrival of the emissaries set off the usual run-around and we found ourselves immediately facing the threat of factionalism and demoralization" (Habbas 1954, 75).

Expressions such as "we're all in the same boat" and "all Jews are comrades" are very accurate when applied to the atmosphere among the immigrants on *Exodus* and the deportation ships, but their loyalty to political movements never faded away – and not necessarily with negative connotations. It was there all the time and the various movements and political parties served as objects to identify with and a framework of belonging and mutual care. They were an organizational, even more than ideological, basis to the immigrants' lives, and to the Holocaust survivors in general. We remember that people had been organized for boarding *Exodus* according to their political affiliations and it was only during the transfer to the deportation ships in Haifa and the attending confusion, which caused members of organized groups to be separated from each other. Nonetheless, the splinters of the original frameworks still did their best to preserve social cohesion and tried to contact their friends on the other ships. Altogether, during the Port de Bouc period, the people were not detached from the political problems which held the attention of the

Jews in Palestine and in the DP camps in Europe. Debates were held on the ships on issues such as the partition of Palestine, the terrorist activity of the dissident groups and other matters on the world agenda. And we have already mentioned the tension between the various movements and the emissaries on the one hand and the Revisionists, on the other.

Tension and anger were also caused by the ultra-Orthodox party, Agudat Israel, which brought its struggle with the Jewish Agency on the matter of immigration certificates right into the holds of the deportation ships and sent a message to its people, calling on them to disembark and not to oppose the British. The Aguda even applied to the Colonial Office on this matter, informing it both verbally and in writing that the party approved of the immigrants' disembarking in Europe and that it was willing to order its own people to disembark, in return for the Government's intervention on the issue of immigration certificates to Agudat Israel members.[1]

While taking care of the *Exodus* community as a whole, each of the movements made sure to look out for their own supporters. The emissary previously quoted denouncing the disruptive effect of the emissaries in the camps in Germany had written before from *Empire Rival*: "First of all, we are doing our job with the public in general, but we are also helping our own members conduct their movement activity." On *Empire Rival* Vanchotzker considered himself primarily an emissary for his movement, and "I hope," he wrote to his counterparts in Palestine, "that my behavior here will bring credit to our movement." He even felt the need to report to his party leaders on his activity during his stay on the deportation ships.[2]

Vanchotzker's attitude was typical of Mapai – there is unity, so long as the situation is being controlled by people of the party; but activity on the part of other movements creates a situation of political factionalism and disunity. We have seen for ourselves that Vanchotzker's own activity was not free of a party political attitude. If we compare this with Roseman's activity (who was at once the recognized leader of the immigrants, while also devoting his energy to his own, ha-Shomer ha-Tza'ir, movement), we must differentiate between activity organized by the immigrants themselves and that of an emissary who boarded the ship as a representative of the Haganah. However, with Mapai being the leading force in the Histadrut, the Yishuv and the Zionist organization, the line dividing general activity and party oriented activity was very fine indeed. For example, Vanchotzker and Perlson set up direct and informal contact with Shaul Meirov and David Ben-Gurion from their ship. This could, of course, be seen as an *ex officio* approach to the head of the Mossad and the Chairman of the Jewish Agency Executive. Still it is clear that belonging to the same party, and the personal, even family, connections of these two emissaries with high-ranking Mapai officials, created the kind of familiarity which did not exist between ha-Shomer ha-Tza'ir activists and the Yishuv leaders, for instance.

It was mainly Mapai which continued to speak out about the factionalism caused by the emissaries. Mapai was especially concerned at the activity of Achdut ha-Avodah and ha-Shomer ha-Tza'ir, which in the autumn of 1947 was more than ever a threat to Mapai's hegemony. These appeared as a single faction at the meeting of the Zionist General Council at the end of August and beginning of September and later negotiated on forming a joint party. The tension between Mapai on the one hand and these left wing parties on the other, increased and reached a peak with the formation of the United Worker's Party ("Mapam") in January 1948. Mapai took its attack as far as Germany, and the *Exodus* camps became an important arena. Ha-Shomer ha-Tza'ir's power was relatively greater there than in Palestine and among the Holocaust survivors, both because the *Exodus* immigrants included a large contingent of movement members, which had a deep effect throughout the long voyage and also because Mordechai Roseman, who was recognized by all as the leader of *Exodus*, was himself a ha-Shomer ha-Tza'ir member. Mapai tried to undermine that movement's hegemony in the camps – mainly with the help of emissaries from without, but these efforts failed, and Roseman's standing remained as strong as ever (Rabinowitz 1961, 628).

All in all the story of the *Exodus* immigrants teaches us that in times of crisis, the people knew how to close ranks and stand firmly united for the common cause, while not losing hold of their party affiliations and loyalties. And just as they knew how to organize themselves in places and cases where there were no emissaries available, so, too, they did not require the influence of emissaries to help them preserve movement frameworks. And indeed, by the time the new emissaries had arrived at the camps, the immigrants were already reorganized, all by themselves, in their new living quarters, in accordance with their political affiliations. Nonetheless, this careful preservation of their party framework, within their own society, had no effect on the *Exodus* immigrants when it came to presenting a united front to the rest of the world, both at sea and on land.

On the eve of the deportees' arrival in Germany, the British appealed to various Jewish welfare organizations for food supplies for the returning immigrants.[3] The official request was made to the Joint Distribution

Committee, which was a recognized organization in the DP camps in Germany. Although the request related to a region in which the JDC had been active for a long time and to activity which was similar to that conducted by the organization in Cyprus for a year or more, the JDC found itself facing an unprecedented situation. It was clear that the situation's political repercussions would be much more significant than the actual welfare problem involved, and these repercussions demanded that all the Jewish organizations agree on a mutual policy. Representatives of the JDC, the Jewish Agency, the Jewish Relief Unit and the Central Committee of Liberated Jews in the British zone held day and night consultations in Belsen. A uniform policy was finally decided upon at a tense meeting between all these organizations, which took place on 5 September at the home of Joseph Rosensaft. It was agreed that the British would receive no help whatsoever, either in disembarking the *Exodus* immigrants or in bringing in supplies or staff to the camps as long as these remained detention prisons.[4]

All efforts on the part of news-hungry reporters to glean any information on the line of action decided upon by the Jewish organizations proved fruitless. However, the British Command, who knew the way the wind was blowing, presented an ultimatum to the JDC, that if no aid was forthcoming, "His Majesty's Government would reconsider the status of the JDC in the British zone" (*Davar*, 5 Sept. 1947). The organization found itself facing a difficult dilemma. As an international Jewish relief organization, it was the JDC's duty to see to the welfare of the *Exodus* exiles, especially the children among them, to feed them, clothe them and see to their medical needs. But, under the political circumstances of the time, the organization was not in a position to supply aid unconditionally, according to British dictate.

It would seem that news of all the *Exodus* leadership (in fact, only the leaders on *Runnymede Park*) having been arrested by the British gave the Jewish organizations a ladder, down which they could climb from their non-cooperative stance. Under the new circumstances, it was decided that Dr Levin, head of the Jewish Agency delegation in the British zone, would request permission of the military authorities to visit the camps, to examine the possibility of sending out a medical team on behalf of the Jewish voluntary organizations. The British, who were interested in the material side of the help offered, presented their concurrence as a humane gesture, a reward for the fact that the transfer of immigrants to the camps had been less violent than anticipated.

Representatives of the Jewish voluntary organizations entered the camps on 13 September, bringing with them supplies from the JDC warehouses – food, soap, religious books, artifacts for the forthcoming high holidays, and books and newspapers in Hebrew and Yiddish. The JDC pointed out to the authorities that they were willing to help the immigrants on the mutual understanding that the main brunt of responsibility rests on the British, who brought them to Germany in the first place.[5]

The assistance received by the immigrants consisted of three main types – food, clothing and medical services. Their adventures over the past three months had left them in a state of general exhaustion and malnutrition. Their food during the two-and-a-half week voyage from Port de Bouc to Hamburg had been insufficient and of poor quality. Their tattered clothing only added to the miserable impression they made on the representatives of the welfare organizations who came to visit them. The immigrants had set off on their journey in the middle of summer and were dressed accordingly. Their warmer clothes had been packed away in their baggage, which had been taken from them in Haifa and most of which had been subsequently lost, stolen or destroyed during the journey from Haifa to Hamburg. The men wore shorts and torn shirts. Many of them went around dressed in robes sewn from the blankets supplied to them at Port de Bouc. Their shoes were worn through and no one had any socks. Most of them were not suffering from any serious illness, but about 150 pregnant women did need special medical care. Most of the people were in dire need of dental treatment.

The food rations decided upon in September for the *Exodus* immigrants consisted of 2,800 calories a day,[6] and included the basic rations allotted to DP camp inmates (1,500 calories), with an additional half of the supplement supplied to hospital inmates. Children under six received a daily milk supplement and children and young people, aged between seven and 20, were given skimmed milk. Pregnant women and nursing mothers received other small supplements as well. An immigrant who was not included in one of the above categories received an average of 827.3 gr. of food a day, of which 375 gr. were bread, 317.1 potatoes, 46.4 gr. dried peas and beans, 16.1 gr. jam, 12.3 gr. fresh meat, 10.7 gr. fish, 9.1 gr. salami, 9.0 gr. sugar, 7.1 gr. butter and 4.5 gr. cheese. The official ration also included 107.1 gr. skim milk or 26.3 gr. cream and 4.5 gr. coffee – but these last were never supplied. The JDC representatives considered the rations to be insufficient in quantity and nutritional composition and lacking in proteins and vitamins. The bread supplied by the British was of poor quality and the potatoes were frozen. Cereals were supplied regularly, but there was never enough milk, butter, sugar, meat and fish, and on the rare occasions when cheese was supplied, it was moldy.

The JDC decided to compensate the immigrants for the poor rations over the previous months and to build them up for the long journey ahead. By adding components to the daily diet, the calorific value was raised from 2,800 to 3,500. When, at the end of September, the British re-issued the French Government's invitation, they threatened that those who chose to remain in Germany would receive a daily food ration comprising only 1,500 calories. Right away, Eliezer Kaplan (the Jewish Agency treasurer) asked the JDC to supplement the official food rations and bring them to a reasonable level.[7] After consulting with Shertok, Joseph Schwartz (JDC head in Europe) ordered his people to supply the *Exodus* group with food, like the other DPs in the British zone.[8] Thanks to the plentiful food supplied by the JDC, Britain's 1,500-calories-a-day cut back (from the beginning of October) caused no response from the immigrants and peace prevailed in the camps.[9]

The JDC supplied the immigrants with some 75 tons of food during the month of September. In October, this was reduced to 60 tons, and a further 40 tons were donated to the immigrants by the Central Committee of Liberated Jews in the American zone. What happened in fact was that the DPs in the American zone donated some of their JDC food supplies to the *Exodus* immigrants. The food was transferred to the British zone in JDC trucks.

Before that, the Jews of Belsen had supplied the *Exodus* people with bread, fruit, fresh vegetables and other items. By October the entire Jewish population in the British zone had donated half of the JDC food for the benefit of the *Exodus* immigrants.[10] After the immigrants had been moved to new and better camps at the beginning of November and were somewhat recovered from their long journey, the JDC came to the conclusion that they could live nicely on a daily ration of 3,000 calories. Thus each month a 60 ton supply of food was sent by the JDC office in the American zone and there was no longer any need for the additional 24 tons of food the Jews in that zone were prepared to donate to their brethren from the *Exodus*.[11]

The JDC also supplied the immigrants with warm winter clothing, new shoes, and equipment for study and recreation. The list of supplies brought during the first month to the two camps ranges over eight closely typewritten pages. It included, among other things, 45,000 tins of condensed milk, 1,300 kg powdered milk, some 5,000 kg margarine and some 40,000 kg fresh vegetables. The JDC supplied 28,000 packets of cigarettes, 7,000 bars of laundry soap and clothing: 3,000 T-shirts, 700 brassieres, 4,800 pairs of shoes with an additional 2,800 heels and 1,700 soles for repairing the immigrants' worn-out shoes and 3,600 pairs of laces. There were 4,500 toothbrushes, 10,000 laxative pills and 2,000,000 units of penicillin. Also supplied were 7,500 school books, an accordion, and a great deal more cooking utensils, items of clothing, etc.

Some of the supplies came from the JDC's warehouses in the British zone, certain things were locally produced, but most of the stuff came from the JDC in the American zone. Usually, the JDC in the American zone was capable of caring for ten times the number of people than were in the care of the organization's offices in the British zone. The JDC was there, helping, until the very last of the *Exodus* immigrants was out of Germany. Supplies were transferred in suitable quantities, as and when needed, and health, cultural and educational programs were handled in an orderly manner (Dallob 1948).

The swift and efficient way in which the JDC went to the aid of the *Exodus* immigrants in Germany contrasted with the organization's hesitant behavior at Port de Bouc. In order to understand this, it would be necessary to consider not only the character of the organization and its objectives, but also its rather tense and complex relationship with the Mossad. At the end of 1945, an informal understanding had been reached between the Mossad and representatives of the JDC, whereby the latter would pay the former £40 per Jew removed from camps in Europe and brought to Palestine via Aliyah Bet. The traditional national-humanitarian considerations which had heretofore motivated the JDC, were joined now by financial considerations, since each immigrant leaving the camps on the way to Palestine reduced the population of the camps, which the JDC was partner in maintaining. Since the beginning of 1946, most of the illegal immigration ships had been apprehended and the British deducted the number of their passengers from the quota of certificates. Thus, in the middle of April the JDC informed the Mossad of its intention to cease its contribution according to the number of immigrants on the Mossad's ships, since illegal immigration was harming legal immigration and not easing the situation for the DPs in Europe. The JDC was not blind to the absurdity of the situation, whereby in fact, illegal immigration had swallowed up the quota of immigration certificates and brought Jews to Palestine at a much greater cost than legal immigration. Legal immigration was aided by the JDC to the tune of £15 per immigrant – as compared with the £40 per head allotted to illegal immigrants. This was the basis for the JDC's claim that there was no further need for the Mossad, since it was bringing in immigrants at an inflated cost (Hadari 1991, 44–52).

A new understanding was reached between the JDC and the Mossad about six months later, with regard to the transfer of funds for financing the illegal immigration operation (Hadari 1991, 44–52). But then, right in the middle of the Exodus Affair, problems re-arose between the two sides. The uncertainty during the last days of July and throughout August 1947 as to the fate of the immigrants and their final destination reduced the chances of the JDC continuing to support Mossad activity exactly when preparations were underway for huge illegal immigration operations, which reached a peak with the sailing of the "Pans".[12] And in the meantime, they found themselves having to face a new and urgent problem – feeding the *Exodus* immigrants at Port de Bouc.

The JDC's assistance to the deportation ships was too little and too late (Reichman 1947; Roseman 1947; Habbas 1954, 124; Einor 1985). At first food had been supplied by a French welfare organization,[13] and it was to be a while before the JDC began financing this supply.[14] As a Jewish welfare organization, which took care to conduct all its activity within the limits of the law, the JDC had not been qualified to handle this necessity to supply food for illegal immigrants on British deportation ships. These were people who did not comply with a recognized definition of "refugees", nor did they fit the JDC's criteria for aid. In mid-August, J. Schwartz rejected the proposal put forward by the President of the Hebrew University, Judah Magnes, to drop hints to the British that the JDC would be willing to undertake financial responsibility for the *Exodus* immigrants.[15] Intervention was needed from afar and from above – the JDC Management in New York – in order to unravel the tangle of problems and to set the wheels of aid in motion. Probably, the official excuse for the JDC's intervention in the matter was the need to supply kosher food for the 1,000 observant Jews among the immigrants. In the meantime, the he-Halutz organization was sending limited supplies to the ships, for which they hoped the JDC would pay (Reichman 1947). When the JDC received the bill, they agreed to pay only part of it, because it seemed to them to be "very heavy".[16]

However, the need to supply aid to the *Exodus* immigrants back on German soil was tailor-made for the JDC. The organization went into action at once, even though they did not disregard the political implications of the matter, and were conscientious in coordinating and cooperating with the Jewish Agency. This had become easier because of the recently renewed understanding between the two organizations, following the tension over the Emigration Office in Germany. The JDC had wanted to open its own emigration offices for candidates to Palestine, similar to those it operated for emigrants to other countries, but the

Jewish Agency opposed this. On 22 June 1947 they came to an agreement, whereby the Jewish Agency's Palestine offices would continue dealing with all matters concerning emigration to Palestine, and the JDC would finance emigration expenses (i.e. for legal immigrants), including the immigrants' food and dispatch of their baggage (Barlas 1947a).

JDC reports summarizing the handling of the *Exodus* immigrants, make frequent reference to the "very good" attitude of the immigrants toward the JDC. Considering the commendable activity of the JDC in the DP camps in general and the especially bountiful assistance forwarded to the *Exodus* immigrants, it would be easy enough to take this gratitude on the part of the immigrants for granted. Nonetheless, here and there signs of dissatisfaction were obvious, as Roseman wrote to J. Schwartz after the transfer to the new camps: "I won't go into any detail at the moment. No doubt you understand that here and there, supplies have arrived late and they were not quite up to scratch – but we realize all this is connected with the fact that you were unprepared for the matter."[17] The reason behind the JDC's surprise at the friendly attitude shown them by the *Exodus* people was probably that their past experience with DPs in Europe and the exiles in Cyprus had been less than easy. Some of the Cyprus exiles harbored bitter feelings toward the JDC and the way the organization conducted its activity. The immigrants' secretariat there had demanded, in vain, to be included in considerations and decisions regarding the spending of the budget (Bogner 1991, 86–89).

Things were different in the *Exodus* camps. Unlike the Cyprus exiles, who had inadvertently entered a situation in which they felt themselves to be objects of charity, cared for by the complex bureaucracy of a welfare organization, the *Exodus* immigrants were full of self worth, aware that they were bearing the flag of the Jewish national struggle, a shining halo of heroism above their heads. Their lives on camp were mostly self-existent, free of direct dependence on the JDC and from the beginning their secretariats made it clear that they would not agree to any form of categorization or inequality based on anything other than health. They refused to accept any supplies which could not be distributed equitably among them all, nor would they accept charitable donation or handouts from private persons or from DP camps. The JDC agreed to these standards, and they discussed all questions of supply and distribution with the secretariats in a spirit of true comradeship (JDC 1947a).

During their first few months in Germany, the *Exodus* people led a semi-socialist way of life. All supplies arriving at the camp were pooled and distributed equally among all the inhabitants, so as to avoid distinctions in wealth or position among the immigrants. Eventually, however, a perceptible change took place in the social set-up in the camps, rules became less stringent and the secretariats made it possible for individuals to receive parcels.[18]

The JDC's welfare teams which entered the camps on a permanent basis on 7 October (previously, the visits had been random) found a fairly well-organized community. Kitchens had been set up in the camps, in which the communal midday meal was cooked. The people were supplied with raw materials for preparing their morning and evening meals in their living quarters. Children received special mid-morning meals. One of the first things the immigrants saw to was school for the children, a continuation of the lessons at Port de Bouc. The camp at Poppendorf also offered religious education. Most of the day the children and teenagers were busy. The kibbutz members took part in sports, held concerts, political meetings and lectures. Still, many of the adults were inactive and bored. The new camps – Emden and Sengwarden – provided workshops to keep people occupied and to prevent them from regressing into undesirable profiteering activity. The *Exodus* immigrants impressed the staff of the JDC by not involving themselves in black market activity, but as far as the JDC were concerned, the best thing of all was the way in which the immigrants managed to keep up their morale and discipline (JDC 1947a). But in time this too became somewhat lax.

At first, when all their energies were directed toward getting the immigrants back to France as soon as possible, the British tried to nip in the bud all the immigrants' attempts at setting up their own leadership. The Foreign Office ordered its people in Lübeck to do "everything possible ... to prevent the mass of illegal immigrants from being organized again by the leaders who sought to prevent them from disembarking".[19] This time, too, as in the past, there were inconsistencies in Britain's assessment of the immigrants' determination and the degree to which their leaders could influence them and their decisions. The perpetrators of "Operation Oasis" were convinced that all the refugees had been thoroughly schooled in the reply they were to give if the back-to-France offer was made.[20] The Foreign Office, well experienced in the Exodus Affair, already knew that the number of volunteers to step forward would be small whatever conditions were offered in Germany, since these people were very disciplined and had a strong sense of mission.[21] About a month after the immigrants' arrival in Germany, when it was clear that they were not about to return to France of their own accord, the British accepted their special status and recognized their leaders. Before the transfer to the new camps the British tried to feel out the leadership's reaction and even agreed – if requested to do so – to permit them to look over the new place, once it was free of its previous inhabitants.[22]

The Am Stow and Poppendorf camps were not suitable winter quarters, and in the middle of October it was decided to transfer the immigrants to Emden and Sengwarden camps (north of Wilhelms-haven).[23] The British Command presented the issue to the camp's leadership on 20 October 1947, and these responded thus: "Nothing will deter us from going to Palestine. Which jail we go to [a reference to Emden and Sengwarden] is up to you [the British]. We did not ask you to reduce our rations, we did not ask you to put us in Poppendorf and Am Stow, we will tell you by 14:30 hours tomorrow, 21st October, whether we will send an advance party or not."[24]

In this letter of reply, which he wrote on behalf of the inhabitants of both camps, Roseman stuck to the line he had adopted during the stay at Port de Bouc: cool politeness would be used at all times in negotiations with the British on the question of living conditions, while stressing the fact that the real struggle is for the right to immigrate to Palestine. He informed the British that the immigrants were willing in principle to transfer to better camps, but pointed out that "our decision was not reached under pressure of the threats to transfer us forcibly. We have already shown on more than one occasion that physical force and acts of violence do not scare us and are not able to break our will to live." The immigrants rejected the idea of being left in Germany for a further winter and made it clear that "our immediate departure to Palestine remains a burning issue and until this happens, we are your prisoners and you are our gaolers and oppressors".[25]

What happened in the end was that representatives of the immigrants accepted the proposal to send an advance party to check out the new camps. The visits took place on 22 and 23 October and included representatives of the JDC. There was housing for some 2,000 people in the Sengwarden camp in permanent buildings. These were in generally good condition, but repairs were needed to the plumbing and floors, white-washing, furniture and electrical appliances, central heating and a water supply. The buildings which had been meant for housing sick people, as well as the central kitchen were adequate and suited their new objective. The seven barracks in Emden could house some 2,500 people. Some of the buildings were in need of basic repairs, electricity and washrooms. The kitchen and health services buildings were in reasonable condition and there was plenty of space for schools, workshops and club rooms.

Transfer of the immigrants began on 2 November and was completed in three consecutive loads, accompanied by Jewish medical teams. The inhabitants of Poppendorf (ex-*Ocean Vigour* and *Runnymede Park*) were taken to Emden; the ex-*Empire Rival* people, who had been at Am Stow, were transferred to Sengwarden. The trains they were taken in were dirty, unheated and unlit. When they arrived at their new camps, it was apparent that very little had been done to improve conditions since the visit of the advance party. Sanitary conditions were appalling. Piles of rubbish had been left behind by the previous residents, the lavatories did not work, the living quarters were filthy and more than half the windows were either broken or missing altogether. It was raining and cold, but there was no fuel to fire the heating. The delivery rooms were primitive and the nearest hospital was 30 km away.

The *Exodus* people never ceased to maintain their special status and remained apart from the rest of the DPs. On the eve of their transfer to the new camps their secretariat issued official ID cards declaring that the bearers were ex-*Exodus 1947* immigrants, forced back to Germany from the port of Haifa and currently in exile on the way back to Palestine. A stamped passport photograph was attached to each card.[26] They also sealed their letters with a special stamp, bearing the ship's name in Hebrew and English and a drawing of a ship breaking through a wall with its flags flying.[27]

There was a material aspect also to their special status. Fund raising was organized on their behalf in Palestine, an operation which began with a loud fanfare and ended in a weak whisper. First of all news came from the Mossad in Palestine that the Committee for the Cyprus Exiles had PP6,000 to put at the disposal of the *Exodus* immigrants and the question was, what did they want and need to have the Yishuv send them?[28] A week went by with urgent cries coming in from Europe describing the desperate state of the immigrants in their camps, but there was no reply on the matter of the financial aid offered from Palestine. After further questioning,[29] the emissaries in Europe suggested that the PP6,000 be placed at the disposal of the two camp secretariats. The secretariats were respected by the Mossad because they were comprised of responsible people who acted under the supervision of the emissaries from Palestine. The money was to be used for improving conditions for the children, pregnant women and nursing mothers, and for cultural activity.[30]

At this point, things took an about turn. From then on, urgent telegrams were sent from Europe – send the money, what's holding it up so long?[31] But replies from Palestine explained that the money was not yet in the possession of the Mossad.[32] The emissaries in Europe were becoming impatient during the last week in October: "You should know that this money has already been counted upon to cover essential expenses."[33] And, as if to force their colleagues to face a *fait accompli* the emissaries were quick to inform the immigrants that PP6,000 were on their way from the Yishuv.[34] After great effort, only PP1,000 were sent and the Mossad emissaries and the Jewish Agency were forbidden to spend any more than this sum,[35] and in the meantime, the Mossad continued in their efforts to raise at least another PP2,000 on behalf of the *Exodus* immigrants.[36]

The Committee for the Cyprus Exiles was formed in January 1947 with a modest budget. By December that year its expenses had reached PP15,000, of which PP10,000 were used to help illegal immigrants and PP5,000 were spent on organization, advertising and office expenses. Considering the Committee's limited budget, it is not quite clear how the Mossad came up with the impressive sum of PP6,000 for the benefit of the *Exodus* immigrants. In fact, right from the beginning the Mossad had asked the Committee for PP3,000 only. But the need to help the *Exodus* immigrants seemed to give the Committee a new lease on life, and it decided not to let the Mossad or the immigrants themselves have the money, but to keep to itself the right to decide how the money was to be spent.

Thanks to the financial contributions and parcels sent by relations in Palestine and America, the *Exodus* immigrants enjoyed a kind of material plenty way beyond that of their brethren in the DP camps. This brought about requests for handouts. In January 1948, for example, the head of Youth Aliyah in the German camps informed Roseman that a 16 ton consignment was about to arrive for the immigrants, with things from Palestine. "We don't know what kind of things, but we have been told that they are all new .... If possible, I would ask you to consider letting the children's houses in the American zone have some of the things that you can spare."[37]

The Yishuv found other ways to show solidarity with the immigrants. One of them consisted of publishing notices in the press for the Jewish New Year. Institutions, organizations, kibbutzim and others sent messages of encouragement and "well done!" to the immigrants. For example, the daily, *Davar* (14 Sept. 1947) blessed all the *Exodus 1947* immigrants and all those making their way to the shores of the homeland, that they would achieve imminent immigration and complete salvation in the Hebrew state. The Histadrut Executive Committee sent a greeting to the *Exodus* immigrants, who, "with their agonies, blessed Israel's right to immigration and deliverance".

Another way of expressing solidarity consisted of planting young trees in the names of the immigrants and registering them in the Jewish National Fund's "Golden Book". Some years later this was described in a cynical and bitterly realistic way in a conversation between two immigrants:

> "And in Eretz Israel, they say, the Jewish National Fund has decided to plant a new forest of four thousand five hundred trees in our name ... in the name of the *Exodus* refugees."
>
> "And they have also inscribed us in the Golden Book of the Fund ... ."
>
> "So it is more comfortable for me to lie in my nice bed of troubles! ..." (Perlov n.d., 295–96)

From mid-September onward the headlines were taken over by new items and by the end of the month, after France's invitation had been rejected, the Exodus Affair disappeared from the press. The embittered immigrant just mentioned wrote in his book: "I have received several newspapers. But yesterday they wrote about us with screaming headlines, on the very front pages ... . Today they are silent and we have been forgotten as though there had been no *Exodus* at all in this world. ... We have stopped being a sensation" (Perlov n.d., 294).

19 · *The Second Aliyah*

Even before their arrival in Germany, attempts were being made to find a way to return the immigrants to Palestine. But clearly this time there would be no resort to the tiresome route of illegal immigration, which had been made even more complicated by the Exodus Affair. France had been erased almost completely from the illegal immigration map since July 1947, as British pressure had caused the French to be very strict in checking the documentation of ships leaving from their ports. The French also restricted the movement of all foreigners on French soil.[1] The Mossad in France was obliged to be extremely devious in its activity,[2] and everything had to be kept top secret. Only four months after the *Exodus* had sailed from Sete, were two small ships – *Aliyah*, with 182 illegal immigrants and *Ha-Portzim*, with 167 – able to get out of a French port. This was followed by a further three month break in sailing out of France (Slutzky 1972b, 1903). And with France blocked, there was nowhere left but Italy. However, in order to get to Italy, the would-be immigrants were required to hike 30 kilometers over difficult roads, over tall hills and rocks, across rivers, always in danger of being caught at the border and returned to their point of departure – only to go through the whole procedure all over again. Everyone agreed that the *Exodus* immigrants could not be expected to undertake this dangerous journey. An easier way would have to be found for them to make their "second aliyah".

Moreover, it was clear that the *Exodus* people stood at the head of the immigration-to-Palestine queue. It was while they were still in Port de Bouc that Jewish Agency representative, Moshe Sneh, had given them his word of honor that the Jewish people would not rest until they were brought to Palestine, and no matter at what destination they ultimately ended up, the Haganah would be there to see to it that they were brought to Palestine (Habbas 1954, 294). This promise was rather general and not really binding and Perlson wrote (14 August 1947) to the Mossad head asking "to know what were the chances of receiving legal immigration certificates from the place at which we are about to arrive. And if this possibility exists – can we let our people know about it and start making some promises?" (Habbas 1954, 192–94). Meirov's reply was: "You can promise all the immigrants that their right to immigrate to Palestine will be preserved for them wherever they go to. We shall make sure that a special decision on this be taken at the next meeting of the Zionist General Council which will be convening at the end of the month in Zurich and we shall let you know the results as soon as we have them" (Habbas 1954, 292–93). In the meantime, the ships had set sail for Hamburg and contact with them had been severed. Still, the promise in general and the moral obligation to bring the *Exodus* people to Palestine as soon as possible remained sound.

The JDC had its own reasons for trying to find ways to bring the *Exodus* immigrants to Palestine. Aware that the British, too, were interested in getting the Jewish DPs out of Germany as soon as possible, the JDC suggested that His Majesty's Government allot a specific monthly quota of visas to Palestine to Jews in France, and the JDC would then make sure the *Exodus* immigrants returned to France. But the JDC made it quite clear that unless there was a firm promise that the necessary immigration certificates were issued, they could not cooperate in bring-ing the immigrants to France.[3] This proposal was never discussed on a practical level, since it contradicted the prevailing concept among the Foreign and Colonial Offices – that the immigrants had to be taught a lesson, not given a prize, for pushing their way to the head of the queue.

The Jewish Agency made several attempts at obtaining certificates for the *Exodus* immigrants. They tried, for example, to get the immigrants priority in obtaining "Grand National" certificates (which were issued for immigrants from the British zone in Germany). An alternative possibility was for a limited number of certificates to be placed at the disposal of the *Exodus* immigrants, in symbolic recognition of the group's uniqueness and right to immigrate to Palestine (JDC 1947a). When it became clear that the British had no intention of giving the *Exodus* group any kind of priority, on the contrary, a proposal was made to give them a status similar to that of the Cyprus exiles and to integrate them into one immigration queue, arranged according to the order in which they arrived in Cyprus or at the camps in Germany. Special cases, such as pregnant women and children would receive permits immediately (Levin 1947c). The British rejected all these proposals out of hand.

And in the meantime, gloomy, pessimistic tales were arriving in Palestine, about the sad state of the immigrants in the detention camps, and there was concern that they would be unable to endure the situation much longer. In the middle of September Meirov made an emotional appeal to his friends in Palestine and to Ben-Gurion: "Tension is increasing in the *Exodus* immigrants' camps .... They feel they have been deserted. Our people are fearing a break down." He demanded that, "in light of the tension," the Mossad should be "authorised to announce on behalf of the Jewish Agency, that *Exodus* people will be given priority on any sort of immigration to Palestine channel."[4] Roseman wrote to his fellow movement members that "there is appalling neglect" with regard to *Exodus*, which he related to an exaggerated evaluation of the immigrants' inner strength.[5]

Sneh was another prophet of doom. He had the idea, together with the Central Committee of Liberated Jews in the British zone, that the Jewish Agency should propose to the British Government to put aside 500 certificates out of each monthly immigration quota for use by the *Exodus* people. According to this idea, these certificates would come from the following sources: 150 from the British zone; 250 from Cyprus (with the approval of the Cyprus exiles); 100 from certificates designated for people with relatives awaiting them in Palestine.[6]

The executive of the Jewish Agency in Jerusalem then decided to announce that *Exodus* immigrants would receive priority in immigration, and to discuss with the Cyprus exiles the possibility of allotting 250 certificates out of their own quota for this purpose (21 Sept. 1947). It should be noticed that the sides were not broadcasting on the same wavelength. Sneh was talking about a *continuous* monthly donation of 500 immigration certificates, while the Jewish Agency had decided that this donation would be a *one off* affair.

The Jewish Agency's decision was declarative in nature and symbolic in scope and its implementation had to rely on the exiles in Cyprus agreeing to relinquish their place in the queue in favor of the *Exodus* immigrants. The job of contacting the people in Cyprus and persuading them to take part in the plan was delegated to Moshe Kolodni (later Kol), chairman of The Committee for Cyprus Exiles.[7] He was still deep in negotiations with the exiles, and the Mossad and the Jewish Agency in Europe were losing their patience. Sneh, Meirov and Pomerantz seemed to be competing among themselves over who could supply the gloomiest description of the immigrants' situation in Germany and putting pressure on the policy makers in Palestine – they sent telegrams directly to Ben-Gurion – to take action quickly, even if this meant bypassing those involved, who happened to be the exiles in Cyprus.[8]

At the beginning of October Meirov sent another telegram to the Mossad in Palestine, to Ben-Gurion and to Golda Myerson, giving a grim and pessimistic account of the situation in the *Exodus* camps. "Tension is at its highest. The British are about to remove the guards at the gates. There is an immediate danger of disintegration if no hope is given to the people that they are to receive immigration certificates, and that promises by the Jewish Agency and the Haganah to do their utmost to bring in the immigrants very soon, are kept." Meirov feared that the situation would end in "deep disappointment and would deal a fatal blow to the immigration movement in Europe". He served as spokesman for the *Exodus* immigrants by expressing their feeling that "they have won all the battles but may well lose the war", and demanded that maximum pressure be put on the Cyprus people to do the same as the residents of the camps at Belsen did, by agreeing to relinquish their place in the immigration queue, for the benefit of the *Exodus* immigrants. At the same time, the Mossad head called on the Jewish Agency to arrange fund raising for the *Exodus* people.[9]

Yet again, the deep commitment felt by the leaders of illegal immigration in Europe toward the *Exodus* immigrants went hand-in-hand with a low estimation of their staying power, and a fear that the affair would have a negative effect on the entire illegal immigration operation. The somewhat hysterical tone of the telegrams reflects a blend of honest concern for the fate of the immigrants, a real fear of the negative repercussions of their condition and a deliberate attempt to create panic, with the objective of speeding up their exit from Europe. The pressure placed on the Cyprus exiles was intensified since the DPs in the British zone in Germany had already announced their willingness to step down the immigration queue. But the DPs in Germany were different from the exiles in Cyprus. In summer 1947, there were some 12,000 Jewish DPs living in the British zone in Germany. Some 5,000 of them wanted to remain in Germany anyway, while the number of hard-core "pioneers" was not large – only about 1,000 in March 1948.[10] For those interested, the chances of immigrating to Palestine were relatively high. Three hundred and fifty immigration certificates were issued each month for the British zone and residents of this zone who had invitations from relatives in Palestine were given priority in receiving certificates.

In contrast, by September 1947 there were already some 14,500 Jewish exiles on Cyprus (Sha'ari 1981, 363). These had spent many months in exile camps, waiting for their turn to immigrate, on a first to arrive, first to leave basis. But they had been plagued for several months by a series of frustrating setbacks. In April 1947 the British cut back 400 permits from the monthly quota, at the expense of the immigrants from the ship *Shabtai Lojinsky*, who had landed on the Palestine coast and succeeded in being "swallowed up" in the Yishuv (Hadari 1991, 293). Riots had broken out in the camps in Cyprus; one immigrant was killed and several wounded. That summer arrangements for immigration from Cyprus underwent some changes and priority was given to children, mostly orphans (Sha'ari 1981, 144–53). Tension in the camps grew. And at the very time that efforts were being made to persuade the Cyprus exiles to give up their place in the immigration queue in favor of the *Exodus* immigrants, they were joined by another 4,500 immigrants from three ships captured by the British. Notwithstanding all this, and thanks to a great degree to the atmosphere created by the pioneer youth movements, the elected authorities of the Cyprus exiles decided, in the middle of October, to donate one entire monthly quota – 750 certificates – to the people of *Exodus*. They called on the Jewish Agency in Jerusalem to implement this decision and to "tell this to our brethren far away in the camps at Lübeck and Poppendorf, together with our best wishes" (Exodus File b).

The British refused to take part in this web of generosity and concession, and the prospect of letting *Exodus* immigrants enter Palestine at the expense of certificates allotted to Cyprus exiles, was abandoned (Jewish Agency Executive, 31 Oct. 1947). In Germany, where it was possible to dupe the British, half the quota of certificates at the disposal of the British zone was transferred to the *Exodus* people (Yahil 1981, 147). Another method of ensuring the swift and direct immigration of *Exodus* immigrants, was one known as "Aliyah Dalet", which involved the use of forged documents.[11] At the beginning of November the Mossad and the Jewish Agency took advantage of the move to the new camps and picked out candidates for immigration.[12] These people infiltrated from the British zone into the American zone, where they had the necessary documentation prepared for them. At the beginning of December 170 of the *Exodus* immigrants set off on their way to Palestine, equipped with certificates originally intended for DPs in the British zone; and on 20 January 1948, a further 167 took the same route.[13] Women in advanced stages of pregnancy (so that the babies would be born in Palestine) and their spouses were among the first to leave, together with the pioneer groups from England and France.[14]

Not everyone was pleased with the "second aliyah" arrangements. For example, one of the "individual" immigrants noted that immigration queues were based mainly on discrimination and favoritism:

> Most of the secretariat members, though almost all of them were young people, allocated certificates to themselves, leaving the non-party families with children to migrate in "aliya D". Those with certificates were able to

take along their belongings and the trip was human, normal, while "aliya D" people, on the other hand, could take only one knapsack or one valise per person, and they had to travel along the same route upon which they had already been when they had gone from Heidenheim to Marseilles, to the *Exodus*. (Perlov n.d., 308)

This last should be read with care, since it might not be devoid of vindictiveness. The author, Yitzchok Perlov, and his wife, the singer Lola Fulman, did not see eye-to-eye with the leaders on their ship the *Runnymede Park*. On the way from Port de Bouc to Hamburg, the singer gave a concert to the British crew, as a nonpolitical gesture of goodwill to the ship's doctor and the British authorities for taking care of the sick people on board.[15] Still, even if we don't accept Perlov's story as an accurate and factual description, it certainly expresses the feelings of some of the immigrants. "Aliyah Dalet" was based on false documents or authentic certificates issued to residents of Palestine and then adapted for people in Europe, who had characteristics similar to those of their original owners. It was quicker and easier to change an existing document than to produce a new one, so that use was made first of documents which arrived from Palestine and if these had belonged to families with children, they had to be used accordingly. New documents were issued mainly for young men, "fit to fight for their country", while families with children were sent in order to balance out the population of "returning residents", so as not to raise the suspicions of the British.[16]

From the moment they landed in Germany, the immigrants and their escorts were troubled by the question of how they were to determine who was to be the first to immigrate, since here, unlike in Cyprus, the principle of "first to arrive first to leave" did not hold. Some claimed that the first to leave should be those who had taken part in the fighting with the British near the coast of Palestine; others believed that "the woman with the sick child, who maintained a brave spirit and did not land at Port de Bouc – she is the real heroine and she had all the rights to first place in the immigration queue" (Habbas 1954, 51). Indeed, it was thanks to women such as this one that the *Exodus* immigrants won a victory at so decisive a point in their struggle. But that particular battle belonged to a previous war and it was soon evident that the queues would have to be adapted to suit the next war, the one in Palestine with the Arabs. And this was hinted at in the orders sent to the immigrants on the eve of their voyage from Port de Bouc to Hamburg: "Try to preserve your strength and your health ... we are counting on your strength in Palestine."

And in the meantime, the emissaries who had accompanied the *Exodus* immigrants, had left the camps, each to his own affairs. Some went on to continue working in illegal immigration and arms acquisitions in Europe and others returned to Palestine. Soon after his arrival in Palestine, Vanchotzker met with Ben-Gurion to present an emotional account of his encounter with the Holocaust survivors, his experiences at Port de Bouc, the voyage to Hamburg and the stay in the deportation camp in Germany, which he defined a "concentration camp". Full of youthful enthusiasm, he told Ben-Gurion all about his adventures and described the heroism of the illegal immigrants, "'their fight for the honor of Israel, which made them courageous and proud'. And suddenly I received a blow. I got the feeling that I did not have his full attention. I asked myself: 'What's going on here?' and then I turned to him and asked: 'Aren't you interested?' Ben-Gurion replied: 'It's in the past. It's over. Now there's a future. We have to think of the future. We've got other problems, serious ones.' I was shocked" (Bar-Zohar 1977, 656).

For some time, Ben-Gurion had had reservations about the way illegal immigration was being handled, but his position was not accepted. Since the autumn of 1947, however, he had been able to stamp his concepts on the character of the operation, albeit gradually. In the middle of November, the Jewish Agency decided to be careful in selecting immigrants, and to take into consideration their suitability for the country's labor and military needs. At that stage, this new order applied only to Romania, Hungary and Bulgaria,[17] and it was only during the winter months that it was extended to encompass all the illegal immigration operation, to comply with priorities determined by Ben-Gurion at the beginning of December: "The *security* issue takes priority even over *immigration*! Even before the state! Since without an existing Yishuv, there can be no immigration, no state, nothing."[18]

Thus the *Exodus* people were able to enter Palestine at a reduced speed not only because of British produced obstacles, but due also to pressures of the time and changes in Zionist policy. At the end of December all the Jewish Agency and Haganah activists in Europe came together for a series of closed and secret meetings, to determine future activity in accordance with events in Palestine.[19] Haganah chief in Europe, Nachum Kremer (later Shadmi), expected a prolonged state of war, especially after 15 May 1948, "in which we shall count our fallen in four figure terms", and it was most urgent that reinforcements be brought in. The change in priorities was so sharp that not everyone was able to take it in at once. Yehoshua Levy, Jewish Agency treasurer in Germany, was convinced that the decision to focus all of "Aliyah Dalet" on defense, meant that "we should be committing a wrong toward the *Exodus* people, who could rightly be referred to as soldiers, who were of great help to us in our political battles and we should also be doing ourselves a wrong" (Slutzky 1972a, 1464–65; 1972b, 1915–18). No clear-cut decisions had been taken at the time, as to the changes to be made in Haganah and Mossad activity in Europe, so that the *Exodus* people kept their special rights to immigrate and all that could have been done, technically, to facilitate their move through the "Aliyah Dalet" program was done without differentiating between potential fighters and others.[20]

By the beginning of March 1948, around a thousand *Exodus* immigrants were already in Palestine. Some 300 of these had come with certificates and six or seven hundred more via "Aliyah Dalet". A further 1,000 were awaiting their turn in France and about 2,000 were still waiting in Germany. Two hundred and sixty children were supposed to be leaving shortly, using some of the 461 children's permits issued at Belsen.[21] From France, the Mossad reported optimistically the hope that by April, more than 2,680 of the *Exodus* immigrants would be in Palestine and "in May, we shall try to make a last ditch effort to solve the problem of the *Exodus 1947* people".[22]

Under the new circumstances, the *Exodus* immigrants, heroes of the previous set, had become – heaven forbid – a "problem". Mossad activists encountering those of them stuck in France on their way to Palestine, felt that the people's pride at being part of the *Exodus* story was diluted somewhat by bitterness at the delay in their immigration, as well as a touch of protest, "but we were promised" (Teiber testimony; Arlozoroff testimony). Our friend, the writer Yitzchok Perlov, describes a conversation between two immigrants, in which one says: "'Well, you must not say, nevertheless, that Haganah, that has promised us something, has forgotten about us entirely,' Raphael says again, 'but our mood is yet of soldiers who have been left to winter in the posts of a distant quiet position ....'" (295). A few pages on, the two discuss the reasons behind this change and they seem to understand and accept the new order of priorities. There is a war in Palestine, and there is a need for soldiers: "Haganah, therefore, is busy mobilizing help. Haganah had to interrupt temporarily the aliyah of families, of older people and children, in order to bring in as many army-suitable people as possible" (311).

Which is the way it happened. It was clear that the British were not about to honor the clause in the UN decision, calling on them to clear a sea port and an area of hinterland by 1 February 1948 in what was to become the Jewish state, in order to enable immigration to be conducted on a significant scale. The significance of this was, that until the middle of May, all legal immigration from Europe and Cyprus, would continue to be almost entirely under the control of the Mandatory Government, which did its utmost to prevent the entry of people of military age. Thus, the only way to increase the Yishuv's military reserve was through various channels of illegal immigration – "Aliyah Bet" and "Aliyah Dalet". It was obvious, of course, that all attempts at illegal immigration of the "Aliyah Bet" type would end up in Cyprus, but there at least they would be only a few hours away from Palestine and there was every chance that the British would sooner evacuate Cyprus than allow Jews to come in from Europe. Therefore, at the beginning of February 1948, Ben-Gurion informed the Mossad in Europe of the Jewish Agency Executive's decision that future illegal immigration had to consist of young, able-bodied and militarily fit people and not just ordinary immigrants (old people and children) (Ben-Gurion 1982, 8 Feb. 1948).

At the same time, the draft in Palestine was getting larger. At first – the day after the 29 November 1947 – orders were issued to call up 17–25 year-olds. In early February 1948 this became a full recruitment order, encompassing all men in that age group. Later that month, the maximum recruitment age was raised to 35 – for single and childless married men. About a month before the end of the Mandate, a call was issued for single and childless married women, aged between 18 and 25, and on 4 May all men aged between 26 and 35 were recruited – including men who had children. Simultaneously, at the end of February, a call was issued for young Jewish people in Europe, male and female, aged between 17 and 32, who were asked to get ready (trained and organized) for imminent immigration to Palestine. Recruitment allocations were placed on all the countries in Europe. In Cyprus immigrants were being trained in "Shurot ha-Meginim" (defenders' lines) (Slutzky 1972a, 1465).

March 1948 was one of the grimmest months in the Yishuv's history. Waves of violence washed over the towns. On 11 March a car bomb exploded in the National Institutions compound in Jerusalem, three weeks after the explosion in Jerusalem's Ben-Yehuda street. The Jews suffered heavy blows in battles to keep the roads open. In one week, the last in March 1948, the Negev was cut off; convoys from Jerusalem to Neve Ya'akov and to Gush Etzion were attacked, as well as one to Kibbutz Yechi'am in the western Galilee; and the road was blocked near Hulda to a convoy making its way to Jerusalem. Things were going from bad to worse in the North with volunteers flowing in from the Arab countries to join the "Army of Salvation". And a new front was opened in the political arena, when the United States backed out of its support for the UN decision of 29 November 1947 and proposed to set up an international trusteeship in Palestine.

This was the background to the instructions issued by the Jewish

Agency Chairman and the Commander of the Haganah to the Mossad in Europe, regarding the composition of immigrant groups setting off for Palestine:

> The war depends on immigration, because there is not enough manpower here. The Arabs have enormous reserves and we are now in need of people from abroad for this war, but we cannot welcome immigration which is not directed entirely – from beginning to end – to the needs of war. And you must understand that all your activity, like that of the Yishuv, must be aimed now toward the needs of war. In other words, send out only people aged between 18 and 35. You can make exceptions of men, able to take up arms, aged up to 40 (Ben-Gurion 1982, 18 March 1948).

The situation in Palestine and the cost of absorbing immigrants not in the desired age bracket, caused angry responses when immigrants arrived who did not fill military requirements. "This time, we'll get no thanks for sending in 860 children. Anyway, don't send in any more children, until further notice,"[23] the Mossad cabled to France on 29 March. And another, more direct, telegram was sent to all the emissaries in Europe: "Everyone is furious at the … transports. The agent [Jewish Agency] categorically demands that you bring in [Aliyah] Bet and Dalet for the conscription purposes only. The agent demands that you stop bringing in *Exodus* people until May, and give preference to trained people and others for the war effort. We are warned that the funding of immigration will cease, if this immigration does not serve war needs. Confirm forthwith."[24]

At the same time, information came from Pomerantz in France, that *Exodus* immigrants were being sent to Palestine in "Aliyah Dalet" together with young people.[25] The message which was sent in return was clear: "Our orders on the selection of immigrants for military recruitment only are not open to any kind of interpretation and change. You are to act exactly as ordered."[26] That day a promise was received from France: "We are fulfilling your firm order not to send out immigrants aged below 17 and above 35."[27] And to further placate fears, it was made clear that "so far no potential recruit has been denied immigration because of anyone else".[28]

Throughout winter and spring of 1948, the Mossad staff who had handled the various stages of the Exodus Affair, were torn between their commitment to the immigrants and their duty to obey orders. The Mossad in Palestine, too, did its best to lessen the blow to the immigrants. About a month after the founding of the state, they ordered the emissaries in France: "In case you take on non-recruits – first priority goes to *Exodus* people."[29] Within three months this priority was realized and exactly one year after the three deportation ships had arrival in Hamburg with the 4,294 ex-*Exodus* immigrants on board, the following message was cabled from Paris: "We have removed the last of the *Exodus* people from Amos [Germany]. With the exception of a few sick people, no one remains. With the immigration of the last seventy on the *Kedma* we have fulfilled our promise to bring the *Exodus* people home. Inform everyone involved."[30]

20 · Who, Then, Was the Victor?

The Exodus Affair is commonly considered a victory for Zionism. It is also the custom to point out Britain as the overall loser in the struggle against illegal immigration to Palestine and the blow was especially harsh in the Exodus Affair, which was one of the highlights and an outstanding symbol of the whole operation. British historians are not quite so conclusive and tend to ponder – and question – the wisdom of the decision to expel the immigrants to Germany (Monroe 1961, 36; Bullock 1983, 450). Now, from a perspective of time and research, it is pertinent to examine once again whether the winner/loser division is as clear cut as it seemed; and if, indeed, one side or the other achieved a partial, or complete, victory over the other, in what way was this victory expressed, what were its limitations, who and what were responsible for it. In order to provide answers to these questions, it is necessary first to define the objectives of each of the sides, then to compare the objectives with the achievements, taking into consideration the price paid by each side.[1]

The British objective in the war against illegal immigration was to prevent the arrival in Palestine of illegal Jewish immigrants and to maintain the monthly quota of 1,500 immigrants entering the country through legal channels. They had been doing this very successfully since January 1946. The new, more intimidating method of deporting immigrants to the port from which they had sailed, depended on ships being apprehended in mid-sea, with all their cargo of illegal immigrants on board. "Operation Mae West" on 18 July 1947, indeed successfully prevented the landing of *Exodus* on a sand bank and the arrival of its thousands of passengers to Palestine. The cost, in terms of damage to British naval vessels was heavy, and it was decided not to repeat such operations.

By returning illegal immigrants to the country from which they set sail, the British hoped to avoid overcrowding the deportation camps in Cyprus. A ship carrying thousands of immigrants would have created a necessity for new camps to be set up on the Mediterranean island. At the beginning of September 1947, the architects of the war on illegal immigration were convinced that, by returning the *President Warfield* passengers to Europe, they had removed the danger of overcrowding in Cyprus for the foreseeable future. They pointed out with satisfaction that there would be no need to build new camps on the island for many months to come.

The British expected their main gain in returning the immigrants to Europe to be the total blocking of illegal immigration at source, in other words: a situation whereby no ships at all set sail for Palestine. They assumed that refoulement would serve as a deterrent to everyone involved. The coastal countries would be more careful to prevent illegal sailings from their ports; potential immigrants would be discouraged from setting off on a voyage which would turn out to be useless; the organizers, i.e. – the Mossad and in fact the Zionist leadership, would discard this expensive channel and find it difficult to raise money for illegal immigration, after it became evident that all the money they had invested in the purchase and fitting out of ships had gone down the drain.

The ultimate aim – blocking illegal immigration at source – was not achieved. Illegal immigrant ships continued to sail right up to the last week of the British mandate on Palestine. The return of the *Exodus* immigrants to France and their subsequent expulsion to Germany did little to dilute the reserves of potential illegal immigrants. Even if there were those who preferred not to set out on the long hard journey in the wake of *Exodus*, there were plenty of candidates for illegal immigration even in the autumn and winter of 1947–48. On the contrary, the immigrants' firm stand and the worldwide publicity caused by their disembarkation in Hamburg, only made "Aliyah Bet" more attractive to the Jewish DPs in Europe, who were encouraged by the fact that those who set off in ships after *Exodus* were not returned to Europe, but were deported to Cyprus, as before. It was clear that the return of illegal immigrants to Europe was a unique event. Also, the Exodus Affair did not act as a deterrent to the organizers of illegal immigration, nor did it harm the operation's financial sources. On these fronts, the British suffered defeat.

They did enjoy a certain success on the Arab front. In the period following the Second World War, the British had no clear and long term policies on Palestine and these were defined in negative rather than positive terms. One of Britain's main objectives was to prevent the Palestine issue from harming her relations with the Arab world (Monroe 1961). In this respect, the Exodus Affair had a positive significance. There was nothing that aroused Arab fury more than Jewish immigration into

Palestine, and all the more so when this was illegal immigration. Even if all Britain's attempts at blocking illegal immigration turned out to be useless, the mere show of determination in turning the immigrants back to Europe could be seen as something of an alibi on the part of the British toward the Arabs.

The French front also supplied Britain with a success of sorts. France imposed increased surveillance of foreigners on her soil and imposed stricter control on ships sailing out of her ports. After *Exodus* it took almost four months for sailings out of France to resume, and when they did, they were "black" – or top secret, and small. The situation in France toward the end of 1947 rendered the success of the Jewish side of the Exodus Affair something of a Pyrrhic victory, and in this respect there was a similarity between this event and the La Spezia Affair about a year and a half previously. In both cases, it was the success in one operation which caused the Mossad trouble on the entire front, first in Italy and this time in France.

In all their communications with Britain, throughout the various stages of the Exodus Affair, the French Government made sure to stress that their agreement to accept the immigrants was no more than a one-time gesture of goodwill, which should under no circumstances be seen as a precedent. Thus only three candidates remained for the refoulement policy: Italy and two communist Balkan countries, Romania and Bulgaria. Why were no attempts made to return illegal immigrants to those countries, and with respect to the current discussion, to what extent did this result from the repercussions of the Exodus Affair?

Deportation of immigrants to Romania and Bulgaria was rejected for political reasons, which had nothing to do with *Exodus*. On the one hand, it was impossible to return immigrants to a country that had agreed for them to set sail from her shores; on the other hand, the British hesitated to send people back behind the Iron Curtain – Jews or otherwise – where the Communist authorities were opposed to their activity. Another difficulty in sending immigrants back to these countries was imposed by the Montreux Convention (1936) on the matter of transferring military vessels through the Dardanelles. For example, the necessity for a warship to give long-advance notice of its intent to enter the Straits, would have forced the British to hold the deportees in Haifa for a long time, a possibility which was rejected out of hand.

Things were different on the Italian front. When the refoulement policy was still in its planning stage, the British hoped that France's agreement to accept the returned immigrants would serve as a positive precedent when they approach the Italians with a similar request.

France's behavior made it quite clear that the chances of forcing immigrants to land in Italy were virtually nil, since at the time when Britain was making great efforts to improve relations with Italy, she was reluctant to take any steps which might be interpreted as discriminating against her. Thus Britain was prevented from demanding that Italy do what France had already refused to do. In other words, even if the British could prove beyond a shadow of a doubt that an illegal immigrant ship had set sail from Italy, and these immigrants were returned to that country, this would be no more than a repeat of the Exodus Affair and the question would remain, what would happen if the immigrants refuse to land in Italy of their own accord.

The discussions in which Britain weighed the pros and cons of her refoulement policy and the chances of implementing it successfully a second time show us the heavy price the British had to pay over *Exodus*, as well as the coincidences and circumstances which made it possible for them to return the passengers of this particular illegal ship to their port of exit. An essential condition to the return of illegal immigrants to their port of origin was the availability of certain and irrefutable proof of where exactly they had set sail from. For this condition to be fulfilled, it was necessary to keep a close watch on all suspicious ships, a task which placed a heavy burden on the navy and air force and one which used up large quantities of fuel. The British had been following *Exodus* – while she was still sailing under the name *President Warfield* – constantly, from the United States, through the Azores and throughout her wandering from port to port along the Mediterranean coast. *Exodus* was thus "privileged" because of the noise and publicity surrounding her in America and the write-ups she received in the press, especially after the aborted journey eastward in February 1947. Among themselves, the British complained about the heavy cost of the various stages of the *Exodus* operation: the close watch on the ship; air and sea reconnaissance on the ports at which she anchored, followed by the two-month period in which three deportation ships were effectively tied up and out of action. In short, as far as the British Navy in the Mediterranean was concerned, the Exodus Affair was a thorn in the flesh and burned up a significant amount of their yearly fuel allotment. The British could not afford to put a watch on each and every ship they suspected of being potentially involved in illegal immigration and this reduced their chances of implementing their refoulement policies.

A second vital condition to the successful implementation of the refoulement policy consisted of the availability of suitable vessels for transporting the immigrants to their return destination – vessels which would be capable of reaching an alternative destination, further away.

The *Exodus* immigrants had the misfortune of arriving in Palestine after a two-month break in illegal immigration, during which the deportation ships had been anchored aimlessly at the port of Haifa. Even if the deportation of the immigrants to France had been conducted on schedule, from the British point of view, it would have been impossible to implement a consistent and continuous refoulement policy, because of the arrival of other illegal immigration ships immediately after *Exodus* and the reluctance of the British to hold the immigrants temporarily in Palestine before returning them to Europe. While the immigrants were still on their way westward to France, and before it was known that they would be refusing to land, the British had decided against implementing refoulement against the next two immigrant ships – even if their port of exit were known – for lack of deportation ships on which to make the return journey.[2]

The British were worried at their own inconsistency in implementing their new policy, and pondered the question the publication of which consideration would harm them the least – the lack of deportation ships or the fact that they were not sure of the port of exit.[3] But there was no point in evasiveness. On 27 July *The Manchester Guardian* published an item by the Jerusalem correspondent, saying that the immigrants on board the ships which arrived immediately after *Exodus* had not been returned to the port from which they had set sail because this port was unknown; because the means necessary to transfer them were unavailable; and because even if the port were known, chances were that the country in question would not be willing to accept them, as France had.[4] In other words, within a short time – even before the *Exodus* immigrants had issued the news that they were refusing to land in France – it was clear that the return of immigrants to their port of origin was a sporadic, even one-time event, and not a regular ongoing policy, like the deportation of immigrants to Cyprus which had been going on since August 1946.

Among the voices heard in discussions on refoulement, there were also those who opposed its continuation. It was claimed, for example, that the assignment of four ships for the express purpose of transporting illegal immigrants was far too expensive and that it would be much better to put these ships, or some of them, to commercial use where there was a profit in dollars. Another argument was the lack of alternative destinations, in case of failure. Exiling the deported immigrants to far-flung British colonies was out of the question because of the unsuitability of the ships to lengthy ocean voyages; it was also out of the question to bring them to Cyprus, after announcing that they would be returned to their country of origin; the possibility of taking them to England was never seriously considered.

And to expel them to Germany? Participants in the discussions were in one mind over the impossibility of bringing another group of immigrants to Germany. First and foremost because the Foreign Office opposed this, and also because of the fury of world public opinion. Interestingly enough, the reaction of the Yishuv was never a factor raised in opposition to the continuation of refoulement. In the end, the decision not to send more returned illegal immigrants to Germany came not from a consideration of world public opinion, but as a result of the commitment made to the military authorities there before the expulsion of the *Exodus* immigrants – that this was to be a once-only event. After all, it was in Britain's interest to empty Germany of Jewish DPs.

In spite of all the obstacles and notwithstanding the fact that there were no great hopes of its succeeding, the British never decided to abandon the refoulement policy. They simply came to the conclusion that conditions were not right to implement it. A review of the Exodus Affair in its various stages teaches us that here too the necessary conditions did not prevail for the success of refoulement. Thus, by returning the immigrants to France Britain was placing herself, almost knowingly, in a "no win situation", in which the key to success or failure was not in her hands at all, but in those of a third party who was expected to cooperate in being taught a lesson.

Up till now, criticism of Britain's behavior has focused on her decision to expel the *Exodus* immigrants to Germany. Elizabeth Monroe labeled as "wrong" the "act of sending Jews back to a former charnel house" (1961, 36); Allen Bullock defined the expulsion as a mistake, a blunder, as something which played completely into the hands of the Zionists (1983, 450); Arthur Koestler believed that the matter could not be explained by any rational motives (1949, 180). The moral faults in the decision to expel the immigrants to Germany were so obvious, as to make it politically deficient as well. The return to France, on the other hand, was not seen as heavy punishment or as an inhuman act against the immigrants, so that less attention was paid to its inherent political faults. In fact, and the British became aware of this during the unfolding of the Exodus Affair, their greatest mistake was in the very implementation of a policy which was doomed to failure, and in the fact that no alternative plans were made should complications arise. Bullock's opinion that the expulsion to Germany shows how far the judgment of experienced politicians like Attlee and Bevin and other senior ministers "had been clouded by anger and frustration with the situation in which they found themselves placed in the summer of 1947" (1983, 450), can be applied also to the decision to return the immigrants to France.

How is France's position in the affair to be explained? With their quiet and half-open aid in allowing the *Exodus* to set sail, the French were continuing their traditional trend of informal assistance to Jewish illegal immigration to Palestine in the years following the Second World War. The demand to accept the returned immigrants placed the French Government in a dilemma between preserving her own interests, which meant refusing Britain's request, and her desire to improve relations with her neighbor across the English Channel. The observation that "in the Exodus Affair the French could allow themselves, with a smile of revenge, to put a spoke in the British wheels, without causing any untoward damage to themselves" (Bar-Zohar 1964, 24), is more indicative of the situation before the ship set sail and less of the next stage of the affair. The reference is, of course, to attitudes and personal feelings, and not to any rational consideration which guides the policies of a government. Furthermore, the French, who helped in the illegal immigration operation, did so from humanitarian motives and did not see their activity as leading to the formation of a Jewish state; and France's stand on the Exodus Affair was guided by the concept that this was a solution to a human problem, which lay within the scope of French–British relations and it had nothing to do with the Middle East and the Palestine issue. This, by the way, was unlike the position taken by the United States, who refrained from intervening in the French phase of the Exodus Affair because of the repercussions it would have on the question of Palestine.

An illustration of the way France differentiated between the Exodus Affair and the Middle East issue, can be found in a conversation which took place in Lyons in the middle of August 1947 between the French Prime Minister, Paul Ramadier, and a member of the Jewish Agency Executive during the French Socialist Party Convention. Berl Locker, who had been invited to represent Mapai at the convention, thanked Ramadier for France's stand on the Exodus Affair and the latter replied that his Government had done what it considered to be the right thing to do from a humanitarian point of view. When they reached the main subject of the conversation – France's position on the United Nations debate on the Palestine issue – Ramadier made it clear that France, with her many Arab subjects, was obliged to consider Arab interests and the growing power of the Arab League.[5]

Where France's position is concerned, the Exodus Affair took place at the very last moment, only weeks before she, like all the other UN member nations, had to take a stand on the question of the future of

Palestine. During the months of July and August, it was still possible to disregard the Middle East aspect of the Exodus Affair. Within a short time considerations relating to the Middle East joined the vintage French interest of maintaining good relations with Britain and a new French line was born. On the question of illegal immigration this was expressed in a hardening of the means for preventing sailings from France. On the wider issue of the political future of Palestine, France was undecided in November 1947 between sympathy for the Jews and her Arab considerations, and up to the last moment it was unclear as to how she would behave at the United Nations vote on the partition proposal. France's hesitation and her parliamentary maneuver almost caused a defeat for Zionism in this historic vote, even though, in the end France did vote in favor of the partition of Palestine and the formation of a Jewish state (Eban 1977, 95–99; Bar-Zohar 1964, 9–36).

In conclusion, in the Exodus Affair France took the almost obvious line, the only one possible under the circumstances, and it happened to be compatible with Zionist interests. France succeeded in preserving her own interests and even if this annoyed the British, they were not able to put too much blame on her, since they were aware that the refusal to permit the forced landing of immigrants was a "natural" step (Beith 1947b). France forged her natural and easily conceivable position (considering her own interests) in such a way as to appear to everyone in the best possible light. She did not totally reject Britain's request; she avoided using force against the survivors of the Nazi sword; and at the same time she did not lock her gates to these refugees, victims of a cruel fate. There is nothing in this to minimize France's decisive role in turning the Exodus Affair into a Zionist victory, and from the debt of thanks owed to her by the Zionists for her part in the illegal immigration operation in general and in the Exodus Affair in particular.

The seeds of Britain's failure in the Exodus Affair, which had been contained in the refoulement policy by its very nature, and which sprouted thanks to France's position, flourished into a victory for the Zionist cause due to the illegal immigrants. Flung into a campaign for which they had been unprepared, these people fulfilled their role in it above and beyond what was expected of them. Everyone involved in this operation, in one way or another, were favorably surprised at the way in which the immigrants conducted themselves. The emissaries from Palestine expressed themselves in terms of astonishment: "The massive steadfastness of these immigrants – this was the greatest revelation for us. We asked ourselves, where did these people draw their strength from to live and persevere under the horrific conditions in which they lived?"

This man's surprise was all the greater because he had been prepared to encounter "people of a certain kind, especially difficult" (Habbas 1954, 66–69). The "he-Halutz" emissary in the south of France wrote to his friends in Palestine right after the deportation ships had left Port de Bouc: "We had no faith in these people ... we were shaking in anticipation of the ships. What shape would the people be in, how great was their desperation, what did they want for the future ... and were surprised anew" (Reichman 1947).

Years later one of the immigrants gave his reply to the surprise and suspicions expressed by the Palestinians: "We got to know later that in the Yishuv, in the Haganah, they were very afraid that our resolve in so endless a test of our strength, would falter. Those who had not been cast in the furnaces of the Holocaust may not have been able to conceive the depths of agony, insult, anger, longing and yearning which drove the Holocaust survivors" (Peker 1964). Even in 1947 there were those who tended to use the high-flown phrases and flowery language common in those days, when describing the forbearance of the illegal immigrants. Immigrants and Palestinians talked about the sense of mission which guided them, of the legacy of the generations of the Jewish people who placed upon them a special responsibility, and of the national order which called them to fight and to fulfill their mission – to prevent the British from dealing a fatal blow to the illegal immigration operation.

We must not let high-flown rhetoric mislead us into believing that these are empty words. In the context of that period in time, when the events of the Second World War and the Holocaust cast a heavy shadow and a deep impression on the way people thought and acted, it would be wrong to deny the powerful feelings of nationalism and yearning for the homeland which were aroused at the sight of the beautiful Carmel mountain, as the immigrants drew close to the coast of Palestine that Sabbath eve, after wandering for so long, after a voyage at sea and a night of battle. Many were the people involved in the Exodus Affair who mentioned the excitement and emotional turmoil which this sight aroused in the hearts of the immigrants and contributed to their determination not to disembark in France.

All these made Palestine even more attractive as a land of aspiration and hope. Add to these the elements which pushed the immigrants out of Europe: The near-crisis situation in the camps in Germany and the sense of having reached a dead end. People who had been taken out of Europe and led to Palestine by the young men and women of the Haganah, had thrown their lot in with this organization, which would see to getting them to a safe haven, albeit through winding roads. And it was clear to everyone that landing in France meant a severance of ties with the Haganah, abandoning its protective auspices and even relinquishing the right to immigrate to Palestine. A high price to pay.

Haganah people in France worked hard to convince the immigrants that they were taking care of them. They sailed boats close to the deportation ships, offered encouragement to the immigrants, promised them that the Yishuv in Palestine was firmly behind them and swore that they would indeed immigrate to Palestine. More conclusive proof of the Haganah's concern for the immigrants was supplied by the boarding of additional emissaries in France, and, most important of all, perhaps, were the "dumplings", the improved food rations they received at Port de Bouc, which was far better and in greater quantity than anything they had been served at sea. And who was responsible for all this plenty if not the omnipotent Haganah?

One of the elements which made up the decision not to land in France, was the *esprit de corps* which prevailed among the immigrants, not only the alliances which bound the groups prior to embarkation, but also the fellowship which developed during the voyage at sea, in the battle, on the way back to France and during the trying days at Port de Bouc. People did not want to be separated from their friends, as was evident from the fact that those immigrants who had succeeded in obtaining legal immigration certificates chose – even in Gibraltar, on the way to Hamburg – to pass them up and remain with their friends on the deportation ships. Another more prosaic factor was their emotional ties with their material belongings. We shall recall that their things had been taken from them for searching in Haifa and reloaded at random on all three deportation ships, not necessary on the same ship as their owners. Those who considered the possibility of landing in France had to take into account that this would cost them the loss of their personal belongings

And let us not denigrate the power of "no choice". Where could they have gone? The same reasons which had made Palestine the preferred destination for Jewish displaced persons after the war, were several times more valid with regard to the *Exodus* immigrants after what they had gone through. If they were still able to think in terms of "home", then Palestine was their home. It was there that they could meet up with relatives and people from their home towns, people with a common background and similar ambitions. Circumstances increased the commitment to Palestine, even among those of the *Exodus* immigrants who, in the past, had signed up for emigration to other countries. In Palestine they would be able to rebuild their lives as Jews among their brethren, either family members in every sense or members of the same nation. Whereas France was a strange place. What would they do there? Who would look out for them there? Who was waiting for them there? It was not on French soil that they would find solace.

And their constant wishful thinking that any minute now they would be making their way to Palestine, worked wonders for the morale of the immigrants and prevented some of the irresolute among them from landing (Habbas 1954, 212–13). Some of them believed that perhaps their persistence would pay off and in the end they would be returned to Palestine. As time passed and their hopes and illusions dissipated, the escorts began to worry that the people's spirit would break and their patience and strength would be lost (Exodus Diary 1968, 9 August 1947). The escorts, who did their best to prevent the landing of those who had no patience, those who sought more comfortable conditions, and those who had set themselves a date by which they would land if no change had taken place, organized several forms of "Zionist propaganda activity" (Exodus Diary 1968, 13 August 1947). The immigrant leaders and the emissaries from Palestine worked on dissuasion; here and there physical violence was applied by the immigrants against people they suspected of wanting to land (Habbas 1954, 172), and there were threats that anyone who landed would have to face trial on shore (Habbas 1954, 211–12), and may even be executed (Exodus Diary 1968, 9 August 1947).

The threats did not go unheeded by the British, who even noticed that force was used by "extremists" and "hooligans", and not by the leaders. They also noticed the constant pressure the immigrants were subject to from people on shore and they believed that the large Jewish crowd at Port de Bouc had the effect of increasing the fears of those thinking of landing, that the threats directed at them on board would be implemented by the people waiting for them on land.

All in all, testimonies from the British and the Jewish sides complement each other and present a similar picture: Only an insignificant minority of immigrants considered going ashore at Port de Bouc. Although they were aware at a very early stage and admitted to themselves that most of the immigrants would not land, the British made a point of spreading around that the people were refusing to land because they were being threatened and pressured into staying aboard. Those involved on the Jewish side denied such allegations: "It was not Zionist propaganda which influenced them – *they themselves* decided" (Reichman 1947, original emphasis); "rumors that the Haganah are responsible for forcing the immigrants to remain on board ... are untrue" (Habbas 1954, 66). These claims are surely more accurate than the British ones, which they were meant to contradict, although they were not completely unfounded. We have seen that here and there threats were sounded and hands were raised. Even if these were isolated cases, it is still possible that they prevented the landing of some at least of the hesitants.

Members of the youth movements and the kibbutzim, those for whom ha-Shomer ha-Tza'ir's order of the day, just before setting off from the port of Sete (see Chapter 4), expressed their attitude to the illegal immigration operation and their own task in it, were the hard core among the immigrants, whose ability to persevere in the struggle is almost self-evident and in whom there were no cracks or breaks. In addition to their ideological and organizational commitment, they were also young people, most of them had boarded the ships by themselves, without any family members, each to his own. Inspired by the group of pioneers and the personal example set by the emissaries, an anti-disembarkation atmosphere was created on board the ships which infected others – family members, "individuals", those who had been defined "ordinary Jews" and "every-day Jews". The reference here is to a moral influence, to the organization of day-to-day life, willingness to help, maintaining social and cultural activity, and creating a mood which, notwithstanding all its manifestations, is hard to describe in words.

When the *Exodus* immigrants first set out on their way to Palestine, they were no different, neither better nor worse, from illegal immigrants before or after them. During the battle near the Palestine coast, they split up into a front and a rear, according to age, family status, group membership and the ability of each of them to make their way to the battle zone, when the fighting broke out suddenly, sooner than had been expected. The line dividing the front and the rearguard had been flexible and changed according to fluctuations in circumstances. At Port de Bouc, even those people who had seemed defeatist in their behavior during the battle, now refused to land and held on adamantly to their decision for a long time. Not every immigrant was able to take part in a physical confrontation with the soldiers of the British Navy, but when the struggle involved a cause which the public understood and could participate in, be this passive resistance, a hunger strike or a stubborn decision: "We shall not land!" – the entire ship became the "front". When the immigrants recognized the importance of the task they were faced with, and the importance of their own contribution to it was evident (and it was within the scope of their ability), they stood up to it with distinction.

After facing so many trials together at Port de Bouc, many immigrants joined in the refusal to land at Hamburg – even those who had not taken an active part in the battle on the approach to Palestine. In Hamburg, as in Palestine, it was clear to all that the British would have the upper hand, since this was a struggle between two totally unmatched forces. None-theless, many who for various reasons refrained from taking an active part in the fight on the way to Palestine, now offered passive and even active resistance to being landed at Hamburg.

Above and beyond all the reasons listed so far, the immigrants' will throughout the Exodus Affair seemed to be consistent with the *Zeitgeist*, the prevailing mood after the Second World War. Their strength was forged not only during the harsh war years, but also by the circumstances afterwards. Ha-Shomer ha-Tza'ir leader, Meir Ya'ari, was extremely frank in his description following his visit to Europe in autumn 1946:

> Here we have a new movement in Germany, with thousands of members … gifted with one virtue, which is of outstanding importance. They do not have too many choices. They came to us not of their own free will, nor will they turn their backs on us out of capriciousness or should the mood so take them....
>
> Only one way remains. There is no more volunteerism in the Diaspora. Free choice remains only to the movement in America or Palestine: Their pioneers can buy a boat ticket in order to return to America, or a bus ticket home. The people of Bavaria have no such choice. They are not free to choose, but this is by nature a kind of "joy of the poor". It was thus that they were saved, the way they found themselves together, forged one ideological family, immigrating by all ways and means possible, in rickety boats, via Cyprus, to Palestine. There is compulsion here, but there is no subjection … when our movement's orphans spend a year or two in our own educational atmosphere, the movement becomes their mother and father. They do not meet a few times a week for a group discussion, but rather spend all their time together. Whoever devotes himself to them – dresses the naked, liberates the imprisoned and breathes into them new life.
>
> This is the portrait of the new wave of immigration, which we are currently bringing in from the Diaspora. If the gates are opened to immigration, or if they leave only a tiny crack [these people] will make their way here in all sorts of ways, but they will come; and leading them will be those partisan elements, the like of which we have not known for a long time. (1947, 288–89)

In retrospect, Shaul Meirov explained the illegal immigration operation as "the exploitation of the indefatigable power of the im-migrants. What we were faced with was a 'grass roots power', sometimes latent, sometimes obvious, of people who had no choice. And, in the final analysis, we depended on the existence of this non-surrendering power" (1959). Indeed the immigrants had no choice – all other ways of immigration were closed to them and they did not wish to remain in Europe, but they were not facing a choice between life and death. Here

Ya'ari's description is more to the point: "There is a compulsion here but there is no subjection." This can be explained with the help of a paraphrase of a saying taken from elsewhere: We are not talking here of a proletariat which had nothing to lose but their chains, but of a group of people with a firm national consciousness, for some of them this took the form of post-catastrophic Zionism.

The seemingly clear and obvious objective of illegal immigration during the years following the Second World War was to bring Jews to Palestine. Since the British deducted the number of illegal immigrants entering Palestine from the officially issued immigration certificates, the illegal immigration operation did little to raise the overall number of immigrants who entered the country during the 36 months between the end of the Second World War and the founding of the State of Israel. But this does not label the illegal immigration operation a failure, since this was not its main objective at the time.

In the years immediately following the Second World War, the illegal immigration operation was intended first and foremost to serve as a lever for founding a Jewish state in Palestine. Zionist policy makers designated the operation a central role in proving the connection between solving the problem of the displaced Jews in Europe and founding a sovereign Jewish state in Palestine. In other words, the operation was *not* a struggle over the opening of the gates of Palestine and canceling out the 1939 White Paper. The issue was the foundation of a state, and the question is worn from over-use over what would have happened to Zionism had the British concurred to President Truman's 1945 request to allow the entry of 100,000 displaced Jews into Palestine, within a short period of time? The illegal immigration operation was meant to prove the Jews' desire to immigrate to Palestine no matter what. It was meant to keep the headlines and world public opinion busy with the problem of the Jewish DPs who were rotting away in Europe many months after the war was over. This operation could have embarrassed the British, who were blocking the way of Holocaust survivors to their homeland, by exploiting the moral advantage of the Zionist cause.

In addition to these two objectives, the illegal immigration operation was also a bridge between the Yishuv and the Diaspora, a tool of national solidarity crossing oceans and continents. And it was meant to reinforce both sides of this bridge. In the Diaspora, it was meant to maintain the morale of the Jews in the DP camps, instill in them the hope that they would one day leave the valley of tears, and save them from despair and ideas of emigration to other countries. Being an issue of wide public

consensus, the job of illegal immigration in Palestine was to cohere the
population around its leadership and the objectives set by this leadership
and the ways in which they were to be achieved. The operation was
particularly important in its ability to capture the imagination of the
young and to prevent them from running off after the terrorist dissident
groups.

The priorities of the illegal immigration operation and the ways in
which these were carried out did not enjoy general agreement. Opinions
were divided, for example, on the desirable size of the ships. *Exodus* was
larger than all her predecessors, although some of these had been big,
with cargo-loads of up to 4,000 people. And at the time of her sailing, the
Mossad was engrossed in the "Pans'" operation – two huge ships, each
bearing some 7,500 illegal immigrants. The move to larger ships was the
result of circumstances and supply of ships on the European and
American markets at the time, rather than of a debate and a decision on
new ways (Sereni 1975, 126–27). Latent disagreements as to the size of
the ships deepened and exploded at full force on the eve of the "Pans'"
sailing. Ben-Gurion pointed out that for the past year and a half, he had
been protesting the line taken by the Mossad. He said: "Not large ships,
but small boats, 200 passengers in each! And many such boats! ... It's
much more trouble, because to apprehend a ship with 1,500 people on
board ... all it takes is one cruiser, but if we send 20 small boats, they'll
need to activate their entire naval fleet in the Mediterranean ... and then,
possibly, out of 20 small boats, three or four will succeed in entering
Palestine."[6]

Ironically, it was *Exodus*, who by her size was the antithesis of Ben-
Gurion's concepts, which succeeded more than all the others in achieving
what he considered to be the aims of illegal immigration. As far as he
was concerned, illegal immigration was not going to increase the Yishuv
demographically, but was to serve as a means in the struggle against the
British and for the founding of a Jewish state. The advantages of *Exodus*
were revealed as a sort of "cloud with a silver lining", and rather than
being the result of careful Zionist planning, they dropped into Zionist
hands like ripe fruit, because of the series of mistakes made by the other,
British, side.

And the strange irony of history is that during the Exodus Affair –
the apex of illegal immigration operation from a propaganda point of
view and its potential to reap the political fruit – at the very same moment
when the immigrants were making their way from Port de Bouc to
Hamburg, the operation exhausted its political objective. Until August
1947, *Exodus* had contributed to each of the objectives described here,

apart from actually bringing Jews to Palestine. And then she almost became a burden instead of an asset.

The change in attitude of the Zionist leadership to illegal immigration is usually related to the UN decision on the partition of Palestine. One of the new claims made by this book is, that this change took place earlier, at the time the *Exodus* immigrants were making their way to Hamburg, when it was already known which direction the UNSCOP conclusions would be taking and the Zionist leadership, with Ben-Gurion at its head, navigated the affair's end in such a way as not to harm Zionism's political achievements. Not only was *Exodus*, therefore, one of the highlights of the illegal immigration operation, it was also a watershed between two periods in its history. Up to then, illegal immigration had served the purpose of founding a Jewish state in Palestine by political means; later on, its purpose was to help the war effort, by bringing as many young people as possible to the vicinity of Palestine, from where, in due course, they would be able to join the forces against the Arabs in Israel's War of Independence. But care had to be taken to avoid harming the political gains already achieved. Up to now, illegal immigration had been accompanied by loud fanfares. From now on, it had to keep a low profile.

In the summer of 1947, Ben-Gurion was virtually the only one to see things this way, although he ultimately had the upper hand. The commanders of the illegal immigrant ships were ordered to make do with no more than symbolic protest to being captured (Sha'ari 1981, 116). In the end, the "Pans" sailed straight to Cyprus, by agreement with the British; and the Mossad sent out specific orders to its people in Europe, to send out only people who would be of use in the war effort.

Even before it was over, scores of people were inspired to sum up the chronicles of the Exodus Affair. Anyone who had a connection of any kind with the affair, was eager to have it mentioned favorably and to become part of the myth which was already in the making. The Mossad in France asked to be sent copies of *Davar* and *Ha-Aretz* for Jarblum, who was writing a book about *The President*,[7] and in Palestine they were swift to comply.[8] Earlier, the Mossad in Palestine asked to be told if any photographs remained of the *Exodus'* voyage and the battle, and offered to provide each of the immigrants ships with a cine-camera.[9]

No sooner had the immigrants landed in Germany, than the various parties and movements set to writing down the history of the Exodus Affair to ensure their part in the glory. Each movement asked those of its members who had been on the *Exodus* to save every bit of material connected with the affair and to write down their own stories. A ha-Shomer ha-Tza'ir emissary applied to Roseman to see to it "that all people who know how to hold an author's pen, sit down and begin the task of writing. There are already signs of historical writing of the worst kind."[10] Roseman, for his part, asked the movement's leadership in Germany to keep all the material he had given them, "since it will be necessary in the future. The material includes valuable documents." Over and over again, he asked that newspapers be collected which contained material on *Exodus*. It is interesting to note that as soon as it became evident that Mordechai Roseman had taken a central role in the *Exodus* leadership, ha-Shomer ha-Tza'ir's journal *Mishmar*, which until then had been covering events briefly compared with *Ha-Aretz* and *Davar*, using material supplied by news agencies, began to publish lengthy descriptions and special articles on Roseman's speeches and activity.

The ha-Shomer ha-Tza'ir Supreme Management in Palestine sent repeated requests to Germany to keep material – "diaries, lists, orders-of-the-day, literary efforts, whether in poetry or prose, etc" – and to send it to Palestine for publication or preservation in archives.[11] One of the letters said: "The Exodus Affair in Poppendorf is something that should be brought to the public's notice. And we have no information at hand. We ask of you not to save any effort or time on the matter and make sure that we receive detailed information on the situation there."[12] The eagerness of ha-Shomer ha-Tza'ir people to write up the *Exodus* story and to preserve every scrap of information connected with the affair stems from a fear that their part in the developing myth and the history-in-the-writing, might be left out. Sediments of the not-so-distant past and the conflict between the movements and the parties over hegemony of the DP community and the need to be seen as leading heroes in the Jewish struggle – then, in the ghettoes and on the *Exodus*, now – produced analogies, like the one included in the movement emissary's letter, which informed Roseman of the "efforts made by the other parties to push us aside. It irritates them to see that we are once again showing initiative, and as far as you are concerned they are prepared to do as they did to the holy memory of Mordechai A[nielewicz, commander of the Warsaw ghetto uprising]. This is no surprise to us and we are not in a position to amuse ourselves by feeling hard done by."[13]

At first, movement members in Germany considered publishing a booklet on the Exodus Affair. In a sort of self effacement so typical of the Diaspora people toward their colleagues in Palestine, or perhaps through respect for the movement's hierarchy, they asked to have a preface sent to them from Palestine. The movement's Supreme Management in

Merchavia discussed the matter, approved publication of the booklet and concluded that, instead of a preface it would begin with excerpts of editorials from *Mishmar*.[14] But the program never materialized and in the end it was ha-Shomer ha-Tza'ir that lagged behind in the historiographic race, and made do with devoting a few pages to the Exodus Affair in the volumes of *Sefer ha-Shomer ha-Tza'ir* (Book of ha-Shomer ha-Tza'ir). At the beginning of 1948, the Dror youth movement in the German camps published a book based on the stories of the children and their counselors who took part in the voyage, and at the end of 1947, the journalist Bracha Habbas (who was identified with Mapai) began preparing an ostensibly general book, on behalf of the Histadrut.

When ha-Shomer ha-Tza'ir in Germany found out that Habbas was collecting material for her book, they consulted their movement leadership in Palestine and were answered: "If the Histadrut publishes a book and Bracha Habbas will be the editor-in-chief, we shall of course be willing to take part in it, but on the specific condition that they include us on the editorial board."[15] An editorial board was never formed and Habbas was the only editor of the book, *Ha-Sefina she-Nitzha* (The Ship that Won), which was first published in 1949; and its second edition (1954) became the official account of the Exodus Affair. The head of the Mossad, who was one of the initiators of the idea to produce the book, was personally involved in its preparation. He supplied the author with material and advised her on ways to present it. For example, he was quick to send her the telegram of 7 September 1948, informing that the last of the *Exodus* people had immigrated to Israel, together with a handwritten note saying that, "it would be a good idea to place this in a suitable place in the book", and added: "I am especially interested that emphasis be laid on the fact that the Haganah's promise to bring all the *Exodus* people was *fulfilled* in its entirety. Perhaps you could write a title, 'The Promise that was Fulfilled'" (Exodus File a). The telegram was included under the title: "The Haganah Promise was Fulfilled".[16]

There is an obvious trend in Habbas' book to give extra credit to the Mossad, even at the expense of other participants, and to glorify the emissaries from Palestine while playing down the part played in the affair by the immigrants. The book was one of the forerunners in the first wave of historical writings on the period of the struggle over the founding of the state, which came as a direct continuation of the conflicts dividing the Yishuv at the time under review. This wave was also meant to supply *post factum* reinforcement for the position of this or that side in the conflicts which split the Yishuv and to strengthen it in its present and future political struggle. As the editor of another book in this first wave,

Sefer ha-Palmach (Book of the Palmach) wrote: "May this book fulfill its mission not only as a volume of history of the period it describes ... but also as an educational tool and as a weapon for *times to come*" (Gil'ad 1953, ix, original emphasis).

Three specific characteristics were evident in the first phase of recording the history of illegal immigration. One: In the context of the debate on "who drove out the British", emphasis was placed on the contribution of the illegal immigration operation to the struggle, while playing down the part of the dissident organizations and denouncing terror. The coincidence of the Exodus Affair and the execution of the two sergeants seemed to illustrate the polarity of methods used by the two camps in the Yishuv, and *Exodus* served as a tangible and heartrending medium in the actual and historiographical struggle over supremacy in the leadership of the struggle against the British.

The second one: The Mossad, as a Mapai stronghold, and the Palmach, in which members of Mapam ruled supreme, competed with each other over the contribution made by each to the illegal immigration operation. The *Exodus* aspect of this competition consisted of underestimating the part played by the Palmach in Habbas' *The Ship That Won*, while in *The Book of the Palmach* stress was placed on the independence shown by the Palmach in handling the resistance to the British – for example, the case of the bomb on the *Empire Rival*. In those days, at the beginning of the state, there was growing tension between Mapai and Mapam in the wake of Ben-Gurion's decision to disband the Palmach.

The third characteristic consists of glorifying the Yishuv's role at the expense of the immigrants. The first books to be written on the Exodus Affair and on the history of the period in general, tended to gross overemphasis when describing the Yishuv's participation in the illegal immigration operation. This was done to such an extent as to disclose attempts at "smoothing things over", even when the picture presented of the Yishuv's behavior and attitude is a complex and unflattering one, and the caption describing it does not lack a critical tone. The opposite is true where the immigrants were concerned. They, who were treated at first as survivors of the sword, who had to be saved, became in no time virtually the lone fighters in the struggle against the British. Many noticed this, but alongside the rebukes against the Yishuv and feelings of guilt toward the immigrants, there were expressions of concern that the "weak shoulders" of the immigrants would be incapable of withstanding the efforts required of them. The Exodus Affair changed the immigrants' image for the better and the Yishuv was swept away on a collective catharsis of admiration toward them. But with time the glory of their courage was dulled. Of all the Seventh Column poems written by Alterman on illegal immigration, in which there is praise for the courage of the immigrants and criticism of the indifference of the Yishuv in Palestine and the Jews in America toward the struggle, of all those poems there remains in the collective, and selective, memory, the one on "our lads", the Palmachniks, the Jews of Palestine, who "bore their nation on their shoulders" (Halamish 1988, 51).

And when the story of illegal immigration was put down in writing, the immigrants themselves all but disappeared. The reason for this is that the role they had been delegated was a passive one – even that of "film extras" – in the inter-Yishuv conflict, which directed not only events in the period but also the way its history was written. In this respect, the historiography of the Exodus Affair and the illegal immigration operation in general is compatible with a more general trend in the history of the Jewish people over recent generations and the way they are recorded – especially in Israel – whereby focus is laid on the Jewish Yishuv in Palestine, and the Diaspora remains in the shadow. In the case of *Exodus*, the role enacted by the immigrants – with the significance of ha-Shomer ha-Tza'ir among them – is understated because of a blend of two trends: One – the Palestinocentrism in the historiography of the period; and second – Mapai's hegemony during the first stages of the official historiography of the Exodus Affair.

The faults inflicting the first stages of writing the history of the period prior to the founding of the state were also the result of the fact that this was an official and semi-official historiography of a national liberation movement, which was creating its national myth, striving to establish its role as "master of its own destiny" and victor in the struggle against foreign rule. Of course, this kind of writing stresses the role played by the Zionist struggle in the foundation of the state, while understating the significance of international events and of economic, global and strategic considerations. A further distortion was caused by the fact that the British documents had not been revealed at the time of writing, which made it impossible to know the overall balance of considerations which guided the decision makers on the issue of Palestine.

The same weak points in the first stages of writing the history of the period in general, are also evident in writing the history of the Exodus Affair. Its closeness to the dramatic developments on the political front resulted in immediate and retrospective comments on its contribution to the UNSCOP conclusions; to Britain's decision to leave Palestine; to the United Nations 29 November 1947 decision; and to the foundation of the state in general. *Exodus* was a symbol and it was easy to attach coronets to an event as impressive and dramatic as this was, some of which were deserved by the entire illegal immigration operation, and others, the fruits of wishful thinking and a search for replies to questions, the answers to which are complex and complicated. It was tempting to latch on to the Exodus Affair as the key to understanding theses processes and changes.

For example, in *Sefer Toldot ha-Haganah* (History of the Haganah): "The illegal immigration operation, which, in the passing of time became something gray and routine, which ceased to cause reverberations in the world, became once again a bleeding wound, crying to high heaven. The world could not disregard it. The cry of the *Exodus* immigrants echoed through the halls of Lake Success, where the political fate of Palestine was being discussed at the time" (Slutzky 1972a, 1165). However, in truth, it is hard to find traces of the Exodus Affair and of the illegal immigration operation altogether in the debates of the United Nations General Assembly and its committees between September and November 1947, and we have already pointed out that *Exodus* had no effect on the recommendations of UNSCOP.

Today, after British archive material has been made available, the view is that illegal immigration, including the Exodus Affair, did not play a major role in Britain's decision to bring the Palestine issue before the United Nations and to leave the country. Even those who delegate importance to the illegal immigration operation and other forms of struggle used by the organized Yishuv and the dissident organizations, do so in the sense that these activities only reinforced the trend to which Britain tended anyway as a result of economic, strategic and imperial considerations (Kolat et al. 1980; Cohen 1982, 278; Bullock 1983, 367).

Another example, inter-Zionist this time, of a historiographic contortion, is the following description of the contribution of the Exodus Affair to founding of the state and of Ben-Gurion's part in it: "Ben-Gurion was aware, that more than any 'historical right', more even than moral obligation on the part of the world toward the Jewish people, as expressed in the Balfour Declaration and the Mandate – the tragedy of the Jewish DPs in Europe was the most convincing argument for the members of UNSCOP to recommend founding the state. Thus he was not satisfied only with the testimony he himself presented to the committee. He took a big part in preparing the most devastating 'testimony' of all to be presented to the members of the international committee – the *Exodus*." After describing the way the ship had been prepared, her voyage to Palestine, the mid-sea battle, the three casualties and her arrival at the port of Haifa, Ben-Gurion's biographer writes: "The death of the three, and the tragedy of the 5,000 *Exodus* immigrants were not in vain; on the quay in the port of Haifa, watching in agitation, stood members of the United Nations inquiry committee. Ben-Gurion was absolutely certain that the Jewish state was knocking at the gates" (Bar-Zohar 1977, 575–76).

Due to his position and standing Ben-Gurion played an important part in determining the activity of the Zionist movement and the Yishuv, and he was the chief architect of the Zionist policy of attaching the problem of the Jewish DPs in Europe to the founding of a Jewish state in Palestine. But in what way was he directly involved in *Exodus*?

The author of the above quoted paragraph, Michael Bar-Zohar, also wrote: "At every phase of his life and in the history of his people, Ben-Gurion sensed clearly the focal point of activity and decision. And at each stage, he knew how to place himself at the center of this focal point, to pick up the reins and to lead" (Bar-Zohar 1977, 573). When the ship *President Warfield* was purchased and restored in the Unites States, Ben-Gurion undertook the Security Portfolio in the Jewish Agency Executive. During the long weeks in which the ship was being prepared for her journey to Europe, he sat in his home in Tel Aviv and made plans for the next stage in the struggle – war with the Arabs. He showed very little interest in the whereabouts of the Exodus Affair. This could be explained by his illness during the months of July and August 1947 and the fact that he was even hospitalized.[17] And, of course, from its very beginning, the Exodus Affair had been in direct opposition to his own concept of the illegal immigration operation. However, the more significant reason was that throughout the summer and autumn months of 1947, illegal immigration was not at the center of Zionist activity according to Ben-Gurion's concepts. He was already one step ahead. However, since the Exodus Affair was one of the cornerstones in the heroic struggle for the founding of the state, it was quite proper to present Ben-Gurion as senior partner in its preparation.

The struggle over the glory of *Exodus*, which had begun with the landing of the immigrants on German soil continued for many years, both verbally and in writing. One of its peaks was the *Exodus* rally in 1964, as part of the officially organized "Ha'apalah Year". The stage was taken by members of Mapai who had taken part in the affair. The rally ended with cries from the crowd: "Bring on Mordechai Roseman", and "We want Mordechai". Written accusations were then flung by the participants at each other. These claimed that the immigrants had been overlooked at the rally and that amendments had been made to the events, in order to "make compatible with the spirit of the time and the interests of the reigning party" (Peker 1964). On the other side, complaints were made that "there had been deliberate incitement on the part of someone who had not been satisfied and honored" (Perry 1964).

Twenty-three years later, the fortieth anniversary celebrations for *Exodus* were held in a relaxed and amiable atmosphere. The immigrants had already become veteran Israelis, of equal status with those who had been their escorts. And a quarter of a century had passed, rich with events and new conflicts, which had produced long standing political alliances between sides which in the past had been rivals, and united them against common adversaries. All these helped old arguments to be forgotten – "historic", in every sense of the word – which may have been no more than the fruit of the historians' imagination. And in a kind of peace which comes from seeing things from the perspective of years, all came together in the true partnership they had known during those difficult days, those trying days at sea and on land, in the summer and autumn of 1947.

Notes

1 CRISIS

1. In the spring of 1947 distribution of the Jewish DP population in Germany was thus: the American zone, some 157,000; the British zone, some 15,000; the French zone, some 2,000; in West Berlin, some 10,000; in Austria, some 44,000; in Italy, some 19,000 (Proudfoot n.d., 341; Wischnitzer 1948, 264).
2. Major-General R. H. Dewing. To the British deputy War Minister. 18 August 1945. PRO. FO 945/599.
3. Wischnitzer 1948, 266. The statement was made by General Joseph MacNarney, who replaced General Dwight D. Eisenhower as Commander of the American Forces in Europe.
4. No accurate statistics are available on the numbers of people who left the camps. According to Slutzky, at the end of 1946, about half of the Jews in Germany were living in towns or villages (1972a, 1027). This is obviously exaggerated. In a report written in October 1947, two months after completing a 15 month term of office as advisor on Jewish affairs to the Commander of American Forces in Europe, Rabbi Philip Bernstein points out that in the summer of 1947 some 80 percent of the Jews in Germany were living in camps and DP centers and not in towns.
5. Head of the DPs Administration in the American HQ in Germany, General Stanley Michaelson, claimed that, based on military sources, 60 percent of the Jewish DPs would choose emigration to Palestine if they had the choice; 20 percent would choose countries overseas; 14 percent had not yet made up their minds and only 1 percent expressed the desire to return to their country of origin (Bauer 1970, 202–203). In advance of the Anglo-American Committee, the United Nations Relief and Rehabilitation Agency (UNRRA) distributed a questionnaire among 19,311 people, of whom 96.8 percent replied that they would choose Palestine, and only 393 expressed the desire to emigrate to the United States (Bauer 1970, 202).
6. An internal British document, 13 August 1947. PRO. FO 371/61821; Foreign Office. To Paris. 11 Sept. 1947. Ibid; answers sent by the secretary of the Jewish Agency's Immigration Department to people in Palestine, who requested certificates for their relatives. CZA. S6/1103.
7. Correspondence between the Foreign Office, which was responsible for the British zone in Germany, and the Colonial Office, which was responsible for distributing the certificates. 6 August 1947. PRO. CO 537/2277.
8. *News Bulletin of the Jewish Agency Immigration Department* (Hebrew), no. 56. 25 June 1947. CZA. S6/5045.

9. The number ten thousands is the result of calculations based on: Yahil testimony; "Departure for Palestine" (undated report). Brichah file/Germany. HHA; Habbas 1954, 23.

10. Menachem Braun. Letter. 28 July 1947. CZA. S6/262; Habbas 1954, 23–24; Bernstein 1947; Braginsky 1965, 374.

11. Wischnitzer 1948, 273–75; Bernstein 1947; "Letter", signed by "Alexander from Revivim". 4 July 1947. *Zror Yedi'ot*. 3 August 1947. CZA. S6/262.

12. Yitzhak Tabenkin, who visited the camps in Germany at the beginning of 1947, got the impression that "despair was rampant in the camps, and many of the inmates had begun seeking out relatives in America, who would help them financially, and especially send them the permits necessary for entry into the United States" (Braginsky 1965, 374).

13. The law went into effect on 1 July 1948. The President signed it, heavy-heartedly, on 25 June 1948. His reservations were that the law discriminates against DPs of the Jewish faith (Devine 1957, 110–29; Hartmann 1971, 23 and 175–79).

14. Haim Hoffman. Letter, 7 June 1946. CZA. S6/4685; Moshe Shertok at a meeting of the Jewish Agency Executive in Jerusalem. 14 March 1947; meeting of the Jewish Agency Executive in Jerusalem. 21 July 1947.

15. Shertok at a meeting of the Jewish Agency Executive in Jerusalem. 14 March 1947.

16. "A review of the 'Nocham' situation, May–June 1947" (Hebrew). Munich, 16 July 1947. CZA. S6/262.

17. This kind of advertising was published at the time in the American press by "The Political Action Committee for Palestine". For example, *PM*. 4 May 1947.

18. Wording of the interpellation, consultation between the Foreign Office and the Colonial Office on the issue, and Bevin's reply: PRO. FO 371/61806.

2 "THE YANKS ARE COMING"

1. Cunningham (Palestine). To Secretary of State for the Colonies. 28 Feb. 1947. PRO. FO 371/61839.

2. Morris Bernstein. 23 July 1947. CZA. F41/119.

3. Bill Bernstein. To his mother. N.d. Ibid. Partially quoted in Gruber 1948, 45. Similar sentiments are expressed in a letter to his brother in which he wrote of his desire to "spend a few months looking around Palestine and I suppose on my way back, I'll drop back into Europe for a quick look around" (15 May 1947. CZA. F41/119).

4. The second non-Jewish American in the crew was the chief engineer, Frank Stanzac.

5. Rome. To Foreign Office. 9 May 1947. PRO. FO 371/61841.

6. Bill [Bernstein]. To his brother. Undated, but apparently written before the ship left North America. CZA. F4/119.

7. Bill [Bernstein]. To his brother. 9 March 1947. Ibid.

8. Arnon. To Leonard. 5 June 1947. HHA. 14/530.

9. Arnon. To Yis'ar. 29 June 1947. Ibid. There were many such messages: Arnon. To Yis'ar. 3 July 1947. HHA. 14/702; Hofi. To Arnon. 29 June 1947. HHA. 14/530.

10. Arnon. To Sidney. 3 July 1947. HHA. 14/532.

11. Arnon. To ha-kli. 14 July 1947. Exodus File a.

12. Amnon. To Arnon. 16 July 1947. Ibid.

13. Hofi. To Arnon. 25 July 1947. HHA. 14/533.

14. Arnon. To Yis'ar and Sidney and Leonard. 17 Sept. 1947. HHA. 14/537.

3 CRESCENDO

1. Washington. To Foreign Office. 11 March 1947. PRO. FO 371/61839.
2. Note on illegal immigration. 3 March 1947. PRO. FO 371/61750/E2009.
3. Meetings of the Cabinet. 10 and 19 Dec. 1946. PRO. Cab 128/6.
4. John Higham (Colonial Office). To J. G. S. Beith (Foreign Office). 12 Feb. 1947. PRO. FO 371/61801.
5. Palestine (Cunningham). To Secretary of State for the Colonies. 9 Feb. 1947. PRO. FO 371/61838.
6. Internal document, Defense Office. 18 Jan. 1947. PRO. FO 371/61894; Palestine (Cunningham). To Secretary of State for the Colonies. 9 March 1947. PRO. CO 537/2334; Commander-in-Chief Mediterranean. To Admiralty. 9 March 1947. PRO. FO 371/61804.
7. John Balfour (British embassy in Washington). To Don J. J. Vallarino (ambassador of Panama in Washington). 10 March 1947. PRO. FO 371/61839.
8. PRO. FO Files 371/61839-61840, contain countless instances of correspondence relating to the *President Warfield*.
9. Foreign Office. To Lisbon. 3 April 1947. PRO. FO 371/61840.
10. Document. 25 April 1947. PRO. FO 371/61805; Teguciagalpa. To Foreign Office. 9 May 1947. PRO. FO 371/61806.
11. Defense Office. To Commander-in-Chief Mediterranean. 14 March 1947. PRO. FO 371/61803.
12. Meeting of the Cabinet. 20 March 1947. PRO. Cab 128/9.
13. C. J. Jeffries. To J. G. Lang. 5 April 1947. PRO. FO 371/61804; T. I. K. Lloyd. To J. G. Lang. 16 April 1947. PRO. FO 371/61805.
14. Meeting of the Cabinet. 1 May 1947. PRO. Cab 128/9.
15. Bevin. To Attlee. 2 May 1947. PRO. FO 371/61806.
16. Ibid.
17. Washington. To Foreign Office. 21 April 1947. PRO. FO 371/61805.
18. Foreign Office. To British delegate to the United Nations, New York. 25 April 1947. Ibid.
19. Foreign Office. To Rome. 30 April 1947. PRO. FO 371/61840.
20. Rome. To Foreign Office. 10 May 1947. PRO. FO 371/61841.
21. Rome. To Foreign Office. 12 May 1947. Ibid.
22. Cabinet Illegal Immigration Committee. 13 May 1947. PRO. FO 371/61811.
23. Cabinet Illegal Immigration Committee. 7 June 1947. Ibid.
24. Yis'ar. To Arnon. 26 April 1947. HHA. 14/331; Neter. To Arnon. 27 April 1947. HHA. 14/704; Ehud Avriel at a meeting of Mapai Central Committee. 26 June 1947. LPA. 23/47.
25. Neter. To Arnon. 18 May 1947. HHA. 14/530. Original emphasis.
26. Ibid.
27. Ibid.
28. Ibid.; E. Avriel at a meeting of Mapai Central Committee. 26 June 1947. LPA 23/47.
29. E. Avriel at a meeting of Mapai Central Committee. 26 June 1947. LPA 23/47.
30. Ibid.; Neter. To Arnon. 18 May 1947. HHA. 14/530.
31. Neter. To Arnon. 18 May 1947. HHA. 14/530; Leonard. To Arnon. 5 July 1947. HHA. 14/532.
32. Leonard. To Arnon. 5 July 1947. HHA. 14/532; Braginsky 1965, 376.
33. Rome. To Foreign Office. 12 May 1947. PRO. FO 371/61841.
34. Rome. To Foreign Office. 13 June 1947. PRO. FO 371/61811.

35. British embassy, Paris. To French Foreign Ministry. 17 May 1947. PRO. FO 371/61842.
36. Document submitted to the Cabinet Illegal Immigration Committee. 7 July 1947. PRO. FO 371/61845.
37. Marseilles. To Foreign Office. 18 June 1947. PRO. FO 371/61812. In a debate in the Working Party of the Cabinet Illegal Immigration Committee, 2 July 1947, mention was made of six suspicious ships (PRO. FO 371/61814), five of which, including the *President Warfield*, were indeed illegal immigrant ships.
38. Paris. To Foreign Office. 23 June 1947. FO 371/61813.
39. Paris (Duff Cooper). To Foreign Office. 12 May 1947. PRO. FO 371/61807; and 13 May 1947. PRO. FO 371/61806; meeting of the Cabinet Illegal Immigration Committee. 16 May 1947. PRO. FO 945/494.
40. Meeting of the Cabinet Illegal Immigration Committee. 9 June 1947. PRO. FO 371/61811.
41. 27 June 1947. Ibid.
42. Meeting of the Cabinet Illegal Immigration Committee. 9 June 1947. Ibid.
43. Foreign Office. To Paris. 9 July 1947. PRO. FO 371/61814.
44. Foreign Office. To Paris. 14 June 1947. PRO. FO 371/61811.
45. Paris. To Foreign Office. 16 June 1947. PRO. FO 371/61812.
46. Marseilles. To Paris. 16 June 1947. Ibid.
47. Paris. To Foreign Office. 23 June and 3 July 1947. PRO. FO 371/61813.
48. Paris. To Foreign Office. 23 June 1947. Ibid.
49. Paris. To Foreign Office. 3 July 1947. Ibid.
50. Foreign Office. To Marseilles. 25 June 1947. Ibid.; Marseilles. To Foreign Office. 26 June 1947. PRO. FO 371/61814; Foreign Office. To Marseilles. 1 July 1947. Ibid.
51. Foreign Office. To Paris. 27 June 1947. PRO. FO 371/61813.
52. Bevin. To Bidault. 27 June 1947. PRO. FO 371/61811.
53. Document prepared for a meeting of the Cabinet Illegal Immigration Committee. 7 July 1947. PRO. FO 371/61845.
54. In a document titled "Refoulement – Future Policy", 3 Sept. 1947 (PRO. FO 371/61825), which was prepared toward the completion of the *President Warfield* affair, specific mention was made that the original objective was to implement the refoulement with regard to Italy and not to France.

4 A SHIP FOR ALL JEWS

1. Eliyahu Dobkin at the Zionist General Council, 1947.
2. Appendix to weekly report no. 51 of the Sixth Airborne Division. PRO. WO 275/60. The document bears no date, but it is clear that it was written immediately following the capture of *Exodus* in July 1947.
3. "A review of the 'Nocham' situation, May–June 1947" (in Hebrew). Munich, 16 July 1947. CZA. S6/262.
4. Yis'ar. To Itay. 7 July 1947. HHA. 14/532.
5. France. To Arnon and Itay. 25 June 1947. HHA. 14/704.
6. Diary 1947a; appendix to weekly report no. 51 of the Sixth Airborne Division. PRO. WO 275/60; Habbas 1954, 60; Exodus File a.
7. Amnon. To Arnon. 15 July 1947. Exodus File a.
8. Cunningham (Palestine). To the Secretary of State for the Colonies. 19 July 1947. PRO. FO 371/61816.
9. Some 600 members of Nocham and Gordonia; some 550 members of Dror; some

550 members of ha-Shomer ha-Tza'ir; some 300 members of ha-No'ar ha-Tziyoni; some 250 members of Po'alei Agudat Israel; some 300 members of Bnei Akiva; some 70 members of Betar; as well as members of Mizrachi, Agudat Israel, Po'alei Zion Left and Pahah (Exodus File a; Reichman 1947; "A review of the 'Nocham' situation, May–June 1947" [in Hebrew], Munich, 16 July 1947. CZA. S6/262; notes preserved by Mordechai Roseman).

10. Shadmi 1964. Speaking 17 years after the events took place, Shadmi talked about the waiting period as having taken a number of weeks, while, in fact the period had been only a few days.
11. MA. D.1.5943.

5 THE BIRD FLEW THE COOP

1. Neter and Ur. To Arnon. 16 June 1947. HHA. 14/704.
2. To Delphi. 13 June 1947. HHA. 14/530.
3. Arnon. To Neter. 18 June 1947. HHA. 14/702.
4. Allon 1947, 841; Elisha. To Hofshi. 20 April 1947. HHA. 14/331; Sereni 1947.
5. To Delphi. 15 June 1947. HHA. 14/530.
6. George Lichtheim. To Gershon Hirsh. 4 May 1947. CZA. S25/2233. Cited by Nussinov 1969, 184.
7. Paris. To Marseilles. 10 July 1947. PRO. FO 371/61815.
8. Ibid.
9. The account from the British side: Paris. To London. 22 July 1947. PRO. FO 371/61818.
10. Main points of a report presented by Jules Moch to his Prime Minister at the end of July on the Exodus Affair, quoted in: Yanai. To Arnon. 12 Dec. 1947. Exodus File a.
11. Amnon. To Rudy. 11 July [1947], 07:30, no. 5. HHA. 14/702.
12. Bevin. To Bidault. 27 June 1947. PRO. FO 371/61811.
13. Bevin. To Bidault. 12 July 1947. Ibid.; Bevin's conversation with Bidault. 12 July 1947. PRO. FO 371/61815.
14. Bevin. To Bidault. 12 July 1947. PRO. FO 371/61811.
15. British Embassy Paris (Duff Cooper, in the name of the Secretary of State). To French Foreign Ministry. 13 July 1947. PRO. FO 371/61816.
16. Foreign Office. To Paris. 15 July 1947. PRO. FO 371/61815.
17. Creech-Jones. To Cunningham. 14 July 1947. Ibid.
18. Document. 16 July 1947. PRO. FO 371/61816.
19. British Embassy in Paris. To Foreign Office [Bevin was in Paris at the time and the message was from him]. 12 July 1947. PRO. FO 371/61815.
20. Creech-Jones. To Cunningham. 14 July 1947. Ibid.
21. Palestine (Cunningham). To Secretary of State for the Colonies. 15 July 1947. PRO. FO 371/61816.
22. Secretary of State for the Colonies. To Palestine (Cunningham). 16 July 1947. Ibid.
23. Paris. To Foreign Office. 16 July 1947. Ibid.
24. Secretary of State for the Colonies. To Palestine (Cunningham). 16 July 1947. Ibid.
25. Foreign Office. To Paris. 15 July 1947. PRO. FO 371/61815.
26. Paris. To Foreign Office. 16 July 1947. PRO. FO 371/61816.
27. Creech-Jones. To Cunningham. 14 July 1947. PRO. FO 371/61815.
28. Secretary of State for the Colonies. To Palestine (Cunningham). 16 July 1947. PRO. FO 371/61816.

29. Paris. To Foreign Office. 16 July 1947. Ibid.
30. Document. 16 July 1947. Ibid.; Paris. To Foreign Office. 18 July 1947. Ibid.
31. Internal Foreign Office document. 17 July 1947. Ibid.

6 SEVEN DAYS ON THE SEVEN SEAS

1. Summary of the casualties of the illegal immigration operation. CZA. S6/4304.
2. Tel Aviv. To Paris. 26 May 1947. HHA. 14/702.
3. Yis'ar. To Arnon. 12 July 1947. Exodus File a.
4. Amnon. To Arnon. 14 July 1947. Ibid.
5. Arnon. To ha-kli. 15 July 1947. Ibid.
6. Report by commander of the British Forces. 17 July 1947, 10:15 hours. PRO. Adm 1/20685.
7. Foreign Office. To Paris, no. 1209. 23 Sept. 1947. PRO. FO 371/61825.
8. Amnon. To Ben-Yehuda and Rudy. 11 July 1947. HHA. 14/702.
9. Amnon. To Arnon. 13 July 1947. HHA. 14/705.
10. The President. To the people of the division. 13 July 1947. HHA. 14/702.
11. Amnon. To Rudy and Ben-Yehuda. 12 July 1947. Ibid.
12. Amnon. To Arnon. 15 July 1947. Exodus File a.

7 THE BATTLE

1. The President. To Mossad office in France. 11–13 July 1947. HHA. 14/702.
2. Amnon. To Arnon. 17 July 1947. Exodus File a.
3. Arnon. To ha-kli. 14 July 1947. Ibid.
4. Amnon. To Arnon. 14 July 1947. Ibid.; Arnon. To ha-kli. 15 July 1947. Ibid.
5. Amnon. To Arnon. 15 July 1947. Ibid.; Arnon. To Amnon. 16 July 1947. Ibid.; Amnon. To Arnon. 16 July 1947. Ibid.
6. Amnon. To Arnon. 16 July 1947. Ibid.
7. Arnon and Matityahu. To Amnon. 17 July 1947. Ibid.
8. Arnon. To ha-kli. 17 July 1947. Ibid.
9. 13 July 1947. HHA. 14/705.
10. Conversation between Bevin and Bidault. 12 July 1947. PRO. FO 371/61815.
11. The President. To Arnon. 18 July 1947. Exodus File a.
12. For example, so claimed the judge in the "Habeas Corpus" trial which took place in London at the end of August 1947. PRO. CO 537/2403. This claim appears also in Wilson 1949, 135.
13. Commander-in-Chief Mediterranean. To Admiralty. 12 August 1947. PRO. Adm 1/20789; British report which reached the Haganah at the beginning of Sept. 1947. Exodus File a.
14. Paris. To Foreign Office. 18 July 1947. PRO. FO 371/61816; Cunningham. To Secretary of State for the Colonies. 20 July 1947. Ibid.
15. Foreign Office. To Prague and Washington. 24 July 1947. PRO. FO 371/61817.
16. For example: *Yagur, Henrietta Szold, Katriel Yaffe* and *Kaf Gimel Yordei ha-Sira*, the first ships whose passengers were deported to Cyprus (Gil'ad 1953, 580); the ship *La-Negev* ("Mercia") was intercepted 22 miles off-shore (Cunningham. To Secretary of State for the Colonies. 9 Feb. 1947. PRO. FO 371/61838).
17. Description of the battle, preparations and preliminary conclusions, from the British point of view, based on "Report on Interception".

18. Commander-in-Chief Mediterranean. Report. 1 August 1947. PRO. Adm 1/20789.
19. British report on the capture of the ship, Exodus File a; British response on broadcasts from the ship. 19 July 1947. PRO. FO 371/61817.
20. "Report on Interception"; British response on broadcasts from the ship. 19 July 1947. PRO. FO 371/61817.
21. Commander-in-Chief Mediterranean. To First Sea Lord (Personal). 26 August 1947. PRO. Adm 1/20789.
22. Report to the Mossad on a meeting with high ranking officer. 23 June 1947. HHA. 14/531.
23. British report on capture of the ship. Exodus File a.
24. Palestine command. To Commander-in-Chief Mediterranean. 19 July 1947. PRO. FO 371/61817.
25. Mossad report. 18 July 1947. HHA. 14/533; reports by two British officers. PRO. Adm 1/20685.
26. Report prepared by Admiralty for the purpose of a discussion on ways to capture illegal immigrant ships, following the experience gained in the *President Warfield* battle. N.d. PRO. Adm 1/20789; Palestine command. To Commander-in-Chief Mediterranean. 18 July 1947. PRO. FO371/61817.
27. Commander-in-Chief Mediterranean. To Secretary of the Admiralty. 15 Sept. 1947. PRO. Adm 1/20685.
28. The personal letter to the First Sea Lord was sent on 26 August 1947 (see note 21 above) and then was quoted by his secretary in a letter to the Head of the Military Department at the Admiralty. 1 Sept. 1947. PRO. Adm 1/20789.
29. Commander-in-Chief Mediterranean. To Admiralty. 1 August 1947. Appendix 2. PRO. Adm 1/20789.
30. Undated Admiralty document. PRO. Adm 1/20789.
31. Arnon. To Yis'ar and Leonard. 28 July 1947. HHA. 14/533.
32. See note 29 above.
33. In Exodus File a there are no records of wireless broadcasts on 18 July 1947 between the hours 02:42 and 06.46. The decision to cease resistance was taken at around 5:00. See also Habbas 1954, 49: "At five o'clock on Friday morning, *following* a night of fighting, we renewed communications with the coast" (emphasis added). Elsewhere, the radio officer tells how "at about three in the morning ... we suddenly heard a terrific noise and we were informed that we were under attack by destroyers of the British Navy. I ordered the wireless operator to call the coast urgently in order to renew communications. However, since this call was not made during communications time, we received no reply for a couple of hours" (Einav 1947).
34. To ha-kli. 18 July 1947. Exodus File a.
35. Derogy 1972, 142–43. Accuracy is very important here, since this source has been used for other books. It appeared in Bethell 1979, 331–32; and then Bethell's book served as the main source in describing the battle in Bevin's biography (Bullock 1983, 449).

8 WHERE NOW?

1. To Delphi. 2 June 1947. HHA. 14/530.
2. To Delphi. 4 June 1947. Ibid.
3. To Delphi. 6 June 1947. Ibid.
4. Yishai. To Hillel. 23 June 1947. HHA. 14/531.
5. Documents. 20 and 21 July 1947. Exodus File a; documents at Exodus File b; CZA.

S25/1695; meeting of Jewish Agency Executive in London. 21 July 1947. CZA. Z4/302/32.

6. Paris. To Foreign Office. 18 July 1947. PRO. FO 371/61816.
7. Foreign Office. To Paris. 19 July 1947. Ibid.
8. To all British Ambassadors in the world. 19 July 1947. Ibid.
9. United Kingdom. Parliamentary Debate (Commons), 5th ser., vol. 440 (1947), 1044–45. The question was raised by Silverman following an initiative on the part of the Jewish Agency in London, who approached him on the matter previously (Jewish Agency, London 1947. 21 July).
10. Exchange of messages between the Foreign Office in London and the British embassy in Paris. 21–22 July 1947. PRO. FO 371/61817.
11. Ibid.; communication between Palestine and the Colonial Office. 23 and 30 July 1947 (PRO. FO 371/61819), and 22 August 1947 (PRO. FO 371/61821).
12. Shertok. To Epstein. 22 July 1947. CZA. S25/1695.
13. Bogota. To Foreign Office. 22 July 1947, no. 164. PRO. FO 371/61817.
14. Paris. To Foreign Office. 22 July 1947. Ibid; Paris. To Foreign Office. 25 July 1947. PRO. FO 371/61819; Crossley 1947. On the element of corruption in the way the visas to Colombia were issued, i.e. the consul was paid several dollars for each visa, and he gave the Mossad free hand in stamping the passports: Har'el 1985.
15. Meeting in Colonial Office. 24 July 1947. CZA. S25/7567. From the British side: Document. 25 July 1947. PRO. CO 733/491/1.
16. Cunningham. To Secretary of State for the Colonies. 19 July 1947. PRO. FO 371/61816.
17. Gregson (D3). To Admiralty. 25 July 1947. PRO. FO 371/61819; Gruber 1948, 84–85.
18. Paris. To Foreign Office. 24 July 1947. PRO. FO 371/61818; Foreign Office. To Paris. 25 July 1947. Ibid.; Paris. To Foreign Office. 26 July 1947. PRO. FO 371/61819. Negotiations between France and Britain on the use of force and composition of the French announcement to the illegal immigrants is repeated frequently in PRO. FO 371 files: 61818, 61819 and 61821.
19. Shertok. To Sneh. 22 July 1947. CZA. S25/1695; Shertok. To Epstein. 23 July 1947. Ibid.
20. G. R. To Shertok. 23 July 1947. Ibid.
21. Paris. To Jewish Agency in Jerusalem. 22 July 1947. Ibid.
22. Yis'ar. To Arnon. 22 and 23 July 1947. HHA. 14/533.
23. Yis'ar. To Arnon. 23 July 1947. Ibid.
24. Paris. To Foreign Office. 23 July 1947. PRO. FO 371/61818.
25. Paris. To Foreign Office. 28 July 1947. PRO. FO 371/61819.

9 WE SHALL NOT LAND!

1. Arnon. To ha-kli. 14 and 16 July 1947. Exodus File a; Amnon. To Arnon. 16 July 1947. Ibid.
2. Paris. To Foreign Office. 25 July 1947. PRO. FO 371/61818.
3. Foreign Office. To Paris. 26 July 1947. PRO. FO 371/61819 (original emphases).
4. Foreign Office. To Paris. 26 July 1947. PRO. FO 371/61818.
5. Internal British Foreign Office document. End of July 1947. PRO. FO 371/61821.
6. Paris. To Foreign Office. 25 July 1947. PRO. FO 371/61818.
7. Foreign Office. To Paris. 26 July 1947. PRO. FO 371/61819; To Commander-in-Chief Mediterranean. 29 July 1947. Ibid.

8. Yis'ar. To Arnon. 26 July 1947. HHA. 14/533.
9. Paris. To Foreign Office. 28 July 1947. PRO. FO 371/61819.
10. To Commander-in-Chief Mediterranean. 24 July 1947. Ibid.
11. Yis'ar. To Arnon. 23 July 1947. HHA. 14/533; Paris. To Foreign Office. 24 July 1947. PRO. FO 371/61821.
12. Report. 26 July 1947. PRO. Adm 1/20684; Perry 1985.
13. From the British side: Marseilles. To Foreign Office. 1 August 1947. PRO. FO 371/61821.
14. The following description is based on: Internal British report. 29 July 1947. PRO. FO 371/61819; Marseilles. To Foreign Office. 29 July 1947. PRO. FO 371/61820; Marseilles. To Foreign Office. 1 August 1947. PRO. FO 371/61821; Habbas 1954, 82; Roseman 1985; Einor 1985.
15. Marseilles. To Foreign Office. 29 July 1947. PRO. FO 371/61820.
16. Marseilles. To Jerusalem. 29 July 1947. PRO. FO 371/61846.
17. 21 August 1947. Exodus File b.
18. To Commander-in-Chief Mediterranean. 29 July 1947. PRO. FO 371/61819; internal British report. 29 July 1947. Ibid.; Paris. To Foreign Office. 29 July 1947. Ibid.
19. Description of the French delegation's visit to the *Empire Rival* is based on: Habbas 1954, 87, 95–96, 123–24; Leichter 1985; Perry 1985; Tubul 1985; Marseilles. To Foreign Office. 30 July 1947. PRO. FO 371/61819; internal British document. 1 August 1947. PRO. FO 371/61821. The story of the youth and the flag is repeated in almost all the testimonies by Haganah activists and immigrants, but no mention is made of it in British documentation.
20. Description of visit to *Ocean Vigour* is based on: Habbas 1954, 87; Ganuz 1985, 206–207; Marseilles. To Foreign Office. 30 July 1947. PRO. FO 371/61819; internal British document. 1 August 1947. PRO. FO 371/61821.

10 A FLOATING CONCENTRATION CAMP

1. There were small differences in the length of the ships. *Empire Rival*, 446 feet; *Ocean Vigour*, 442 feet; *Runnymede Park*, 425 feet. Palestine. To Colonial Office. 19 July 1947. PRO. FO 371/61816.
2. Paris. To Foreign Office. 30 July 1947. PRO. FO 371/61819.
3. Commanders-in-Chief Mediterranean. To Chiefs of Staff. 28 Jan. 1947. PRO. FO 371/61894.
4. Crew of *Ocean Vigour*. To British consul in Port Said. 8 Jan. 1947. PRO. FO 371/61801; the ship's captain confirmed the crew's complaint in a letter to the consul. 9 Jan. 1947. Ibid.
5. Crew of *Ocean Vigour*. To British consul in Port Said. 8 Jan. 1947. Ibid.
6. Report of Jewish Agency representative, I. Linton. 3 August 1947. Exodus File b.
7. Paris. To Foreign Office. 30 July 1947. PRO. FO 371/61819.
8. Yis'ar. To Arnon. 23 July 1947. HHA. 14/533.
9. Almost every day a report was sent from Marseilles to London on the number of immigrants who had landed, and on days when none had landed, this too was reported (PRO. FO 371/61822).
10. Marseilles. To Foreign Office. 1 August 1947. PRO. FO 371/61820; Marseilles. To Foreign Office. 2 August 1947. Ibid.
11. Colonial Office. To Bevin. 14 August 1947. PRO. FO 371/61822.
12. According to Mossad documents, eight people disembarked on the day of sailing

(Yis'ar. To Arnon. 23 August 1947. HHA. 14/535). According to British reports – six (Marseilles. To Foreign Office. 22 August 1947. PRO. FO 371/61822).
13. Colonial Office. To Bevin. 14 August 1947. PRO. FO 371/61822.
14. *Ha-Olam* reported, that out of 129 people who disembarked, 112 were hospitalized (14 August 1947).
15. Habbas 1954, 190: 1,200; the JDC estimated that of the *Exodus* passengers to reach the German camps after landing at Hamburg, 800 were orthodox Jews in need of kosher food (JDCJA. Geneva files, S-1405, box 22b).
16. Report by I. Linton. 3 August 1947. Exodus File b.
17. PRO. Adm 1/20684; Gruber 1948, 114.
18. Reports by British Naval Officers. PRO. Adm 1/20684.
19. Marseilles. To Foreign Office. 3 August 1947. PRO. FO 371/61820.
20. Foreign Office. To Marseilles. 29 July 1947. PRO. FO 371/61819. The censor in Jerusalem prevented the publication of an item from Paris: "In the case of resistance on the part of the immigrants to landing at the French shore, the army will cease all supply of food and water to the immigrants and will destroy all food on board ship in order to force the immigrants to leave the ship." To Delphi. 23 July 1947. HHA. 14/533.

11 NOT BY BREAD ALONE

1. The matter is mentioned several times in PRO. FO 371/61821.
2. Avi (Schwartz). To *Runnymede Park*. 19 August 1947. MA. C.17.
3. Excerpts from letters from *Exodus* immigrants were published in *Dvar ha-Po'elet*, 14 Oct. 1947; many letters were included in Habbas 1954.
4. Summary of the Exodus Affair as reviewed in the American press. 25 Sept. 1947. Exodus File b. List of articles on *Exodus* published in the American press: Holly 1969, 294–98.
5. Paris. To Foreign Office. 21 August 1947. PRO. FO 371/61822.
6. Commanding Officer, HMS *Phoebe*. To Commander-in-Chief Mediterranean. 31 August 1947. PRO. Adm 1/20684.
7. Marseilles. To Foreign Office. 18 August 1947. PRO. FO 371/61822.
8. Marseilles. To Foreign Office. 19 August 1947. Ibid.
9. This information was distributed by *Reuters*: PRO. CO 733/491/1. About "The Hebrew Committee for National Liberation" see Baumel 1995, 82.
10. This claim has appeared elsewhere, e.g. the story of the French delegation's "interpreter" (who was a Mossad activist), Habbas 1954, 92.
11. Office of Commander-in-Chief Mediterranean. To Secretary of Admiralty. 13 Sept. 1947. PRO. Adm 1/20684.

12 IN THE SHADOW OF UNSCOP AND TERROR

1. Documents prepared in the Colonial Office. 5 April 1947 (PRO. FO 371/61804), and on 16 April 1947 (PRO. FO371/61805).
2. First quoted in *The New York Herald Tribune*, 19 July 1947; then included in Kirk 1954, 244; then quoted in Slutzky 1972a, 982; and so on.
3. The decision was accepted on 30 July. In favor of the visit: Australia, Uruguay, Guatemala, Holland, Canada and Sweden; against: Iran, India, Yugoslavia and Peru; the Czech representative abstained (*United Nations Weekly Bulletin* 3, no. 7, 12 August 1947).
4. The visit took place 8–14 August (United Nations 1949, 229).

5. As recorded in his book, 1949.
6. Iran and India voted against the visit, in favor of the minority recommendations and against the partition plan; Uruguay, Guatemala, Holland, Canada and Sweden voted in favor of the visit, in favor of the majority recommendations and in favor of the partition plan; Yugoslavia voted against the visit, in favor of the minority recommendations and abstained on 29 November 1947; Australia voted in favor of the visit, abstained at the end of August and voted in favor of the partition plan; the exceptions were: Peru, who voted against the visit but in favor of the majority recommendations and in favor of partition; Czechoslovakia, who abstained on the visit vote, voted in favor of the majority recommendations and the partition.
7. Shertok. To Epstein. 22 July 1947. CZA. S25/1695.
8. Epstein. To Shertok. 24 July 1947. Ibid.; Exodus File b.
9. Bevin. To Bidault. 12 July 1947. PRO. FO 371/61815.
10. For example, Ivor Thomas at a meeting with Jewish Agency representatives in London. 24 July 1947 (CZA. S25/7567).
11. London. To Jerusalem. 22 July 1947. CZA. S25/1695; Shertok. To London. 23 July 1947. Ibid.
12. Cunningham. To Secretary of State for the Colonies. Monthly report, July 1947. C.P. Box II, file 2.
13. Arnon. To Yis'ar. 21 July 1947. HHA. 14/553; Gil'ad 1953, 586–595.
14. Cunningham. To Foreign Secretary. 2 August 1947. C.P. Box II, file 2; and see note 12 above.
15. Shertok at a meeting of the Jewish Agency Executive in Jerusalem. 28 July 1947; Shertok. To Epstein. 22 July 1947. CZA. S25/1695; Shertok. Cable. 23 July 1947. Ibid.
16. Report by Golda Myerson on a conversation with the High Commissioner. 31 July 1947. CZA. S25/5601; Cunningham. To Foreign Secretary. 1 August 1947. C.P. Box II, file 2.
17. Meeting between Bevin and American ambassador in London. 2 August 1947. PRO. FO 371/61821.
18. Epstein. To Myerson. 2 August 1947. CZA. S25/1697; Shertok (Geneva). To Myerson. 4 August 1947. Ibid.
19. Lovett. To American ambassador in London. 22 August 1947. *FRUS* 1947, 1140; Marshall. To Bevin. 7 August 1947. Ibid., 1136–37. Bevin's letter to Marshall was sent on 27 June 1947. PRO. FO 371/61811.
20. Epstein. To Myerson. 2 August 1947. CZA. S25/1697; Shertok (Geneva). To Myerson. 4 August 1947. Ibid.; meeting of Jewish Agency Executive in the United States, New York. 5 August 1947. CZA. Z4/302/32.
21. Marc Jarblum, at Zionist General Council. 27 August 1947.
22. Crossman met Bevin on 4 August 1947 and told Aubrey (Abba) Eban about it at the beginning of August (Report by Aubrey Eban on his visit to London, CZA. S25/3891).
23. Cabinet 66 (47). 31 July 1947. PRO. Cab. 128/10.
24. Document. 3 Sept. 1947. PRO. FO 371/61826.

13 FROM CATHARSIS TO APATHY

1. Report by G. Myerson on a conversation with the High Commissioner. 31 July 1947. CZA. S25/5601.
2. Cunningham. To Foreign Secretary. 1 August 1947. C.P. Box II, file 2.

3. Document prepared in Colonial Office. 5 April 1947. PRO. FO 371/61804.
4. Report by Myerson on a conversation with the High Commissioner. Jewish Agency Executive, Jerusalem. 9 Feb. 1947.
5. Meetings at Colonial Office: (1) 21 July 1947. Exodus File b; (2) 23 July 1947. CZA. S25/7567; (3) 24 July 1947. Ibid.
6. Document. 4 June 1947. HHA. 14/530; to Delphi. 8 June 1947. Ibid.
7. Security Conference. 12 August 1947. CP. Box IV, file 1.
8. Report of the Sixth Airborne Division. 1 Sept. 1947. Exodus File a.
9. See Chapter 7.
10. Arnon. To Danny. 20 July 1947. HHA. 14/533; Arnon. To Yis'ar. 23 July 1947. Ibid.; Schind's reply was transferred to the Mossad in Tel Aviv via France on 25 July 1947. Exodus File a.
11. Letters sent by the secretary of the Immigration Department of the Jewish Agency to residents of Palestine who requested immigration certificates for their relatives. CZA. S6/1103.
12. It was decided in Sept. 1946, to raise PP100,000 from the Yishuv's urban population, to help fund the illegal immigration operation. Fundraising dragged on for many months and faded away in the end (Slutzky 1972a, 962–63).

14 THE LAST WEAPON: DEPORTATION TO GERMANY

1. See Chapter 8.
2. *JTA* report from London. 31 July 1947. Exodus File b.
3. Paris. To Foreign Office. 5 August 1947. PRO. FO 371/61820.
4. For example: War Office. To Commander-in-Chief Mediterranean. 28 July 1947. PRO. FO 371/61819.
5. 9 Sept. 1947. PRO. FO 371/61825, P7770/48/31 and E 8057/48/31.
6. Report prepared by Foreign Office for Cabinet meeting, 31 July 1947. PRO. FO 371/61820.
7. Paris. To Foreign Office. 1 August 1947. Ibid.
8. Report. Signed: J. G. S. Beith. 1 August 1947. Ibid.
9. To the Eastern Department. 6 August 1947. Ibid.
10. Report. Signed: J. G. S. Beith. 11 August 1947. PRO. FO 371/61821.
11. Creech-Jones. To Bevin. 14 August 1947. PRO. FO 371/61822.
12. Jewish illegal immigrants ex-*President Warfield*; meeting of Cabinet Committee on Illegal Immigration. 22 August 1947. PRO. Adm 1/20789.
13. See Chapter 3.
14. See note 6 above.
15. Internal document. 13 August 1947. PRO. FO 371/61821; Jewish illegal immigrants ex-*President Warfield*.
16. Foreign Office. To Berlin and Lübeck. 16 August 1947. PRO. FO 371/61822.
17. Paris. To Foreign Office. 1 August 1947. PRO. FO 371/61820.
18. Report. Signed: J. G. S. Beith. 13 August 1947. PRO. FO 371/61821.
19. Report. Signed: J. G. S. Beith. 22 August 1947. PRO. FO 371/61822.
20. See note 6 above.
21. Creech-Jones. To Bevin. 14 August 1947. PRO. FO 371/61822.
22. Document. Signed: Sir Orme Sargent. 19 August 1947. Ibid.
23. Document. Signed: J. G. S. Beith. 23 August 1947. Ibid.
24. Cunningham. To Secretary of State for the Colonies. 14 August 1947. Ibid.
25. Report. Signed: G. A. Exodus File b.

26. Golda Myerson. To Sir Alan Cunningham. 1 Sept. 1947. Exodus File b.
27. Creech-Jones. To Bevin. 14 August 1947. PRO. FO 371/61822; internal document. 14 August 1947. PRO. FO 371/61821.
28. Foreign Office. To Paris. 19 August 1947. PRO. FO 371/61822.
29. Colonial Office. To Palestine. 21 August 1947. Ibid.; Berl Locker. To Trafford Smith. 21 August 1947. PRO. CO 537/2403; *Davar*, 22 August 1947.
30. Foreign Office. To Marseilles. 20 August 1947. PRO. FO 371/61822.
31. Marseilles. To Foreign Office. 19 August 1947. Ibid.
32. Marseilles. To Foreign Office. 18 August 1947. Ibid.; Foreign Office. To Marseilles. 19 August 1947. Ibid.; Foreign Office. To Marseilles. 20 August 1947. Ibid.
33. MA. C. 17.2.5.
34. Marseilles. To Paris. 26 August 1947. PRO. FO 371/61825.
35. Paris. To Foreign Office. 21 August 1947. PRO. FO 371/61822.
36. Ibid.
37. Report of naval man. 21–31 August 1947. PRO. Adm 1/20684.
38. Avi Schwartz. MA. C.17.
39. MA. C.17.6.

15 A CHANGE OF SCENE

1. Telegrams and letters on this issue are concentrated in PRO. CO 733/491/1 and 491/2. By 5 Sept. 1947 84 letters and telegrams had been received; by 4 Oct. 1947 the number had grown to 199. Mrs Weizmann's telegram: PRO. CO 733/491/1.
2. Robert Lovett (Acting Secretary of State). To American ambassador in London. 22 August 1947. *FRUS* 1947, 1140.
3. Washington. To Foreign Office. 5 Sept. 1947. PRO. CO 733/491/2.
4. Washington. To Foreign Office. 26 August 1947. PRO. FO 371/61824.
5. Washington. To Foreign Office. 14 August 1947. PRO. FO 371/61822.
6. Bevin. To ambassador in Washington. 16 August 1947. Ibid.
7. Cabinet meeting. 29 July 1946. PRO. Cab 128/6.
8. Cabinet meeting. 20 June 1946. PRO. Cab 128/5.
9. Cabinet meeting. 8 July 1946. PRO. Cab 128/6.
10. Louis Douglas (American ambassador in UK). To Secretary of State. 26 August 1947. *FRUS* 1947, 1141–42; Epstein. To Shertok. 27 August 1947. CZA. S25/1697; Epstein. To Myerson. 3 August 1947. Ibid.
11. Internal Foreign Office document. Signed: J. G. S. Beith. 2 Sept. 1947. PRO. FO 371/61824.
12. American embassy in Paris. To Washington. 4 Sept. 1947. *FRUS* 1947, 1142.
13. Acting Secretary of State. To American Embassy in France. 31 August 1947. *FRUS* 1947, 1142 (emphasis added).
14. Epstein. To Myerson. 28 August 1947. CZA. S25/1697.
15. Washington. To Foreign Office. 21 August 1947. PRO. FO 371/61822.
16. See Chapter 1.
17. Robert Macatee (American consul-general in Jerusalem). To Secretary of State (Washington). 21 July 1947. *FRUS* 1947, 1130.
18. CZA. S25/3889; PRO. CO 537/2403.
19. Goldman. To Sandstrom (Geneva). 21 August 1947. Exodus File b.
20. Exodus File b, and PRO. CO 733/491/1.
21. Epstein. To Myerson. 30 August 1947. CZA. S25/1697.
22. Paris. To Foreign Office. 22 August 1947. PRO. FO 371/61823.

23. Ibid.
24. Internal document. 25 August 1947. Ibid.
25. Foreign Office. To Paris. 27 August 1947. Ibid.
26. Announcement no. 127. 21 August 1947. Exodus File b.
27. CZA. S25/6671.
28. Speech at a party for surviving members of the First Zionist Congress. 17 August 1947. Ben-Gurion 1950, 213–15.
29. Zionist General Council 1947. 26 August. Ben-Gurion made a point of mentioning that he was referring to the meeting as a closed one, and the chairman instructed the participants not to take notes.
30. Daniel Levin. To Shaul Avigur [Meirov]. 19 Sept. 1966. HHA. 4613.
31. Haim Yahil [Hoffman]. To Shaul Avigur. 31 July 1966. HPIC. Temporary symbol 20.4.
32. Circular issued by the Va'ad Le'umi (the National Council). 3 Sept. 1947. Exodus File b.
33. Weizmann's version of this can be found in a letter he sent to the Jewish Agency Executive in London. 6 August 1947 (1980, 4–7); Ben-Gurion's version: Letter to the members of the Executive in London. 7 Sept. 1947. Diaries.
34. PRO. FO 371/61826.
35. Shertok (Geneva). To Myerson (Jerusalem). 23 August 1947. CZA. S25/1697.
36. Jewish Agency Executive (Zurich). To Prime Minister of Denmark. 26 August 1947. Exodus File b.

16 "EACH AND EVERY ONE OF YOU IS DEAR TO US"

1. Berl Locker. To Bevin. 1 August 1947. PRO. FO 371/61820.
2. MA. C.17.6.
3. Sources describing the disembarkation of the *Ocean Vigour* immigrants in Hamburg: *Davar*, *Ha-Aretz*, 9 Sept. 1947; JDC 1947b; Schwartz 1965, 96–97; Ganuz 1985, 281–87; Report on Disembarkation; Hamburg. To Foreign Office. 8 Sept. 1947. PRO. FO 371/61827; Commonwealth Relations Office. To Governments of Canada, Australia, New Zealand and South Africa. 12 Sept. 1947. Ibid.
4. Sources describing the disembarkation of the *Empire Rival* immigrants in Hamburg: JDC 1947a; Report on Disembarkation; Disembarkation of the Jewish illegal immigrants from the *President Warfield* on arrival at Hamburg. 9 Sept. 1947. PRO. FO 371/61827.
5. HHA. 14/713.
6. Meeting of Mapai secretariat. 9 Dec. 1947. LPA. 23/47. On the "Pans" episode see Hadari and Tzahor 1985.
7. In the following files, which are stored in the HHA, the following time-divisions are missing: In files 14/702 and 14/703 (incoming cables, Mossad le-Aliyah, Paris) – 31 August to 23 Sept. 1947; in files 14/704 and 14/705 (outgoing cables, Mossad le-Aliyah, Paris) – 20 August to 28 Sept. 1947. Unable to find file: 14/536 (Mossad Journal, first half of Sept. 1947). File 14/107 (France), makes no mention of Hamburg matters between 1 August and 14 Sept. 1947.
8. Description of struggle on *Runnymede Park*: Dror 1948, 49–57; Roseman 1985; Report on Disembarkation; Disembarkation of the Jewish illegal immigrants from the *President Warfield* on arrival at Hamburg. 9 Sept. 1947. PRO. FO 371/61827.
9. Letter. Signed: B. A. B. Barrows. 30 Sept. 1947. PRO. FO 371/61827.
10. Ernest. To Venia. 25 August 1947. HHA. 14/702.

17 THEY'VE DONE IT AGAIN

1. Sidney Silverman, MP. To Arthur Greenwood, MP. 2 Sept. 1947. PRO. FO 371/61825; JDC 1947a.
2. Foreign Office internal document. Signed: J. G. S. Beith. 2 Sept. 1947. PRO. FO 371/61824.
3. Foreign Office. To Paris, no. 1209 (Draft). 23 Sept. 1947. PRO. FO 371/61825.
4. Duff Cooper. To Foreign Office. 27 August 1947. PRO. FO 371/61824; Paris. To London, no. 843. 30 August 1947. Ibid.; Paris. To Foreign Office, no. 877. 8 Sept. 1947. PRO. FO 371/61826; Foreign Office internal document. 11 Sept. 1947. Ibid.; *Ha-Olam*, 4 Sept. 1947.
5. Foreign Office. To Lübeck, no. 4698. 6 Sept. 1947. PRO. FO 371/61824.
6. Document. Signed: J. G. S. Beith. 9 Sept. 1947. PRO. FO 371/61826.
7. Lübeck. To Foreign Office (German Dept.). 26 August 1947. PRO. FO 371/61824 (press release prepared by General Bishop in advance of arrival of the deportation ships in Hamburg).
8. Sidney Silverman, MP. To Arthur Greenwood, MP. 2 Sept. 1947. PRO. FO 371/61825.
9. Foreign Office. To Lübeck. 19 Sept. 1947. PRO. FO 371/61826.
10. Foreign Office document. 10 Sept. 1947. PRO. FO 371/61825.
11. Lübeck. To Foreign Office (German Dept.). 26 August 1947. PRO. FO 371/61824.
12. See note 10 above; Lübeck. To Foreign Office, no. 11107, "Operation Oasis". 12 Sept. 1947. PRO. FO 371/61826.
13. See note 10 above.
14. Foreign Office. To Lübeck, no. 4698. 6 Sept. 1947. PRO. FO 371/61824; Lübeck. To Foreign Office, "Operation Oasis". 12 Sept. 1947. PRO. FO 371/61826.
15. Instructions to the authorities of the British zone of Germany, with regard to the dispatch to France of Jewish illegal immigrants from among the *President Warfield* party. 16 Sept. 1947. PRO. FO 371/61826; Foreign Office. To Lübeck. 19 Sept. 1947. Ibid.
16. Foreign Office. To Lübeck, no. 5539. 18 Sept. 1947. Ibid.; Commonwealth Relations Office. To Governments of Canada, Australia, New Zealand and South Africa. 24 Sept. 1947. Ibid.
17. Commonwealth Relations Office. To Governments of Canada, Australia, New Zealand and South Africa. 16 Oct. 1947. Ibid.
18. J. W. L. Ivimy (Foreign Office). To J. D. Higham (Colonial Office). 25 Nov. 1947. PRO. FO 371/61832.
19. Ibid.
20. Ibid.

18 ALL JEWS ARE COMRADES

1. H. A. Goodman (Agudat Israel). To T. Smith (Colonial Office). 22 July 1947. PRO. CO 733/491/1; summary of meeting between Goodman and Smith. 25 July 1947. PRO. CO 537/2277; Yis'ar. To Arnon. 19 August 1947. HHA. 14/535; Ganuz 1985, 242.
2. Giora [Elhanan Vanchotzker]. To secretariat of Mapai Young Guard. 17 August 1947. Exodus File a.
3. Lübeck. To Foreign Office (German Dept.). 26 August 1947. PRO. FO 371/61824.
4. JDC 1947a. Unless otherwise stated, this report is the main source for description of the situation in the camps and the activity of the JDC.
5. JDC Paris. To New York. 17 Sept. 1947. JANY. #97.

6. Lübeck. To Foreign Office. "Operation Oasis". 12 Sept. 1947. PRO. FO 371/61826.
7. E. Kaplan. To J. Schwartz (JDC New York). End of September 1947 (no exact date). JANY. #97.
8. J. Schwartz. To Kaplan and Paris. 30 Sept. 1947. Ibid.
9. Commonwealth Relations Office. To Governments of Canada, Australia, New Zealand, South Africa. 16 Oct. 1947. PRO. FO 371/61826.
10. Report from Paris. 10 Nov. 1947. JDCJA. Geneva files, S-1405, box 22b.
11. JDC Internal document. 19 Nov. 1947. JANY. #97.
12. Yis'ar. To Arnon. 28 July 1947. HHA. 14/533; Neter. 12 August 1947. HHA. 14/534.
13. Marseilles. To Foreign Office. 1 August 1947. PRO. FO371/61820.
14. Marseilles. To Foreign Office. 18 August 1947. PRO. FO 371/61822.
15. J. Schwartz. To Magnes. 14 August 1947. JDCJA. Geneva files, S-1405, box 22b.
16. To JDC Accounts. 4 Sept. 1947. Ibid.
17. Report from Paris. 10 Nov. 1947. Ibid.; draft of the letter, in Yiddish, kept by M. Roseman.
18. S. Dallob. To H. Katzki. 10 Feb. 1948. JDCJA. Geneva files, S-1405, box 22b.
19. Foreign Office. To Lübeck. 10 Sept. 1947. PRO. FO 371/61826.
20. Lübeck. To Foreign Office, no. 11107. 12 Sept. 1947. Ibid.
21. Foreign Office. To Lübeck. 18 Sept. 1947. Ibid.
22. Lübeck. To Kiel and Hannover. 12 Oct. 1947. PRO. FO 371/61830.
23. Ibid.
24. Lübeck. To London. 21 Oct. 1947. Ibid.
25. Material kept by M. Roseman.
26. HHA. 14/713.
27. MA. C.17.4.
28. Arnon. To Ur and Yis'ar. 24 Sept. 1947. HHA. 14/538.
29. Arnon. To Yis'ar. 1 Oct. 1947. Ibid.
30. Yis'ar, Ovadia. To Arnon. 4 Oct. 1947. Ibid.
31. Yis'ar. To Arnon. 15 Oct. 1947. HHA. 14/539.
32. Arnon. To Yis'ar, Berg. 16 Oct. 1947. Ibid.
33. Yis'ar. To Arnon. 23 Oct. 1947. Ibid.
34. Yis'ar, Ur. To Arnon. 26 Oct. 1947. Ibid.
35. Ur. To Hannan, Haim H. 30 Oct. 1947. HHA. 14/705.
36. Arnon. To Yis'ar, Ur. 29 Oct. 1947. Exodus File a.
37. Material kept by M. Roseman.

19 THE SECOND ALIYAH

1. Yanai. To Arnon. 12 Dec. 1947. Exodus File a.
2. Yis'ar. To Arnon. 3 Nov. 1947. HHA. 14/540.
3. Paris. To Foreign Office, no. 878. 8 Sept. 1947. PRO. FO 371/61826.
4. Ur. To Arnon, Ami, "urgent!". 19 Sept. 1947. Exodus File a.
5. Galoni. N.d. MA. C.17.3.
6. Sneh's proposal was passed on to Myerson via Locker. 18 Sept. 1947. CZA. S25/1696.
7. Arnon. To Ur and Yis'ar. 16 Oct. 1947. HHA. 14/539.
8. Yis'ar and Ur. To Ami. 26 Sept. 1947. Exodus File a; Ur. To Arnon, Ami. 26 Sept. 1947. HHA. 14/537; Sneh. To Ben-Gurion and Myerson. 29 Sept. 1947. CZA. S25/1696.
9. Ur. To Arnon, Ami, Zehava. 6 Oct. 1947. HHA. 14/538.

10. Immigration of Exodus people and data on the situation in the British zone (Hebrew). 2 March 1948. Exodus File a.
11. Yis'ar. To Arnon. 17 Oct. 1947. HHA. 14/539; Yis'ar. To Arnon. 3 Nov. 1947. HHA. 14/540.
12. Haim Hoffman. To Ben-Yehuda. 23 Oct. 1947. HHA. 14/703.
13. Hillel Chomsky (Palestine Office in Belsen). To Barlas (Immigration Department, Jerusalem). 25 Feb. 1948. CZA. S6/1628.
14. Kinzler testimony; Tubul 1985; and see note 10 above.
15. Report by *Reuters* correspondent, Boyd France. PRO. CO 733/491/2.
16. Some problems of Aliyah Dalet (Hebrew). Signed: Tal. 1 April 1948. HHA. 14/345.
17. Arnon. To Yis'ar et al. 19 Nov. 1947. HHA. 14/703.
18. Meeting of Mapai secretariat. 9 Dec. 1947. LPA. 23/47 (original emphasis).
19. Dov. To Yis'ar, Itay. 19 Dec. [1947], HHA. 14/703.
20. Yis'ar. To Arnon. 3 Nov. 1947. HHA. 14/540; Arlozoroff testimony.
21. See note 10 above.
22. Tal (Paris). To Arnon. 3 March 1948. CZA. S6/5067.
23. Arnon. To Yis'ar, Ben-Ya'akov, Tal. 29 March 1948. HHA. 14/345.
24. Mossad in Palestine. To Mossad abroad. 30 March 1948. CZA. S6/5067.
25. Yis'ar-Hadari. To friends in Arnon. 19 March 1948. Ibid.
26. Arnon. To Sidney. 2 April 1948. Ibid.
27. 2 April 1948. Ibid.
28. See note 16 above.
29. Mossad. To Yis'ar and Tal. 17 June 1948. Exodus File a.
30. Ben-Ya'akov (Paris). To Mossad. 7 Sept. 1948. Exodus File a.

20 WHO, THEN, WAS THE VICTOR?

1. The British side is henceforth presented on the basis of summaries, evaluations and conclusions made by those responsible for the war on illegal immigration during the summer and autumn of 1947: (a) Colonial Office. To Cunningham (Palestine). 29 July 1947. PRO. FO 371/61818;(b) Meeting of the Illegal Immigration Cabinet Committee. 22 August 1947. PRO. Adm 1/20789; (c) Cable 1947; (d) Refoulement – Future Policy [3 Sept. 1947]. PRO. FO 371/61825; (e) Beith 1947a; (f) Memorandum by the First Sea Lord to the Chiefs of Staff Committee, Palestine – Illegal Immigration. 9 Oct. 1947. PRO. FO 371/61830; (g) Beith 1947b.
2. Cunningham. To Colonial Office. 22 July 1947. PRO. FO 371/61818.
3. Colonial Office. To Cunningham. 24 July 1947. Ibid; Cunningham. To Colonial Office. 25 July 1947. Ibid.
4. Colonial Office. To Cunningham. 7 August 1947. Ibid.
5. Conversation between Berl Locker and Paul Ramadier in Lyon. 16 August 1947. CZA. S25/3889.
6. Meeting of Mapai secretariat. 9 Dec. 1947. LPA. 23/47.
7. Yis'ar. To Arnon. 25 Sept. 1947. HHA. 14/108.
8. Arnon. To Yis'ar. 4 Oct. 1947. Ibid.
9. Arnon. To Ur. 8 Sept. 1947. Exodus File a; Arnon. To Sidney. 10 Sept. 1947. HHA. 14/108; Sidney. To Arnon. 27 Sept. 1947. Ibid.
10. Chaim. To Mordechai. 19 Sept. 1947. MA. C.17.28.
11. S. Schwartz (Supreme Management, Merchavia). To Itzhak Weissbrod, Munich. 6 Nov. 1947. SHA. 7.13.2.

12. M. Talmi. 3 Oct. 1947. SHA. 7.13.2.
13. See note 10 above.
14. See note 11 above.
15. S. Schwartz (Supreme Management, Merchavia). To Top Management, Munich. 25 Dec. 1947. SHA. 7.13.2.
16. Habbas 1954, 151; in Slutzky, published many years later, the title was: "The Haganah promise was fulfilled in its *entirety*" (1972a, 1165; original emphasis), exactly as Avigur had requested.
17. Ben-Gurion, Diaries. 1 August 1947; *Davar*, 24 July 1947 and 4 August 1947. From 18 July to 1 August 1947 there are no entries in Ben-Gurion's diary. Later, too, the *Exodus* matter is mentioned very infrequently, and only marginally.

Glossary

Agudat Israel: Association of Israel. An Orthodox religious anti-Zionist political party, founded in 1912.

Aliyah: Ascent. The Hebrew term for immigration of Jews to Palestine.

Aliyah Bet: Immigration B. Organized illegal Jewish immigration to Palestine, in violation of British regulations. Same as Ha'apalah.*

Aliyah Dalet: Immigration D. Illegal immigration of Jews to Palestine based on forged or borrowed documents.

Betar (Brit Yosef Trumpeldor): Joseph Trumpeldor Alliance. Revisionist* youth movement.

Black Sabbath, The: 29 June 1946. The first day of a comprehensive cordon and search conducted by the British in order to break the military power of the Yishuv.*

Bnei Akiva: Akiva's Sons. Pioneering religious youth movement.

Brichah: Flight. Mass movement of Jewish survivors out of Eastern Europe in the wake of the Second World War; also the name of the underground organization that helped Jews in 1944–48 to move out of Eastern Europe into southern and western parts of the continent as a step toward immigration to Palestine.

Davar: The Histadrut's* daily. Founded in 1925, it was the most widely circulated paper in pre-State Palestine.

Dror: Freedom. Pioneering youth movement affiliated with ha-Kibbutz ha-Me'uchad and ha-Tenu'a le-Achdut ha-Avodah.*

Eretz Israel: The land of Israel. Palestine.

Gordonia: Pioneering youth movement affiliated with Mapai.*

Ha'apalah: Arduous ascent. Organized illegal immigration of Jews into Palestine in violation of British Mandatory regulations. Same as Aliyah Bet.*

Ha-Aretz: The Land. Liberal Zionist daily, published in Tel Aviv.

---

* The term is identified elsewhere in the Glossary.

Haganah: Defense. The underground military organization of the Jewish community in Mandatory Palestine, under public control.

Ha-Mossad le-Aliyah Bet: Organization for Immigration B. In short: The Mossad. The Haganah* branch responsible for the illegal immigration operation.

Ha-No'ar ha-Tziyoni: Pioneering youth movement affiliated with the General Zionists.

Ha-Olam: The World. The official organ of the Zionist Organization, published weekly in Jerusalem.

Ha-Shomer ha-Tza'ir: The Young Guardsman. A pioneering socialist-Zionist youth movement and since 1946 also a political party. Affiliated with the kibbutz movement ha-Kibbutz ha-Artzi. Merged in January 1948 with ha-Tenu'ah le-Achdut ha-Avodah* and Po'alei Zion Left* to form Mapam.*

Ha-Tenu'ah le-Achdut ha-Avodah: Movement for Labor Unity. An activist leftist political party founded in 1944 after the split in Mapai. Affiliated with the kibbutz movement ha-Kibbutz ha-Me'uchad. Merged in January 1948 with ha-Shomer ha-Tza'ir* and Po'alei Zion Left* to form Mapam.*

"Ha-Tikvah": The hope. The Zionist anthem, and later the national anthem of the State of Israel.

Ha-Va'ad ha-Le'umi: The National Council. The excecutive of the Yishuv.*

Hebrew Resistance Movement, The: An umbrella organization in which the Haganah,* IZL* and Lehi* cooperated under a common command, between October 1945 to July 1946.

He-Halutz: The Pioneer. A non-partisan association of pioneers preparing for immigration to Palestine. Affiliated with the Histadrut.*

Histadrut: General Labor Federation of Jewish workers in Palestine.

IZL (Irgun Zva'i Le'umi): National Military Organization. Underground Jewish military organization associated with the right-wing Revisionist party.* Acted in defiance of the recognized Jewish authorities in Palestine. Known also as the Irgun.

Jewish Agency: International body of Zionists and non-Zionist Jews founded in 1929, whose aim is to assist the building of the Jewish National Home in Palestine. Recognized by the League of Nations, the United Nations and Britain as the representative of the Jewish people in all matters concerning Palestine.

Kol Israel: The Voice of Israel. Israel's state radio station.

Kol Zion ha-Lochemet: The Voice of Fighting Zion. Underground radio station of Lehi.*

Lehi (Lohamei Herut Israel): Freedom Fighters of Israel. A radical anti-

British military underground organization associated with the right-wing Revisionist party.* Acted in defiance of the recognized Jewish authorities in Palestine. Also known as the Stern Gang.

Ma'apilim: Jews who came to Palestine via Ha'apalah.*

Mapai (Mifleget Po'alei Eretz Israel): Palestine Workers Party. The dominant party in the Yishuv* and the Zionist Organization since the early 1930s, blending Zionism and reform socialism.

Mapam (Mifleget ha-Po'alim ha-Me'uchedet): United Workers Party. A leftist pro-Soviet Zionist party, founded in January 1948 by ha-Shomer ha-Tza'ir,* ha-Tenuah le-Achdut ha-Avodah* and Po'alei Zion Left.*

Mizrachi: Religious Zionist party, founded in 1902. In the early 1920s the left wing of the party formed ha-Po'el ha-Mizrachi: The Mizrachi's Worker.

Mossad, The: See Ha-Mossad le-Aliyah Bet.

1939 White Paper: Issued by British Colonial Secretary Malcolm Mac-Donald. Stipulated stiff restrictions on Jewish immigration to Palestine.

Nocham (No'ar Halutzi Me'uchad): United Pioneering Youth. Short-lived postwar youth movement.

Pahah (Partizanim, Hayalim, Halutzim): Partisans, Soldiers, Pioneers. Non-political organization affiliated with the left-wing pioneering youth movements, founded in 1945.

Palmach (Plugot Mahatz): Shock Troops. Striking arm of the Haganah.*

Palmachnik: Member of the Palmach.*

Palyam (Ha-Pluga ha-Yamit): Naval troop of the Palmach.*

Po'alei Agudat Israel: Agudat Israel's* Workers. An Orthodox religious party with Zionist inclination and social awareness.

Po'alei Zion Left: Worker of Zion, left-wing. Marxist Zionist party. Merged in January 1948 with ha-Shomer ha-Tza'ir* and ha-Tenu'ah le-Achdut ha-Avodah* to form Mapam.*

Revisionist Party: A right-wing militant party, founded in 1925 by Ze'ev Jabotinsky. The Revisionists seceded from the Zionist Organization in 1935 to form their own New Zionist Organization, but returned in 1946.

Yishuv: Settlement. The Jewish community in pre-State Palestine. During the British Mandate the term was more specifically referring to the Zionist segment of the Jewish population of Palestine. In the late 1930s and during the 1940s the term "organized Yishuv" excluded the dissident Revisionists.

Works Cited

Allon (Peikovitz), Yig'al (alias: Yiftach). 1947. Letter. 21 June. In *Sefer ha-Palmach* (The Book of the Palmach). Vol. 1, edited by Zerubavel Gil'ad, 838–41. Tel Aviv: Ha-Kibbutz ha-Me'uchad, 1953.

— 1953. "Megamot u-ma'as". In *Sefer ha-Palmach* (The Book of the Palmach). Vol. 1, edited by Zerubavel Gil'ad, 529–613. Tel Aviv: Ha-Kibbutz ha-Me'uchad.

"Alternative Destination for the Jews of *President Warfield*". 1947. 13 August. PRO. FO 371/61821.

Aran (Aharonowitz), Yitzhak (alias: Ike). 1947. Report (Hebrew). 4 June. HHA. 14/132.

— 1963. Testimony. HHA. 4271.

— 1985. Interview with author. Tel Aviv, 14 Feb. HPIC. General Testimonies, 278.

Arlozoroff, Shula. 1983. Testimony. HPIC. General Testimonies, 1.

Avigur, Shaul. 1959. Testimony, recorded by Bracha Habbas. HHA. 3403/278.

Bain, Kenneth Ray. 1979. *The March to Zion: United States Policy and the Founding of Israel.* College Station, Texas: A. and M. University Press.

Barlas, Chaim. 1947a. "Report on matters of immigration, training and rescue in Europe, May–September 1947" (Hebrew). CZA. S6/1169.

— 1947b. Speech at a party at his home for the staff of the Jewish Agency Immigration Department (Hebrew). 20 Oct. CZA. S6/1169.

Bar-Zohar, Michael. 1964. *Gesher al ha-Yam ha-Tichon* (Bridge Over the Mediterranean). Tel Aviv: Am ha-Sefer.

— 1977. *Ben-Gurion* (Hebrew). Vol. 1. Tel Aviv: Am Oved.

Bauer, Yehuda. 1970. *Flight and Rescue: Brichah.* New York: Random House.

Baumel, Judith Tydor. 1995. "The IZL Delegation in the USA, 1939–1948: Anatomy of Ethnic Interest/Protest Group." *Jewish History* 9, no. 1: 79–89.

Ben-Amotz, Dan. 1950. "Those Were Forgotten" (Hebrew). In *Arba'ah ve'Arba'ah* (Four and Four). Merchavia: Sifriyat ha-Po'alim.

Beith, J. G. S. 1947a. Unaddressed letter. 10 Sept. PRO. FO 371/61825.

— 1947b. "Return of Jewish Illegal Immigrants to Palestine to Their Country of Embarkation". 19 Nov. PRO. FO 371/61852.

Ben-Dor, Chaim. 1949. *Mivchar Ketavim u-Reshimot* (Selected Writings and Papers). Merchavia: Sifriyat ha-Po'alim.

Ben-Gurion, David. Diaries. BGA.

— 1950. *Ba-Ma'archah*. Vol. 5. Tel Aviv: Mifleget Po'alei Eretz Israel.

— 1975. *Be-Hilachem Israel*. Tel Aviv: Am Oved.

— 1982. *Yoman ha-Milchama*. Vol. 1. Edited by Gershon Rivlin and Elchanan Oren. Tel Aviv: Misrad ha-Bitachon.

Bernstein, Philip. 1947. Report. JDCJA. Box 6A, file C45.069.

Bethell, Nicholas William. 1979. *The Palestine Triangle: The Struggle between the British, the Jews and the Arabs, 1935–48*. London: Andre Deutsch.

Bett, D. C. S. 1947. Report. 26 July. PRO. Adm 1/20685.

Biber, Shaul. 1964. Group interview on Kol Israel. 5 April. HHA. 4744.

— Testimony. HPIC. General Testimonies, 135.

Bogner, Nachum. 1991. *Iy ha-Gerush: Machanot ha-Ma'apilim be-Kafrisin 1946–1948* (Deportation Island: The Camps of the Illegal Immigrants in Cyprus 1946–1948). Tel Aviv: Am Oved.

Braginsky, Yehuda. 1965. *Am Hoter el Hof* (A Nation Striving to Coast). Tel Aviv: Ha-Kibbutz ha-Me'uchad.

Bullock, Allan. 1983. *Ernest Bevin: Foreign Secretary 1945–1951*. Vol. 3 of *The Life and Times of Ernest Bevin*. London: Heinemann.

Cable, J. E. 1947. Document. 25 August. PRO. FO 371/61824.

Cohen, Michael J. 1982. *Palestine and the Great Powers 1945–1948*. Princeton: Princeton University Press.

Coulson, J. E. 1947. Document. 1 August. PRO. FO 371/61821.

Crossley, G. A. 1947. "An account of the *President Warfield* episode". 5 August. PRO. FO 371/61822.

Crossman, Richard. 1947. *Palestine Mission: A Personal Record*. New York: Harper.

Crum, Bartley C. 1947. *Behind the Silken Curtain*. New York: Simon & Schuster.

Cunningham, Sir Alan. Papers. Middle East Center. St Antony's College, Oxford (Microfilm at ISA).

Dallob, Sam. 1948. Report. 21 January. JDCJA. Geneva files, S-1405, box 22b.

Dalton, Hugh. 1962. *High Tide and After: Memoirs 1945–1960*. Vol. 3 of *Memoires*. London: F. Muller.

Derogy, Jacques. 1972. *Parashat Exodus be-Or Hadash* (The Exodus Affair Reconsidered). Translated by Zvi Arad. Tel Aviv: Am Oved. (Originally published in French: *La loi du retour*. Paris, 1969.)

Diary 1947a. Written in French by a female immigrant on the *Exodus*, was taken by the British at Haifa and translated into English. Appendix B to the weekly report no. 51 of the Sixth Airborne Division. PRO. WO 275/60.

Diary 1947b. Written in Polish by a female immigrant. Translated into Hebrew by Hanna Shlomi. HPIC.

Divine, Robert A. 1957. *American Immigration Policy 1924–1952*. New Haven: Yale University Press.

Dror. 1948. *Yetzi'at Eiropa Tashaz: Parashat ha-Ha'apalah ve-ha-Gerush shel Ma'pilei* Exodus 1947 *Mesuperet be-Fi Yaldei Dror u-Madricheihem* (Exodus from Europe 5707: The Affair of the Illegal Immigration and the Expulsion of the Illegal Immigrants of *Exodus 1947* told by the Children of Dror and Their Instructors). Munich: Bafreiung-Dror.

Dror, Levi, ed. 1961. *Sefer ha-Shomer ha-Tza'ir* (Book of ha-Shomer ha-Tza'ir). Vol. 2. Merchavia: Sifriyat ha-Po'alim.

Eban, Abba. 1977. *An Autobiography*. New York: Random House.

Eilat, Eliyahu. 1982. *Ha-Ma'avak al ha-Medina* (The Struggle for State). Vol. 2(a). Tel Aviv: Am Oved and ha-Sifriya ha-Tziyonit.

Einav, Azri'el. 1947. Radio officer's testimony, 31 July. YBZA. 4/1/3.5.
— 1988. Testimony. HPIC. General Testimonies, 392.

Einor (Sonnenborn), Hannan. 1985. Interview with author. Jerusalem, 18 Feb. HPIC. General Testimonies, 124.

Exodus Diary. 1968. "Yoman Exodus", *Yalkut Moreshet* 8, 84–103. Original manuscript: MA. D.2.190.

Exodus File a. HHA. 14/234b.

Exodus File b. CZA. S25/2630.

Frank, Ephrayim (Erich. Alias: Ernest). 1947. Speech at the second European Haganah gathering, 5–8 Nov. (Hebrew) HHA. 14/713.
— 1963. Testimony. OHC. (4)20.

FRUS. 1947. *Foreign Relations of the United States*. Vol. 5: The Near East and Africa. Washington, 1971.

Ganuz (Ganuzovich), Yitzchak. 1985. *Kisufim ve-Sa'ar* (Yearning and Turmoil). Tel Aviv: Misrad ha-Bitachon.

Garcia-Granados, Jose. 1949. *The Birth of Israel: The Drama As I Saw It*. New York: Alfred A. Knopf.

Greenstein, Chaim. 1964. Group interview on Kol Israel. 5 April. HHA. 4744.

Gruber, Ruth. 1948. *Destination Palestine: The Story of the Haganah Ship* Exodus 1947. New York: Current Books Inc., A. A. Wyn.

Habbas, Bracha, ed. 1954. *Ha-Sefina she-Nitzha* (The Ship that Won). 2d. edn. Tel Aviv: Ma'arakhot.

Hadari, Ze'ev Venia. 1991. *Second Exodus: The Full Story of Jewish Illegal Immigration to Palestine, 1945–1948*. London: Vallentine Mitchell.

— Pomerantz, Venia [Ze'ev]. 1949. *Yetzi'at Eiropa* (Exodus from Europe). Tel Aviv: Israel Defense Forces Cultural Services.

—and Ze'ev Tzahor. 1985. *Voyage to Freedom: An Episode in the Illegal Immigration to Palestine*. London: Vallentine Mitchell.

Halamish, Aviva. 1986. "United States' position on the illegal immigrant ship, *Exodus 1947*" (Hebrew). *Yahadut Zemanenu* 3, 209–225.

— 1988. "Illegal Immigration: Values, Myth and Reality." *Studies in Zionism* 9, no. 1: 47–62.

— 1995. "American Volunteers in Illegal Immigration to Palestine, 1946–1948." *Jewish History* 9, no. 1: 91–106.

Har'el (Hamburger), Yosef (alias: Yossi). Testimony. HHA. 4272.

— 1964. Group interview on Kol Israel, 5 April. HHA. 4744.

— 1985. Interview with author. Tel Aviv, 3 Feb. HPIC. General Testimonies, 272.

Hartmann, Susan M. 1971. *Truman and the 80th Congress*. Columbia: University of Missouri Press.

Histadrut Executive. Protocol of meetings. LA.

Holly, David C. 1969. *Exodus 1947*. Boston: Little, Brown and Company.

Horowitz, David. 1953. *State in the Making*. Translated by Julian Meltzer. New York: Alfred A. Knopf.

Hurewitz, J. C. 1950. *The Struggle for Palestine*. New York: W. W. Norton.

JDC 1947a. "Review of JDC Activity in the British Occupied Zone in Germany, January–November 1947". JANY. #97 (microfilm in HPIC).

— 1947b. "JDC Activities in the American Zone of Germany, March–September 1947". JANY. #97 (microfilm in HPIC).

The Jewish Agency Executive, Jerusalem. Protocol of Meetings. CZA. S/100.

The Jewish Agency for Palestine. The Delegation to Germany. 1949. *Din ve-Heshbon 1946–1949* (Report for the Years 1946–1949). Munich.

The Jewish Agency. London. 1947. "Activities Diary". In Exodus File b.

"Jewish Illegal Immigrants ex-*President Warfield*, Who Have Been Returned to Port de Bouc". 14 August 1947. PRO. FO 371/61821.

Katzanelson, Zvi (alias: Miri). 1961. "Exodus 1947" (Hebrew). In *Sefer ha-Shomer ha-Tza'ir* (Book of ha-Shomer ha-Tza'ir). Vol. 2, edited by Levi Dror, 612–14. Merchavia: Sifriyat ha-Po'alim.

— 1985. Interview with author. Kibbutz Kfar Menachem, 22 Jan. HPIC. General Testimonies, 273.

Kimche, John and David. 1954. *The Secret Roads: The "Illegal" Migration of a People 1938–1948*. London: Secker and Warburg.

Kinnarti, Hanna. 1947. To Ze'ev Haklai. 23 Nov. CZA. S6/262.

Kinzler, Chaim. Testimony. HPIC. General Testimonies, 4.

Kirk, George. 1954. *The Middle East 1945–1950*. Vol. 5 of *Survey of International Affairs 1939–1946*. London: Oxford University Press.

Koestler, Arthur. 1949. *Promise and Fulfillment: Palestine 1917–1949*. New York: Macmillan.

Kol Israel. 1964. Group interview. 5 April. HHA. 4744.

Kol Zion ha-Lochemet. 1947. JIA. "Kaf" 4–7/13.

Kolat, Israel, Amitzur Ilan, Michael J. Cohen, Gabriel Cohen and Yosef Heller. 1980. "The decision on the British exit from Palestine" (Hebrew). *Cathedra* 15, 140–189.

Leichter, Yoseph. 1985. Interview with author. Kibbutz Sarid, 7 Feb. HPIC. General Testimonies, 282.

Levin, Kurt (Daniel). 1947a. To Y. Bachar. 2 July. CZA. S6/3658.

— 1947b. To Y. Bachar. 24 July. CZA. S6/3658.

— 1947c. To M. Shapira, Immigration Dept. 23 Nov. CZA. S6/3659.

— Testimony. HHA. 4613.

Lie, Trygve (General Secretary of the United Nations). 1947. To Lord Cadogan (British Ambassador to the UN). 29 May. PRO. FO 371/61811.

Limon, Eli'ezer (alias: Yuzek). 1985. Interview with author. Kibbutz Beit Alpha, 6 Feb. HPIC. General Testimonies, 281.

Lippman, Eugene (Yehuda). Testimony. OHC. 9(2).

Livyathan, Nissan. Testimony. HPIC. General Testimonies, 219.

Locker, Berl. 1970. *Me-Kitov ad Yerushalayim* (From Kitov to Jerusalem). Jerusalem: Ha-Sifriya ha-Tziyonit.

Meir, Golda. 1975. *My Life*. London: Imprint Futura Publications.

Mills, Dov. 1986. Conversation with author. Be'er Sheva, 26 Feb.

Monroe, Elizabeth. 1961. "Mr Bevin's Arab Policy." *St Antony's Papers* 11, edited by Albert Hourani, 9–48. Oxford: Oxford University Press.

Nussinov, Nanna. 1969. *Ha-Holchim al ha-Yam: Ha'aplah me'Italya 1945–1948* (Walking on the sea: illegal immigration from Italy 1945–1948). MA thesis. Jerusalem: Hebrew University.

Ofer, Dalia. 1990. *Escaping the Holocaust: Illegal Immigration to the Land of Israel, 1939–1944*. New York: Oxford University Press.

Peker, Yehuda. 1964. Written Testimony. MA. D2.228.

— 1985. Interview with author. Kibbutz Sarid, 7 Feb. HPIC. General Testimonies, 282.

Perlov, Yitzchok. n.d. *The People of 'Exodus'*. Translated by Jeannette E. Shoham. Tel Aviv: Yechiel (1960).

Perry (Perlson), Micha. 1964. Letter to the Editor. *Ma'ariv*, 25 Nov.

— 1985. Interview with author. Tel Aviv, 14 Feb. HPIC. General Testimonies, 271.

Porat, Dina. 1986. *Hanhagah be-Milkud* (An Entangled Leadership: The Yishuv and the Holocaust, 1942–1945). Tel Aviv: Am Oved.

Proudfoot, Malcolm J. n.d. *European Refugees, 1939–1952*. London: Faber & Faber.

Rabinowitz, Eli'ezer. "On German soil again" (Hebrew). In *Sefer ha-Shomer ha-Tza'ir* (Book of ha-Shomer ha-Tza'ir). Vol. 2, edited by Levi Dror, 627–28. Merchavia: Sifriyat ha-Po'alim.

"Report on the Disembarkation of Jews ex-*Exodus 47* at Hamburg". PRO. FO 371/61827.

"Report on the Interception and Arrest of *President Warfield*". PRO. Adm 1/20685.

Reichman, Hannan. 1947. Letter. Marseilles, 26 August. CZA. S25/2630.

Roseman, Mordechai. 1947. Letter to Dr J. Schwartz. 9 Nov. Material kept by Roseman.

— 1984. Interview with author. Kibbutz Ha-Ogen, 18 Dec. HPIC. General Testimonies, 225.

Schind, Ze'ev (alias: Danny). 1947. Letter. 2 April. HHA. 14/331.

Schwartz, Meir. 1965. "From the diary of a Haganah man on the deportation ship *Ocean Vigour*" (Hebrew). *Bi-Tfutzut ha-Gola* 7, no. 3 (34): 83–102.

— 1986. Public group interview with author, Beth Hatefutsoth, Tel Aviv. 23 March. HPIC. General Testimonies, 346.

Sela, Yehuda. 1987. "The role of American pioneers in the illegal immigration operation." (Hebrew). *Me'asef le-Heker Tenu'at ha-Avodah ha-Tziyonit ve-ha-Sotzialism* 17, 149–68.

Sereni, Ada (alias: Kalir). 1947. To Yiftach and Arnon. 20 July. HHA. 14/533.

— 1975. *Sefinot le-Lo Degel* (Ships With No Flag). Translated by Deborah Ayalon-Sereni. Tel Aviv: Am Oved.

Sha'ari, David. 1981. *Gerush Kafrisin 1946–1949* (Deportation to Cyprus 1946–1949). Jerusalem: Ha-Sifriya ha-Tziyonit.

Shadmi (Kremer), Nachum. 1964. Group interview on Kol Israel. 5 April. HHA. 4744.

Shapira, Anita. 1986. "The Yishuv and the Survivors of the Holocaust." *Studies in Zionism* 7, no. 2: 277–301.

Slutzky, Yehuda. 1972a. *Sefer Toldot ha-Haganah* (History of the Haganah). Vol. 3, part 2. Tel Aviv: Am Oved.

— 1972b. *Sefer Toldot ha-Haganah* (History of the Haganah). Vol. 3, part 3. Tel Aviv: Am Oved.

Stone, I. F. 1946. *Underground to Palestine*. New York: Boni and Gaer.

Sykes, Christopher. 1965. *Cross Roads to Israel*. London: Collins.

Teiber, Rami and Ada. 1983. Testimony. HPIC. General Testimonies, 3.

Troper, Harold. 1985. "Canada and the Survivors of the Holocaust: the Crisis of Displaced Persons". Paper presented at the 6th Yad va-Shem International Conference, Jerusalem.

Tubul, Sara and Shlomo. 1985. Joint interview with author. Omer, 21 Feb. HPIC. General Testimonies, 291.

United Kingdom. *Parliamentary Debates* (Commons), 5th Ser., vol. 440 (1947).

United Nations. 1947. *Resolutions Adopted by the General Assembly During Its First Special Session*. New York.

United Nations. 1949. *Yearbook of the United Nations 1946–1947*. New York.

United Nations Weekly Bulletin 3, 1947.

(UNSCOP) United Nations Special Committee on Palestine. 1947a. *Report to the General Assembly*. 4 vols. Geneva.

— 1947b. *Annexes, Appendices and Maps to the Report to the General Assembly*. Geneva.

Weizmann, Chaim. 1980. *The Letters and Papers of Chaim Weizmann*. Vol. 23, edited by Aaron Kleinman. Jerusalem.

Wilson, R. D. 1949. *Cordon and Search: With 6th Airborne Division in Palestine*. Aldershot: Gale & Polden Limited.

Wischnitzer, Mark. 1948. *To Dwell in Safety: The Story of Jewish Migration Since 1800*. Philadelphia: Jewish Publication Society of America.

Ya'ari, Meir. 1947. *Be-Derech Arukah* (On a Long Road). Merchavia: Sifriyat ha-Po'alim.

Yahil, Haim. 1946. Letter. 7 June. CZA, S6/4685.

— 1947. Letter. 6 April. CZA, S6/4676.

— 1980. "Activity of the Palestine delegation among the Holocaust survivors 1945–1949" (Hebrew). Part 1. *Yalkut Moreshet* 30, 7–40.

— 1981. "Activity of the Palestine delegation among the Holocaust survivors 1945–1949" (Hebrew). Part 2. *Yalkut Moreshet* 31, 133–76.

— Testimony. OHC. 1(12).

Yishai (Vanchotzker), Elhanan. 1964. Group interview on Kol Israel. 5 April. HHA. 4744.

Zionist General Council. 1947. Zurich. 25 August – 2 Sept. CZA. S5/320.

Zionist Organization Executive. n.d. *Ha-Kongress ha-Tziyoni ha-Kaf-Bet, Basel 9–24 December 1946, Din ve-Heshbon Stenographi* (Proceedings of the 22nd Zionist Congress 1946). Jerusalem.

Index